# THE MULTIAGE HANDBOOK

## A Comprehensive Resource for Multiage Practices

# Contents

# ARE MULTI-AGE GROUPING PRACTICES A MISSING LINK IN THE EDUCATIONAL REFORM DEBATE?

by William Miller

*The practice of grouping by age and grade may be creating a significant barrier to meeting the goals of equity and instructional excellence in schools.*

Public education programs in the United States contain a wide variety of organizational patterns. There is, however, one striking similarity. They are almost all organized by age.

## The Age-Graded Structure

The age-graded structure has endured for almost 140 years without being described as an important reason for some of the current ills of the U.S. education system (Owen, 1987).

Our current age-graded organizational structure is based on three assumptions:

- That students of the same chronological age are ready to learn the same objectives
- That students require the same amount of time, as in an academic year, to master predetermined content
- That students can master predesigned objectives for a grade level for all curricular areas at the same rate (Stainback and Stainback, 1984).

As a result of these assumptions, pupils whose educational needs do not match this age-graded structure or who otherwise interfere with the flow of instruction are either excluded from school or placed into "special" classes or schools, thus creating parallel but isolated systems (Stainback, et al., 1985).

In their 1987 report, Knoblock and Berries offer evidence that the current age-graded systems may be promoting failure. According to Knoblock, where public education fails to address the needs of children, the failure might properly be traced to the erroneous assumption that a single curriculum can serve all children. A review of current research indicates that students may gain greater educational benefits from multi-age classroom grouping than single-grade configurations (Brown and Martin, 1989; Villa, 1989).

Many studies have criticized age-graded schools as being seriously out of phase with society (Goodlad and Anderson, 1963; Coleman et al., 1966; Tyler, 1985). Certainly, grouping students strictly by age does not reflect a naturalistic life-like setting in which people of different ages learn from each other.

In order to make schools accessible to all students and to maximize student learning, we must examine organizational trends in schools that hamper the ability of school personnel to educate students of varied needs together. The practice of grouping by age and grade may be creating a significant barrier to meeting the goals of equity and instructional excellence in schools.

## Child Development

The realities of child development defy the rigorous ordering of children's abilities and attainments to the conventional graded structure. In any first grade class, there will be a four-year span in pupils' readiness as suggested by mental age data. Furthermore, children progress in all subjects at different rates. Some children tend to spurt ahead in one area faster than others. Consequently, the difference in any one grade between reading attainment and arithmetic attainment by an individual may extend to a three or five-year difference in each grade.

A central problem, then, emerges out of the conflict between long-established graded/age structures on one hand and trying to meet the variation in children's abilities and attainments on the other.

In reviewing the major reform reports that have been written during the past 10 years, not much suggests that the age-graded organizational structure might be a valuable area to examine for potential solutions to the identified problems within public education. Only one reference is made to the age/graded structure in *A Nation at Risk* (1983). In that report, the suggestion is made that placement and grouping of students, as well as promotion and graduation policies, should be guided by students' academic progress and instructional needs rather than by rigid adherence to age.

---

*Certainly, grouping students strictly by age does not reflect a naturalistic life-like setting in which people of different ages learn from each other.*

---

Although not frequently discussed in school reform movements in the United States, the education literature abounds with references to class grouping in which students of different ages and identified age levels are grouped together in a single classroom for the purpose of providing effective instruction.

Multi-age grouping is but one term used in education literature to describe the practice of placing students of different ages and/or identified grade levels together to meet instructional or administrative goals. The terms inter-age, mixed-age, nongraded, ungraded, primary units, mixed grade, split grade, combination, continuous progress ungraded, multi-graded, and family grouping have also

been used to describe organizational patterns that group students of different ages.

Studies on the value and efficacy of single-age group gradedness are inconclusive. However, the majority of studies have found that a reduction of age ranges and student abilities does not increase achievement (Way, 1981; Pratt, 1986; Veenman, 1987; Raschke, 1988).

In contrast, the development of multi-age or cross-age groupings, sometimes coordinated with olders teaching youngers in tutoring programs, has produced promising outcomes. Pratt (1986) summarized evidence from experimental research, ethnology, and history about the merits of multi-age groupings in the affective and social skill areas. In similar research by Way (1981), the effects of multi-age grouping on achievement and self-concept were explored. No significant differences were found between children in multi-age and single-age classrooms in any areas of achievement. In the area of self-concept, multi-age classroom groups had higher mean scores in some areas.

## Research Summary

A summary of comparative research reveals that grouping by age or single grade levels yields no benefits over multi-age/grade groupings. On the other hand, multi-age grouping can yield benefits for students in the affective domain. The general pattern that emerges from these studies is one of increased competition and aggression within same-age class groups and increased harmony and acceptance within multi-age groups; younger members or high-need populations appear to benefit the most.

Closely related to multi-age or multi-grade grouping is the concept of cross-age and peer-tutoring instruction. Coupling multi-age grouping with peers or cross-age tutoring has been found to produce a positive, cost effective impact on learning.

The success of cross-age and peer-tutoring is well-documented. The overwhelming conclusion is that the children made significant gains in achievement when the techniques were employed (Berliner and Casanova, 1988; Cotton, 1988; Villa and Thousand, 1988). In an exciting study by Cloward in 1967, older secondary school students successfully raised achievement scores for previously low-achieving elementary school students through tutoring. In these studies, the tutoring program had the greatest positive impact on the tutors themselves.

Grouping by age continues to be the major method of organizing children for instruction in U.S. schools despite ample evidence that other forms of heterogeneous grouping by multi-age/graded, mixed ability, and cross-age tutor programming yield better student outcomes.

Despite 65 years of information on the effectiveness of these techniques, despite more information about teaching to individual differences and learning styles, and despite the proliferation of instructional strategies and technology, there is little evidence that the practice of multi-age grouping for instruction is used in our schools for reasons other than to enhance economic efficiency or to balance class size.

Educators have merely accepted the age-graded organizational structure as a way of doing things within the system of public education, and it would appear that efforts to modify the age-graded organization significantly have been generally unsuccessful except on a small scale.

Though the graded school had many advantages, we should not close our eyes to the fact that it is open to the serious charge that it does not properly provide for the individual differences of our pupils and that it is not sufficiently pliant to accommodate itself to the pupils.

As our society has changed, so must our schools. The grading of schools, which was intended to serve children, may now be restricting their educational opportunities.

## References

Anderson, Robert H., and Goodlad, John I. *The Ungraded Elementary School,* rev. ed., 1967.

Berliner, David and Casanova, Ursula. "Peer Tutoring: A New Look at a Popular Practice." *Instructor,* January 1988.

Brown, Kenneth, and Martin, Andrew. "Student Achievement in Multigrade and Single Grade Classes." *Education Canada,* Summer 1989.

Carbone, Robert F. "A Comparison of Graded and Nongraded Elementary Schools." *The Elementary School Journal,* November 1961.

Cloward, Robert D. "Studies in Tutoring." *Journal of Experimental Education,* Fall 1967.

Coleman, James S., et al. *Equality of Educational Opportunity.* Washington, D.C.: U.S. Government Printing Office, 1966.

Cotton, Kathleen. "Peer Tutoring: Lake Washington High School, Benjamin Rush Elementary School, Effective Practices in Place, Snapshot No. 5." *School Improvement Research Series,* Portland, Oreg., February 1988.

Dufay, Frank R. *Ungrading the Elementary School.* West Nyack, N.Y.: Parker Publishing Co., 1966.

Freeman, Jayne. "How I Learned to Stop Worrying and Love My Combination Class." *Instructor,* March 1984.

Gillespie, Ross J. "A Study of the Continuous Progress Curriculum of Leonard Elementary School; Southfield, Michigan." Doctoral dissertation, Eastern Michigan University, June 1974.

Goodlad, John I., and Anderson, Robert H. *The Non-Graded Elementary School.* New York: Harcourt, Brace, and World, 1963.

Hunter, Madeline. "The Dimensions of Nongrading." *The Elementary School Journal* 1(1964): 80-82.

Knoblock, Peter and Berries, Michael. *Program Models for Mainstreaming.* Rockville, Md.: Aspen Publishers, 1987.

Nachbur, R. "A K/1 Class Can Work — Wonderfully." *Young Children,* July, 1989.

National Commission on Excellence in Education. *A Nation At Risk.* Washington, D.C.: U.S. Government Printing Office.

National Education Association. "Grade Organization and Non-Grading Programs." *Research Bulletin,* Washington, D.C., 1963, pp. 52-92.

Owen, Richard. "Identifying an Underlying Rationale for the Development of the Age-Graded Organizational Structure Within American Public Education." Doctoral dissertation, Michigan State University, 1987.

Pratt, David. "On the Merits of Multi-Age Classrooms." *Research in Rural Education* 3 (1986): 111-16.

Raschke, Donna. "Cross-Age Tutorials and Attitudes of Kindergarters Toward Older Students." *Teacher Education,* Spring 1988.

Stainback, W. and Stainback, S. "A Rationale for the Merger of Special and Regular Education." *Exceptional Children* 52 (1984): 102-11.

Stainback, W.; Stainback, S.; Courtnage, L.; and

Jaben, T. "Facilitating Mainstreaming by Modifying the Mainstream." *Exceptional Children* 51 (1985): 144-52.

Tyler, L.E. *Reorganizing American Public Education*, Eugene, Oreg. EDRS, 1985.

Veenman, Simon. "Classroom Time and Achievement in Mixed-Age Classes." *Educational Studies* 1 (1987): 75-84.

Villa, Richard. "Administrative Supports Which Promote the Education of All Students in the Mainstream." Burlington, Vt. University of Vermont Press, 1989.

Villa, Richard and Thousand, Jacqueline. "Enhancing Success in Heterogeneous Classrooms and Schools: The Powers of Partnership." *Teacher Education*, Fall 1988.

Way, Joyce. "Achievement and Self-Concept in Multi-Age Classrooms." *Educational Research Quarterly* 2 (1981): 69-75.

# Voices

*Dear Ms. Class:*

*I am a second-grade teacher, working on a primary-grade curriculum committee. We hope that if students see school as a job, we will get them ready for life, ready to enter the work force as productive members of our twenty-first century society, and they will be more serious about their assignments. We have set up a market economy linking mathematics and social studies. We wonder if you can suggest some resources for real-life curriculum in language arts.*

*— Baltimore, MD*

*Dear Baltimore:*

*No, no, a thousand times no. Please dismiss any notion of getting second graders ready for life. A second-grade teacher should not even worry about getting her students ready for third grade. The proper concern of every primary-grade teacher must be the current lives of the children in her care.*

*Ms. Class entreats you to nurture children as children, not as miniature stockbrokers and bankers. Life is today, not tomorrow. Primary teachers should concern themselves not with good results, but with good beginnings.*

*A good place for your committee to start is to place a moratorium on the use of the term twenty-first century.*

*— **Susan Ohanian, Ask Ms. Class. York, ME: Stenhouse Publishers, 1996.***

# IT STARTS FRONTLINE

The Comprehensive Communication Newsletter for Your School September 1995

## Problem Parents Buy Into Multi-Year 'Relationships'

Today's principals don't have to be told how different things are compared with 15 years ago. Many parents carry a lot of baggage — divorce, dysfunctional families, substance abuse, problem children and financial difficulties — and their anger is often transferred to the school because their expectations are way out of sync with what the school could possibly provide.

These parents' children, of course, come to school with similar emotional baggage and start further behind academically than their counterparts of a decade ago. As a result, today's principal wears many hats — nurse, social worker, police officer, banker, innkeeper and lawyer. Instructional manager barely makes it onto the list.

> *"We don't change doctors or dentists every year, and for good reason. So why should we change teachers? ... Everybody knows each other and what to expect, and they get right to work without spinning their wheels for days or even weeks."*
>
> **Jim Grant**

"I've had many principals tell me they took the job because they want to help children learn. They love to read to kids," said Jim Grant. "With today's high-maintenance kids, many principals don't get to do that any more." And so Grant offers a solution: "We may have to change the structure of the school."

Grant is executive director of the Alliance of Multi-Age Educators — teachers and principals who have found that keeping students and teachers together longer than the traditional one school year builds "trust, belonging and bonding."

"We don't change doctors or dentists every year," Grant said, "and for good reason. So why should we change teachers?" Under the system espoused by Grant and his organization, teachers, parents and kids stay together for two or even three years, creating a "family" at-mosphere that inspires parent involvement and gives children a more positive attitude about school.

Matching a student and a teacher for two or three years, Grant said, means (for student and teacher alike) no sad farewells in the spring, no anxiety during the summer and no difficult adjustments in the fall. "September 2 is the 181st day of school," Grant said. Everybody knows each other and what to expect, and they get right to work without spinning their wheels for days or even weeks.

Grant, who works out of Peterborough, N.H., feels this type of program makes an enormous difference to parents. He titled a recent presentation to NAESP, "Turning Problem Parents Into Program Supporters," because experience shows that this "bonding" with the teacher brings parents into the school to volunteer much more frequently, and spurs their enthusiasm to work with their children.

But even where the parent is a non-factor in the child's education — such as in broken families — this same concept helps children tremendously because it brings a sense of continuity and security to the child, resulting in better discipline and better attendance, Grant said. For teachers, it means more stability in the classroom, smoother transitions, and much more time to teach and to implement instructional strategies.

He said that principals who have tried it love it, but it does require a major philosophical shift. It can work in two different ways. In what Grant calls "looping," the teacher is "promoted" to the next grade along with the students. The other way is to return to the old one-room schoolhouse concept, where a half or a third of the class cycles in and out each year, offering younger students mentors and older students the chance to become "seniors," boosting their self-esteem.

Obviously the teacher has to make some adjustments too, which is the basis of Grant's answer to the question of what happens when there is a "bad" teacher. "Poor teachers rarely volunteer," he said, "because its harder work. There are some potential downsides," he conceded, "but they are far outweighed by the benefits."

# STRAIGHT TALK FROM MULTI-AGE Classrooms

## Why these teachers favor nongraded classes and how they make them work

### By Meg A. Bozzone

**M**ulti-age classrooms are nothing new. They've been around since the days of the one-room schoolhouse, when children of many ages studied side by side under the same roof with the help of one teacher. But in the 1990s, multi-age classrooms have taken on a dynamic new meaning.

In Iowa City, Iowa, groups of children in Vicki Bachman's one-two class develop familylike ties because they work together for two years on thematic units that Vicki develops with a six-teacher team. Students returning to Paula Cramer's two-three class in Mount Washington, Kentucky, hit the ground running and lead newcomers in classroom projects. Children in Judy Darcy's four-five-six class in Tucson, Arizona, tackle the three-level curriculum by delving into an eclectic mix of topics from the Aztecs and Mayas to the heart. Kids communicate with ease in Lockport, New York, because

It's no secret that these Urbana, Illinois, students feel at home in their multi-age class. Here they act out Shel Silverstein's poem "Hug O' War."

Susan Myers and two colleagues, who team-teach a three-four-five class, have gone so far as to knock holes through the walls of their adjoining classrooms and create doorways.

Whatever the style, these teachers are convinced that multi-age (or nongraded) classes are a developmentally sound way to teach—whether their school embraced this approach because of low student enrollment, because it's the law (as in the case of primary classes in Kentucky), or because they believe

in it. "Multi-age classrooms make sense," affirms Jim Grant, director of the National Alliance of Multi-Age Educators. "They don't link learning to the stop-and-go of a clock or school calendar, but focus on children as they grow on a continuum, independent of rigid grade-level divisions."

Still, the idea of teaching a multi-age class has many teachers scared. It's hard enough, they reason, to cover one curriculum while meeting the diverse needs found in any single-grade class. How could they do justice to several curricula and an even wider range of kids? Below, voices of experience explain the benefits kids reap in nongraded classes and outline the linchpins of successful programs.

## WHAT RESEARCH SAYS

Although the jury is still out, according to Robert H. Anderson and Barbara Nelson Pavan, authors of *Nongradedness: Helping It to Happen* (Technomic, 1993), the majority of studies find that students generally perform better academi-

MEG A. BOZZONE, *a former substitute teacher in upstate New York, is a senior editor at* Instructor.

cally and are healthier mentally in multi-age classrooms. Also, in nongraded environments, boys, African-Americans, underachievers, and students of lower socioeconomic status are more likely to perform better and feel more positive about themselves and school. The longer students stay in nongraded programs, the greater the improvement in their achievement scores. Better attendance and fewer discipline problems are also pluses.

## WHAT TEACHERS SAY
Teachers who have made the switch to multi-age classes see a host of benefits.

● **More student rapport—** Maggie Siena, who teaches a kindergarten-one class at P.S. 234 in New York City, says teachers get to know the ins and outs of their students' learning styles. "Because I keep students for two years, I'm able to tune in to their individual needs," she affirms. "I don't start over from scratch at the beginning of the year with a new group of children, so I'm way ahead of the game in terms of helping students."

● **Better parent relations—**Vicki Bachman notes that parents are more comfortable not having to adjust each year to new homework expectations, class routines, and so on. Vicki feels more at ease with parents she's gotten to know, too.

● **Wider comfort range for kids—** According to Paula Cramer, students who are low- or high-achievers don't feel a stigma or stand out in the wider range of ages and abilities. "Children know they're among others who match, complement, or supplement their needs and abilities," she observes. Marcy Vancil,

who teaches a kindergarten-one class in Urbana, Illinois, points out, "Students know that not everyone is *supposed* to be the same, so kids are less likely to compare themselves to classmates or put others down." That means that when kids in Rusty Bresser's three-four class in

**Cooperative learning groups and friendships cut across the lines of age in Paula Cramer's two-three class in Mount Washington, Kentucky.**

Oceanside, California, discuss a book, they're not concerned that some classmates read the book on their own, while others partner-read it, were read aloud to, or "echo read" (repeated sentences after they were read aloud).

● **Stronger social skills—**Nongraded classes are not as prone to cliques, says Anna Switzer, principal of P.S. 234 in New York City. "Kids get the message that relationships should cut across the lines of age," she says. "That helps them understand that friendships should cut across the lines of race, gender, economic class, and ability level, too."

According to Don Rehlaender, who teaches a two-three class in Corte Madera, California, another advantage is that students from multi-age classes adjust more easily

to middle school. "They're less likely to be intimidated by the new environment," he notes, "because many of their new schoolmates are former classmates."

Multi-age classes, teachers report, allow students more latitude in terms of social development. Older children who are less mature may play with younger classmates, while at the same time observing the behavior standards more mature children set. Also, according to bilingual teacher Brenda Mercado in Tucson, Arizona, multi-age classes allow teachers room to focus on developmental needs. "My older students crave independence," she says, "but the younger kids need *cariño* (Spanish for affection or attention). I can give the little ones *cariño* because I don't have 25 kids at that same developmental stage."

## MAKING THE TRANSITION
Mixed-age classes may have many benefits, but what is it like for a teacher to make the switch from a single grade? Kay Perrine, who teaches a three-four class in Copley, Ohio, admits, "I was scared to death of teaching a nongraded class. I thought I was going to bite off more than I could chew." But to her surprise, she found that teaching a multi-age class wasn't much different from teaching a single-grade class. Rusty Bresser concurs. "In single-grade classes I taught, I had gifted, special-education, and ESL students," he remembers. "I had as wide a spectrum of abilities as I have now."

Quiz: Is this a sea anemone or a nongraded class in Urbana, Ilinois? Answer: Both, and the kids are having a ball.

## 10 WAYS TO MANAGE A MULTI-AGE CLASS

To make their nongraded classes work, teachers from Arizona to Ohio recommend the following.

**1. Prepare students for what to expect.** Older students may feel that being placed in a multi-age class is a form of retention, while younger kids may feel uneasy about interacting with older schoolmates. To alleviate these anxieties, acquaint students with the nongraded approach to learning the spring prior to their entering a multi-age setting. The following spring, ask students to write down their feelings about the experience to share with newcomers.

**2. Enlist parental support.** To ease parents' concerns, hold an informational open house in the spring to communicate what your program is. Anticipate questions about assessment, curriculum, social issues, and so on. Stress that in a single-grade class you're likely to have as wide a range of student abilities as in a multi-age class. Keep the lines of communication open year-round. Recruit an advisory council of parents; follow up with a "Day in the Multi-Age Life of…" open house; have kids create a book of welcome letters for visitors; and so on.

**3. Keep children in two- or three-year programs.** Design your multi-age program so that children who start in a kindergarten-one class, for example, remain in that class with the same teacher for both years. Children who stay in a nongraded class for the full two- or three-year cycle have a better opportunity to see how they're progressing. Research shows that more growth occurs during the second year. And younger students can see where they're heading.

**4. Give parents and kids options.** Let parents know that your two- or three-year program is not a life sentence for their child. If at the end of the first year they decide they want their child switched into another class, accommodate them. Most schools report that it's rare for parents to ask for a transfer for their child. They see the benefits multi-age classes offer, too.

**5. Team up with a colleague.** Teachers who have tested the multi-age waters say it helps to have a colleague or group of colleagues to work with. For example, every other day Rusty Bresser teaches a science unit to his students while his colleague teaches a social studies unit to her class. After two weeks, they switch—Rusty's colleague teaches his students the same social studies topic, while Rusty teaches her class the same science subject.

**6. Think developmentally.** Instead of focusing on grade-level academic and social expectations for all your students, look at them as individuals on a continuum. Then decide how to best meet their needs. ➤

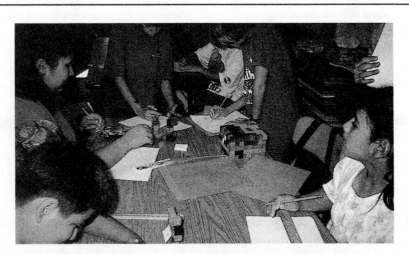
Judy Darcy's students in Tucson, Arizona, tackle open-ended math problems that are accessible to children with a wide spectrum of abilities.

**7. Teach one curriculum.** Multi-age classrooms are not combination classes where students in each grade study a different curriculum. They are environments in which all students study the same topics.

To create your curriculum, first keep in mind the milestones you want kids to reach and the skills your district expects them to acquire. Then spin off your curriculum from there, choosing depth over breadth. Before Kay Perrine taught a nongraded class, for example, she carefully examined the graded courses of study for both levels of students, noted essential learning targets, and then highlighted the areas that overlapped. She found that what the curriculum called for in English, handwriting, health, and, in most cases, the social sciences were nearly the same for each grade. Marcy Vancil chose to alternate teaching the kindergarten curriculum one year and the first-grade the next. Rusty Bresser proceeds by subject area: His district's third-grade science curriculum calls for the study of geology, plants, and matter; the fourth-grade, meteorology, animals, and the environment. He selects three subjects to do one year and then covers the remaining three the next.

**8. Adapt your instructional style.** If you teach from the textbook, a multi-age classroom may seem like a tall order. Instead of relying on the math and reading books for each grade level you teach, think of ways to use textbooks to supplement a more flexible instructional program.

**9. Present a range of activities. (Hint—learning centers help.)** Because you'll have a wide spectrum of abilities, present a range of open-ended activities that are accessible to the least advanced student,

When Kay Perrine (left) of Copley, Ohio, tested the multi-age waters, she found that it was smooth sailing.

while rich enough to challenge the most advanced. Rusty Bresser, for example, creates math menus that feature a range of problems. The focus of his geology learning center is a rock weighing station where kids compare the weights of rocks and record their thinking in words, pictures, and numbers. (Advanced students, Rusty observes, meticulously calculate weights to the nearest gram, while less-advanced kids place rocks on balances and record what happens.)

**10. Intersperse whole-class with small-group activities.** Class meetings and discussions in which ideas are shared are the cornerstones of successful multi-age programs. In Maggie Siena's classroom, for example, after one-on-one conferencing, the class convenes for a writing meeting. Younger or less-advanced kids have the opportunity to hear older or more advanced kids share their strategies for spelling and other techniques.

Because communication is essential for learning, especially in an environment of diverse abilities, make use of cooperative teams. Give students room to interact, talk about ideas, and hear other points of view. Group heterogeneously. Students who can't read as well as others but have advanced thinking skills, for example, may have a lot to contribute to a discussion. ■

## IF YOU WANT TO KNOW MORE

*Nongradedness: Helping It to Happen* by Robert H. Anderson and Barbara Nelson Pavan (Technomic, 1993), $24; (800) 233-9936

*The Multiage Classroom: A Collection* edited by Robin Fogarty (IRI/Skylight, 1993), $19.95; (800) 348-4474

*A Common Sense Guide to Multi-Age Practices* by Jim Grant and Bob Johnson (Crystal Springs, 1995), $16.95; (800) 321-0401

*How to Change to a Nongraded School* by Madeline Hunter (Association for Supervision and Curriculum Development, 1992), $6.95; (703) 549-9110

*The Multi-Age Classroom* by Bev Maeda (Creative Teaching Press, 1994), $14.98; (800) 444-4287

National Alliance of Multi-Age Educators (NAME). Annual dues are $9 (individual); (800) 924-9621

# TRAVELING COMPANIONS:
# THE VALUE OF COOPERATION
## Providing Professional Support When Implementing Multiage Practices

*"The teachers are very much present in each other's lives and they intentionally support each other's individual and collective work."*

— Dr. Charles Rathbone
***Multiage Portraits: Teaching and Learning in Mixed-age Classrooms***

In this quote, Dr. Rathbone is describing multiage teachers in the Shelburne Village School in Vermont. He goes on to say, "They meet regularly to plan and coordinate and support each other professionally and at times, personally." He is describing the working relationship of a team of four effective teachers in an ongoing multiage program that began in 1972.

This kind of professional support is one of the most critical factors in making multiage happen. The road to multiage continuous progress is not a trip to take alone. Those who want to take this journey need to support and work with each other.

## It's Not for Everyone

With the support of their principal, teachers also need to build as much understanding and good will among their colleagues as possible. That's not always easy to achieve. Innovators need to be sensitive to the fact that multiage is not for every teacher. This kind of major change is difficult and can be threatening to many people. We've talked with older teachers who are near retirement and candidly admit they haven't the energy to make such big changes. We have talked to teachers who, having been slapped down hard for some earlier change, will never risk another. There are teachers who not only don't want to change but who don't want to see anyone else succeed for fear the same program will then be forced on them. These teachers may not want to teach

multiage, but those who do need to make an effort to enlist their good will.

In her study of the social organization within schools and how it affects teachers, Susan J. Rosenholtz (1989) points out the kind of rationalization people will use to defend themselves against change: "it's unreasonably difficult"; "it can't possibly work." Unfortunately, with this kind of rationalization goes the need to undermine the particular innovation, because only when it fails are the naysayers vindicated.

Professional envy is also deadly to the change process. It is not uncommon for this to isolate the one or two teachers who are trying something different. Like quicksand, colleagues' negative feelings can sap teachers' energy and leave them sinking in discouragement. Such envy needs to be understood and tempered as much as possible.

## Mutual Support Can Be a Powerful Force

Multiage benefits from cooperating and collaborating. In fact, it often starts when two or three teachers in a school find they share a similar philosophy and begin sharing ideas and going to workshops together.

We've had people say to us:

"I was on the verge of quitting, but then I was allowed to collaborate with another teacher. It was so invigorating."

"Cooperative teaching may require more time, but it brought back some of the excitement I used to feel when I first started."

"It was hard at first, but it added another dimension to teaching."

Collaborating can start small. A first-grade teacher and a second-grade teacher might swap half of their children for a special project or a certain period each week. A first- and a fifth-grade teacher might set up a cross-age tutoring program. These are examples of low-risk ways to try out cooperating and bringing children of different ages together.

Another form of collaboration is co-teaching. Marilyn Friend (1992) interviewed a fifth-grade teacher and special-education teacher from Maplewood School in Cary, Illinois, who co-teach four mornings a week. When they meet for an hour each week to plan, they bounce ideas off each other. They like this arrangement for a number of reasons. It gives them energy and time to provide a balance of presenting lessons to the whole group, individuals, and small groups. It gives the students two perspectives. And there is someone with whom to share and work out the problems that come up. In talking about starting this kind of co-teaching, both teachers spoke of needing time not only to plan but to become comfortable with each other's style of teaching and to build mutual trust. Both agreed that it was helpful to have a mentor. As one teacher commented, "Co-teaching is like a marriage, and once in a while you need a marriage counselor."

## The Principal's Support

An enthusiastic, supportive principal is vital to introducing a multiage program into a school. The principal's leadership is needed to pave the way for cooperation, for parent understanding, for the materials and scheduling that will make it work.

If a teacher doesn't have an administrator who is going to give support and be an advocate for the program, s/he should think carefully about pushing ahead with major changes. Teachers need to make sure administrators are in their camp. Don't do it by yourself. It is too high-risk, too stressful.

A good administrator can help remove obstacles and establish ways for teachers to cooperate and support each other. When all the teachers are involved in trying something new, it becomes legitimate to seek and offer assistance. It is possible to acknowledge problems without appearing inadequate.

Cooperation should begin in the planning stage of developing a multiage continuous progress program. But it needs to be ongoing, and that requires time. Teachers need time and a format within which they can share projects, discuss problems, assess the changes that are being made, and develop ways in which they can cooperatively strengthen their program. This can't be accomplished over a cup of coffee between classes. It requires "quality time" and must be a part of the week's schedule.

## Team Teaching

As a school moves ahead in implementing a multiage continuous progress program, teachers will also want to explore the possibilities for team teaching. Team teaching goes beyond informal cooperation in that it tries to ensure the effectiveness and continuity of these working relationships. As Judson T. Shaplin writes in *Team Teaching*, this is done "by formalizing responsibilities and restricting team members from returning at will to an independent classroom and schedule. They may elect, within terms of their contracts, to leave the team, but the formal organization and the formal delegation of responsibilities remains, to be taken up by new members."

With this more formal organization of cooperative teaching comes more flexibility in scheduling and grouping. More trust and involvement is required from the teachers, but, in return, more support is available.

Robert T. Anderson has a helpful chapter in *Team Teaching* on "The Organization and Administration of Team Teaching." He points out that even though this form of cooperation is more structured, "each community will have its own specific reasons for undertaking team teaching and must work out an essentially unique solution to its recognized problems. Over the past 30 years, many schools have discovered the advantage of team teaching. Though team teaching is not necessary for a successful multiage continuous progress program, the two are a natural fit.

One benefit of teachers working together is that they can draw on each other's strengths. But perhaps the greatest personal benefit to any teacher wanting to try something innovative is that of having a supportive partner, someone with whom to share the frustrations and successes of trying something new. It helps you keep up your courage.

From *A Common Sense Guide to Multiage Practices*, by Jim Grant and Bob Johnson. Columbus, Ohio: Teachers' Publishing Group, 1994. All rights reserved. Available from Crystal Springs Books, Ten Sharon Road, Peterborough, NH 03458 1-800-321-0401.

# How Strong Is the Support System in Your School?

The following questionnaire has been adapted from one developed by Irv Richardson, former principal and multiage teacher at Mast Landing School in Freeport, Maine.

|  | **To Whom Would You Go if You . . .** | **Who Would Come to You if They . . .** |
|---|---|---|
| • need help planning a unit? | | |
| • need some new ideas for teaching a lesson? | | |
| • need some extra materials to teach a lesson next period? | | |
| • want a colleague to observe your teaching? | | |
| • want to co-teach a unit? | | |
| • want to share a successful lesson? | | |
| • want another opinion about something a student has done? | | |
| • need someone to take a duty for you on short notice? | | |
| • had a problem with a family and needed to talk about it? | | |
| • had a bad day and needed to talk about it? | | |
| • had a problem with another teacher? | | |
| • needed help with strategies to work with a particularly difficult student? | | |
| • needed someone to watch your class for a few minutes? | | |
| • had concerns about a change that was happening in your school? | | |
| • had a great idea about how to improve your school? | | |

**Reproducible Page**

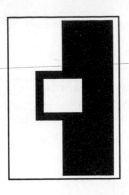

# ON CLASS SIZE: LESS IS MORE

by Debra Viadero

Ask a parent or teacher to name the most important factor in children's learning, and you're likely to hear about small classes. But ask a principal or superintendent, and you may get a different response. Administrators sometimes play down the benefits of reducing the number of students in classrooms. "Research has not conclusively shown that small classes are linked to improved student learning," they might say, or "Learning gains only show up when classes get down to 15 kids."

Well, not quite, say researchers from the Student/Teacher Achievement Ratio project, or Project STAR for short. As part of a two-phase study, the researchers have been tracking classes of 15 to 17 students in 79 schools scattered across Tennessee since 1985. Their efforts make up the largest and longest-lasting experiment ever conducted to examine the effects of small class sizes on student learning and development.

Not only do students in the early grades learn more in smaller classes, the project's investigators say. But they continue to have an edge over the rest of their peers years after they return to normal-sized classrooms.

What's more, they add, the data they have collected are beginning to show that every time a student is added to a classroom, learning is diminished for the rest of the class.

"This is one of the great experiments in education in United States history," Frederick Mosteller, a Harvard University statistics professor, says of the project. "It definitively answers the question of whether reduction from this size to that size does make a difference, and it clearly does."

But some education researchers are skeptical that Project STAR's findings make the definitive case for small classes. They point out that more than 1,100 studies on class size have been conducted over the years

and that the findings have been mixed.

"I don't think a single study proves all that much," says one such skeptic, Herbert J. Walberg, a professor at the University of Illinois at Chicago. "You can find some studies that indicate that *bigger* classes have better effects on learning."

Walburg also suggests that other kinds of intervention, such as cooperative learning, may be more effective and less expensive. Even if smaller classes do make a difference, critics ask, are they worth the expense?

## Testing It Out

Before Project STAR, the landmark study used to argue for small classes was an analysis Gene V. Glass and Mary Lee Smith conducted in the 1970's. They reviewed dozens of studies on the subject and concluded that reducing the number of students in a class does have a modest effect on learning.

Their findings also implied that the benefits would not show up until classes had been reduced to 15 or fewer students. But the study was controversial, partly because it mixed different grade levels and kinds of classes including graduate seminars and one-on-one tutorials.

When the class-size debate reared its head in the Tennessee legislature several years later, lawmakers decided to test out the hypothesis themselves. Spurred by then-Gov. Lamar Alexander's pro-education agenda, the legislature allocated $3 million to four of the state's top universities to launch Project STAR.

"All educators and parents know that, with fewer children, you can do a better job," says Helen Pate-Bain, who lobbied for the project when she was an associate professor at Tennessee State University. She says that 30 years of teaching high school taught her that. "But when you talk to the people that hold the purse strings, they all said to us that research says that small classes don't make a difference."

"The reason for doing the study was to once and for all show that class size does make a difference," adds Pate-Bain, who is now retired. She later became one of four principal investigators in the project.

Unlike the studies that came before it, Pate-Bain and her partners wanted Project STAR to be a true experiment in the most scientific sense of the word. Investigators decided to focus their efforts on students in Kindergarten through 3rd grade, reasoning that small classrooms could have the biggest effect on young learners.

"If you can give a child a good beginning, if they learn to read, nobody can take that away from them," says Pate-Bain, who is also a former president of the National Education Association, which has pushed hard to make smaller classes part of union contracts.

Of the 79 elementary schools that took part in the study, 25 were located in urban areas, 16 were in suburbs, and 39 were in rural areas. To participate, schools had to have at least 57 students in a grade — enough for one small experimental class of 13 to 17 students and two normal-sized classes of 22 to 25 students, one with an aide and one without.

"That way, whatever else might be happening at the school would happen under all three conditions," says Barbara Nye, who is the director of a follow-up study that became the successor to Project STAR.

Students were assigned to their classes randomly.

Through all four years of the study, the researchers found, students in all four grades on average outscored their peers in both types of large-class settings on a battery of standardized tests. Those tests included the Stanford Achievement Test, Tennessee's Basic Skills Criterion Tests, and another basic-skills-type test developed especially for the project.

Students in the inner-city schools appeared to have the greatest leaps. But their counterparts in suburban and rural schools made gains as well.

In reading and mathematics, the size of the gain was about a quarter of a standard deviation. To understand what that means, Mosteller says, think of a child who, without any special treatment, might score about the 50th percen-

tile on a test. A gain in score of a quarter of a standard deviation would raise that child from the 50th to the 60th percentile. In other words, now 60 percent of the testing population scored lower than that child.

"And we didn't do anything to schools other than reduce class sizes," adds Jayne Boyd-Zaharias, who took part in both Project STAR and the follow-up study.

Having a teacher's aide in the classroom, on the other hand, produced only slight improvement in student achievement.

## But Does It Last?

By the end of Project STAR, researchers had collected data on 7,000 students and spent $12 million. But questions arose over whether the documented gains would last. So, with continuing support from the state, the researchers launched a second study.

That project, called the Lasting Benefits Study, is less rigidly controlled than Project STAR. Through it, however, researchers were able to track students after they returned to normal-sized classes in the 4th grade and for years afterward.

In grades 4, 5, 6, and 7, the investigators have thus far found, students who had been in smaller classes in grades K-3 continued to outscore their peers who had been in larger classes. The differences in those scores, however, diminished somewhat as the years went on.

Moreover, the benefits were not limited to reading and math. Students from smaller classes outscored their grade-mates from larger classes in science, social studies, and other subjects, too. Other studies suggest that those students also participated more in class and took part in more extracurricular activities than their peers from larger classes.

Researchers are still tracking more than 4,000 of those students and hope to continue to do so after they leave high school to go on to college or start a career. Results on 8th graders are expected to be completely analyzed later this year.

Charles M. Achilles, a principal investigator on both projects, is also analyzing the data to see whether 15 or 17 is a "magic number" — the threshold at which real learning gains start to occur — or if any reduction in class size helps. Would adding or taking away a child in a class of 24 or 25 make a difference?

"It looks as though the addition of a child to a class decreases the class's average scores by about one-tenth of one month," in terms of the expected learning progress, he says. But, he warns, "we're still tinkering with this."

The results from Project STAR and from the early years of the Lasting Benefits Study persuaded the Tennessee legislature to take the plunge and pay for small classes. In 1989, lawmakers set aside funds to reduce class sizes in kindergarten through 3rd grades in 17 of the state's 138 school districts with the highest proportions of poor students.

More recently, the American Academy of Arts and Sciences, spurred by Mosteller's review of the project, has begun to tout the study as proof that small classes matter. The researchers also traveled to London in May to present their findings to educators weighing the matter there.

"It's time that we quit asking the question, 'Does it make a difference?' and begin to ask why it makes a difference and how we can begin to use this information," says Achilles, who is also a professor of educational administration at Eastern Michigan University.

But the question keeps coming up. Eric A. Hanushek, a University of Rochester economist and public-policy professor, is one of the critics to raise it most recently. Hanushek analyzed 300 studies and concluded that across-the-board reductions in class size are not worth the expense.

Although Project STAR wasn't included in that analysis, Hanushek does have an opinion about the study's findings. "Those people are zealots," Hanushek says of the STAR researchers. The problem with Project STAR, he explains, is that there is not much "value added" beyond the achievement gains that come about in kindergarten. The size of the effect in grades 1 through 3 is about the same.

On the other hand, Hanushek points out, the expense is considerable. "Dropping a class from 25 to 22 students increases classroom expenditures by more than 10 percent," he writes in his 1994 book, *Making Schools Work: Improving Performance and Controlling Costs.*

Project STAR's investigators counter that Hanushek, in his analysis, looked at overall student-staff ratios. That meant he included in his calculations, for example, librarians and special-education teachers — neither of which figure much in reducing the actual size of classes in a given school.

It is true, they concede, that the greatest gains come in the first year or two that students have smaller classes. But the point, they say, is that those gains remain just as strong as long as classes continue to be small.

The researchers also point out that, by 1st grade, the sample of students in small classes included students who were retained as well as 250 students who had not gone to kindergarten. (Kindergarten attendance was not mandatory in Tennessee at the time.) If anything, the STAR researchers say, their numbers are probably conservative.

They also suggest that, contrary to what Hanushek says, the benefits are cumulative. In kindergarten, 55 percent of the top-scoring classes in the project's sample population were small classes. By 3rd grade, small classes accounted for 78 percent of the top 10 percent.

As for the cost, the STAR researchers point out that reducing the number of students that are held back each year or that require remedial service through the federal Title I program for disadvantaged students translates to cost savings in the long run.

"Is it worth it to spend $1,500 extra for a child not to fail," Nye asks, "rather than spend $10,000 for a child to repeat a grade?"

Reprinted with permission from *Education Week.*
Volume 14, Number 39, July 12, 1995.

*If a plant is to unfold its specific nature to the full, it must first be able to grow in the soil in which it is planted.*

— *Carl Jung*

# Managing the Change to Multiage: "How Do I Get There From Here?"

Changing from a graded structure to a multiage structure involves shifting people's ideas about school.

It also means implementing policies and procedures that do not rely on grade levels as a method of grouping students and as a way to organize curriculum.

Because the lock-step graded structure is such a part of how we view education, it is often difficult for people to consider "school" without specific grade levels. It is interesting to note how important grade level designation can be when describing children between the ages of five and eight. More often than not children are defined by their grade level attainment— "Jamie is a third grader," for example. The notion of grade levels becomes much less important after graduation from high school. None of us would consider asking another adult his current grade.

To begin the change to multiage, a first step is to research the topic of multiage by reading professional literature and by attending conferences and workshops.

It can also be beneficial to visit schools which have successfully implemented multiage programs to discuss their change process and to examine the beliefs and structure of their multiage program.

After obtaining a solid foundation of multiage practices and philosophy, educators must work with community members to decide whether or not a multiage structure will benefit the students enrolled in that school system. If a school decides to implement a multiage program, then the members of the school community must begin to plan for the transition from a one-year, single-grade, timebound organization to a multiage continuous progress structure.

## Our Best Advice ✔

Understanding and following the various elements of the change process is the beginning point for all reform efforts. The change process enables stakeholders to clearly focus on the shared vision to create multiage continuous progress programs.

# Take Your Time When Implementing a Multiage Classroom

Imagine a farmer who wants to harvest his crops in a fraction of the usual time. To do this, he plants the seeds, waters them without stopping for two weeks, spends the next week weeding, fertilizes, and then harvests. It sounds silly, for we all know that it takes a certain period of time to harvest a crop—even with good agricultural practices.

Growing a good multiage program also takes time. The foundation for any good early childhood education program must be a staff that is knowledgeable about developmentally appropriate practices. With knowledge about child development, appropriate curricula and teaching strategies, and a love for children, educators have the requisite skills to implement a strong multiage program.

With a strong foundation in appropriate education and support from the school community and parents, some educators choose to implement multiage programs. The decision to implement is made by teachers, administrators, and community members. The decision is made after considerable research about multiage philosophy and multiage programs that function well. Most schools investigate the multiage philosophy for at least a year before implementing a multiage program.

Taking the time to investigate multiage, making the decision to start a multiage program, choosing the staff, making the necessary adjustments to curriculum and launching the program can take a year or more. It may take another four years to iron out wrinkles and get the program running smoothly.

## Steps to Success

1. Attend an awareness session on multiage practices.
2. Present your plans to create a multiage classroom to your parent group, and invite them to participate in the process.
3. Form a multiage study team to do the following:

   - Read and discuss articles and professional books, review videos and audiotapes on multiage practices.
   - Attend workshops, conferences and various staff development opportunities.

4. Secure administrative, fellow staff, school board, and broad community support.
5. Investigate and visit successful multiage models that would be appropriate for your community.
6. Assign willing teachers to staff the multiage classroom
7. Budget appropriate financial resources for training, related costs, travel, professional books, furniture, classroom remodeling, etc.

8.  Select a well-balanced, heterogeneous student population and secure permission from parents to include their children in the multiage classroom.

## Our Best Advice

The more time taken to carefully plan and implement multiage practices, the greater is the likelihood of your program having longevity. The faster you implement your program the more likely you will have overlooked very important elements necessary to the program's well-being. High-speed implementation usually results in high speed unraveling, leading to the eventual dismantling of your program.

I nitiating and maintaining a multiage program will require resources. Perhaps the most important needed resource is time. The teachers and administrators who are starting the multiage program will need time to discuss how the new program will be set up and how it will function. In addition to all of the organizational demands of a single classroom such as room arrangement, supplies, and curriculum, educators beginning multiage programs often must adapt curriculum, decide how students and staff will be selected for the program, and work to create positive transition steps from the graded structure to a multiage one.

# Allow Enough Planning Time Before Implementation

There are many ways to create common planning time for staff members. If the program is started through grant funds, part of the funds can be used to hire teachers during the summer months for program planning and curriculum writing time. Money from staff development can also be used to buy time for teachers.

During the regular school day, substitute teachers can be brought in to allow teachers, parents, and administrators time to meet. If a school has art, music, and physical education or library periods for students, it may be possible to schedule these specials so that one teacher's students are at art while another teacher's students are at music. This will allow the teachers time away from their students to work on planning and implementation of the multiage program.

## Our Best Advice ✔

Murphy's Law states, "Everything takes longer than expected," and the change from a one-year single-grade classroom to a multiyear, multiple grade blend is no exception. The multiage classroom is a more complex classroom structure and therefore requires a great deal of time to think, reflect and plan. In order for teachers to make this reform as stress-free as possible and to end up with a high-quality program, we must prioritize and set aside planning time to do the job.

# Allow Teachers to Become Agents of Change, Rather Than Targeting Them for Change

One of the worst mistakes a school system can make is to force a teacher to teach in a multiage classroom against his or her will. To do so is a fast track to disaster. Such a teacher can undermine the concept of multiage education and cause the program's demise.

Many teachers make wonderful, hard-working, dedicated single grade teachers, yet are not well-suited to teaching in a multiple grade, multiyear classroom. This teaching assignment requires an enormous amount of energy and commitment, and is a great deal more work than teaching in a single grade classroom. Principals are advised to carefully select and assign only willing staff to teach in a multiage continuing progress classroom.

In rare instances a principal will come across a teacher who is not only against teaching in a multiage classroom, but is adamantly opposed to anyone else in the building doing so. In this situation, a principal should consider transferring the teacher to another school or teaching assignment. Keeping this individual on staff could create unnecessary staff dissension and impede necessary education reform.

Teachers who find themselves assigned to teach in a multiage classroom, or who have volunteered for a multiage classroom but discover they are not meant for it, should take steps to get out of the situation as soon as possible.

We suggest the teacher ask to be reassigned to a single grade classroom; in some cases it may be necessary for the teacher to request a transfer to another school.

Principals are advised to seek out the cause of the teacher's distress. It may be that the student population in the classroom is too diverse, or that there have been too many high-impact, special-needs students fully included. Redistributing some students, providing aide support, reducing class size or placing a special educator in the room full time may be viable alternatives to reassigning or transferring a teacher.

## Our Best Advice ✓

A teacher forced to teach in a classroom against his or her will is still of the same mind. By assigning only willing staff to participate in multiage education, you greatly increase the likelihood of a successful multiage program.

# Don't Assume Everyone Can Teach in A Multiage Classroom

One multiage teacher summed it up nicely when she said, "Teaching in a multiage classroom ain't for sissies!" It is hard work—harder than teaching a single grade—and it takes very special people. We are often asked what attitudes and qualities a prospective multiage classroom teacher should possess. The following criteria, while not exhaustive, are fairly inclusive, and would be a good place to start a discussion on teacher selection.

When you are selecting the right person to teach in a multiage classroom, it is important that a teacher answer yes to the following:

- Be a veteran classroom teacher.
- Want to teach in a multiage setting.
- Think developmentally about how students learn best.
- Have experience teaching several different grade levels.
- Be a risk-taker and not fearful of trying something new.
- Be open to "good" education change.
- Be well-versed in whole child instructional strategies.
- Love hard work and long hours.
- Be comfortable challenging the status quo.
- Not be afraid to jettison what doesn't work.
- Not be a consumer of education fads, trends or waves
- Love developmental diversity among students
- Be a high energy person with great sustaining power
- Possess a great deal of common sense
- Like collaborating with fellow teachers
- Be skilled at working with parents

The above attributes should serve to focus discussion among school personnel involved in selecting the staff who might be well suited in a multiage program.

## Our Best Advice ✔

Only uniquely qualified, motivated members of the teaching staff should be assigned to teach in a multiage setting.

We do not think it is advisable for first year teachers to be assigned to multiage classrooms unless their student teaching has prepared them for such assignments.

# Provide Adequate Staff Development

Few of us feel comfortable implementing those practices/strategies which we do not fully understand. The same is true for a teacher trying to implement a multiage classroom program. In order to initiate and maintain a successful multiage program, a teacher must have a strong foundation in the principles of child development and a high degree of knowledge about developmentally appropriate curricula and pedagogical practices. A teacher implementing a multiage classroom should also be comfortable with the following classroom practices:

- School readiness
- Teaching skills in context
- Ages and stages
- Cooperative learning
- Manipulative math
- Writing process
- Literature-based reading programs
- Developmentally appropriate practices
- Thematic teaching
- Learning centers and work stations
- Authentic assessment and evaluation
- Computer technology
- Developmental discipline
- Multiple intelligences
- Conflict resolution/Responsibility Training
- Team teaching
- Inclusion of differently-abled children

Without the necessary foundation in child development and appropriate instructional strategies, it will be extremely difficult, if not impossible, for a teacher to make a multiage program work. Without major curriculum modifications to allow multiage students to make continuous progress, the program will not succeed.

## Our Best Advice ✓

The greater the preparation for teaching in a multiage classroom, the greater likelihood of success. We should not expect teachers to become involved in practices they have not been trained to do. Initiate a staff development plan before implementing your multiage program.

# Q.

Will the older, gifted child be adequately challenged in a multiage classroom?

A. Yes. As a matter of fact, a good multiage classroom can be a more challenging environment, with greater opportunities for advanced students.

One reason is that the multiage setting has a higher ceiling on the curriculum to reflect the needs of the wide range of abilities. There are also opportunities for the more knowledgeable students to teach others. Students who teach other students often retain as much as 90% of the material taught.

On an interpersonal level, older, more knowledgeable students who may be socially and/or emotionally young have an opportunity to socialize with younger class members.

Multiage students get the chance to be the oldest members of a group every two or three years. (Some students in a single-grade classroom may go through childhood without ever experiencing this.) It is beneficial for students to have experiences in different social strata. Older, more knowledgeable students also have more opportunity to be placed in leadership roles. Being needed and admired by younger, less able students increases a student's self-concept.

## Gifted and Talented Children

| Single Age/Grade Classroom | Multiage/Multiyear Classroom |
|---|---|
| · Extended learning program | · Extended learning program |
| · Tutoring opportunities offer a "teaching" role | · Tutoring opportunities offer a "teaching" role |
| | **AND** |
| | · There are younger children to socialize with. |
| | · Students can gain "senior citizen" status. |
| | · The older, more knowledgeable have the chance to practice being in a leadership role. |
| | · Multiage classrooms have a higher ceiling on the curriculum. |

# Q.

## Should kindergarten be separated or mixed in with first grade?

 **A.** If your school is adopting a multiage philosophy, it is important to include the kindergarten in some way for a number of reasons:

· If you want your school community to believe in this philosophy, it's best to be consistent; leaving kindergartners out of a multiage experience when they are a part of the multiage building sends a mixed message.

· Often, the kindergarten teachers in elementary buildings have the most experience in creating developmentally appropriate, child-centered classrooms. Their expertise will be invaluable to teachers who are making dramatic changes in their teaching practices and classroom organization. Don't leave them out!

· Five- and six-year-olds will benefit from a mixed-age environment just as much as seven-, eight-, nine-, and ten-year-olds do. If the priority is a superior, mixed-age environment, then kindergartners deserve to be a part of this experience just as much as any other group.

However, there is no one correct way to group the children in a multiage setting. The most important thing is to consider the specific needs of your students and what your district offers for them, and plan accordingly for your situation.

Combining kindergarten with first grade can be done in a variety of ways. If kindergarten is offered as a full-day program in your school district, there is no reason to separate the kindergartners from the older children.

Many programs combine kindergarten, first, and second grades into one unit with success. One option is to include half-day kindergartners with first graders. The younger children come for the morning only, and the teacher is left with a very small group of six- and seven-year-olds in the afternoon. As the kindergartners mature and possibly need a full-day option, it is available to them.

One classroom arrangement that has drawn some negative response is the combination of two half-day kindergarten programs with one first grade. In this situation, half the children, the first graders, are in the classroom all day, while the other half of the class, the kindergartners, are there either in the morning or in the afternoon. Teachers involved in this situation have not been enthusiastic about the mixed-age grouping. This arrangement adds much more assessment responsibility, recordkeeping, and parental contact to a teaching situation that is already very complex.

Teachers exposed to this arrangement felt it was very difficult to form a cohesive classroom community, and that the older children were often overlooked. It seemed a confusing situation to everyone involved, and so it is not a practice that is recommended.

Another option is combining kindergarten, first, and second grades. While this age span might seem too great, many teachers who have tried it have been very positive about it, especially when there was a team teaching situation. The fact that they had such a variation in levels forced them to give up old "total group" habits and plan their lessons for small groups and/or individual children. This actually made the transition to multiage classrooms less difficult, for they were not falling back on their former, more traditional teaching styles, trying to make the children conform to a new "middle of the road" curriculum, teaching a total group lesson to a nonexistent group of "average" children.

Montessori schools in the United States traditionally have their kindergartners in a multiage classroom with three-, four-, and five-year-olds. This grouping, called preprimary, creates a multiage setting for young children in a half-day program. When children are developmentally ready, they are moved to the primary classroom, another three-year grouping. This situation is nice for several reasons, one of which is the consistency of the multiage, family grouping from the very beginning of school. If your school district offers nursery school and half-day kindergarten, you might consider combining these age groups, rather than K-1.

One of the most appreciated aspects of the multiage school is that it offers alternatives. In your planning, you should consider many options, and choose those that are best for your community.

From *Multiage Q&A : 101 Practical Answers to Your Most Pressing Questions*, by Jim Grant, Bob Johnson, and Irv Richardson. Peterborough, NH: Crystal Springs Books, 1995. 1-800-321-0401.

# Perceived Advantages of a Kindergarten/First Grade Blend

- Mixed-age eavesdropping opportunities
- There is a higher ceiling on the curriculum
- There are peer modeling opportunities
- There are over a dozen multiyear placement benefits
- There can be an additional year of learning time without the stigma of "staying back"
- Grade one is afforded more play opportunities
- There is additional time available for "kid watching"
- In some schools kindergartners go home at noon reducing the class size for first grade in the PM
- There are real benefits to proximal development
- There are tutoring opportunities for both groups
- There are 50% fewer new first graders to teach to read

# Perceived Disadvantages of a Kindergarten/First Grade Blend

- Kindergartners may be denied play opportunities
- Many of today's kindergartners have very high needs
- Class is too diverse developmentally
- First graders may be shortchanged academically
- Some schools have four-year-olds in kindergarten due to a late entrance date
- The needs of five-year-olds are very different from six-year-olds
- Kindergartners may be overwhelmed by more experienced first graders
- There may not be enough quality kid watching time
- Kindergarten is time intensive to teach
- Some entire kindergarten classes are too disjointed to keep together as a group for multiple years
- Kindergartners who are learning-handicapped, yet unidentified, may not qualify for special needs intervention
- If there is an AM and PM kindergarten (2 groups) there may be too much lost time transitioning

# Getting to Know You— Multiyear Teaching

Barbara J. Hanson

**When teachers and kids are together for two years in a row, they reap both academic and emotional bonuses.**

It's the first day of the new school year, and even before the Willett School bell rings, groups of children are gathered on the playground in Attleboro, Massachusetts, eagerly clustered around teachers to share their summer adventures like old friends. What makes this school year so different for these children and teachers is "multiyear assignment": these students will have the same teacher for two years.

As school systems from coast to coast look for innovative ways to restructure schools in order to improve student performance, many are looking to multiyear assignment as a way of shaking up existing paradigms. The Attleboro School System is a case in point.

## What It's All About

Under the direction of school superintendent Joseph Rappa, this New England school system began to move quietly in the direction of multiyear assignment during the late 1980s. In a pilot program, a few teachers were asked to follow their classes for a period of two years. The pilot proved to be successful, and the school system now requires all classroom teachers from grades 1–8 to spend two years with their classes. First grade teachers move to 2nd grade, 3rd grade teachers move to 4th grade, and so on. Even high school staff are now considering the idea.

As with any break with tradition, many parents and staff questioned the rationale behind the change. Was multiyear assignment a radical new trend or an old chestnut left over from the days of the one-room schoolhouse? Where did this idea originate and did it have merit?

Faced with the exciting yet scary prospect of spending two years with my students, I decided to research the concept. I found that there's only a limited amount of information. Early 20th century Austrian educator Rudolf Steiner, founder of the Waldorf Schools, felt that the teacher should follow the class throughout the elementary grades much like a "third parent" (Ogletree 1974). Multiyear assignment has also been successful in middle schools in Germany, where teams of six to eight teachers work with the same students from grades 5–10 (Koppich 1988).

The concept of multiyear assignment as we now know it apparently first appeared in New York in 1974. There, award-winning educator Deborah Meier considered the practice an essential component in her ideal school because it enabled children and teachers to get to know one another well (Goldberg 1991).

## Continuity and Familiarity

In a recent survey of some teachers in Attleboro's pilot group, responses to multiyear assignment were quite positive, for many reasons. For example, teachers agreed that children are less anxious about the new year. They know both the teacher and the expectations. Parents happily report that preschool jitters are a thing of the past, especially during the second year of the cycle.

A bonus for teachers is that they gain almost an extra month of teaching time. Getting-to-know-you time becomes virtually unnecessary during the second year, enabling us to get to learning without much review. We also find it easy to build on the experiences we shared the first year.

Children are also able to continue their learning throughout the summer. We furnished our students with packets of ideas for summer reading, writing, and exploration, taking care to keep the activities short, interesting, and fun. Children study insects, collect rocks, and observe and graph weather patterns. Most parents have enthusiastically supported these activity packets, especially for those rainy summer days.

Barbara J. Hanson

**These 4th graders needed only a quick review to begin a project. They learned the how-to's as 3rd graders last year.**

In the fall, on the first day of school, our 4th graders proudly brought in their handmade bug houses (a product of their summer homework), and our insect unit was off and running.

Teachers also report that time spent on developing social skills and cooperative group strategies really pays off during the second year of the cycle. Students are better able to resolve conflicts and they are more skillful in working as team members to solve problems. These skills will be especially important as schools across the United States move to group-based performance assessment.

From the perspective of the whole language teacher, multiyear assignment offers enormous advantages. Vermont educators Mazzuchi and Brooks (1992) write that this policy provides teachers and students alike with the "gift of time" for observing social and language development. As 1st/2nd grade teachers, the two have found multiyear assignment to be invaluable in assessing growth. Because each child develops at a unique pace, teachers can experience the joy of seeing even the late bloomer blossom. And with two years to nurture and reflect upon our students and our instructional objectives, we can be certain that our instruction will be constructivist, or child-centered, rather than curriculum-centered.

Multiyear assignment is increasingly vital to the countless children whose lives are riddled with change—change of residence, change in family structure, change of economic status. Our kids come from broken homes, or go home to empty houses, or see parents only on weekends: they seem to really benefit from having a teacher as a role model, mentor, and friend.

Multiyear assignment appears to provide a strong support system for these children.

Parents have generally supported the policy. They say that, like their children, they appreciate the chance to become familiar with a teacher's instructional style and expectations for classwork and homework. They also report feeling more comfortable during the parent-teacher conference, especially the second year. By that time conferences are more meaningful, given the perspective of the past and present.

## Not Without Flaws

It would be unfair and unrealistic to suggest that this approach has no problems. Many of the teachers surveyed included words of caution.

Several teachers warned that the particular makeup of a class might adversely affect the group's potential to learn. They suggested that such classes may need to be split up (a good example of why teacher input is essential). Teachers also advised that two-year classes need to be extra sensitive to students new to the class, lest they feel like outsiders. We have found family meetings and "circles of friends" to be excellent avenues for dealing with this problem.

Teachers expressed their own anxieties as well, particularly over the fact that their job performance over two years might be assessed based on their students' performance on standardized tests. This policy, they said, left them with an enormous sense of responsibility.

Finally, on an emotional note, teachers reported that it becomes very difficult to separate from the class at the end of the cycle.

## My Favorite Year

I am currently in the second year of my two-year cycle. I look back upon my first year with satisfaction. As a 30-year veteran of the teaching profession, I can say that it was one of the most rewarding and exciting years of my career. My original fears about changing to a new grade quickly disappeared as I moved from a curriculum-centered to a student-centered classroom. Best of all, the month of June did not mark an ending; it was merely an interlude.

My students returned this September fully equipped with familiar skills and strategies for responding to literature, for process-writing, for group problem solving, and for using learning logs. They understood the importance of portfolios and of reflecting on their personal growth. Perhaps the very first entry in the daily journal of Larry, one of my 4th graders, best sums it up:

> This is the best first day of school. I can be with my teacher from last year. I can see my friends. I like school. ■

## References

Goldberg, M. F. (December 1990/January 1991). "Portrait of Deborah Meier." *Educational Leadership* 48, 4: 26–28.

Koppich, J. E. (1988). "Redefining Teacher Work Roles." Eric Document, ED 326 930.

Mazzuchi, D., and N. Brooks. (February 1992). "The Gift of Time." *Teaching, K–8*: 60–62.

Ogletree, E. J. (March 1974). "Rudolf Steiner: Unknown Educator." *The Elementary School Journal*: 344–351.

**Barbara J. Hanson** is Head Teacher and a grade 3-4 teacher at the Willett School in Attleboro, Massachusetts. She can be reached at P.O. Box 3264, South Attleboro, MA 02703.

# LINCOLN MIDDLE SCHOOL:
## A case study in long-term relationships

by Paul S. George with Melody Spreul and Jane Moorefield

Excerpt from **Long Term Teacher-Student Relationships: A Middle School Case Study**, by Paul S. George with Melody Spreul and Jane Moorefield.

At Lincoln Middle School, in Gainesville, Florida, attempts to capitalize on the quality of more lengthy human relationships have been underway for more than a decade. Previously a segregated high school, when it became a middle school in 1972 Lincoln was one of the few schools in the nation to organize so that teachers and students stay together on interdisciplinary teams for up to three years. Lincoln Middle School, under the leadership of Principal John Spindler, has utilized two similar but significantly different ways of doing so. Both appear to have worked well.

## Multiage Grouping

For about a decade after the opening of the school *almost 15 years ago*, Lincoln organized its teachers and students for learning according to what came to be called multiage grouping. Approximately 1,000 predominantly lower middle and lower socioeconomic status students and 50 teachers were organized into six interdisciplinary teams of 150 students and four teachers per team. Each team took on the characteristics of the school as a whole, with approximately 150 sixth, seventh and eighth graders on each team, served by a team of teachers from the areas of language arts, reading, social studies, science, and mathematics.

Each spring, one third of the team's students moved on to the ninth grade; each fall a new group of sixth graders joined the team. Accordingly, teachers and students remained together on the same team for a period of three years, instead of the customary nine months which most early adolescents experience in

relationships with teachers. Not only did an individual child's relationships with teachers last three times as long, but three-year relationships also were the rule among the students on the team. Often, relationships persisted even longer for the teachers who comprised the adult members of the team. For the entire decade during which multiage grouping existed at Lincoln, the effects were almost entirely positive.[1] After ten years of positive experiences with multiage grouping, the process became an unintended casualty of school board policies aimed at centralizing and standardizing the school organization process within the district's six middle schools.

In 1982, all six of the middle schools in the district were placed on the same traditional chronological-age, grade level grouping format, so that students in the same grade at different schools in the district used the same textbooks in every class. The school board's requirement for standardization and Lincoln's process of multiage grouping were incompatible. At Lincoln, after 1982, sixth graders for instance, could no longer study foreign language even if they were ready to do so. Students who, although in the eighth grade, required remediation in mathematics or reading, were unable to be grouped with students from the same team in so-called regular classes. The curriculum could no longer be dramatically adapted to the needs of the individuals and groups of students. Long term relationships appeared doomed.

## Student-Teacher Progression

After unsuccessfully petitioning the school board to permit them to depart from the policy that brought an end to multiage grouping, the

[1]The details of how the teams were organized and the benefits of this process are discussed elsewhere. See, for example, Alexander and George (1981), **The Exemplary Middle School**, New York, Holt, Reinhart and Winston.

staff of the school so lamented the absence of long-term teacher-student relationships that they voted, almost unanimously, to implement a new program. This new feature of organization at Lincoln, while retaining grade level grouping, would permit the existence of three year teacher-student relationships. "Student-Teacher Progression" (STP) came to Lincoln Middle School at the end of its eleventh year of operation.

Student Teacher Progression at Lincoln is based on grade level team organization, two sixth grade teams, two seventh grade teams, and two eighth grade teams. Teachers who make up a sixth grade academic team (five subjects including reading) move with their students at the beginning of the next year to become a seventh grade team. The following year, these same students and teachers become an eighth grade team. At the end of the three year period, students move on to the high school and the teachers rotate back to pick up a new group of sixth graders and renew the STP process. Lincoln is one of only two middle schools currently known to be practicing this form of teacher-student grouping, the other being Bunche Middle School in Atlanta, Georgia.

## Organization of the Study

In the autumn of 1984, a research team of university and public school educators decided to conduct an initial exploratory study of long-term teacher student relationships at Lincoln, as they existed in the STP process. Since virtually nothing has been done to describe the process and the outcomes of STP, and the long-term relationships it established, this became the point of departure for the year's exploration.

During the summer of 1984, prior to beginning the exploratory study, all members of the research group participated in a graduate level course in middle school education, at the University of Florida. In the beginning of the 1984-85 school year, this group initiated a process of intermittent observation and visitation that lasted throughout the entire school year. Weekly teacher team meetings were observed regularly during the first quarter of the year. Conversations were held with many members of the teaching and administrative staff, with students and with

parents. Classes were observed. One member of the research team spent a week as a substitute teacher on one of the eighth grade teams. Other members of the research group attended the weekly meetings of the school's Program Improvement Council, a policy-making representative group of team leaders and school administrators. One member of the research group became a member of the school's guidance services during the second half of the year.

As the first quarter of the school year ended, members of the research group interviewed teachers, students, and administrators to assist in determining the items that would comprise the detailed questionnaires that would be administered in the winter. Separate questionnaires were designed for and administered to teachers, students, administrators, and parents. Following the collection of completed questionnaires, the data were examined cursorily for suggestions to be incorporated into a second round of more in-depth interviews to be conducted in the late spring with representatives of each of the four groups involved in the study. A final round of observations, visitations, and interviews completed the exploratory process in the late spring near the end of the school year.

## Long-Term Relationships with Students: The Teachers' Point of View

Sixty-one faculty members at Lincoln completed the 85-item written questionnaire, then 15 representative teachers were interviewed following a brief analysis of the data from the teacher questionnaire. Because of the nature of the university community in which they live, teacher attrition is fairly high; the average number of years teachers had taught at Lincoln was 2.9, with a sizeable number in their first year and only two teachers who had been on the faculty the entire time the school has been organized as a middle school. In terms of the range of teaching experience, the average years of experience as a teacher was 7.8, from first year teachers to veterans of 24 years experience. Fifteen teachers had taught at Lincoln for their entire teaching career.

Teachers at Lincoln, almost unanimously, were strongly positive in their evaluation of the effects of STP. The results of the questionnaires and interviews in which teachers participated point to the existence of at least ten possible advantages which teachers believe are a product of the long-term close relationships encouraged by the STP process. These advantages are listed below. The teaching staff at Lincoln sees long-term relationships existing in several different forms (teacher-student, teacher-teacher, teacher-parent), from each of which emanates important positive outcomes for the learning program.

## 1. Classroom Management

Teachers at Lincoln saw the STP program as instrumental in producing better classroom discipline. Because of the length of time they would spend with the same students, teachers saw themselves as being much more willing to attempt behavior management alternatives when conventional or accustomed techniques failed to achieve the necessary results. Many

---

*Students came to know and care about each other more fully . . .*

---

teachers agreed that they came to trust their students more during the three year period they spent with them. Others found it less necessary to make constant reference to classroom rules.

Teachers in the STP program tended to use seating charts and other formal behavior strategies less often. Approximately 70% of the teachers found themselves able to use more positive approaches to classroom management. A majority of the teachers also believed that the in-depth knowledge of their students, gained over more than year, made it possible for teachers to act more fairly when enforcing rules and levying consequences. Finally, the faculty saw themselves as more able to effectively reduce classroom management structure appropriately, as the students matured.

## 2. The Advisory Role

A central feature in the middle school concept is the advisory role that brings the teacher to a point of concern and advocacy for a special group of students. As far back as the first junior high schools in the nation, many educators of early adolescents have recognized the need for teachers to act as special guides for certain of their students, as the students moved from the self-contained classroom of the elementary school on to the complexity of the high school's departmentalized system. It appears the long-term close relationships actualized within the STP program at Lincoln significantly enhanced the performances of teachers in the role of the advisor.

Teachers identified a number of very positive ways this happened. Because teachers and their advisees stayed together in the same advisory group for three years, as well as in the academic classroom, 92% of the teachers said that they had become much more aware of the students' personal lives, in and out of the classroom. Students seemed, to teachers, to be more positive about discussing out-of-school problems with the teacher. More open and frank communication was reported to have occurred between teachers and students. The amount of time teachers spent talking with students about the students' personal lives increased. Teachers said this occurred without detracting from academic efforts. Teachers, it appears, came to care more about each individual student as a person, not just in terms of academic achievement. More and more students, teachers said, came to know and benefit from a continuing relationship with at least one adult who demonstrated authentic caring for them. Teachers believed students were more likely to see the faculty members as concerned about the student's future. They also saw students as more likely, during the three years together, to perceive teachers as role models, especially when appropriate role models may have been missing from the home. Teachers became much more than academicians or instructors.

## 3. Group Involvement

The closeness that developed among the advisors and their advisees, combined with the senses of identification with the team over a period of three years, contributed a great deal to the students' and teachers' sense of unity and group involvement. Eighty-five percent of the faculty thought that students were more able, as a result of the three year relationship, to come to see themselves as important members of a special group, exhibiting more pride in the advisory group, the interdisciplinary team they were on, and in the school as a whole.

Students on the teams and in the advisory groups were much more likely, teachers believed, to get to know each other very well. The number and the depth of important student-student friendships also increased. Students came to know and care about each other more fully, teachers perceived.

The sense of unity that emerged during the three year life of the team also encouraged both teachers and students to take team-related activities more seriously. Some teachers felt a greater willingness to participate in the extra-curricular activities that were available. Teachers perceived the students as being more appreciative of the efforts that teachers made on their behalf.

Symbols of group identification assumed greater prominence in team life as a result of STP. Names for advisory groups, banners exhalting the life on the team, special team t-shirts, bulletin boards and other signs of a feeling of cohesiveness were abundant, colorful, and free of graffiti. Special events, assemblies, intramurals, field trips, camp-outs and almost every other school activity was connected, in important ways, to life on the teams and in the advisory groups. Team spirit and pride were present in almost every aspect of school daily life. Teachers laid the willingness of students to participate more fully in planning special classroom and team events to the students' three year experience.

### 4. Teacher Investment

Conventional wisdom holds that close interpersonal relationships are more likely to encourage one person to spend time and energy contributing to the welfare of another. Research in school effectiveness, referred to the above, indicates that academic achievement is related to the capacity of teachers to make this kind of more intense investment in their students. The results of the present exploratory study indicate that the three year relationship with students does, in the teachers' view, stimulate a more intense level of commitment to the students and their progress.

Teachers more clearly recognized the special needs of their students and reported greater levels of persistence in getting special help for those who required it. Teachers believed that, because they knew students more thoroughly, they were likely to take their students' successes and failures more personally. The teachers were more likely to persist in working through problems with students rather than avoiding the problems or giving up as

quickly as they might have had they not had three years to spend with the same students.

In every classroom, in every school, teachers encounter students who seem to resist every effort the teachers make on their behalf. Often, teachers shudder at the thought of having these students in their classes for three years. At Lincoln, the faculty was almost equally divided on the question of what the three year relationship did to their ability to continue to invest themselves in these exceptional students. Almost 40% of the teachers argue that in spite of this lengthy relationship, and the accompanying constant rejection by these students, they did not give up on these students and redirect their energy to others.

Almost an equal number, however, reported that these very different students did exhaust their capacities to persist and that the teachers had a tendency to give up on these students. The teachers who felt this need to invest themselves where the energy was likely to pay dividends, believed that after two years of trying to help certain students, it would be better for those students to be moved to another team for a fresh start with teachers who were willing to begin anew with them.

The STP program also requires that some members of the teaching team teach a new subject each year. In social studies, for example, teachers would begin with world history, then switch to geography in the seventh grade, and then were responsible for teaching American history during the last component of the three year cycle. This was also the case in science, where the rotation went through earth science, physical science,

*. . . the three year relationship with students does, in the teacher's view, stimulate a more intense level of commitment to the students and their progress.*

and life science during the three years. Over 60% of the teachers reported that this rotation helped them avoid the boredom associated with teaching the same subject every year.

Ninety-two percent of the faculty believed that teaching the same students for three years, in the same general subject areas, made it possible for them to observe continuous progress and to accept some personal responsibility for that progress. Teachers described a greater sense of efficacy than they believed would have been possible if they had their students for only nine months instead of three years.

---

*Because the teachers invested themselves more heavily in the lives of their students as time went on, they saw themselves as much more likely to learn about, pay attention to, and share important information about the life situations of their students.*

---

Typically, in the middle schools, and in most other schools around the nation, the phenomenon known as "spring fever" erodes the persistence of both teachers and students. Time on task suffers significant decrements. This did not appear to be quite as serious at Lincoln; teachers and students continued to work hard, significantly beyond the time when spring fever should have taken a greater toll. Teachers reported that the STP program was responsible for their ability to keep students working so late into the spring.

The staff believed that, because in two-thirds of the teams, all of the students would be returning to the same teachers next school year, their commitment to each other was not at an end even though one school year was over; their contract, as it were, was perceived as a three year commitment. This meant that time wasted in May, for example, would reflect badly on the progress they would attempt to make during the next year or two.

In the same way, teachers and students who were finishing their third year together had established, teachers believed, a strong enough bond that teachers were more effective in keeping their eighth graders on task far longer than they otherwise might. Because of the close relationships that had been established in the three years, students were less eager to leave the school and were, therefore, more responsive to the needs of teachers to keep order and to continue academic work.

## 5. Individualized Perception

Few educators quarrel with the idea that the more teachers are able to view their students as individuals the more likely they are to be successful in educating them. When teachers are faced with upwards of 150 students per day and at least 450 different students over the course of a three year period, however, the likelihood that teachers will be able to see students as individuals may be slight. When the number of students whom teachers must come to know over a three year period is reduced sharply, by more than two-thirds, one would expect them to be able to develop a heightened sense of individual differences.

At Lincoln, 80% of the teachers reported that they were able to separate their capacity to care for students as individuals from the issue of academic achievement. A similar number believed that the long-term relationship made it possible for them to develop greater respect for low-achieving students. Teachers saw themselves as more able to discover and build upon the personal strengths of individual students.

Seventy-two percent of the teachers were able, they believed, to be more aware of the needs of new students at the beginning of the year and to continue their concern for these students throughout the year. Because they had, for two of the three years, so few new students, they could concentrate their available energy on these students. Teachers knew they could enlist the support of other students in helping new students adjust more effectively to the Lincoln situation.

It was easier in the STP program, reported 86% of the teachers, for the faculty to base their expectations for student performance on the characteristics of individual students, rather than relying on the more stereotypical data from the sex, race, age, or the grade level of the students. Teachers felt somewhat freed from the need to make snap judgments of the abilities and interests of their students. They were more able, therefore, to dispense positive reinforcement more accurately. Teachers believed they were more able to focus on the progress of individuals rather than on the progress of groups and to recognize individual progress when it occurred.

On the negative side, teachers reported a tendency for the problem of "teachers' pets" to be more serious than it would have been in more conventional circumstances. Teachers believed that, unless they were very careful, it was too easy for them to rely on certain students for leadership and support, excluding others from the opportunity to develop the skills and attitudes that other students already possessed.

### 6. Diagnosis

The three year plan at Lincoln did more than structure long-term close relationships between individual teachers and students. It meant that a team of teachers worked with the same common group of students for that period of time.

The team organization made it possible for teachers to share a common planning period during the school day. With the opportunity to talk together, and without their all instructing the same subject as would have been the case in a departmentalized situation, the teachers tended to talk about what they did have in common, their students. Teachers talked about the students, sharing data about their characteristics, home situations and school performances. This lengthy and almost daily exchange of information about the students on the team, most teachers believed, dramatically increased the amount of knowledge that teachers possessed about individual students on the team. Because the teachers invested themselves more heavily in the lives of their students as time went on, they saw themselves as much more likely to learn about, pay attention to, and share important information about the life situations of their students.

Further, because they knew they would have the same students for an extended period of years, teachers perceived themselves as much more eager to solicit information regarding student characteristics from their peers in the early months of the first year, and to be more interested in sharing information about the progress of their students as the months turned into years. This could, of course, become a negative experience, depending on the nature of the expectations that are formed.

Teachers at Lincoln saw themselves as less likely, in the process of diagnosis, to make invidious comparisons between the group of students currently on the team and students which they might have had in previous years. Group-to-group comparisons which were made were likely to be with their current students as they were now and as they were in an earlier year than with how these students compared to another group in the school or to other students teachers had known.

The STP program also encouraged teachers to contact parents more frequently, in problem-solving situations regarding students. Rather than merely reporting progress or its absence, 84% of the Lincoln teachers believed that they spent more time with parents in cooperative efforts aimed at improvement.

### 7. Instruction

Teachers reported that the STP program enabled them to use their class time more efficiently and effectively. They saw themselves as more able to reduce time spent in class on diagnosis and, instead, to devote this time to instruction. Teachers identified their improved relationships with students as a

---

*Seventy-eight percent of the faculty recognized that, for better or worse, the STP program required them to have a broader and more current familiarity with their general subject area.*

---

factor in enabling them to increase the general levels of time on task during classes.

The three year curriculum plan also made it possible for teachers to avoid unnecessary and unknowing duplication of instruction from previous years. Teachers knew what students had been taught, because they had taught it to them. At the same time, however, teachers recognized that the STP program made it impossible, or at least difficult, to repeat successful lessons each year, because of the need to teach a new or different subject. Seventy-eight percent of the faculty recognized that, for better or worse, the STP program required them to have a broader and more current familiarity with their general subject area. It was impossible for teachers to be successful by restricting their preparations to American history, for example, when they would be teaching different social studies topics for the next two years.

The three year relationship also encouraged teachers to attempt to be more innovative in the instructional strategies they chose. Variety becomes much more important, teachers reported, when you have the same students for three years. Teachers tended to share with one another the methods that worked with particular groups and to encourage their colleagues to try them. The three year cycle also gave

---

*A fourth of the teachers saw especially increased involvement with school from parents of poorer children.*

---

teachers time to get around to experimenting with those alternatives.

Sixty-nine percent of the teachers saw their students as being more willing to take part, voluntarily, in class discussions and activities. The same portion of the faculty believed that the three year period gave them the encouragement to provide more success experiences for their students in classroom and team activities.

### 8. Achievement

Teachers at Lincoln Middle School believed that long-term relationships with students are likely to be connected to some important concerns in the area of academic achievement. Teachers believed, for example, that the STP program led to increased achievement for less successful students, due to the teachers' increased ability to identify and prescribe for the needs of these students.

Teachers saw themselves as more able to form long range goals for student achievement and to design their instruction with these goals in mind. They believed that this ability to focus on long range goals, and the clear personal responsibility for reaching them, made it less likely for them to be drawn into devoting time to peripheral issues and concepts.

Because teachers come to know and care about their students more fully, about a third of the teachers were concerned that this might lead to a form of grade inflation. Knowing what a student was capable of doing might become confused with what students were actually accomplishing. Feeling more responsible for the success and the failure of their students also made it more likely, teachers reported, that they would issue fewer failing grades than they otherwise might.

### 9. Teachers' Relationships with Parents

The existence of long-term relationships with students carries with it an equally long relationship with the parents of those students. The STP program is seen, not surprisingly, as having significant and positive effects on their relationship with parents.

Because of the additional concern for students generated by the STP program, teachers identified a need to get to know more parents and to know them more thoroughly. Seventy percent of the teachers said that they devoted more care and sincerity to contact with parents because of the necessity of maintaining a quality long-term relationship. The care and concern teachers demonstrated in their contacts with parents resulted, teachers believed, in increased parent-teacher trust and mutual respect. They concluded that parents and teachers tended to be more mutually self-disclosing when they were involved in a three year effort.

This higher level of effective communication was seen as directly benefiting both teachers and parents. More positive communication about students resulted. Teachers believed that parent support for the teachers' efforts was higher, and that parents' understanding of the team concept and other components of the middle school program was significantly better because of the long-term relationship. Parents at Lincoln (predominantly lower socioeconomic group), said 62% of the teachers, had a higher level of identification with and support for the school in general. A fourth of the teachers saw especially increased involvement with school from parents of poorer children.

Teachers also pointed out benefits for parents. For example, teachers saw themselves as having more support for parents' home situations, having greater empathy for the parents' position. Teachers felt more able to assist parents in understanding more about the characteristics of early adolescence and about responding effectively to the changing needs of children.

### 10. Teacher-Teacher Relationships and the STP Format

Teachers, as members of teams at Lincoln, tended to stay with the same group of colleagues from year to year, finishing one group of eighth grade students and returning together to the sixth grade the next year to begin the process with a new group of students. Teaming at Lincoln requires teachers to work closely over the course of the years: making decisions, carrying out policies with regard to discipline, routines, grades, parent conferences, negotiations with other teams and collaboration with specialists from within and beyond the school. Relationships among teachers on the team, thus, tended to be intense, frequent, lengthy, and diverse. Teachers' individual lives were affected in a variety of ways.

First, teachers tended to have an almost fierce loyalty to and identification with the team. They reported commitment to stay together as a team. The STP format increased the willingness of teachers to compromise and cooperate rather than act purely as individuals; but teachers also saw themselves as being willing, for the sake of their students, to question the decisions of other teachers when it affected their common students. In the same way, teachers saw themselves as being more willing to tolerate inconvenient requests from other teachers, if it appeared to be beneficial to a students on the team.

A majority of the faculty reported that aspects of the STP program made arbitrary status differences among teachers (e.g., higher status for teaching at higher grade levels)

much less important. New teachers reported that belonging to a team that already knew each other, the students, and their families, made their transition to teaching at Lincoln an easier proposition.

Because of the necessity of teaching all three grade levels and a variety of subjects, teachers (75%) reported increased teacher-to-teacher empathy, emerging from the broadened experience they received. Teachers developed better understanding of the concerns and experiences of teachers at other grade levels, and tended to share materials and ideas, more frequently, with teachers of the same subject on other teams.

Teachers cooperated more with teachers at different grade levels because they had or soon would be experiencing the same or similar needs. Sixty-seven percent of the faculty reported an increased tolerance, in general, for perceived human weaknesses in teacher-teacher relationships, and they saw this capacity for tolerance extending into their relationships with students and their parents as well.

---

George, Paul S.; Spreul, Melody; and Moorefield, Jane. *Long-Term Teacher-Student Relationships: A Middle School Case Study*. Columbus, OH: National Middle School Association, 1987. Reprinted by permission. All rights reserved.

# Voices

*Sometimes when I am working with a school district, a board member will question the shift from punishment to discipline. He may say, "My father was tough on us, and I'm a better person for it." In this kind of situation I have learned to ask, "Did you know your parents loved you? Did your father teach you things that have helped you in life?" The answer has always been, "Yes." Then I tell them, "You are a successful person. Punishment does work on successful people because they can absorb it and forgive the Punisher. Punishment does not work on a child who has a failure identity because this course of action merely confirms his inadequacy."*

—— *Diane Chelsom Gossen,*
*Restitution: Restructuring*
*School Discipline. New Chapel,*
*NC: New View Publications, 1992.*

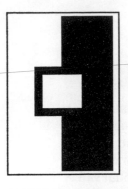

# DIMENSIONS OF THE TIME CHALLENGE

Excerpt from *Prisoners of Time: Report of the National Education Commission on Time and Learning*

There is an urgency about the issue of time and learning that is felt by the public but not yet reflected in the responses of many education officials. On these issues, the American people may be ahead of their schools.

Opinion polls reviewed by the Commission reveal a revolution in public attitudes about time, schools, and the role of schools in the community. According to recent poll findings:

- After nearly 40 years of opposing a longer school year, 52 percent of Americans today favor students' spending more time in school.

- A plurality favors increasing the number of days in the year as opposed to the number of hours in the day (47 versus 33 percent).

- A large majority (62 percent) supports providing after-school care for the children of working parents.

- Americans have reached a national consensus on the importance of pre-school programs to help low-income and minority children get ready for school (85 percent support).

Public opinion experts also report that when Americans are asked to identify their worries about elementary and secondary education, their primary concern is the quality of education provided to their children. Harnessed then, in the public mind, are two powerful forces for reform: a belief that the paramount issue in American education is quality and a dawning consensus, just now being articulated, that school time, broadly conceived, is quality's ally.

The response of America's education leaders to the imperative for school reform is impressive. Both Presidents Bush and Clinton were early advocates of adopting ambitious National Education Goals. These goals enjoy bipartisan support in the Congress and in state houses. The National Council on Education Standards and Testing called in 1992 for the development of new learning standards for all students and voluntary national tests to reinforce them. The content standards movement sweeping American education promises to revolutionize learning.

Based on its 24-month investigation, however, the Commission is convinced that five unresolved issues present insurmountable barriers to these efforts to improve learning. They define the dimensions of the time challenge facing American schools:

- The fixed clock and calendar is a fundamental design flaw that must be changed.

- Academic time has been stolen to make room for a host of nonacademic activities.

- Today's school schedule must be modified to respond to the great changes that have reshaped American life outside school.

- Educators do not have the time they need to do their job properly.

- Mastering world-class standards will require more time for almost all students.

## The Design Flaw

Decades of school improvement efforts have foundered on a fundamental design flaw, the assumption that learning can be doled out by the clock and defined by the calendar. Research confirms common sense. Some students take three to six times longer than others to learn the same thing. Yet students are caught in a time trap —processed on an assembly line scheduled to the minute. Our usage of time virtually assures the failure of many students.

Under today's practices, high-ability students are forced to spend more time than they need on a curriculum developed for students of moderate ability. Many become bored, unmotivated, and frustrated. They become prisoners of time.

Struggling students are forced to move with the class and receive less time than they need to master the material. They are penalized with poor grades. They are pushed on to the next task before they are ready. They fall further and further behind and begin living with a powerful dynamic of school failure that is reinforced as long as they remain enrolled or until they drop out. They also become prisoners of time.

What of "average" students? They get caught in the time trap as well. Conscientious teachers discover that the effort to motivate the most capable and help those in difficulty robs them of time for the rest of the class. Typical students are prisoners of time too.

The paradox is that the more school tries to be fair in allocating time, the more unfair the consequences. Providing equal time for students who need more time guarantees unequal results. If we genuinely intend to give every student an equal opportunity to reach high academic standards, we must understand that some students will require unequal amounts of time, i.e., they will need additional time.

One response to the difficulty of juggling limited time to meet special needs has been the development of "pull-out programs," in which students needing reinforcement or more advanced work are "pulled out" of the regular classroom for supplemental work. Attractive in theory, these programs, in practice, replace regular classroom time in the same subject. They add little additional time for learning. Students deserve an education that matches their needs every hour of the school day, not just an hour or two a week. Pull-out programs are a poor part-time solution to a serious full-time problem.

## Academic Time and Nonacademic Activities

The traditional school day, originally intended for core academic learning, must now fit in a whole set of requirements for what has been called "the new work of the schools" — education about personal safety, consumer affairs, AIDS, conservation and energy, family life, driver's training — as well as traditional nonacademic activities, such as counseling, gym, study halls, homeroom, lunch and pep rallies. The school day, nominally six periods, is easily reduced at the secondary level to about three hours of time for core academic instruction.

Most Americans believe these activities are worthwhile. But where do schools find the time? Within a constrained school day, it can only come from robbing Peter to pay Paul.

Time lost to extracurricular activities is another universal complaint of educators. A 1990 survey of Missouri principals indicated that student activities can deny students the equivalent of seven school days a year. According to these principals, the academic calendar falls victim to demands from athletics, clubs, and other activities. Who is to say that these pastimes are not beneficial to many students? But how much academic time can be stolen from Peter to pay Paul?

## Out-of-School Influences

Over the last generation, American life has changed profoundly. Many of our children are in deep trouble.

Family structure has changed dramatically. Half of American children spend some portion of their childhood in a single parent home, and family time with children has declined 40 percent since World War II.

The workforce is different. Of the 53 million women working in the United States since 1991, 20.8 million had children under the age of 17, including nearly 9 million with children under age six.

Society is more diverse and rapidly becoming more so. By the year 2010, 40 percent of all children in this country will be members of minority groups. The nation's big city schools are already coping with a new generation of immigrant children, largely non-English speaking, rivaling in size the great European immigrations of the 19th and early 20th centuries.

Income inequality is growing. One fifth of all children, and nearly half of all African-American children, are born into poverty today. The United States leads advanced nations in poverty, single-parent families, and mortality rates for those under age 25. Poverty is not simply an urban phenomenon. The number of rural children living in poverty far exceeds the number living in cities.

Technology threatens to widen the gap between the "haves" and the "have-nots." The wealthiest 25-30 percent of American families have a computer at home today, leading to a new phenomenon, pre-schoolers who can use computers before they can read a book.

Anxiety about crime-ridden streets is a daily reality in many communities. Suicide and homicide are the leading cause of death for young men. For some students, the streets are a menace. For many, the family that should be their haven is itself in trouble. Still others arrive at school hungry, unwashed, and frightened by the plagues of modern life — drugs and alcohol abuse, teenage pregnancy, and AIDS.

According to a 1992 study completed at Stanford University, veteran teachers are well aware that today's students bring many more problems to school than children did a generation ago. Today's students receive less support outside school and increasingly exhibit destructive behavior ranging from drug and alcohol abuse to gang membership and precocious sexual activity.

According to a recent Harris poll, 51 percent of teachers single out "children who are left on their own after school" as the primary explanation for students' difficulties in class. The same poll reports that 12 percent of elementary school children (30 percent in middle school and nearly 40 percent in high school) care for themselves after the school day ends.

But the school itself is a prisoner of time. Despite the dedication of their staffs, schools are organized as though none of this has happened. It is clear that schools cannot be all things to all people — teachers cannot be parents, police officers, physicians, and addiction or employment counselors. But neither can they ignore massive problems. It is time to face the obvious. In many communi-ties, when children are not with their families, the next best place for them is the school.

## Time As a Problem for Educators

The corollary to Murphy's Law holds in schools just as it does in life — everything takes longer than you expect. School reform is no exception. While restructuring time, schools need time to restructure. Perversely, according to a recent RAND study, the reallocation of time collides directly with forces of the *status quo* — entrenched school practices; rules and regulations; traditions of school decision-making; and collective bargaining. The greatest resistance of all is found in the conviction that the only valid use of teachers' time is "in front of the class;" the assumption that reading, planning, collaboration with other teachers and professional development are somehow a waste of time.

In light of this, the following findings are particularly troubling:

- According to a RAND study, new teaching strategies can require as much as 50 hours of instruction, practice and coaching before teachers become comfortable with them.

- A study of successful urban schools indicates they needed up to 50 days of external technical assistance for coaching and strengthening staff skills through professional development.

- Resolution of the time issue "remains one of the most critical problems confronting educators today," according to the National Education Association. "For school employees involved in reform, time has become an implacable barrier."

As a representative of the American Federation of Teachers said at a recent Teachers Forum on GOALS 2000 sponsored by the U.S. Department of Education, "We've got to turn around the notion that we have to do everything without being given the time to do it."

Teachers, principals and administrators need *time* for reform. They need *time* to come up to speed as academic standards are overhauled, *time* to come to grips with new assessment systems, and *time* to make productive and effective use of greater professional autonomy, one hallmark of reform in the 1990s. Adding school reform to the list of things schools must accomplish, without recognizing that time in the current calendar is a limited resource, trivializes the effort. It sends a powerful message to teachers: don't take this reform business too seriously. Squeeze it in on your own time.

## *Emerging Content and Achievement Standards*

As 1994 dawned, calls for much more demanding subject matter standards began to bear fruit. Intended for all students, new content frameworks will extend across the school curriculum — English, science, history, geography, civics, the arts, foreign languages, and mathematics, among others. Their purpose is to bring all American youngsters up to world-class performance standards.

The American people and their educators need to be very clear about the standards movement. It is not time-free. At least three factors demand more time and better use of it.

First, subjects traditionally squeezed out of the curriculum now seek their place in the sun. Additional hours and days will be required if new standards in the arts, geography, and foreign languages are to be *even partially attained.*

Second, most students will find the traditional core curriculum significantly more demanding. Materials and concepts formerly reserved for the few must now be provided to the many. More student learning time and more flexible schedules for seminars, laboratories, team teaching, team learning, and homework will be essential.

Finally, one point cannot be restated too forcefully: professional development needs will be broad and massive. Indispensable to educated students are learned teachers in the classroom. An enormous change at hand for the nation's 2.75 million teachers. To keep pace with changing content standards, teachers will need ongoing coursework in their disciplines *while they continue to teach their subjects.*

The Commission's hearings confirmed the time demands of the standards movement:

- **Arts.** "I am here to pound the table for 15 percent of school time devoted to arts instruction," declared Paul Lehman of the Consortium of National Arts Education Associations.

- **English.** "These standards will require a huge amount of time, for both students and teachers," Miles Myers of the National Council of Teachers of English told the Commission.

- **Geography.** "Implementing our standards will require more time. Geography is hardly taught at all in American schools today," was the conclusion of Anthony De Souza of the National Geographic Society.

- **Mathematics.** "The standards I am describing are not the standards I received as a student or that I taught as a teacher," said James Gates of the National Council of Teachers of Mathematics.

- **Science.** "There is a consensus view that new standards will require more time," said David Florio of the National Academy of Sciences.

## *Striking the Shackles of Time*

Given the many demands made of schools today, the wonder is not that they do so poorly, but that they accomplish so much. Our society has stuffed additional burdens into the time envelope of 180 six-hour days without regard to the consequences for learning. We agree with the Maine mathematics teacher who said, "The problem with our schools is not that they are *not* what they used to be, but that they *are* what they used to be." In terms of time, our schools are unchanged despite a transformation in the world around them.

Each of the five issues — the design flaw, lack of academic time, out of school influences, time for educators, and new content and achievement standards — revolves around minutes, hours, and days. If the United States is to grasp the larger education ambitions for which it is reaching, we must strike the shackles of time from our schools.

## Recommendations

As various panaceas have been advanced in the last decade to solve the problems of learning in America, education reform has moved in fits and starts. Indeed, as different helmsmen have seized the wheel, the ship of education reform has gone round in circles. If we have learned anything from these efforts, it is that no single solution exists for the problems of American schools.

Reform can only succeed if it is broad and comprehensive, attacking many problems simultaneously. In that effort, high standards and time are more than simply additional oars in the water. With standards as our compass, time can be the rudder of reform.

In our judgment, educators have created a false dilemma in debating whether additional instructional time can be found within the confines of the current day and calendar, or needs to be sought by extending both. False dilemmas produce bad choices. To meet new demands, the United States needs both — the best use of available time and more time.

## Eight Recommendations

We offer eight recommendations to put time at the top of the nation's reform agenda:

  I. Reinvent schools around learning, not time.

 II. Fix the design flaw: Use time in new and better ways.

III. Establish an academic day.

 IV. Keep schools open longer to meet the needs of children and communities.

  V. Give teachers the time they need.

 VI. Invest in technology.

VII. Develop local action plans to transform schools.

VII. Share the responsibility: Finger pointing and evasion must end.

## I. Reinvent Schools Around Learning, Not Time

*We recommend a commitment to bring every child in the United States to world-class standards in core academic areas.*

By far the most important part of this Commission's charge relates not to time but to student learning. The first issue is not "How much time is enough?" but "What are we trying to accomplish?" As witnesses repeatedly told the Commission, there is no point to adding more time to today's schools if it is used in the same way. We must use time in new, different, and better ways.

The Commission is convinced the following areas represent the common core all students should master: English and language arts, mathematics, science, civics, history, geography, the arts, and foreign languages. This core defines a set of expectations students abroad are routinely expected to meet. American students can meet them as well.

Regular assessment at different stages of students' lives should require every student to demonstrate a firm grasp of demanding material in each of these areas, a grasp extending far beyond the trivial demands of most multiple choice tests. They should assess not only the mastery of essential facts, but also the student's ability to write, reason, and analyze.

## II. Fix the Design Flaw: Use Time In New and Better Ways

*We recommend that state and local boards work with schools to redesign education so that time becomes a factor supporting learning, not a boundary marking its limits.*

The conviction that learning goals should be fixed and time a flexible resource opens up profound opportunities for change.

At a minimum, fixing the design flaw means recognizing that very young children enter school at very different levels of readiness. Some enter kindergarten already reading. Others readily manage computer programs appropriate to their age and skill levels.

But some cannot recognize letters from the alphabet or identify numbers or pictures. Sadly, too many are already abused or neglected. School readiness is the basic foundation on which the rest of the school program is built.

Fixing the design flaw also makes possible radical change in the teaching and learning process. New uses of time should ensure that schools rely much less on the 51-minute period, after which teachers and students drop everything to rush off to the next class. Block scheduling — the use of two or more periods for extending exploration of complex topics or for science laboratories — should become more common. Providing a more flexible school day could also permit American schools to follow international practice — between classes students remain in the room and teachers come to them.

A more flexible time schedule is likely to encourage greater use of team teaching, in which groups of teachers, often from different disciplines, work together with students. Greater flexibility in the schedule will also make it easier for schools to take advantage of instructional resources in the community — workplaces, libraries, churches, and community youth groups — and to work effectively with emerging technologies.

Fixing the design flaw means that grouping children by age should become a thing of the past. It makes no more sense to put a computer-literate second grader in *Introduction to Computers* than it does to place a recent Hispanic immigrant in *Introductory Spanish*. Both should be placed at their level of accomplishment. Although the Commission does not believe 15-year-olds should leave high school early, meeting high performance standards in key subjects should be the requirement for the high school diploma, not simply seat time or Carnegie units. In the case of genuinely exceptional students who meet these requirements while very young, schools should offer them the opportunity to take advanced courses.

Above all, fixing the flaw means that time should be adjusted to meet the individual needs of learners, rather than the administrative convenience of adults. The dimensions of time in the learning process extend far beyond whether one student needs more time and another can do with less. The flexible use of time can permit more individualized instruction.

We should not forget that students are like adults in many ways. Some are able to focus intensely on demanding material for long periods; others need more frequent breaks. Many students, like many adults, learn best by reading; some learn best by listening; others, by doing, or even talking amongst themselves. Offering more frequent breaks, providing more opportunities for hands-on learning, encouraging group work — these techniques and others can parole some of the students who today feel most confined by the school's rigid time demands.

All of these possibilities — and many others — lie within reach if the design flaw is fixed. All of them are much more difficult within the prison of time-bound education.

Reprinted with the permission of the National Education Commission on Time and Learning, 1255 22nd Street NW, Washington, DC 20202-7591 (202) 653-5019.

Copies of the complete report are available from the National Education Commission on Time and Learning, or from Crystal Springs Books, Ten Sharon Road, PO Box 577, Peterborough, NH 03458-0577, 1-800-321-0401.

# Voices

*Suffering teachers . . . are hardly the best people to handle frustrated students. And as long as students are frustrated, teachers will be frustrated too. There is no way a manager can be happy if the workers do not produce. Teachers need to learn that only by choosing to teach in a need-satisfying way can they satisfy both their own needs and the needs of their students.*

— *William Glasser, M.D., The Quality School: Managing Students Without Coercion, New York: HarperPerennial, 1992.*

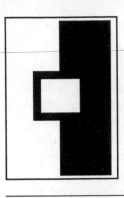

# GROUPING TO FIT PURPOSE

by Ernest L. Boyer

*Ten years ago, Ernest Boyer and The Carnegie Foundation for the Advancement of Teaching launched a study of the elementary schools in the United States, to discover what teaching methods are working. The result of this study is* The Basic School: A Community for Learning, *which offers recommendations based on what the Foundation has learned from the best schools in the country. The following is an excerpt from the chapter entitled, "Patterns to Fit Purpose."*

One of the most controversial issues we encountered was how students should be "grouped" — with some teachers and parents supporting the so-called "graded" classroom and others advocating "nongraded" grouping. One teacher said: "Frankly, I'm convinced that the structured grade level should be abandoned to make way for a system that is more developmentally oriented." Others worry about too much openness. A teacher in a "nongraded" school complained: "It doesn't make sense to put five- and eight-year-olds together all day when their attention spans and levels of learning readiness are so different."

In earlier days, students went to one- or two-room schoolhouses where everyone was grouped together, and where older students often taught the younger ones. The "graded" school — placing students in classrooms based on age — became popular in the nineteenth century as enrollments grew and as schools needed to become organizationally more "efficient."[1] Rigid time blocks and grouping arrangements soon became standardized, creating what some have called "the factory model."

Albert Shanker, president of the American Federation of Teachers, asks the key question: "How do we organize schools and classrooms, given the fact that kids learn differently and at

different rates?"[2] Perhaps students should be mastering material and moving ahead without grade-level restrictions. Otherwise, an enthusiasm for learning may be stifled at an early age.

Clearly, the time has come to move beyond the tired old "graded versus nongraded" debate — just one more false dichotomy in education. What is needed, we believe, is a more *flexible* approach to grouping. In the Basic School, students are grouped in at least five different ways, reflecting the fact that "kids do learn differently and at different rates," as Mr. Shanker put it. Specifically, we recommend for every Basic School:

- *Homeroom grouping*; for placement and sense of family.
- *Mixed-age grouping*; for cooperative learning.
- *Focused grouping*; for intensive coaching.
- *Individual grouping*; for independent study.
- *All-school grouping*; for community building.

## Homeroom Grouping

In the Basic School, we begin, first, with the homeroom. By "homeroom," we mean grouping students initially by age, for a home base. Since birthdays determine when children enroll in school, putting students in a class based on age makes sense administratively, and it's a procedure parents understand. Even more important, homerooms can also give to each child a sense of "family" — a place where children begin and end each day, and in the early grades the homeroom is the place where students do a lot of learning, too.

Some Basic Schools may wish to break out of the "single-age" homeroom and place children of different ages, such as five- and six-year-olds, together. Others may wish to keep a homeroom together, with one teacher, for more than a single year. Researchers Edward A. Wynne and Herbert J. Walberg, after studying student grouping both here and overseas, concluded that the effectiveness of learning in American schools is often tempered because children and teachers are together for only a year, as a rule. They believe that "schools should try and keep discrete groups of students and teachers together over long periods of time."[3]

At Waldorf Schools, an international network of independent institutions, students stay with a "main teacher" for eight years. An intimate, supportive learning community is established. At Seminole Springs Elementary School in Eustis, Florida, students and teachers stay together for educational *and* social reasons for as long as three years. "In our country, the family is not as strong as it once was," said principal Jack Currie. "For those kids who don't have a strong mom-and-dad model, the teacher becomes a significant other."[4] Keeping the group together builds confidence and caring.

Regardless of the length of time together Basic School students most frequently are placed, first, in a homeroom, based on age.

## Mixed-age Grouping

In the Basic School, the homeroom is not an isolated island; it's a staging ground for action. Far from being cut off from other classes, teachers and students in each homeroom regularly work with those in other classrooms, not just at their own level but at other grade levels, too. Fourth-graders and kindergartners, for example, meet together on a science project, while fifth-graders help first-graders with reading or mathematics lessons. Such mixed-age grouping has powerful benefits, both educationally and socially.

By mentoring children in a lower grade, older students develop a sense of responsibility. Younger children, on the other hand, feel more secure as they get to know "a bigger kid." Further, researcher Robert Slavin reports that "cooperative learning" across grade levels is a key component to successful education. In a program called "Success for All," which has spread nationwide from Baltimore, older students tutor younger ones, demonstrating

also that such grouping develops both language and social skills.[5]

Mixing the ages works especially well in the Basic School, with its thematic curriculum that spirals upward — making it possible for first-graders to work together on such themes as the Life Cycle and Connections to Nature. Older students can teach younger ones about good health and safety habits, and in so doing, teach themselves. It also works the other way. In one school where the Core Commonalities curriculum is being used, we overheard a second-grader telling a fourth-grader what it means to "produce and consume."

Students at Ridgeway Elementary School in Columbia, Missouri, have "Learning Communities" that span two grade levels, with three or four teachers in each community. Teachers believe these mixed-age communities have contributed to the academic achievement of their students. They point out that 97 percent of Ridgeway's former students, including those diagnosed as "learning disabled," were on the junior high honor roll after they moved on. Two Ridgeway students were Presidential Scholars in high school.

"We've learned that chronological age doesn't mean everything in terms of learning," notes Susan Fales, the principal. "In our school, you may have seventy to eighty kids interacting with each other on many levels — academic and social — and they clearly spark each other. The focus is on individual success, *within community* — not a single age or grade."

## Focused Grouping

As a third approach, Basic School students with similar aptitudes and interests occasionally are brought together for intensive coaching, an arrangement we've called "focused grouping." Small groups of students concentrate on a special task, skill, or project within a class or across grade levels. The value of such an approach seems apparent. Consider sports: Typically, beginners in tennis are placed in one group, the more advanced in another. In music, beginning piano players do not routinely receive lessons with more proficient players.

Similarly, focused grouping can be helpful in academic learning, too — in reading and writing, mathematics and science, for example. Children who need intensive coaching in one area or another should get it — and those with common interests also should be encouraged to meet together.

At the Key School in Indianapolis, students are organized into special interest groups, called "pods," that meet four times each week. Math, architecture, drama, choir, instrumental music, and the physical sciences are among the offerings. Specialists teach the violin or a foreign language. In the "math pod," students play board games that develop their logical, spatial, and mathematical skills. In the "architecture pod," students with special interests adopt houses in the neighborhood, present reports on them, and go on architectural walking tours.

Focused grouping can, without question, be pedagogically effective. As students with similar interests and skills work together, they gain confidence and encourage one another. But we add a strong word of caution: In the Basic School, focused grouping is *always* a temporary arrangement. Under no circumstances are students to be "tracked," locked rigidly into a class or group that separates them, based on an arbitrary judgment. The Johns Hopkins University researchers report that homogeneous grouping can, in fact, be effective *when it is integrated in the course of a day with other arrangements.*

## Individual Grouping

Many times, throughout the day and week, students in the Basic School also engage in independent study — in an arrangement we call "individual grouping." Working on their own in a classroom or in the school's Learning Resource Center, they gather evidence, write reports, or complete an experiment on a challenging math assignment. Just as a musician must occasionally practice alone, students, too, need time alone to concentrate on a single task, developing skills in independent study.

Individual grouping can also be used for students who need intensive one-on-one assistance, either from a teacher, an aide, or a parent volunteer, and for children with special needs who require extra guidance and support.

In one school in the Midwest, we walked into a classroom midday, and the teacher met us at the door. All students were deeply engaged in self-guided projects. They hardly noticed our arrival. We moved easily from one work station to another, observing one student at a computer writing a story, another checking an experiment, a third reading silently in a corner, all completing their own projects, without distractions.

At another school we visited, the day begins with a fifteen-minute silent reading period. Everyone in the school — the principal, teachers, students, secretaries, and the custodian —sits quietly and reads when the bell rings at 8:15 A.M. The principal announces over the public address system: "DEAR Time — Drop Everything and Read." Each day begins in a climate of concentrated, self-directed learning.

## All-School Grouping

While all students study on their own, there are times when the *whole school* becomes a classroom, when everyone in the Basic School has a shared experience. On such occasions, children in the fifth-grade read their poetry to others, or a third-grade class puts on a play for the entire school, or student musicians, from across grade levels, present a concert. In the Basic School, such celebrative gatherings are scheduled regularly throughout the year. The point of these all-school groupings is, as educator Theodore Sizer elegantly put it, "the gathering of children" — a time to affirm the school as a community for learning.

At the Cambridge Friends School in Massachusetts, everyone comes together every Thursday morning. On the day we were there, students and teachers were joined by parents in the modest-sized gymnasium. Everyone sat on the floor. A performance by third-graders — with African drum music and Japanese dances — began the celebration, with the audience in rapt attention. Hearty applause followed each presentation. Next, a kindergarten teacher led everyone singing, *"If you had potatoes and I had tomatoes, we could have dinner together,"* and *"You know I'd be glad to share what I had, cause that's what friends are for."* Kindergartners were thrilled, of course, and third- and fourth-graders participated wholeheartedly, too. Over two hundred students swayed, sang together, supporting one another, meeting as one class.

**Reference Notes**

1. John I. Goodlad, and Robert H. Anderson, *The Nongraded Elementary School,* revised edition (New York: Teachers College Press, Columbia University, 1987), 48-49.

2. Albert Shanker, "Where We Stand: The Debate on Grouping," American Federation of Teachers advertisement, *The New York Times,* 31 January 1993, sec. E, 7.

   Roberto Gutiérrez and Robert E. Slavin, "Achievement Effects of the Nongraded Elementary School: A Best Evidence Synthesis," *Review of Educational Research* 62, no. 4 (winter 1992), 333-76; see also Roberto Gutiérrez and Robert E. Slavin, *Achievement Effects of the Nongraded School: A Retrospective Review,* report no. 33, Center for Research on Effective Schooling for Disadvantaged Students, The Johns Hopkins University, Baltimore, MD, June 1992.

3. Edward A. Wynne and Herbert J. Walberg, "Long-term Grouping for Better Learning," *Education Digest,* May 1994, 4, citing *Phi Delta Kappan* 75 (March 1994), 527-30.

4. Kenneth J. Cooper, "Florida Principal Seeks to Instill Sense of Family," *The Washington Post,* 28 October 1991, sec. A, 1, 12.

5. Robert E. Slavin et al., *Success for All: A Relentless Approach to Prevention and Early Intervention in Elementary Schools,* Educational Research Service, Arlington, VA, 1992; see also Bruce Joyce and Emily Calhoun, "Lessons in Learning," *The American School Board Journal* (December 1994); 37-38; and Nancy A. Madden et al., "Success for All," *Phi Delta Kappan* 72 (April 1991), 593-99.

*Voices*

*The nongraded school is not for those who would stop with a little organizational reshuffling. It is for those educators who would use present-day insights into individual differences, curriculum, and theories of personality, and who would commit themselves to a comprehensive revision of education.*

*— John I. Goodlad and Robert Anderson, The Nongraded Elementary School. New York: Teachers College Press, 1987.*

# Chapter 4

# THEMATIC PLANNING

Excerpt from:
*Creating and Managing Learning Centers:*
*A Theme Based Approach* by Phoebe Bell Ingraham

*The brain is designed to perceive and generate patterns, and it resists having meaningless patterns imposed upon it. "Meaningless" patterns are isolated pieces of information unrelated to what makes sense to a student. When the brain's natural capacity to integrate information is acknowledged and invoked in teaching, then vast amounts of initially unrelated or seemingly random information and activities can be presented and assimilated.*

—*Teaching and the Human Brain*
by Renate Nummela Caine
and Geoffrey Caine

The first thing I like to do in June, when my classroom is cleaned up and all the activities are put away, is plan my thematic units for the coming year. I come home from my classroom vowing to keep thoughts of school and teaching out of my head for two solid weeks, but it never happens. I sit down, put my feet up, and my brain starts to review the year, immediately jumping into revising the program. I know this sounds like I have no life—I do. Really. But I find that taking the time to revise my plan as my thoughts are pleasantly reviewing the year works well. The things I want to keep, as well as those I need to change, are fresh in my mind.

Also, once my plan is set, I can go about enjoying my summer. I can make the most of any shopping excursions, camping trips, and visits to faraway places, picking up a book or activity that will be perfect for a unit I have in mind. The plan isn't set in stone, but it is there, simmering, until it is ready to use. I can't take advantage of these spur-of-the-moment ideas unless I spend some time coming up with my annual plan first, for creating specific center activities is actually the last stage of my planning.

## Yearly Planning

We educators have made it a habit of beginning with the specifics. We tried to teach children how to read by teaching isolated sounds, chopping up the context of words and text that might have been comprehended. Young children could sit with a book, grunting and uttering lots of isolated sounds, but too often the connection between these sounds and the words on the page was never made for the child.

We're smarter now, and know how to begin with the whole. We've learned to first show children what reading is all about, and how writing can save our thoughts to remember and reread again and again and again. This is magic to a young child, and what young child can resist magic?

When we begin with specific activities, we wind up with lots of little children running around the classroom, enjoying a wide variety of neat projects. The children are busy, but the connections between an activity and its purpose are not there. Without those connections, no learning takes place. The children have a nice time, but their brains aren't ignited, and so they don't build the understanding that will make them feel how powerful learning can be. There is no magic.

I begin my planning with the total picture for the year: What will I need to teach my students this year? What basic concepts and specific objectives are designated for my students in my school district? These are usually found in your curriculum guides. Pull them out. Take not only the objectives for your year(s), but for the years that come before and after, for every class is filled with children who lag behind in something and those who are zooming full speed ahead. Keep these in the back of your mind as you begin to plan your themes.

Now, think of lots of ideas for thematic units. Brainstorm as many as you can. This step is fun to do with other teachers: more people, more ideas. Put them down randomly; be as general and as specific as you wish. Just get those ideas down on paper.

Start with the concepts required by your district. Think of your textbooks, and what you found interesting in them. Consider trips you will take, your students' backgrounds and interests, and books you have read. Put down concepts taught at your level, such as magnetism, weather, the solar system, animals, plants, the history of your local town, mammals, the environment. You can see already that some of these units will overlap, and some might even overlap with several topics. That's okay. Just have fun and get those ideas down!

Now you can group these ideas into units. Draw lines connecting any that might go together, or make webs, or create lists—whatever makes sense to you. The idea is to pull them together into groups that have similar concepts. Those that tie into more than one concept should be placed in all that are relevant. For example, let's say you've written nutrition, butterflies and moths, night and day, animals, seasons, the solar system, owls, plants, bats, clouds, constellations, birds, health, and weather. Let's see how we can group them together (see Figure 4.1).

You can see how they overlap, and how I've come up with some broad themes that might include several mini-units under them. You name each group according to the broad concept, and then you decide which broad concepts you will use during your year. You do not have to decide which specific mini-units you'll bring in, or even in which unit to include them. Your students will determine that, and so your units will change from year to year.

For example, one year you might study owls and bats during the Solar System unit, as your students get interested in nocturnal animals. Another year, you might learn about bats and owls as you study animals, and the children question whether a bat is a bird or not. You might then choose to compare and contrast owls and bats.

These specific topics can be organized into the theme that makes connections for your students, and planned at that time. Knowing they are possibilities will allow you to gather some ideas and materials while planning your main thematic units.

To help you think of how to create broader topics to use for grouping concepts together thematically, I came up with the chart in Figure 4.2). These are not complete, and are certainly not set in stone. But they might help you get started planning broader topics, in order to enable your students to make connections in their learning with prior knowledge and experiences they bring with them from outside the classroom.

The next step of my planning consists of deciding which broad thematic units I will use, and placing them on the calendar. I like to think of a central focus that my year will take

**1.**

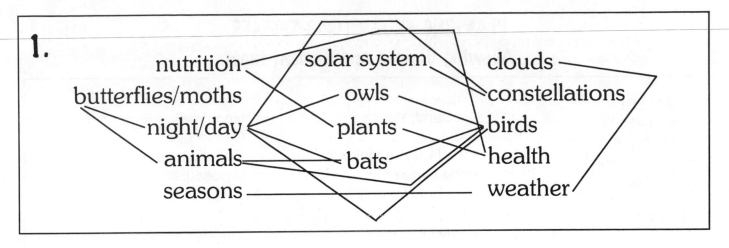

**2.**

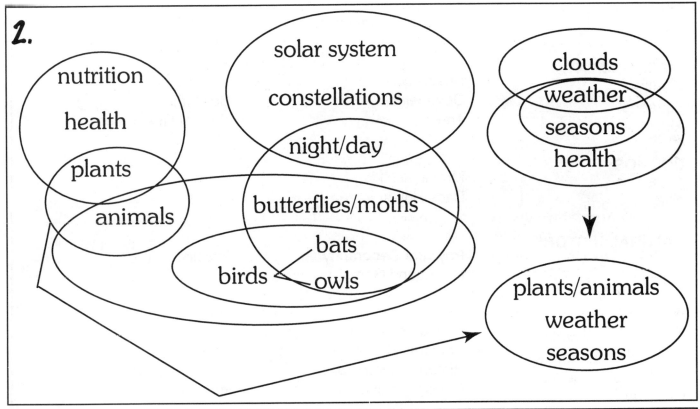

**3.**

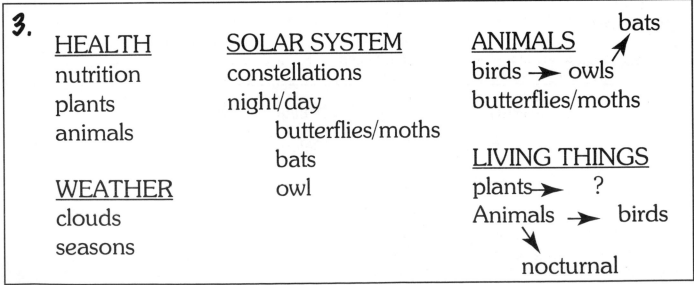

Figure 4.1  Brainstorming theme ideas

# PLANNING BROAD TOPIC THEMES
## Allowing Options and Student Input

**ANIMALS:**
Birds, Reptiles,...
Butterflies & Moths
Farm, Zoo, Pets
Hibernation

Air, Land, Water
Habitats
Insects & Arachnids
Food Chain

Nocturnal
Ocean Life
Endangered
Dinosaurs

**HEALTH :**
Five Senses
Nutrition
Drug Prevention

Physical Fitness
All About Me
Disease Prevention

Plants
Reproduction
New Life

**ENVIRONMENT:**
Weather
Seasons
Air Pressure

Shadows
Continents
Trees

Oceans
Collections
Natural Resources

**COSMOS:**
Suns
Constellations

Moon
Back Holes

Planets
Novas

**NATURAL HISTORY:**
Land Forms
Volcanoes

Physical Geography
Rocks and Gems

Fossils

**PEOPLE:**
Personal History
Authors & Illustrators
Folktales & Legends
Celebrations

Native Americans
Personal History
History of Hometown
Foreign Countries

Occupations
Languages
U.S.A. (States)
Immigration

**INVENTIONS:**
Electricity
Transportation

Communication
Simple Machines

Magnets

## Integrate Thematically Throughout the Year:

**Personal Responsibility**
caring for others
caring for the planet

**Celebrating Diversity**
"cultural imagination"
disabilities
storytelling

**Seven Intelligences**
artistic expression
creative thinking

**Curriculum Objectives**
language arts
math

Figure 4.2

on, and name my units according to that concept. This will allow me to make connections for the children to relate to throughout the entire year. For example, I might focus my year on "The Environment" or "Natural Habitats." Next I divide my year into main units, where I will focus attention on one area of that main theme. I can then place general concepts and the specific skills that my district has designated for my students under those themes. (Figure 4.3)

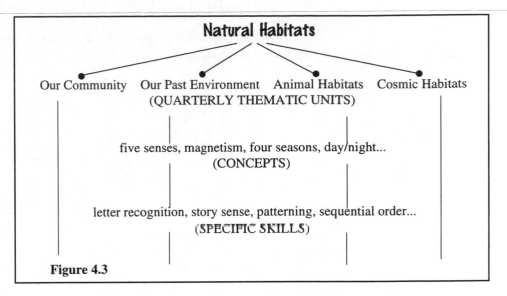

Figure 4.3

The plan I have for next year is included in Figure 4.4. I want my students to feel they can make a difference in the world, and so I've chosen this as my main concept for the year. The four thematic units will allow me to teach the concepts important to my district, as well as the specific skills my students are ready to learn and will need to know to meet with success. The concepts will be chosen by what makes sense to use with each theme. The specific skills will go into the units according to the time of year they should be taught as well as the books and activities that I know will encourage the acquisition of those skills (Figure 4.5).

Now that my year is outlined, I can focus on the activities. Because I began with my goals and planned how I would teach them in a thematic framework, I can plan specific activities for my students that will foster understanding of concepts and knowledge of specific skills. They will learn from interacting with the materials I choose because they will be able to make the connections between what they are doing and how it relates to the lessons I am teaching. They will learn general concepts and use information in meaningful experiences, and they will understand. That information will belong to them, for they have spent time applying what they know.

That's the magic of center time. But as you can see, there must be a firm foundation laid before the games and activities ever enter the room. Without the planning, it's just a lot of stuff. Without the planning, the children will work with the materials, but the connections won't be there, and soon, the activity will become off-task, for there will be no intrinsic motivation to learn and understand.

When this planning is done as a group, it is even better to begin early. If several teachers are working together as a team, school monies might be used to order specific materials to be used in the units. You might choose to create files for each unit, and keep ideas for trade books and interesting activities that you come across in the files, so that they are ready to pull together as you begin to plan the unit in detail. School librarians can also be advised of the units in order to locate resource books that could be included in their ordering. This is particularly important if several classrooms or grade levels will use the same materials. The librarian might wish to focus book displays and pull small collections to be set out for your students.

## Student Involvement in Planning

As I have mentioned, planning general topics allows you the flexibility to include your students in the planning. They can suggest specific topics within each unit for further investigation. For example, in the thematic plan shown in Figure 4.6, students might sug-

# I AM IMPORTANT TO MY WORLD

| MY COMMUNITY<br>1st Quarter<br>Sept-Nov  | MY HISTORY<br>2nd Quarter<br>Nov-Jan | MY UNIVERSE<br>3rd Quarter<br>Jan-Mar | MY ENVIRONMENT<br>4th Quarter<br>Mar-June  |
|---|---|---|---|
| me/my family | dinosaurs | solar system | plants |
| five senses | Inventions | planets | animals |
| opposites | Native Americans | constellations | oceans |
| transportation | pilgrims/pioneers | sun/moon | transformations |
| nutrition/food groups | explorers | weather | butterflies/moths |
| shapes/patterns | celebrations | seasons | tadpoles/frogs |
|  |  |  | rain forests |
| physical geography | Europe | Asia (China) | Africa |
| maps | North America (Mexico) | North America (U.S.A.) | South America |
| nags/symbols | Antarctica | Australia |  |
| **B, A, F, L, P, D** | **I, T, H, Q, C, N, S** | **M, G, V, Y, W, U, O, K** | **E, R, X, J, Z** |
| house | museum | space station | plant store/nursery |
| doctor's office | invention convention | post office | vet's office |
| restaurant | teepee | weather bureau | pet shop |
| bicycle shop | gift shop | library/book shop | zoo |
| grocery store |  |  |  |

© 1995 Phoebe B. Ingraham

**Figure 4.4  The author's lesson plan**

_____
(Yearly Theme)

_____
(Quarterly Thematic Units)

(Listing of possible mini-themes to include under each theme.)

(Listing of important concepts to include under each thematic unit.)

(Listing of specific skills, objectives to teach during each thematic unit.)

(Listing of possible centers, special projects, field trips, visitors to include during thematic unit.)

**Figure 4.5**

gest a mini-unit on endangered animals during the study of animal habitats. You can incorporate this topic into the goals you have already set for this unit.

While you can plan mini-units in response to a wide-spread interest of one class, it is impossible and unnecessary to plan individual thematic units for each child in your class. When only one or a few students are interested in a precise topic, you might suggest they design an individual study unit (discussed in Chapter Two) on that area. This will let your students feel empowered in their learning, and encourage them to take responsibility for it.

When planning activities for each thematic unit, be sure to include a wide variety of experiences specific to your students, their community, special events occurring during this unit, field trips, music, art, drama, and food experiences. There are many ways to insure that you include all subject areas, as well as "extra" experiences, events, and activities. Traditional webs for planning individual thematic units may be used, or you may wish to plan around your centers.

Another way to insure that you have integrated your unit into all areas of your curriculum is to use your contract or center chart (Figure 4.7), and list at least three activities in each area that will make a connection to the thematic topic. You might also choose to incorporate the seven intelligences within your planning, to insure that the abilities of all your students are nurtured in the investigation into this topic (Figure 4.8).

The activities found in each center should be created around activities that the children associate with the theme. Do not try to stretch too far, just to include a food experience or a favorite project. If the activities do not flow naturally from the concepts, your students will not see the connections and their work with them will not be meaningful or have any real purpose. Their work in that center will become thoughtless and off-task.

For example, when studying health and nutrition, it would be a natural extension to operate a small restaurant, designing menus that would include foods they could easily prepare and serve in your classroom. For a kindergarten or primary classroom, the children would focus only on the behavior necessary for ordering, making, and serving the food. For older children, the use of money might be included, and the students might find it necessary to count change and balance the books at the end of each day.

Asking students to complete a worksheet about a balanced diet in the restaurant would not be a natural extension of that area. It would, in fact, detract from the meaningful, purposeful play that the children engage in, and therefore, should not be included in this area.

However, students might be asked before opening the restaurant to design a menu around the food groups, offering food items for each (Figure 4.9). Publishing a cookbook of favorite family recipes is also an appropriate project for this unit; however, it should be placed in a research or publishing center, rather than a dramatic play area.

Again, the task should be placed in a center where the activity is naturally part of your students' activities, or it will detract from the purpose of both the task and the center.

Learning through play does not mean that making connections becomes haphazard or merely by chance. The teacher must know his or her students well, and design activities that are interesting to them, while engaging them in activities that establish an understanding of the skills and concepts that are the goals of the unit. It is important to listen to your students, and allow them to offer suggestions for activities that you can develop into learning tasks.

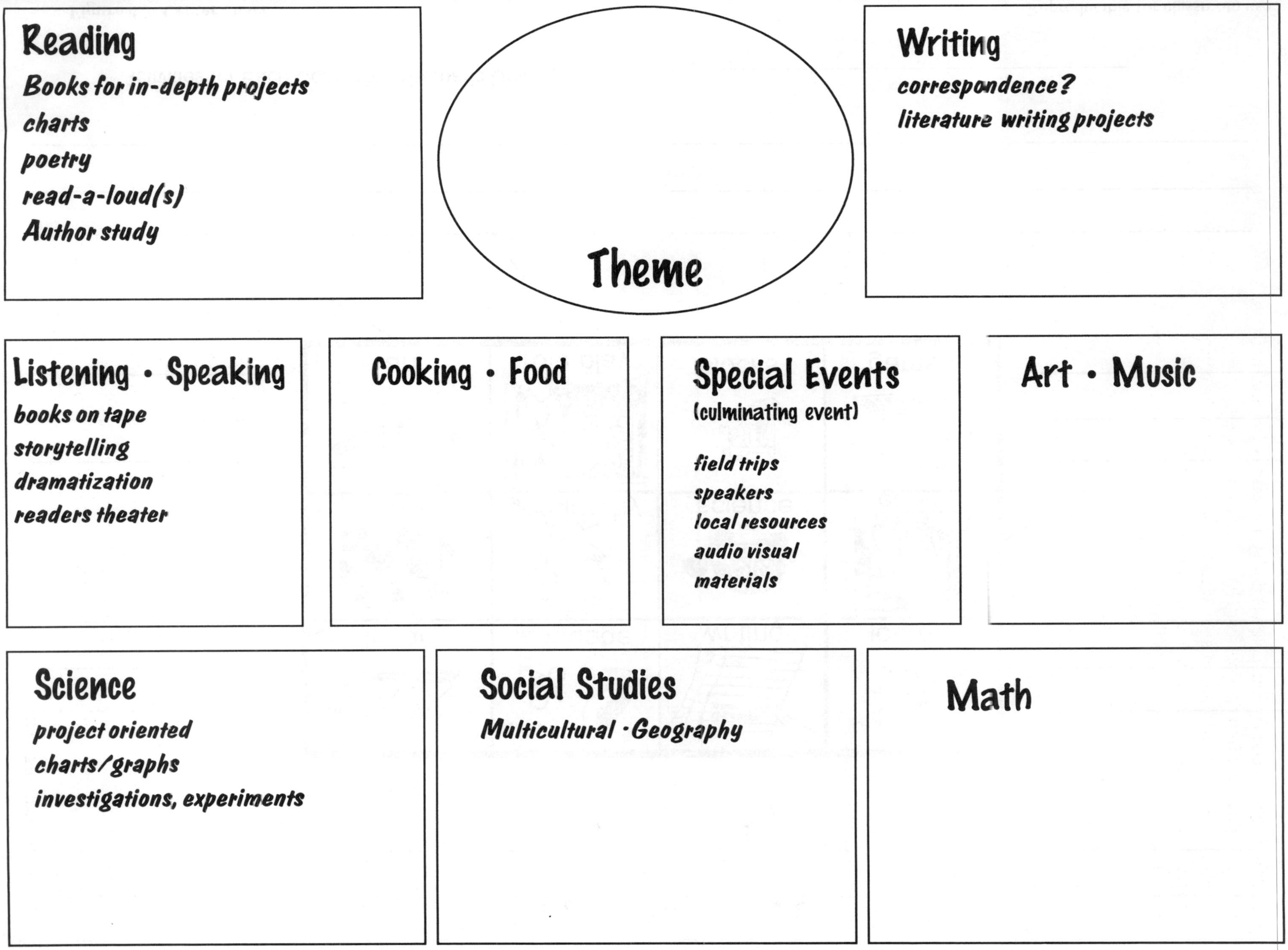

# Reading

*Books for in-depth projects*
*charts*
*poetry*
*read-a-loud(s)*
*Author study*

# Writing

*correspondence?*
*literature writing projects*

# Listening · Speaking

*books on tape*
*storytelling*
*dramatization*
*readers theater*

# Cooking · Food

# Art · Music

## Theme

# Special Events
(culminating event)

*field trips*
*speakers*
*local resources*
*audio visual*
*materials*

# Math

# Science

*project oriented*
*charts/graphs*
*investigations, experiments*

# Social Studies
*Multicultural · Geography*

**Figure 4.6  Thematic plan**

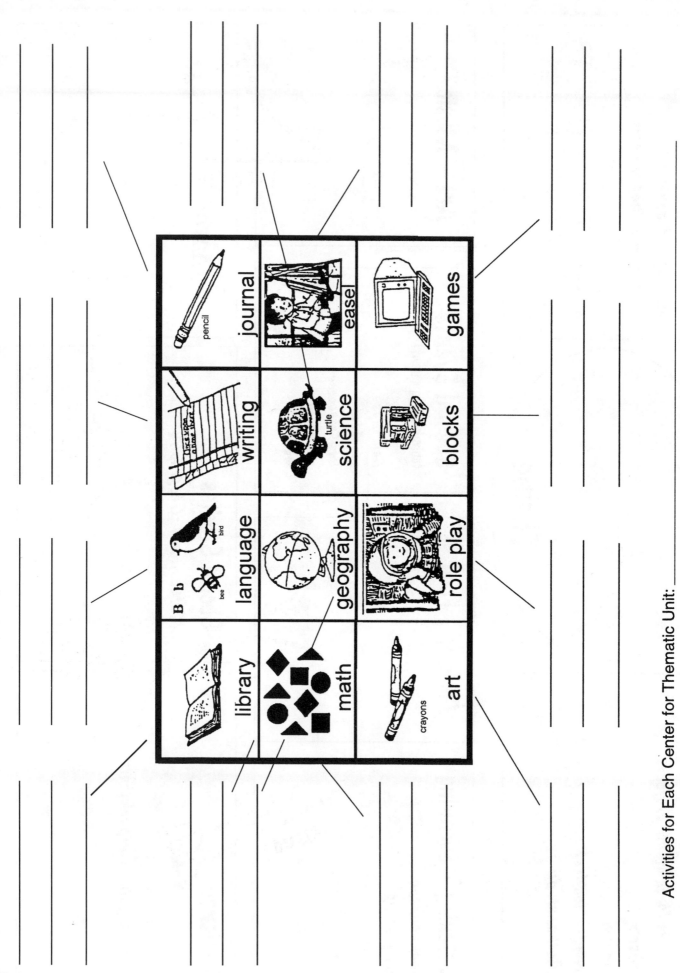

Activities for Each Center for Thematic Unit: _____

**Figure 4.7  Center chart**

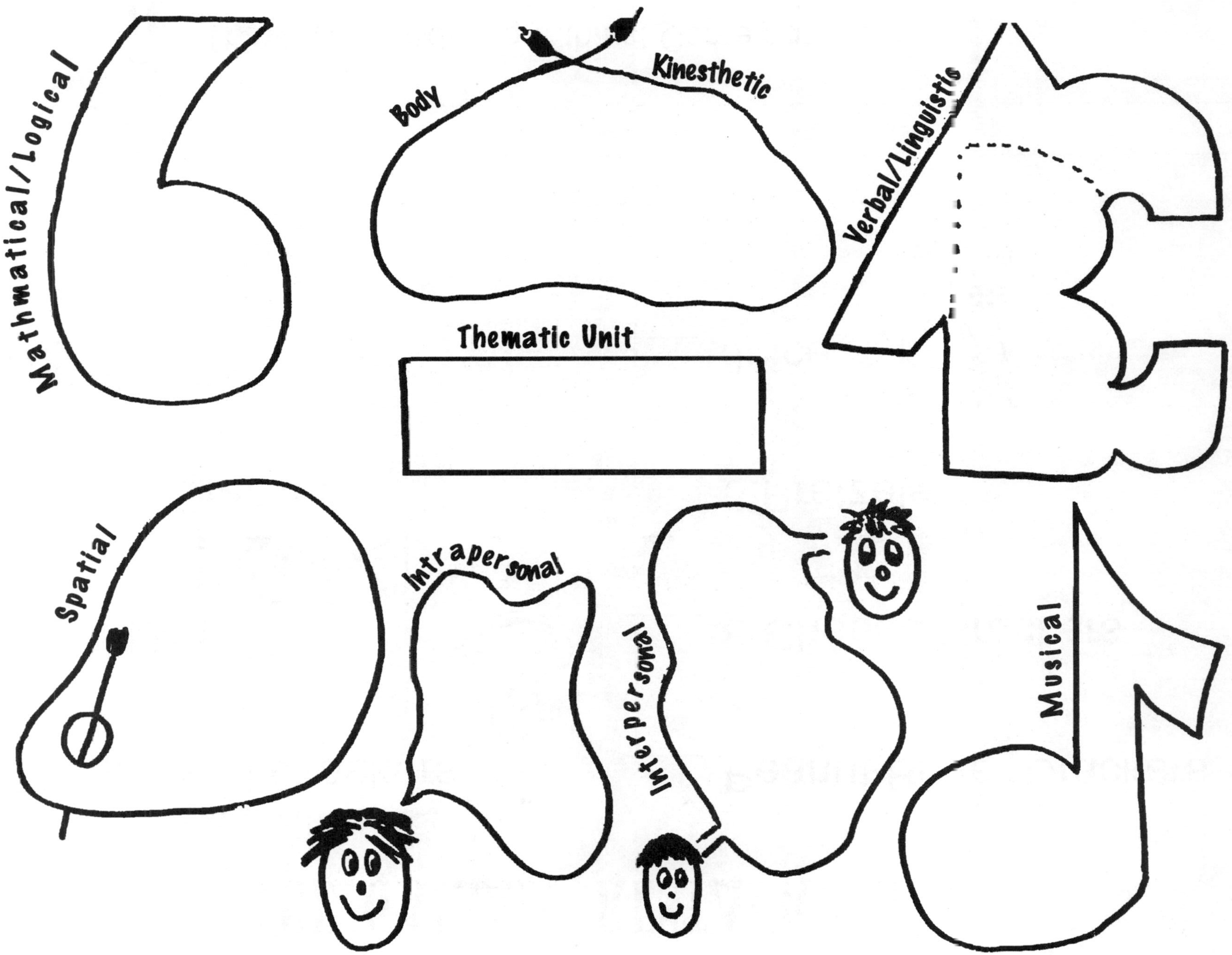

Musical

Verbal/Linguistic

Kinesthetic

Thematic Unit

Body

Interpersonal

Intrapersonal

Mathmatical/Logical

Spatial

**Figure 4.8 Thematic plan incorporating multiple intelligences.**

# THE GARDEN RESTAURANT

____ Cheese and Crackers

____ Peanut Butter Crackers

____ 8 Cheese Crackers

____ 2 Cookies

____ 6 Pretzels

____ 10 Fish Crackers

____ Juice

____ Milk

Thank you for dining with us! Come again soon.

Figure 4.9

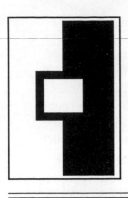

# LEARNING CENTERS FOR MULTIPLE INTELLIGENCES

by Linda Campbell

Four third, fourth and fifth grade boys recently gave an oral report about California to their classmates. The students sang an original rap of the state, played a short video they produced, displayed maps drawn to scale and spiritedly presented a series of facts. Are these students academically advanced or exceptionally creative? No, such multimodal learning is commonplace in multiple intelligence classrooms.

## The Theory of Multiple Intelligences

In 1983, Howard Gardner, a cognitive psychologist at Harvard University, published *Frames of Mind: The Theory of Multiple Intelligences*. This book outlined a new view of human intelligence. In addition to linguistic and logical-mathematical intelligences, Gardner identified five other intelligences. These include: visual-spatial; bodily-kinesthetic; musical; interpersonal intelligence, which refers to getting along with others; and intrapersonal intelligence, which is the ability to know and understand oneself. Howard Gardner was surprised and pleased when educators across the country expressed interest in his work. By the mid-1980s a few educators had applied Gardner's theory to their classrooms. Today, there are thousands of teachers using Multiple Intelligence concepts in instruction, curriculum and assessment.

Howard Gardner states that his theory serves as an ink blot test for educators. There is no single, correct way to implement the Theory of Multiple Intelligences in classrooms or schools. Teachers develop MI approaches that are most appropriate for their students. One thing all MI teachers appear to have in common, however, is their effort to enrich the learning experiences of their students through linguistic, logical, kinesthetic, visual, musical, interpersonal, and intrapersonal teaching strategies.

## Multiple Intelligence Classroom Models

Over the last ten years, numerous multiple intelligences programs have emerged. Many educators provide seven entry points into their lessons by using direct instruction or centers-based options. Some teachers adopt interdisciplinary and thematic curriculum. Others affirm the importance of the arts and dedicate more time to the visual and performing arts in their schools. Some teachers develop project-based classrooms to enhance student autonomy. A few organize apprenticeship and mentor programs to nurture students' intelligence strengths in greater depth.

## A Learning Centers Approach

One classroom program that has been successfully adopted by teachers in Washington, Oregon, Idaho, California, Kentucky, Vermont, Ohio, and Indiana, features seven learning centers, each devoted to one of the intelligences identified by Gardner. The students spend approximately half of their school day rotating through the centers. The morning begins with a brief lecture and discussion of the classroom's current theme. Students then divide into seven groups to begin center work. The groups spend 25 to 30 minutes at each center, learning about the day's topic in seven modalities.

The centers are named after individuals whose lives demonstrated outstanding accomplishments in one of the seven intelligences (see graph on page 62). At the beginning of the year, students learn about each individual, noting how his or her intelligence developed throughout life.

Following center time, students share their work with classmates, attend math groups and spend the remainder of the day completing unfinished center work and pursuing individual or small group activities such as the four boys' California report.

## A Thematic, Integrated Curriculum Design

In this centers-based MI model, the curriculum is thematically organized. At the beginning of the school year, students list topics they want to study. The teacher reviews the district's learning objectives and textbooks. Themes then emerge, integrating district requirements and materials with student interests. Thematic units span four to six weeks and cover such topics as "Art from Around the World," "Our Planet's Problems," and "The Human Brain and Intelligence." Student learning objectives are taught in the thematic units without being tied to textbook sequences.

The curriculum is interdisciplinary, since traditional subject matter areas naturally integrate when teaching to the multiple intelligences. Daily activities are planned to incorporate all seven intelligence areas. Math, reading, music, art, movement and cooperative and independent work are woven into the teaching of each topic. For example, in a recent unit on outer space, the class studied comets for a day. In the Martha Graham Center, students made model comets with sticks, marshmallows and ribbons, and choreographed dances illustrating a comet's orbit around the sun. In the William Shakespeare Center, students read about comets in school textbooks, and in the Albert Einstein Center, solved story problems concerning the lengths of comets' tails. In the Mother Teresa Center, each group created a database file of comet facts on the classroom's computer. In the Emily Dickinson Center, students individually authored poems on pieces of paper cut to resemble comets.

Colorful comets were designed with glue and glitter on graph paper, and comet parts were labeled and drawn in proportion at the Pablo Picasso Center. In the Ray Charles Center, each group created a song incorporating several comet facts. At the end of the day, students bound comet poems in a class book, shared songs, displayed their artwork, and reviewed the progress in other centers.

Because of the variety of student activities, drill and practice is no longer a monotonous, repetitive task. Skills are learned and applied in numerous modes. The work at the seven centers enables children to make informative, multimodal presentations of their studies. It is the norm, rather than the exception, for students to sing, dance, draw, role play, calculate, and write their learnings. It is also the norm for each child to experience daily academic success, since there are numerous opportunities to learn through one's strengths.

## MI Teacher Challenges

Numerous challenges confront a teacher who attempts to engage the multiple intelligences in classroom lessons. Planning in multiple modes is initially arduous; however, the task becomes easier with experience. Ongoing projects at some centers, such as making paper maché globes at the visual station, relieve the necessity of extensive daily planning. Additionally, a developing repertoire or menu of activities for each center simplifies the planning task. Some typical center activities include:

*Intrapersonal Center:* journals, independent research projects, thinking skills, student choice activities, and learning-to-learn skills

*Interpersonal Center:* cooperative learning tasks and problem-solving, conflict management techniques, learning games, group discussions

| GARDNER'S IDENTIFIED | |
| --- | --- |
| INTELLIGENCE | CENTER NAME |
| *Bodily/Kinesthetic Intelligence* | *Martha Graham, Jim Thorpe* |
| *Visual/Spatial Intelligence* | *Pablo Picasso, Georgia O'Keeffe* |
| *Mathematical/Logical Intelligence* | *Albert Einstein, Madame Curie* |
| *Musical Intelligence* | *Ray Charles, Kitaro* |
| *Verbal/Linguistic Intelligence* | *William Shakespeare, Maya Angelou* |
| *Interpersonal Intelligence* | *Mother Teresa, Mahatma Gandhi* |
| *Intrapersonal Intelligence* | *Emily Dickinson, Sigmund Freud* |

*Musical Center:* background music, songwriting, instrument making, rhythmical learning activities

*Visual Center:* diverse art media, charts, collages, murals, videotaping and photography

*Kinesthetic Center:* model building, manipulatives, puzzles, role play, dance activities, scavenger hunts, skits

*Linguistic Center:* reading, writing, speaking, listening, word processing, making books, and storytelling activities

*Logical Center:* math games, manipulatives, timelines, flow charts, science experiments, deductive reasoning, and problem solving activities.

With time, teachers find it becomes second nature to integrate the seven intelligences into instruction. Many claim that after the first year of effort they naturally think and plan multimodally. They realize that not all concepts or skills lend themselves to instruction in seven ways, and instead select how to teach most effectively. Since it is unlikely that an individual teacher is skilled in all seven intelligences, natural limitations are confronted. Some teachers turn to school specialists or parents for support. Many team plan or teach with their colleagues, drawing upon each other's strengths. Some seek community members who volunteer their time and expertise by mentoring individuals or small or large groups of students.

Teachers also realize that multimodal instruction is not their final goal. Since MI teaching requires more time than textbook-based instruction, teachers must identify the most important concepts to teach and adopt a "less is more" philosophy of instruction. When they do, however, students benefit from opportunities to *understand* rather than memorize content. In addition to deepening the curriculum, there are other challenges for MI teachers. These include how to perceive diverse student strengths, how to develop each child's strengths in depth, how to approach each child's weakness through her strengths, and how to assess multi-modal learning.

Even with the challenges confronting them, most MI teachers gladly continue their efforts. The reason is simple. Students are more engaged, motivated, and on task when they are active learners. Through multiple intelligences instruction, students exhibit a joy in learning that motivates their teachers to continue to enrich classroom learning. There are other benefits as well.

## The Results of an Action Research Project

A year-long action research project was undertaken to assess the efficacy of a centers-based MI program. Using daily journal entries, classroom climate surveys, student questionnaires and standardized test scores, a teacher with a multiage classroom of third through fifth graders determined that:

1.  By working in small groups at the seven centers, the students demonstrated increased responsibility, self-direction and independence over the course of the year. They grew skilled at developing their own projects, gathering necessary resources and making well-planned presentations of all kinds.

2.  Discipline problems were significantly reduced. Students, previously identified by other teachers as having behavior problems, showed rapid improvement during the first six weeks of school. By mid-year, many contributed well in their small groups, and some assumed positive leadership roles.

3.  All students developed and applied new skills. In the fall, most students described only one center as their favorite and where they felt most confident. Interestingly enough, the distribution among the seven centers was relatively even. By mid-year, most identified three to four favorite centers. By year's end, every student identified at least five centers which were favorites and at which they felt skilled. Moreover, they were all making multimodal presentations of independent projects, including songs, skits, visuals, poems, games, surveys, puzzles, and group participation activities.

4.  Cooperative learning skills improved in all students. Due to the collaborative nature of the center work, students became skilled at listening, helping each other, sharing leadership, accommodating group changes, and introducing new classmates to the program.

They learned not only to respect each other but also to appreciate and call upon the diverse talents and abilities of their classmates.

5. Academic achievement improved. Standardized test scores were above state and national averages in all areas. Scores for critical thinking skills were above the 85th percentile. Retention of content was also high on a year-end teacher-made test of the topics studied during the previous eight months. Students cited that their preferred methods for recalling information were musical, visual and kinesthetic. Students who had previously been unsuccessful in school became achievers in new areas.

It appears that multiple-intelligences teaching is one approach to meeting the needs of a diverse student population. Talented students, frequently lacking academic challenge, find it demanding to work in several modalities on a daily basis. Being asked to role play or paint one's learnings also demands critical and creative thinking. Those with attention deficit disorders note that just as they begin to lose focus, it is time to move to the next center for a new activity. Children who previously had difficulty working with their peers practice social skills in small groups of three or four. For them, collaboration becomes less threatening and cooperation leads to personal and group success. All students have the opportunity to learn through their strengths, to develop new skills, to engage the broad spectrum of human intelligence, and to become more of who they already are.

*Linda Campbell is Professor and Chair of Teacher Education at Antioch University Seattle, 2607 2nd Ave. Seattle, Washington, 98121, and primary author of* Teaching and Learning through Multiple Intelligences, *published by Allyn and Bacon.*

*Voices*

*Many of the difficulties which we encounter in everyday life are the result of problems that we have working with others or of problems that they have working with us. The ability to get along and work well with others has always been an essential quality for success; with our ever-shrinking world, it will be even more important in the future. Whatever the question, future technological advances will make the answers easier to find; the ability to work collaboratively with others in finding those answers will be what determines whether or not one is successful.*

*A high degree of interpersonal intelligence — being sensitive to the needs and moods of others, understanding them, and being able to work with them — is surely a very important component of this kind of success. Yet our belief is that Intrapersonal Intelligence — knowledge of one's own strengths and weaknesses — is the key, the starting point, the most important intelligence.*

*Possessing a strong Intrapersonal Intelligence means that we know our strengths and our weaknesses. It also means that we know how we are perceived by others.*

*— Faculty of the New City School, Celebrating Multiple Intelligences: Teaching for Success. St. Louis, Missouri: The New City School, 1994.*

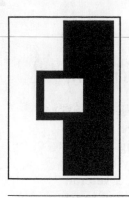

# ARIZONA EDUCATOR FOUNDS MULTIAGE CHARTER SCHOOL

by Aldene Fredenburg

Lynda Rice, a teacher in the public schools for 18 years, who has lectured nationwide on the topics of multiple intelligences, cooperative learning, writing and math, and themes and centers, has founded a multiage alternative school in Chino Valley, Arizona.

The Mingus Springs Charter School began its first year with 72 students in four classes, ranging from first through eighth grade, with a maximum of 18 students in each class. Rice and three other teachers teach a first-second grade combination, as well as a third-fourth, fifth-sixth, and seventh-eighth grade combination. Right now they are doing looping as a transitional phase, but will be fully multiage by the 1996-1997 school year.

"I started a one-room private school last year for students from fifth through eighth grade," Rice said, "primarily because I was frustrated with issues of class size, and because I feel multiage and student-centered learning are so important—all the things I've talked about at my conferences— and they're not allowed to be done here in public schools." The Mingus Springs school is an expansion of her private school.

Rice had quite a response to her private school even with the tuition requirement; she deals with primarily a low-income, rural population, and a lot of the parents "literally did without to scrape up the tuition for school." When the Mingus Springs school opened up on August 28, it was supported with public funds, and with tuition no longer paid by the parents. The children who attended Rice's school last year have been grand-fathered in, along with their siblings; the rest of the students were chosen by lottery. It's impossible at present to accept all students who want in; there are 120 students on the waiting list. Rice has plans to hire more teachers and double the size of the school next year.

The opportunity to create the Mingus Springs school came because of legislation passed in Arizona aimed at providing choices for parents in terms of their children's education. Out of hundreds of applications from people seeking to start charter schools, only 50 were accepted. Rice's was one of them. And of the hundreds of applications, Rice's was one of only two that mentioned multiage education.

"The key word was alternative," Rice said; "They were leaning toward anything that is different." The small class size was a factor

---

*The small class size was a factor that the state board of education found appealing, as well as the multiage component, and the exclusive use of integrated thematic units.*

---

that the state board of education found appealing, as well as the multiage component, and the exclusive use of integrated thematic units. The school will use portfolio assessment to evaluate students' progress, another plus in the state's eyes.

"One stipulation they gave was that students do state [standardized] testing, which I wasn't keen on, but I finally said okay," Rice said.

Asked if it was complicated to obtain the charter from the state, Rice said, "You're not just a-kiddin'." She had to supply missions statements and goals statements, and provide a curriculum that the state "went over with a fine-tooth comb. The state also examined all their proposed policies, including how the school planned to handle special education.

One remarkable aspect of the process was that the new school was not expected to conform to a standard state-mandated curriculum; rather, Rice came up with the curriculum, which was scrutinized and finally accepted by the state.

"The entire proposal went through lots of revisions," Rice said, "Which meant numerous trips to the state board of education. And since the board only meant once a month, if we had to go through another revision it meant waiting another month before we could present it again."

In the end the school got one of the highest amounts of money granted by the Arizona board of education. Rice needed to find a new location for the school, and managed to get a stimulus grant, which helped fund the purchase of modular building units, a well, and a new septic system. "I told the state board, 'When I say a classroom without walls, I hope you're not taking me literally,'" Rice said.

When looking for teachers, Rice was able to find "the best of the best." Since there is currently a lot of frustration among teachers in Arizona, she found she virtually had her pick; one of the women she hired, a veteran teacher, actually took a substantial cut in pay for the opportunity to teach at Mingus Springs school. She has implemented major staff development with the teachers, since none of them have yet taught a truly multiage continuous progress class.

Rice and another staff member will share the responsibilities of director; they will both also teach. "You couldn't get me out of the classroom," Rice said.

*Aldene Fredenburg is the editor of Crystal Springs Books, a Division of The Society For Developmental Education in Peterborough, NH.*

# Voices

*Dear Ms. Class:*

*I keep hearing about authentic assessment but I can't see that it means much more than keeping students' work in a folder. How am I ever going to sell this to parents, who want to know how their children measure up to children around the country?*

*— Pueblo, CO*

*Dear Pueblo:*

*Ms. Class sympathizes with your cynicism. Those who want to be truly authentic let the students choose what goes in the folders.*

*Ms. Class does take offense, however, at your willingness to go along with the idea of measuring children against other children. Why is it that we are so obsessed with measuring children? At the same time we are obsessed with measuring our children from age five to eighteen, we ignore the ability of parents, policemen, politicians, media pundits. Are the parents of your students willing to take a test to see how they measure up with other parents around the country? Do you want your SAT scores posted on the schoolhouse door?*

*The irony of assessment, be it authentic or otherwise, is that it doesn't reveal as much about students as people think it does. The worth of any assessment is in the eye of the perpetrator.*

*— Susan Ohanian, Ask Ms. Class. York, ME: Stenhouse Publishers, 1996.*

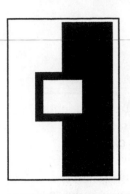

# MINGUS SPRINGS CHARTER SCHOOL: Meeting the Needs of the Children

by Lynda Rice

There are many problems facing our public schools today. One of these problems is overcrowding. Overcrowding in classrooms lends itself to the impersonalization of the teacher/student relationship. One-on-one interaction with the students by the teacher is minimized, which in turn allows many students to slip through the cracks. Some slip because they are quiet, and therefore go unnoticed in a busy, crowded classroom. Some slip because the attention they loudly demand turns into discipline problems that are hard to deal within a full classroom. The teacher becomes a policeman; the students become discipline problems.

Another problem that faces our schools, which can be seen as an offshoot of the overcrowding problem, is the rigid structure of single grade-level classes that can inhibit individual student progress. Developmental and academic levels vary greatly among children in the same age group, yet traditional schools are structured to group all of these differences together under the category of a single, chronological age. The result is that the learning process becomes generalized for the whole class. Again, the students can slip through the cracks—those who aren't ready for the concepts learned at that grade level, and those who are ready to move on but cannot because they are locked into the single-age classroom curriculum. The teacher then "teaches to the middle," and the children at opposite ends are left confused or bored.

The intention of the Mingus Springs Charter School is to address and correct the problems mentioned above. Multiage grouping provides a classroom organization sufficiently flexible to accommodate children at different levels of maturity and with different levels of brightness. Moreover, the younger children will have the experience of being the older children when the older group moves on and a younger group moves in.

Thus, multiage grouping encourages cooperation. There is a growing recognition, at all academic levels, that cooperation is much more effective than competition in improving academic achievement. Multiage grouping also enables a teacher to use the knowledge she or he has gained about a child during the first year to plan learning experiences for the next year. Too often, the knowledge a teacher has gained about his or her students is lost when children move on to the next grade.

The teacher in a multiage classroom can develop a long-term relationship with each of his or her children, which will in turn maximize the teachers' ability to meet their emotional and academic needs.

The Mingus Springs Charter School is designed to provide an alternative learning environment conducive to the development of individual human potential, and quality education that promotes high self-esteem and academic success.

Mingus Springs Charter School consists of four multiage, non-graded classrooms of ages 6-14 (grade level equivalents 1-8). Each class consists of not more than 18 students, and is broken down into the following age levels: Ages 6-7-8, ages 8-9-10, ages 10-11-12, and ages 12-13-14. The bulk of each class consists of two age levels, with an "overflow" on either end of students who need to master skills at a higher or lower level. Each child thus has the same teacher for two to three years consecutively. An integrated curriculum is taught through thematic units, cooperative learning, and the implementation of critical thinking skills.

Coupled with a multiage setting, the Mingus Springs Charter School's intent to keep the classes small, at 18 students per class, alleviates the problems that come with over-crowding. More one-on-one interaction with the students gives the teacher the opportunity to spot potential "at-risk" behaviors. Each child's needs, be they emotional or academic, are met more efficiently because the teacher does not have to spread himself or herself so thin among too many students. With the multiage structure, the students keep the same teacher throughout a two- to three-year block of time. Time-consuming academic review and "getting to know the student" is cut, making for an easy transition from skill to skill over this two- to three-year stretch of time.

## Improvement of Pupil Achievement/ Goals of the School

Mingus Charter School provides a curricular framework that leads to:

1. Improved student achievement
2. Community involvement
3. Responsibility and citizenship
4. Curriculum continuity from class to class
5. Content retention
6. Increased self-esteem and motivation to learn

The process by which these goals are met are:

1. Small classes structured through multiage grouping, allowing the teacher to have the same students for 2 to 3 consecutive years.
2. Content areas taught through thematic integration of subject areas.
3. Cooperative Learning as an integral part of every classroom.
4. Critical thinking and problem solving skills built into the curriculum.
5. Field trips and hands-on workshops within the community integrated in the curriculum to provide "classrooms without walls."
6. Community volunteer services available in the school setting.
7. Mentoring and internships by local colleges and universities welcomed and encouraged.

## Special Program Emphasis or Methodology

With the multiage concept in force, students have the opportunity to progress to higher level skill levels within their own classroom without the restriction of grade levels. This goes along with the Mingus Springs Charter School's philosophy that all students can learn and all students can be successful. Because of the built-in "overflow" of age levels at the top end of the two- to three-year span, older students who need more time to learn are allowed to stay in this block, concentrate on higher skill levels, and still stay within the realm of their peer group.

With this type of individualized flexibility, the students are given the opportunity to advance not only vertically in their skill levels, but horizontally. Enrichment and critical thinking skills are integrated into lessons, so that every child can expand his/her learning outside the texts and outside the walls of the classroom.

## A Comprehensive Program of Instruction

The Mingus Springs Charter School provides a comprehensive program of instruction through a multiage classroom approach to learning. This approach of having different age levels in one classroom allows for the students to excel where they will be uninhibited by the confines of one grade level. In this classroom situation, students are given the opportunity to move through a continuum of skills at their own pace. Children in the classroom who are working at both ends of the spectrum in skills have the benefit of gleaning knowledge from the varying levels of instruction. This in-class spectrum allows for peer tutoring opportunities, and the introduction of skills and concepts that might have otherwise been "saved" for the next school year in a traditional classroom.

The role of the multiage classroom in the Mingus Springs Charter School is to provide this spectrum of instruction via an integrated, thematic and cooperative learning approach to teaching the content areas. These content areas include skills required by the Arizona State Essential Skills for ages 6-14 (The state-mandated skills are categorized by grade levels, so there will be reference to equivalent grade levels, i.e., grades 1-8). The general content areas include the following:

- **Language Arts**
  Reading, Spelling, Grammar, Process Writing, Vocabulary
- **Mathematics**
  General Concepts as per grade level, Arithmetic, Geometry, Consumer Math, Pre-Algebra
- **Science**
  Life, Physical, Earth, and Environmental Science
- **Social Studies**
  Family, Communities, State of Arizona, U.S. History, Geography, World History, Multicultural Education, Future Studies
- **Fine Arts**
  Visual Arts, Painting, Sculpture, Music, Movement/Drama

The content areas listed above are integrated in a thematic, whole language conceptual approach to the classroom curriculum. As stated earlier, individualized approaches to the basic skills in each of these areas is implemented for each child.

Enrichment and critical thinking skills are integrated into lessons through an open-ended, discovery approach to the curriculum. Divergent questioning and problem solving strategies are an integral part of the thematic unit activities.

### Effectiveness Measures

Competence in core academic instruction in correlation with the Arizona State Essential Skills are determined through a minimum proficiency/mastery level of 80 percent via teacher-developed tests, completion of ASAP (Arizona Schools Assessment Plan) tests with a proficiency/mastery level of 75 percent (based on a 4 pane rubric system), and project-based assessment. Skills not mastered are retaught on an individualized basis.

## A Multi-Faceted Assessment Plan

The Mingus Springs Charter School complies with all assessment testing required by the Arizona Department of Education, including ASAP testing and ITBS. Students are also assessed using the methods described below:

- **Portfolio/Authentic Assessment:**
  Portfolios of student work are collected, and this portfolio follows the student through each year of attendance at Mingus Springs Charter School. This assessment illustrates progress in the core subjects over a long period of time. The portfolios include a list of essential skills. There are indications of attainment of proficiency/mastery levels for each essential skill.
- **State-Mandated Assessment:**
  Assessment through state mandated ASAP tests and required norm-referenced tests are administered to the students as required by Arizona law.
- **Teacher-Developed Assessment:**
  Teacher-developed formative and summative tests are administered throughout the school year to assess levels of progress and progression to subsequent skill levels. Pre-tests are administered by each classroom teacher to determine the level at which each student should begin individualized instruction.
- **Project-Based Assessment:**
  Classroom teachers develop integrated, thematic projects to assess learning of skills and concepts.

The Mingus Springs Charter School philosophy is that the elementary and middle school years are of critical importance not only for the children's long-term academic achievement, but also for their abiding sense of self-esteem. By putting into effect all the components of a multiage school as stated above, Mingus Springs Charter School feels that it is dealing successfully with the age effect and is giving the majority of children entering school a chance to develop a healthy and robust liking for themselves, for learning, and for schooling in small, manageable classrooms with multi-age grouping.

*THE ARTS are especially appealing to children. A sense of imagery is with us from birth, and youngsters, responding to this deep urge, paint with their fingers, dance to the beat of drums, sing simple melodies, make sculptures from modeling clay. For young children, art is not a frill; it is an essential language that makes it possible to communicate feelings and ideas words cannot express.*

*—Ernest Boyer, The Basic School:*
*A Community for Learning, Princeton,*
*NJ: The Carnegie Foundation for the*
*Advancement of Teaching, 1995.*

# DEVELOPMENTALLY APPROPRIATE MUSIC IN THE MULTIAGE CLASSROOM — An Interview With Music Specialist Abby Butler

by Aldene Fredenburg

Abby Butler was concerned about the prospect of teaching music in a multiage setting when the first multiage classrooms were created in her school district in rural New Hampshire.

"There wasn't a lot out there on the topic," Butler said. She managed to glean some information from a contact in the music department of Arizona State University, but for the most part had to develop her teaching strategies and curriculum as she went. She now feels that a two-grade blend is a very workable option.

Butler has based her curriculum on a firm developmentally appropriate foundation. She uses many different activities to allow the children to learn the basic steppingstones of musical knowledge.

## Feeling the Beat

"The younger (K-1) kids need to work on developing and maintaining a steady beat," Butler said. It's natural for humans to keep a beat; but, when some kids don't have much life experience with music at home, it takes them longer to feel the beat. Butler uses a lot of movement and physical activities, and a lot of tactile experiences, to help the children feel that sense of beat.

"It's very obvious when they get it," Butler said. In working with one single-age first grade new to her, the kids just weren't together; then, about a month into the school year, they really started to click, and knew it. After the children had performed a particular song, she would ask, "Did you like that?" and the children would say, "We're not together."

In comparison, some of her one-two multiage classes clicked a little sooner. "Part of it was that the older kids helped the younger kids," Butler said, "and part of it was that a lot of the older kids had had me as a teacher the previous year."

## Singing in Tune

Another really big developmental stage is the ability to sing in tune, or match pitches. In order for children to succeed, they need to have lots of listening and echoing activities (where the teacher sings a phrase and children repeat it).

"It's important to use very simple songs with very few skips," Butler said—in other words, use songs with the notes *sol, me*, not skipping a note, as in *do mi sol*. From there children can go into learning Kodaly skips, which are natural for children. "One-two multiage blends are generally more able to do skips than kindergartners," Butler said.

## No Such Thing as Tone Deaf

Butler doesn't believe there's any such thing as tone deafness. Some children may not be hearing enough or not hearing well; others may not understand how to use their voice, or the physical act of singing in a higher register.

"Kids with no experience singing often don't know how to use the voice properly, or open up head tones," she said. Often, when kids don't sing in tune, or when it sounds like they're shouting or speaking, it's because the song isn't in the right key or pitch. Butler suggests that teachers teach songs to children in a higher pitch than they would ordinarily feel comfortable with for themselves.

It's also important, Butler said, to encourage children to sing in a nice voice—strongly, rather than loudly. For many children, "loudly" means shouting.

## Developmental Aspects

There is also a developmental component to being able to sing in tune. By second and third grades, kids are starting to hear;

they're beginning to develop musically.

Third graders generally are more in tune when learning a round, for instance, than second graders. They are beginning to be able to hear and sing two-note harmonies; more advanced harmonies usually are more appropriate for third or fourth grade.

A teacher can do some preparation to get children ready to learn harmonies. For Halloween, Butler had one of her third-grade groups do a song with three different melody parts, which she layered—a step toward singing in harmony.

While some children in second grade are able to do well with harmonies, it's easier to accomplish with third or fourth graders.

## Balancing Developmental Levels

It is difficult sometimes to balance activities so that no age level or experience level is left out; but it can be done. For example, older children, or those with advanced motor skills, can accompany a song on instruments, while younger children can pat the beat with their hands. Children can also be divided into groups who take turns singing different parts of a song.

## Reading Music

Teachers can begin very simple rhythmic reading, which prepares kids for reading music, as early as kindergarten. Butler uses flashcards, and starts with a very simple quarter note/quarter rest pattern. (Kids really enjoy the Kodaly rhythmic symbols—"ta titi ta ta"—when learning rhythm, says Butler.)

As a general guideline, a teacher can use the following when teaching music reading to children:

In Kindergarten, teach quarter notes
" 1st grade " double eighth notes
" 2nd grade " half notes
" 2nd-3rd grade " dotted half and sixteenth notes

This is *only* a general guideline; Butler has successfully taught sixteenth notes to first graders.

Butler also uses a variety of activities designed to help children associate what they hear with what they see. This has lots to do with learning styles; with a group that learns better visually, for instance, she may use charts with stickers.

It's important to have materials that kids can see easily; if there's a Big Book available of a music text, for example, it's better to use that than individual textbooks.

## Connecting with the Class's Personality

Each class has its own personality, which colors the kind of activities they enjoy doing and their successes. It's important to figure out the group's personality and connect with that. Children have their favorite things to sing; some groups want to run the class and choose every song, while some kids are happy to do anything the teacher suggests.

Butler usually gives her classes 10 or 15 minutes where the children can choose songs or games, or gives them a choice of two songs to sing.

## The Lesson Plan

Butler's lessons are pretty structured; her lessons average a half-hour, twice a week; with kindergarten she recommends 20 to 25 minutes per lesson. Beyond that, children find it hard to sit still and pay attention at that age.

A lot of thought goes into a lesson; she tries to incorporate three different types of activities, including singing, some sort of reading and/or instrument performing, and either a listening activity or a movement activity. Sometimes the focus of a lesson will go to singing, sometimes to listening.

She usually presents a single musical concept in a lesson, and builds the activities around that concept. If the musical concept is "loud and soft," for example, then she'll choose a song or game that illustrates that, and may include an additional listening example of the concept, given time.

## Integrating the Curriculum

Butler makes it a point, at the beginning of each school year, to make personal contact with the classroom teacher. She discusses special units or themes the teacher is planning, and asks if there's anything she can do to contribute.

In one class, which was participating in an inter-school World's Fair, she taught the children a song from Brazil, added Latin American instruments to the song, and had the children make rain sticks, which make the sound of rain on leaves. The children performed the song at the closing ceremonies at the Fair.

In another program, the children at the school were having an ethnic extravaganza; Butler taught them songs from different cultures. She has also taught environmental songs in conjunction with classroom themes. She's had very good success especially with music of other cultures, the kids respond very positively, enjoying singing and playing instruments, remaining involved and on-task.

"I enjoy it," Butler says. She often dances around and plays games with the kids, and says, "If the teacher doesn't enjoy the activity, it's hard to sell it to the kids."

Many classroom teachers like to incorporate literature into the music lessons; Butler often reads stories in music class and finds songs to relate to the stories, to tie music and literature together. She also likes to include readings of child-written poetry or stories as part of Christmas or Spring musical productions at her schools.

## Inclusion

Butler has dealt with children in wheelchairs, which is always challenging when dancing or movement is part of the lesson plan. Other children are wonderful about incorporating these kids into the activities. "I've not had a child left out," Butler says. She credits the classroom teachers and their success with acceptance models with that.

## Age-Appropriate Music

It's essential to select music that's age-appropriate so that children are physically and mentally able to handle it. Music teachers should be getting information on age-appropriateness in music method classes at college; teachers can also contact a professor in a good college music program for recommendations. There are many textbooks and articles that are very useful; but perhaps the best way to know whether music is age-appropriate is to watch the kids. If something the music teacher tries is not working, it may be too difficult. The best thing to do in that instance is ask the classroom teacher; usually she will have a good perspective on their children's abilities—and possible distractions.

It is often valuable, if the music teacher has time, to observe the classroom teacher working with her students, and model her methods.

## A Problem With Music Texts

One difficulty with multiage music classes is that the music textbooks tend to have a strong grade-level structure, last year she used a grade two text for her 1-2 multiage classes, but this year her second graders ended up using the same text. This may have implications in the future for textbook manufacturers, who may want to consider revamping their texts.

Also, certain students have special needs; some teachers have individual children on a discipline plan, and if the specialist is informed of that she can help implement it.

## Developmental Appropriateness for Older Kids

Children continue to develop musically as they get older. Serious involvement with musical instruments is usually delayed until a student is in fourth or fifth grade; that is when the body development is far enough along to be able accomplish fine motor skills and breath control. Also, most band instruments are just plain too big for most younger children. The violin and piano, on the other hand, can be begun as early as age three (an example is the Suzuki method of teaching violin to young children, using downsized violins.)

Most schools don't involve children in choirs until fourth grade, when students are able to handle harmonies, and have developed music reading skills. Most schools then limit themselves to two-part music; exceptional students can handle three-part harmonies, but it's unusual to see that in a public school setting.

Butler doesn't usually recommend voice lessons until age 14 or 15; even then students' voices are not mature, but will go through major changes for the next 10 years.

*Anne Butler teaches a 1-2 multiage and a 2-3 multiage at Farwell School in North*

*Charlestown, N.H.; two single-grade first grades and one single-grade second grade in neighboring Alstead; and a 1-2 multiage and 3-4 multiage at Sarah Porter School in Langdon. She also directs the choral program at Fall Mountain Regional High School—a truly multiage chorus of ninth- through twelfth-graders. She has taught grade four in the past; she has never taught more than a two-grade elementary blend, and feels that the developmental range would be too great in the early grades.*

*Aldene Fredenburg is the editor of Crystal Springs Books.*

## Advice for Classroom Teachers—and Specialists

Anne Butler offers valuable advice to classroom teachers and their music specialists:

- It's very important for both the classroom teacher and specialist to have a mutual respect for each other and the job they're doing.

- It's important for specialists to respect the instructional time the classroom teachers have. Specialists should be on time, and be prepared for their lesson.

- The classroom teacher needs to make sure children are available for the lesson, not doing makeup work or being punished by being told, "You can't do music." Withholding music class is not an appropriate punishment for a child.

- The specialist must be consistent with children in the classroom. Try to find out what the classroom teacher's expectations and classroom rules are, and follow them. This is the responsibility of the specialist to find out the rules; but it is also the responsibility of the classroom teacher to communicate with her specialist.

- Communication is paramount; the classroom teacher and the specialist need to talk frequently about individual students, their plans for classroom, and interdisciplinary programs.

  It is especially important for the specialist to know which students are having problems; for instance, the classroom teacher might know that Johnny's having problems at home, so he might not be behaving as he usually would. That is valuable information for the specialist to have.

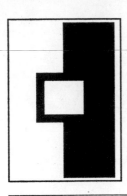

# HOW TO IMPLEMENT DEVELOPMENTALLY APPROPRIATE PHYSICAL EDUCATION
## for Elementary School Children

by Mile Soules

The purpose of this article is to give classroom teachers insight into developmentally appropriate physical education for children, and to provide practical information to help them implement developmentally appropriate practices.

Physical education is unique in the school system in that it focuses primarily on the motor development of the children; therefore, motor development and motor skills should play a major part of the planning of activities. Developmentally appropriate physical education concerns how the children develop their motor skills.

As in other areas of development, not all children progress at the same rate—not all children 9 years of age perform the forward roll the same way; however, the children seem to develop their skills in an orderly and sequential manner.

Realizing that not all children are at the same skill level is an important concept to understand. Just as classroom teachers do not give all of the children the same book and expect them all to be on the same page and improve at the same rate, the developmental physical education teacher needs to make adapations both for children who are less skilled and more skilled. This is the essence of developmentally appropriate physical education for children.

To better illustrate the developmental skill concept, let's look at two eight-year-old children. Brent and Brittany both perform the forceful overarm throw. Brent, who is low-skilled, throws the ball with very little leg, arm and trunk action or movement; while Brittany, who is high-skilled, demonstrates a greater range of motion for the leg, arm and trunk action. The greater the range of motion of the body parts, and the more body parts involved with the action, the more skillful a child is.

Brent is not performing the skill wrong; right now he's just at a lower point on the developmental spectrum than Brittany. A teacher using developmentally sound practices would work with Brent to help him increase his range of movement; the emphasis is on helping Brent get better, not telling him what he's doing wrong.

It is important to be able to observe children and define where the child is developmentally, and where you want him or her to be. This entails knowledge of motor development, motor learning, biomechanics, and pedagogy. Realizing that most classroom teachers are not immersed in motor development literature — there are over 200 textbooks about motor development — I have put together some practical information that should help teachers implement developmentally appropriate physical education for children.

The Council on Physical Education for Children (COPEC) has a pamphlet that really nicely captures the essence of appropriate and inappropriate developmentally appropriate physical education for children. Some components of the pamphlet are as follows:

### 1. Curriculum

*Appropriate practice:* the program has an obvious scope and sequence based on goals and objectives that are appropriate for all children.

*Inappropriate practice:* the program lacks developed goals and objectives and is based primarily on the teacher's interests, preferences, and background, rather than those of the children.

### 2. Active participation for all children

*Appropriate practice:* All children are involved in activities that allow continuous movement.

*Inappropriate practice:* Activity time is limited because the children are waiting in lines for a turn in relay races, to be chosen for a team, or because of limited equipment or playing games such as duck duck goose.

### 3. Fitness

*Appropriate:* Children participate in activities that are designed to help them understand and value the important concepts of physical fitness and the contributions they make to a healthy lifestyle.

*Inappropriate:* Children are required to participate in fitness activities, but are not helped to understand the reasons why.

### 4. Assessment

*Appropriate:* Teacher decisions are based primarily on ongoing individual assessment of the children as they participate in physical education activities (formative evaluation), not on the basis of a single test score (summation assessment).

*Inappropriate:* Children are evaluated on the basis of fitness test scores or on a single test score.

Let's put these ideas to practical use. Suppose your goal is to help children between the ages of eight and nine, one of whom is in a wheelchair, become better at kicking, throwing and catching balls. You organize a game of kickball for the children, creating two teams with ten or so children on each team. After awhile you notice observe seven or eight children on each team who are not "into" the game, because two or three children from each team dominate the action.

Also, it becomes clear that most of the children—at least 15 of them—are not getting a chance to work on any of the skills because they can't get to the ball. Your solution might be to get two more balls and have three games of kickball going, which will dramatically increase the number of chances each child will get to catch, throw and kick. Still, there may be children having difficulties; perhaps one group is confused and needs easier rules, while another group needs further challenge.

What about the child in the wheelchair? Can the children modify the rules or change the equipment to include him or her into the game? Maybe the child can play "catchball" with the group.

After reflecting on the activity, you might conclude that kickball is an inappropriate activity for a large group, but has possibilities

if you make some adaptations. It is critical, no matter what the activity, that we observe carefully and change rules, equipment or whatever is necessary to help the activity work better for all children.

So what should developmentally appropriate physical education for children entail? As a teacher you should strive to:

- allow different children to do different activities in a physical education class
- give feedback to each child during each class
- become a keen observer and have the confidence to change the lesson for some or all of the children; and
- have all of the children active most of the time.

Most of all, we must be committed to accommodating individual differences, no matter how tough the going gets. There is no magical lesson. Teaching from a developmental perspective is challenging; however, it is the children that reap the benefits.

### References

"Developmentally Appropriate Physical Education Practices for Children," COPEC, 1992. A position statement of the Council on Physical Education for Children. COPEC is part of the American Association of Health, Physical Education Recreation and Dance. For materials, call 1-800-321-0789.

Barrett, K. R., Williams, K., and Whitall, J. (1992). "What does it mean to have a Developmentally Appropriate Physical Education Program?" *The Physical Educator* 49,114-118.

Grineski, S., (1992). "What is a truly developmentally appropriate physical education program for children?" *The Journal of Physical Education, Recreation and Dance* 63(60)33-36.

Roberton, M. A. "What is developmental teaching?" Abstract presentation at the Midwest District meeting of the American Association for Health, Physical Education, Recreation, and Dance.   Feb. 19, 1987.

---

*Mike Soules, a teacher at Essex (Vermont) Elementary School, has been teaching elementary school physical education to children for sixteen years. Half of his classes are multiage, and all children are included in the physical education class. Mike has made numerous state- and national-level presentations on developmentally appropriate physical education for children.*

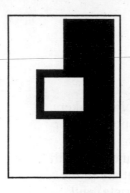

# DEVELOPMENTALLY APPROPRIATE PHYSICAL EDUCATIONAL PRACTICES FOR CHILDREN

*Excerpt from "Developmentally Appropriate Physical Education Practices for Children,"* a position paper of the National Association for Sport and Physical Education (NASPE) and the Council on Physical Education for Children (COPEC).

## Quality Physical Education for Children

The Council on Physical Education for Children (COPEC) of NASPE, the nation's largest professional association of children's physical education teachers, believes that quality, daily physical education should be available to all children. Quality physical education is both developmentally and instructionally suitable for the specific children being served. Developmentally appropriate practices in physical education are those which recognize children's changing capacities to move and those which promote such change. A developmentally appropriate physical education program accommodates a variety of individual characteristics such as developmental status, previous movement experiences, fitness and skill levels, body size, and age. Instructionally appropriate physical education incorporates the best known practices, derived from both research and experiences teaching children, into a program that maximizes opportunities for learning and success for all children. The outcome of a developmentally and instructionally appropriate program of physical education is an individual who is "physically educated."

In 1990, the National Association for Sport and Physical Education (NASPE) defined a physically educated person as one who:

- HAS learned the skills necessary to perform a variety of physical activities

- DOES participate regularly in physical activity
- IS physically fit
- KNOWS the implication of and the benefits from involvement in physical activities
- VALUES physical activity and its contributions to a healthful lifestyle.

Appropriate physical education programs for children provide an important first step towards becoming a physically educated person.

## Premises of Physical Education Programs for Children

In any discussion of physical education programs for children there are three major premises that need to be understood.

### 1. Physical education and athletic programs have different purposes.

Athletic programs are essentially designed for youngsters who are eager to specialize in one or more sports and refine their talents in order to compete with others of similar interests and abilities. Developmentally appropriate physical education programs, in contrast, are designed for every child — from the physically gifted to the physically challenged. The intent is to provide children of all abilities and interests with a foundation of movement experiences that will eventually lead to active and healthy lifestyles — athletic competition may be one part of this lifestyle, but is not the only part.

### 2. Children are not miniature adults.

More than ever before we are in a time of rapid change. Consequently, educators have the challenge of preparing children to live as adults in a world that has yet to be clearly defined and understood. The only certainty is that they will have different opportunities and interests than currently exist. Contemporary programs introduce children to the world of today, while also preparing them to live in the uncertain world of tomorrow. In brief, they help them learn how to learn — and to enjoy the process of discovering and exploring new and different challenges in the physical domain.

Tomorrow's physical activities may look different from today's. Present programs need to prepare children with basic movement skills that can be used in any activity, whether it be popular today or yet to be invented. Mastery of basic skills encourages the development and refinement of more complex skills leading to the ultimate enjoyment of physical activity for its own sake.

## Intended Audience

This document is written for teachers, parents, school administrators, policy makers, and other individuals who are responsible for the physical education of children. It is intended to provide specific guidelines that will help them recognize practices that are in the best interests of children (appropriate) and those that are counterproductive, or even harmful (inappropriate). It needs to be understood that the components described in this booklet are, in actuality, interrelated. They are separated here only for purposes of clarity and ease of reading. It should also be understood that these components are not all-inclusive. They do represent, however, most of the characteristics of appropriate programs of physical education for children.

*I believe that movement is essential to all children. They move to learn, to interact with people and to know objects. Children move throughout their lives, encountering many experiences. Movement is the vehicle through which they obtain experiences, express feelings, receive inspiration and develop concepts. Through body movement, children have life experiences and then respond to these experiences. Body movement plays an important role in the life and learning of children.*

*— Janet Millar Grant, Shake, Rattle, and Learn: Classroom-Tested Ideas That Use Movement for Active Learning, York, ME: Stenhouse, 1995.*

# Appropriate and Inappropriate Physical Educational Practices

## APPROPRIATE PRACTICE

### Component: Curriculum

The physical education curriculum has an obvious scope and sequence based on goals and objectives that are appropriate for all children. It includes a balance of skills, concepts, games, educational gymnastics, rhythms and dance experiences designed to enhance the cognitive, motor, affective, and physical fitness development of every child.

### Component: Development of movement concepts and motor skills

Children are provided with frequent and meaningful age appropriate practice opportunities that enable individuals to develop a functional understanding of movement concepts (body awareness, space awareness, effort and relationships) and build competence and confidence in their ability to perform a variety of motor skills (locomotor, nonlocomotor, and manipulative).

### Component: Cognitive development

Physical education activities are designed with both the physical and the cognitive development of children in mind.

Teachers provide experiences that encourage children to question, integrate, analyze, communicate, apply cognitive concepts, and gain a wide multi-cultural view of the world, thus making physical education a part of the total educational experience.

### Component: Affective development

Teachers intentionally design and teach activities throughout the year that allow children the opportunity to work together to improve their emerging social and cooperation skills. These activities also help children develop a positive self-concept.

Teachers help all children experience and feel the satisfaction and joy that results from regular participation in physical activity.

### Component: Concepts of fitness

Children participate in activities that are designed to help them understand and value the important concepts of physical fitness and the contribution they make to a healthy lifestyle.

### Component: Physical fitness tests

Ongoing fitness assessment is used as part of the ongoing process of helping children understand, enjoy, improve and/or maintain their physical health and well-being.

Test results are shared privately with children and their parents as a tool for developing their physical fitness knowledge, understanding and competence.

As part of an ongoing program of physical education, children are physically prepared so they can safely complete each component of a physical test battery.

## INAPPROPRIATE PRACTICE

### Component: Curriculum

The physical education curriculum lacks developed goals and objectives and is based primarily on the teacher's interests, preferences, and background rather than those of the children. For example, the curriculum consists primarily of large group games.

### Component: Development of movement concepts and motor skills

Children participate in a limited number of games and activities where the opportunity for individual children to develop basic concepts and motor skills is restricted.

### Component: Cognitive development

Instructors fail to recognize and explore the unique role of physical education, which allows children to learn to move while also moving to learn.

Children do not receive opportunities to integrate their physical education experience with art, music, and other classroom experiences.

### Component: Affective development

Teachers fail to intentionally enhance the affective development of children when activities are excluded which foster the development of cooperation and social skills.

Teachers ignore opportunities to help children understand the emotions they feel as a result of participation in physical activity.

### Component: Concepts of fitness

Children are required to participate in fitness activities, but are not helped to understand the reasons why.

### Component: Physical fitness tests

Physical fitness tests are given one or twice a year solely for the purpose of qualifying children for awards or because they are required by a school district or state department.

Children are required to complete a physical fitness test battery without understanding why they are performing the tests or the implications of their individual results as they apply to their future health and well-being.

Children are required to take physical fitness tests without adequate conditioning (e.g. students are made to run a mile after "practicing" it only one day the week before.)

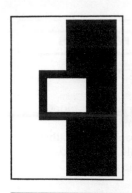

# DEVELOPMENTAL STAGES OF ART IN THE MULTIAGE CLASSROOM

by Deborah Camara

The multiage classroom is an exciting and stimulating environment for all subject areas, but it is especially conducive to integrating art. In the multiage classroom the students are working at a variety of developmental stages, and creating a rich, experimental environment that motivates and expands the growth of their peers. The peer teaching that occurs between the students in a multiage classroom exists on a greater level because of the variety of ages and stages that exist in the classroom. The younger students begin to explore and experiment with art techniques and concepts by observing the older children in the class.

I have been teaching in a multiage R-1 classroom for the past eight years, and I always find it fascinating to watch each child's art development over the course of a year.

It is important to understand that art development begins long before the first mark is placed on the paper. Just as children learn the importance and how-tos of reading by being shown books and being read to long before they can represent or comprehend symbols on a page, they learn about art by seeing it and watching its creation.

It is easy in a multiage classroom to look at a wide range of art techniques and styles represented in children's literature. Some of these art techniques can be explored later in combination with writing assignments. In creating big books with my class we have explored crayon resist, collage and printing techniques so that my students could expand their art vocabulary.

When I work with my students on the writing process, I also work with them on the art process. I give students suggestions on how they can expand their details both in their writing and illustrations.

It is also equally important to look at and understand where the child is in her art process. Just as with writing you would not suggest to a child beginning to work with initial and ending sounds that it is time to begin to work on quotation marks, you would not present a concept beyond the developmental level of the child but would encourage the child to expand on concepts that are appropriate for that stage of development.

For instance, a child who focuses on using one color for all of his illustrations can be asked probing questions similar to the questions that you might ask that child about his writing: What color were you wearing? What color is your house, cat, car? These questions can expand the child's vocabulary of color just as similar questions might assist a child to expand his writing vocabulary.

## The Stages of Art Development

There are primarily three stages of art development. An understanding of these levels will give any educator a better idea of what is appropriate to expect at each level.

Scribbling is the first stage, which begins at the time a child produces the first mark on the page and goes through several evolutions until the age of four.

The second stage, which develops out of the end of the Scribbling stage, is the Preschematic/Schematic stage, which lasts from around the age of four to around age eight; this is when a child begins to create the first representational symbols.

The Gang stage, the third stage of development, usually begins at around age nine and continues throughout the middle school years.

## Scribbling Stage

In this stage, children begin by making random marks on a page and gradually evolve into making drawings that have content adults

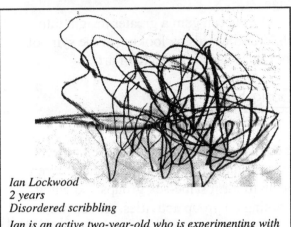

Ian Lockwood
2 years
Disordered scribbling

*Ian is an active two-year-old who is experimenting with making random marks on the paper, often without looking. He is using a gross motor stroke, and line weight varies according to movement.*

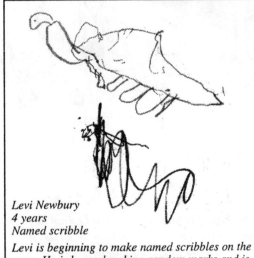

Levi Newbury
4 years
Named scribble

*Levi is beginning to make named scribbles on the page. He is beyond making random marks and is moving from making lines to creating shapes and joining these shapes. Levi is very interested in dinosaurs, and here are two dinosaurs from The Land Before Time.*

can recognize. There are three categories of scribbles: disordered scribbles, controlled scribbles, and named scribbles. At the disordered scribbling stage, a child makes random marks with large strokes, very often not looking at the page. Children use various methods to grasp the drawing implement; fine motor coordination is not very developed. A child in this stage of development, if not given the proper materials, will choose to scribble in inappropriate places using inappropriate materials.

Although it is important to show interest in the child's early marks, parents and teachers should not try to see representations that are not there.

During the controlled scribbling phase, the child will begin to explore making different size marks and using more than one color. As the child begins to show more control in scribbling, there is also an increase in small motor development. Young children will move toward copying lines, circles and then squares during this time.

The last phase in the scribbling stage is when the child begins to name his scribbles. At this point the scribbles are often named before the child begins to draw. The actual scribbles do not look different, but the reason for the marks has changed from a kinesthetic activity to imaginative thinking.

The child usually begins to spend more time exploring and experimenting with scribbling by the age of three.

## Preschematic/Schematic Stage

Although the early part of this stage resembles the scribbling stage the child begins to create forms that have a relationship to the world around him. By four years of age children are making recognizable forms that adults can relate to. One of the earliest forms

Michael Richardson
6 years
Preschematic

*Michael has moved from the scribbling stage and is beginning to create a symbol of a person. He is representing the schema by two circles joined without a neck and stick legs. With some figures he chooses to indicate eyes, and with others he doesn't.*

81

*Molly Rose Newbury.*
*6 years*
*Early Schematic*

*Molly has developed her schema of a person and has indicated a difference between the male and female members of her family. She has worked to create greater details in the shape of the arms and legs.*

At this stage children will also explore symbols for many objects such as houses, cars and natural objects. A spatial schema begins to develop, and children begin to connect the various schema by placing a baseline on the page.

Adults can gain a greater insight into children's worlds by looking at the symbols they have developed in their art.

## Gang Stage

During this stage children begin to see their place in the world and develop peer relationships. This is a time when children begin to form same-sex groups and enjoy working on group activities. At this point

*Lauren Cassidy*
*9 years*
*Early Gang Stage*

*In this drawing you can see that Lauren has developed a schema of a person. She has started to work at showing individualized details on the clothes of the figures. Lauren has also moved away from representing a straight baseline and has indicated a pond.*

the child will represent is a human figure, which will be fully developed by the age of six. By age seven a child has developed a schema/symbol to represent the human form.

When students begin to represent figures, they are trying to understand how the figure gets put together. At this point you can make suggestions by talking to the students about ways of dressing the figure. Children often start with a stick figure and then add clothes and dress the figure.

*Julie Richardson*
*9 years*
*Schematic*

*Julie is at the late part of the Schematic stage but has not entered the Gang stage. She is still indicating a single baseline and a frontal schema of each figure. She has indicated which members of her family are male and female, but is indicating the schema without much variation.*

students also become more interested in the representation of details in their drawings. The schema that were once used are no longer adequate. Children at this time recognize the nuances of color and search for the correct shade of blue to represent the sea and sky. They explore multiple baselines in their drawings and give a greater naturalistic look to their drawings. Children become more aware of overlapping images, and the skyline continues to the baseline.

*Marcus Newbury*
*10½ years*
*Gang Stage*

*In this illustration Marcus has represented a detailed illustration of his family hiking. He has chosen to include a great deal of details showing EMS on the backpack, his brother Len in a backpack, and the figures pointing at the bear in the woods.*

Drawings at this stage show a great deal of decoration and pattern. Students at this stage are interested in working on their drawings for longer periods of time.

## Ways to Assist a Child at Each Stage

Foremost, it is important to realize and respect which developmental stage each child is at. After you have observed a child's drawings, you can assist the child in moving to her next stage of development by being supportive, as you would in any subject area. Providing open-ended assignments which will allow each child to develop at her own rate is essential and will stimulate creativity.

As with reading or writing, you can assist a child to focus on one area at a time by making encouraging comments. [What color dress were you wearing? Does your dog have shaggy or smooth fur?] This can help expand a child's visual vocabulary while at the same time respecting her drawing.

## Gaining Comfort with Art Materials

Step-by-step projects are monotonous and stifle creative growth, but many teachers fall into the trap of relying on them because they aren't comfortable with using art materials. As a teacher in a multiage classroom it is important to explore the characteristics of a variety of art materials so that you won't suggest using tempera paints, for instance, when children want to create a detailed drawing. Instead you could suggest the use of colored pencils.

Along with choosing appropriate materials, mini sessions demonstrating how to use these materials are essential. You can't simply say, "Use watercolors," and expect children to use the materials properly. Art materials are tools and need to be presented in a manner that can assist the exploration and use of these materials. By taking the time to demonstrate art materials you will find that it will allow students to be able to work more independently throughout the year.

There are many picture books dealing with color, shape, and texture which can be read as an introduction to a unit on color or other art concepts. It is also helpful to have resource materials available in the classroom on artists, and Zoo books and other magazines as references. It is useful to have photos of animals and other objects on hand so, for instance, if a child wants to draw a beaver and has never seen one, he can refer to a photo for the appropriate details.

## Appropriate Materials

During the Scribbling Stage I would recommend that children explore materials that can help them use their gross motor control while at the same time be developing their fine motor control—good materials for this include fingerpaints, crayons, tempera with large brushes, colored chalk and play dough. Children can also explore tearing and gluing of paper to develop fine motor control and to prepare for cutting with scissors.

When children are developing symbols during the Schematic Stage they are more interested in exploring color and varying line quality. At this point the introduction of watercolors, markers, Cray pas, and colored pencils can be added to the materials lists. Introducing children to the cutting and gluing of collage elements is very stimulating at this point.

At the Gang Stage, when children become more interested in details and spatial relationships, pen and ink, pencil drawing and linoleum printing techniques can be explored. At this time children can explore multimedia projects and work on larger group projects and murals.

## Good Multiage Projects

**Self Portraits** can be done at the beginning and end of each year, and can reveal a great deal of information and indicate where each child is developmentally. I use the self portrait as one tool to give me an idea as to which students could benefit from a Readiness year.

**Mask Making** is an area that can be explored by children at all developmental stages. These projects are open-ended and can be integrated into the curriculum to create a memorable sharing of a piece of literature. Children can make paper masks at the earlier stages, and later explore plaster and clay masks. Students can also create costumes and instruments to create a dramatic sharing.

**Murals** are an exciting way to incorporate a variety of art styles and techniques in a cooperative environment.

If you are studying an integrated space unit, each students could create his or her idea of a space alien using watercolor and perma-

nent markers. The actual planet could be created by incorporating sponge painting, torn paper and paint. Large 12-foot murals can be created with all the aliens on Planet X. Students can extend this activity by writing about what it would be like to live on Planet X.

A mural can be easily explored on a wide range of themes or topics. Puppets can be explored by incorporating a wide variety of materials. Simple bag and stick puppets can be created by younger children. As students begin to form symbols, they can create papier maché and plaster of paris finger puppets. As children enter the Gang stage, they can explore Indonesian shadow puppets with movable parts, and string puppets.

Puppets are also an interesting way to incorporate art and literature to create a dramatic sharing.

*Deborah Camara has been teaching in an R-1 multiage classroom for eight years at Hancock Elementary School in Hancock, New Hampshire. She has an M.Ed. from Antioch New England in Elementary Education and Art Education. She has worked to integrate art in curriculums working with children from ages 3 to 12. She has worked at the Keene State Children's Performing Arts program and an integrated arts program at a multigenerational camp in Burlington, Vermont, during the summers. In the fall of 1995 she began to teach art workshops to other educators which integrate the arts into the multiage classroom. She finds it exciting and rewarding to assist other educators in feeling more at ease when working with a wide range of art materials and developmental stages.*

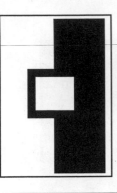

# Student-Directed Learning:
## Children at Sandown (N.H.) Central School Ask for Black History Month

by Cheryl Zanello

In February, our multiage class met at the beginning of the school day to check the progress of our February activities. Everyone was excited and enthusiastic about the topics, when one child raised his hand with a question.

"Mrs. Zanello, why aren't we doing Black history month, like last year?" I reminded him that, since the veterans (nine students who had been in the multiage class the year before) had completed a Black history month last year, they probably would prefer to study other reading topics this year.

Immediately many children raised their hands and gave reasons for another look at Black authors, biographies, folktales and African "Why" books. They also decided they wanted to study Black history in March, because March is longer than February, and a school vacation fell in February.

It certainly seemed logical to combine my curriculum goals for the class with themes based on my class's interest and desire for

*These two-sided charts provide information on black inventors, educators, manufacturers and political leaders.*

more extensive knowledge of the Black experience. I set the following plans in motion:

• I obtained three unique posters from a teacher's book store. They contained pictures

and stories of unknown or unusual African American authors, educators, inventors, and scientists. I put them on the bulletin board as a motivational tool.

• I notified our media specialist, Ellen Beckwith, of our month-long study of the Black experience. She responded by providing hundreds of books for all of the reading levels present in my class. She presented us with African folk tales, biographies (from picture book level to high school level), fiction by African authors and illustrators in America and around the world, stories of sports heroes, and authors' studies.

• I set a display of my own class compilation of black authors and illustrators in a reading center, and created a listening center at the back of the room with tapes and accompanying books. During the course of the month I found many boys reading the book *Jolly Mon* by Jimmy Buffet, and playing the accompanying tape; the boys had headphones on, and were moving to the beat of the music. The book, which depicts Black Caribbean culture, became a big thread in their wanting to learn.

• I consulted the reading specialist, Sharon Hobbs, who planned ways of reaching our goals for March with this self-chosen theme. We developed a poetry project summarizing the Black experience; we held discussion groups; I provided format activities which helped the children expand critical thinking abilities as they wrote about what they read every day.

On the second day of March, I found an excited boy at my side. Joey Assenza had found a challenging book of important African American people. I knew of almost none, and promised I would read a different biography at the start of each day. The children checked the posters on the bulletin board and asked me to see if the book contained these people. We discussed the Black experience and difficulties daily. The book—which was actually suitable for middle school—was passed around the class and read, silently and aloud, by both rookies and veterans.

Miss Hobbs came in two or three times a week. She developed a poetry project aimed at expanding the children's critical thinking; the children had to describe the author or character in the poem they were studying in the first person. An interesting outcome was that the veterans responded wonderfully orally, while the rookies had a finer sense in the written form.

When she (Miss Hobbs) was present during the class's discussion time, she and I were both surprised at the high level of expression on a most difficult topic. I often felt high school teachers would be jealous of such highly enthusiastic participation. Miss Hobbs' real interest in the "Pinkney Family" of writers and illustrators sparked small reading sharing groups.

A common perception amony many children is that Black people get involved in sports and make a lot of money without having to expend any effort. A lot of the independent reading among the boys was biographies of famous sports heroes like Jackie Robinson and Reggie Jackson. Miss Hobbs led a discussion on what truly makes a hero, and the children worked in groups to write hero poems.

As the children learned more about African Americans, they went back through history to the Revolutionary War and early settlements. The children came to the realization that no matter how bright African Americans were, they had to work ten times harder than whites to succeed. The children were sometimes surprisingly thoughtful in terms of "What it must be like to struggle for your goals." They also pondered each biography by thinking of what it would be like to be different in a white culture.

They decided that "You could become successful if you were Black in America, but you had to work hard and may not have personal satisfaction or good health, because some doors might be closed to you."

The children were particularly interested in how long each individual they studied had lived. They understood that many African Americans had difficulty getting adequate

*The children pose with singer-author Jimmy Buffett's book and tape "Jolly Mon," an island tale.*

health care, and that even if an African American achieved multimillionaire status in the 1800s and 1900s he or she might not get the same health care and housing and food that white people did.

A lot of Black history consists of discussions of George Washington Carver and Martin Luther King; I didn't concentrate on Martin Luther King, because it's hard for third and fourth graders to relate to someone who was a religious leader who was assassinated. Instead the children learned about farmers, Revolutionary War heroes, industrialists, women who succeeded in medicine, and cowboys. (A lot of the boys were fascinated by the Black cowboys.) The class eventually developed an interest in Dr. King.

As often happens in multiage classrooms, a genuine unconscious sharing of knowledge occurred. Veterans shared favorite tapes of folktales in the listening center. Many children partner-read and conversed about favorite books. My teaching assistant and I found our format writing projects were being completed with both fiction and nonfiction Black topics.

One learning-disabled child completed a non-fiction format form on a difficult chapter book. He told the class that "He was real interested in the topic and that was why he did such a good job." Another boy said that he did so well in his work because he learned that "you had to keep trying and work hard."

The class did not seem to want to stop

learning at the end of the month, and wanted to know more of the Black experience.

How often do we, as teachers, miss opportunities for real learning experiences by not listening to what children want to know? There was no reason I could not teach the skills demanded by the curriculum in a setting produced by the children. The few days I spent in thinking and gathering materials paid off in a way I did not expect. They showed me that a multiage classroom can produce what we really want: oral and written expression at a higher level than anticipated, because the class had a major part in the formation of their own learning. The children showed me that my thinking was narrow, and that they had keener eye on what was important to them.

We should listen more and faciliate what we hear! I became a listener in a more child-centered classroom. Every day the children all shared more and more of what they learned and thought. Oral expression of very difficult concepts was expressed by very young children.

Often I hear teachers feel overwhelmed when faced with the prospect of teaching Black history; "Do we have to do this?" I feel that their wariness comes from uncertainty about how to approach the subject. But when a teacher allows her students to take the lead, their enthusiasm and natural curiosity will take the teacher far.

*Cheryl Zanello has been teaching whole language for nine years, and has her own vast*

*A detail of the cover of the Big Book the children created for this project*

*personal library of children's books. Her school, Sandown Central School, became involved in multiage education in 1994, and has 1-2, 3-4, and 4-5 combinations, as well as single-grade classrooms. Zanello's class is a whole language classroom; she does not use basals. The learning is theme-based; she follows her curriculum guide and incorporates the required skills into her teaching, choosing a different theme for her class, with the input of the children, each month. She sees her role as teacher as that of a facilitator, and allows her children a lot of say in terms of what they will study. "It's ten times the work," she says, but believes it's worth the effort. Her own attitude is also important; "When you treat any subject with interest and enthusiasm, the children are interested," she says.*

*Voices*

*Strong self-esteem is the flower and fruit of active involvement, emerging competence, exposure to appropriate challenge, and willingness to risk. When we nurture curiosity, creativity, and opportunities for genuine success, self-esteem blooms.*

— *Priscilla Vail, Emotion: The On-Off Switch for Learning. Rosemont, NJ: Modern Learning Press, 1994.*

## Some Important Black Biographies and Fiction Books—American and African Roots

Aaadema, Verna. *Traveling to Tondo.*
—. *Bringing the Rain to Kapiti Plain.*
—. *Crocodile and the Ostrich.*
—. *Why Mosquitoes Buzz in People's Ears.* Tape also.
Adler, David. *Martin Luther King, Jr.*
—. *Jackie Robinson.*
Altman, Susan R. *Extraordinary Black Americans from Colonial to Contemporary Times.*
Barg, Molly Garrett. *Wiley and the Hairy Man.*
Brenner, Richard. *Shaquille O'Neal.*
Buffett, Jimmy and Savannah. *Jolly Mon.*
Cameron, Ann. *More Stories Julian Tells.*
Davidson, Margaret. *I Have a Dream.*
Daynell, E. *Why the Sun and Moon Live in the Sky.*
Dragonwagon, Crescent. *Home Place.* (Illustrated by Jerry Pinkney).
Epstein, Sam and Beryl. *George Washington Carver.*
Freedman, Russell. *Cowboys of the Wild West.*
Goss, Clay. *Baby Leopard.* * Tape.
Greenfield, Eloise. *Nathaniel Talking.*
Griffalconi. *The Village of the Round and Square Houses.*
Hacker, Randi. *Amazing Bo Jackson.*
Hoffman, Mary. *Amazing Grace.*
Johnston, Johanna. *They Led the Way.*
Jordan, June. *Fannie Lou Hamer.*
Kimmel, Eric. *Anansi and the Moss-Covered Rock.*
Lester, Julius. *Tales of Uncle Remus.*
—. *How Many Spots Does a Leopard Have?*
Larungu, Rute. *Myths and Legends From Ghana for African American Cultures.*
Levine, Ellen. *If You Travelled on the Underground Railroad.*
Lowery, Linda. *Martin Luther King Day.*
McDermott, G. *Zomo.*
—. *Anansi the Spider.*
McKissack, Patricia. *Flossie and the Fox.*
—. *Mirandy and Brother Wind.*
—. *Sojourner Truth.*
—. *The Dark Thirty.*
Medearis, Angela. *The Seven Days of Kwanzaa.*
Monjo, F.N. *The Drinking Gourd.*
Musgrove, Margaret. *Ashanti to Zulu.*
Pinkney, Gloria J. *Back Home.*
Polacco, Patricia. *Chicken Sunday.*
Porter, Connie. *Meet Addy.*
Sansousi, Robert. *The Boy and the Ghost.* (illustrated by J. Brian Pickney).
—. *Sukey and the Mermaid.* (illustrated by Brian Pinkney).
—. *Talking Eggs.* (illustrated by Jerry Pinkney).
Turner, Ann. *Nettie's Trip South.*
Vass, George. *Reggie Jackson.*
Woods, H. & G. *Bill Cosby.*

*Artwork provided by Sandown Central students.*

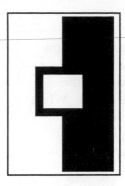

# BUT WHAT DO THEY KNOW? ASSESSMENT

by Jill Ostrow

Excerpt from **A Room with a Different View**

David is writing about his progress in the following areas:

*Challenging Myself:* I think I have been challenging myself at descriptive writing. I used to not have very descriptive writing, now I do.

*Independence:* When I first came into this room I would always ask what to do next. Now I just do everything on my own.

*Confidence:* Right now I am pretty confident. I really don't think I have got more confident.

As I was sitting uncomfortably in my cramped seat, flying from Portland, Maine, to Portland, Oregon, after a conference in May 1994, I turned to Ruth Hubbard and asked, "How can I write a chapter on assessment? I don't do any." She looked at me and shook her head and laughed, as she often does in reaction to the things I say. She reminded me of something Larry, an eight-year-old, had said to me last year. He had just moved into our classroom a few months before from a very traditional classroom. I asked him how reading was different in our room than in his other room. He looked at me smiling and said, "We don't have to do reading in your room." He was obviously extremely excited by this thought. I, on the other hand, was quite puzzled. "Well, Larry," I asked him, "What are you doing with that book?" He looked at the book and then looked back up at me. "I'm reading. We're not *doing* reading."

Later, when he again moved into a very traditional environment, he told me during a phone conversation now that he had to *do* math. I suppose since we don't have math workbooks or a special "math time," new kids from a more traditional curriculum don't think we do it.

Ruth and I generated a long list of assessment and evaluation strategies that I do use in my classroom. Just because something doesn't have a label attached to it, doesn't mean you aren't doing it. The children are reading, writing, and *experiencing* math all day long, and I am assessing them all day long. Yet, not until I sat down and began listing what I was doing, did I realize just how much I do, and how often I do it.

## Everyday Assessment

Every time I talk to the children I am learning about them. I like the words "learning about" much more than I like "assessing." I learn about my children. I get to know them. I want to know *what* they know. I want to know *how* they know. Isn't that what assessment is all about — learning what children know? When I ask a six-year-old to tell me about her weekend, I am learning how this child tells a story. I learn if she can tell a story, if the story makes sense — is there a beginning, a middle, and an end? I am learning what interests the child, what the child talks about, and what is important to the child, and I am learning more about the child. All this from one small question. Observation and listening are the most important strategies I use for learning about the children in my class.

As Carly was presenting her Journey Problem journal, she came to a part in which she needed to mention what countries she had traveled through. She said, "We went through Asia, Europe, and Africa." Now, because I know Carly so well, I could ask the class the following question: "Did Carly just share what countries she traveled through?" Someone noticed her mistake and said, "No."

"Do you see that Carly?" I asked her. I

watched her glance over her journal. She looked up and smiled. "Oh, I looked at the wrong line. These are the continents. The next ones I share will be the countries." That was a quick on-the-spot assessment. I knew that Carly knew the difference between countries and continents, so by asking her to see her mix-up, I could listen to her response and watch her face. I would have been able to tell if she was confused by the expression on her face. I didn't need to give her a test or assign page after page of geography worksheets to find out what she knew about countries and continents. And I knew she'd be comfortable being put on the spot like that. I could not put Megan or Alissa on the spot like that. If I had a similar question for them, I would pull them aside later.

I use these on-the-spot assessments often. As we sat on the grass in front of the school during Quiet Writing one afternoon, after we had finished sharing but before I wanted to go back inside, I asked everyone to find one thing and then another thing that was about four times as big as the first thing. The children went off for about three minutes and then we met back in a circle. What they found was interesting but even more so how they "proved" the bigger item was four times bigger. Clearly, some of the children needed practice estimating, some needed practice measuring accurately, and some had a fairly precise sense of "times-bigger."

The facial expressions of children help me understand the "sense" they have of particular concepts. Watch your students' faces one day as you question them about a concept. I have seen looks anywhere from extreme confidence to total bewilderment. These expressions help me to know when I need to back off or when I need to step in and help a child with a concept they find confusing.

I find myself constantly assessing during Writing and Reading Workshop. Through conferences, I know what a child knows and what a child needs to work on. Dave, who has an uncanny love for writing, was working on a piece that had a section of dialogue. I asked him if he knew what he needs when he writes dialogue.

"Oh yeah, these little things, quotes, right? But I never know where to put 'em." So I showed him. Days later, during another conference with Dave, after he had finished

reading his story to me I concentrated on how he was using quotes. I also find it easy during writing conferences to see the progress the child has made since our last conference. When I notice a skill or concept a child has been consistently using and understanding, I will record that progress on their progress wheels.

## Progress Wheels

The year I taught in England, I was introduced to the National Curriculum (NC). The teachers in my school were trying to understand this new curriculum, not to mention all the new record-keeping sheets. I had never seen so much paperwork. I had seen an example of some sort of recording system in an article or book I was reading. It was in the shape of a wheel and looked very organized. I decided to try to put the Reading, Writing, Speaking, and Listening parts of the NC onto such a recording wheel to make it easier to keep track of the children's progress. I remember it as being quite an intense job. I also helped to create a wheel for the Maths NC. The staff seemed to like using this record-keeping strategy.

When I was back in the States and beginning my teaching at my present school, I decided to make progress wheels for my personal record-keeping system. I created one for reading and writing. These wheels were very useful to me that first year. I was able to explain them easily to parents, who appreciated the fact that the wheels were so visual. I like the fact that the wheels are not linear, since I look at children as "scattered" learners. As *Figure 20a* shows, it is easy to see that these wheels are not linear

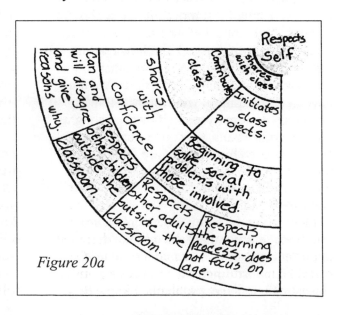

*Figure 20a*

continuums. Children don't learn in neat, straight lines.

The following year I updated the wheels a bit, condensing them more, yet by June I realized that I really wasn't using them as often as I needed to. When I'm not using a tool, I either don't need it anymore, or it is time to update and change it. Last summer I spent time updating the wheels so they would be more useful to me.

I thought a lot about what I would consider important as I ventured into this class of first-, second-, and third-grade children. I knew I did not want to separate them into grade levels! I *couldn't* separate them into grade levels! I made a list of all of the qualities I watch in children as they progress over time. I knew that choice, challenge, independence, and respect were important to me. After I had listed the skills that I thought would be of help to me, I made some lists. What I discovered in the lists was a common theme and consistency. Finally I came up with the two topic headings I use on the most recent wheels, *Progress as an Independent Learner* and *Progress as a Community Learner* (*see Figures 20b and 20c*).

When I was showing the progress wheels to Ruth, she told me she could actually use parts of them for her graduate students. I think that is probably true. There are sections that I wish all adults could shade in, especially the section under Community Learner that says, *can show an appreciation for someone else's point of view.*

I condensed the content areas significantly. I have found that I just don't need to know every writing skill I had listed on the old wheels. All the emergent writing stages on the original wheels seemed trivial. I replaced these sections with *Writes for meaning.* That gives me the same information in less space.

I also took out all the specific math skills. It matters less to me that a child *knows* his math facts to 10 or 20 than how a child *uses* math facts. I added two sections about algorithms: *Sees algorithms as a "shortcut"* and *Uses algorithms to solve problems.* I have noticed that at a certain point, children begin to see algorithms as a shortcut in solving problems. They begin to realize that they don't need to use cubes or ten strips all the time. That is an important realization, so I added it into the wheel. When children begin to use algorithms consistently to solve problems, I know they

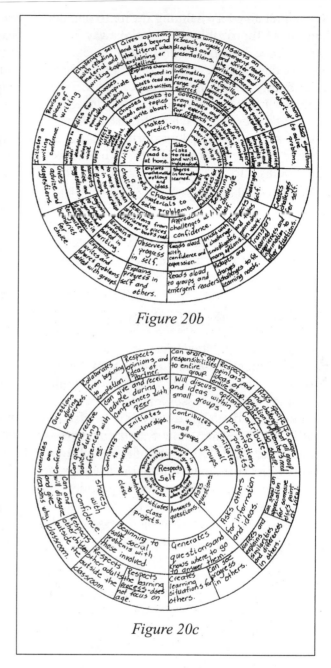

*Figure 20b*

*Figure 20c*

have truly internalized the concept. Because we don't use math workbooks or any commercial math program, this is a vital observation for my records.

The community progress wheel is also a very important and essential record-keeping tool for me. Since I honor a sense of community so strongly, I need a way to record how the children progress as community members. I added a number of comments about respect. No child, or adult, can be an effective community member without respect. And the core of respecting others is respecting oneself, which is why I put *respects self* at the center of the wheel.

These progress wheels have proven themselves effective record-keeping tools this year.

I don't feel an overwhelming desire to change them, but I'll probably add or take away comments as I need to. I don't shade these in every day or even every month. I usually do it just before conferences or reporting time, or whenever I feel I need to look more closely at a child's progress. Each child has a wheel, which I keep in one of their portfolios.

Some parents have asked me, "What now?" when their child's wheels have been completely filled in. I don't see these wheels as learning *goals*, I use them more for observing learning *strategies*. For these children, this kind of record-keeping might have outlived its usefulness to me, and we need to expand further on those strategies.

## "Authentic" Assessment

What could tell a teacher more about a child than assessment that really *means* something? That sounds so simple, but assessment should be simple. Authentic assessments show what a child *knows*. I don't use assessment to discover what a child does not know. Standardized tests so that quite nicely! They are of no use to me.

Authentic assessments force me to look more at the process and less at the product. These assessments should not be standardized in any way, such as the reading assessments the whole second grade does, or spelling assessments for the first grade. I have seen these types of assessments used in schools, but to me there is no difference between them and standardized testing. Neither focuses on *process*, and those little tests are not in keeping with what we know today about good child-centered practice.

A fraction problem turned out to be an authentic assessment that I hadn't intended as an assessment. I discovered it after the children had completed the assignment. I asked the kids to pick a card with a fraction written on it. Then I asked them to do two things with the fraction they had picked:

1. Show the fraction using a picture.
2. Write a story explaining the fraction.

It was clear to me from their response to this problem what each child knew about fractions on both a concrete and an abstract level. I know, for example, that JB has a clear sense of numerical fractions and abstract fractions (*see Figure 21*). He not only understands the concept of mixed fractions, but his written explanation showed that he could find a different way to see the fraction $2^2/_3$. When I questioned him about his written answer, he said, "Well, when I put the picture down, I noticed another way to say $2^2/_3$. It's 1 and $1^1/_3$ and $1/_3$ left over. So I decided to write that instead." He not only challenged himself, but he used what he knew about fractions to look at this one in a new way.

I know that Kyle has a clear sense of numerical fractions abstractly (*see Figure 22*). He was quick to draw and cut the picture of the strawberry. He knew that the bottom number meant "how many in all" and that the top number meant "how many to show," but watching him write his story was very different. He was obviously confused. His writing was actually pretty accurate, but he was very unsure of his answer when it came time to share his problem and answer questions from the class.

Anna is still learning to understand fractions numerically and with pictures (*see Figure 23*). She is learning to represent fractions pictorially. When she picked her fraction card, she took it to a table and sat staring at it for a long time. She saw Kyle making a strawberry and I noticed that she began making a strawberry too. When she had completed cutting out the picture, I walked over to her.

"Okay, Anna," I said, "You have a strawberry. What do you need to do to the strawberry now?"

"Cut it up?"

"Yep. How many pieces do you need to cut it into?"

"Three?" she asked.

"Good guess! What does the 3 mean in $3/_5$?"

"How many in all?" I noticed that all of Anna's answers were asked as questions. This was significant in terms of her confidence with this concept.

"Try again."

"Oh, yeah. The top number is how many you take and the bottom number is how many in all, right?"

"What do you think?"

"I think yes. So the 5 is how many pieces to cut. I'll cut my strawberry into five pieces and circle three pieces." Without this sort of questioning, she would have been confused and frustrated. Through questioning and reinforcement, she became very con-

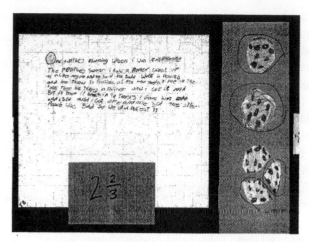

*Figure 21*

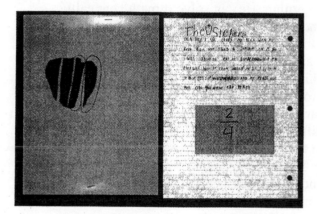

*Figure 22*

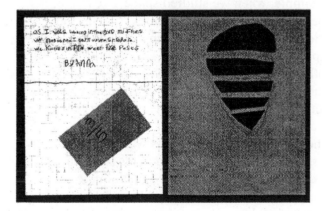

*Figure 23*

fident about her final answer.

Although this sort of questioning was appropriate for Anna, it wouldn't have been for Kyle. He needed to take time to experiment with his knowledge, and was comfortable doing so. These three samples might seem to indicate that these children have a clear numerical and abstract concept of fractions. Yet obviously not all of them do. The reason I call this an *authentic* assessment is that this problem shows me where each child is. Had I given the kids a pencil and paper test that asked them to circle the correct fraction or to shade in the numerical fraction shown, I would not have learned what I did about how much the children do know, how they know it, and what they need to know.

The other point is that I don't always look for the correct answer. I look for the process a child goes through to find the answer to a problem. Even though Anna did finally understand what she was doing, her process was different from that of Kyle and JB, and theirs were different from everyone else in the class. Anna's explanation at the end of my questioning made it clear to her that she did understand what she was doing. As Kyle was sharing, he was aware that his written explanation confused him. He knew he understood the picture, but he also knew he needed to work more on fraction stories. JB was also able to challenge himself to go further and test out his knowledge.

I remember the first time Danny did a play that made sense. That too was a form of authentic assessment. Danny, a first grader, acquired oral language at age six. I know he is beginning to develop an understanding of story in terms of beginning, middle and ending. He made up and performed a short play in which he had these three elements. Every time I see children using or making up new spelling strategies to help them spell, I list those strategies as authentic assessments. Rachel, for example, writes lists for checking her spelling all the time. And when a child moves from writing with only consonant sounds to adding short vowels, I know that child has made a huge step in his writing progress.

Before conferences I borrowed an idea from Allyn Snider. I wrote five addition problems ranging in difficulty from an addition fact to a three-digit problem on a piece of paper. I told the children to choose the one they felt was right for them, solve it, and write about how they solved it. This was a wonderful assessment of many things besides whether or not the children could add. I observed how independent children were in solving the problem, how — and if — they would challenge themselves, and how detailed their writing was.

Chuck chose to do the first problem (*see Figure 24a*). He wrote that he solved it using unifix cubes. Chuck is a second grader and knowing that cubes were available to him was a huge step for him. He also tried to challenge himself by doing the second problem. From his scratch out, it would seem that he felt it was too difficult for him to solve. He then decided to try one that would be better for him. Megan also chose the first problem, but she solved it very differently. She wrote, "I took 17 in my head and added 5 with my fingers." She understands the concept of counting on, yet she didn't need cubes to solve this. She too wanted to try the second problem but didn't begin to try it as Chuck had. She has much less confidence than Chuck, so this seemed right for Megan. Alissa was becoming more comfortable using ten strips. She even drew a picture of what the strips looked like when she had added the two numbers together. The fact that she doesn't need cubes but isn't yet ready

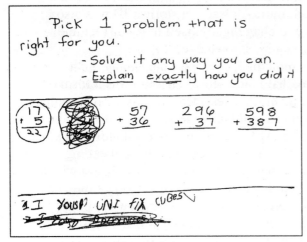

*Figure 24a*

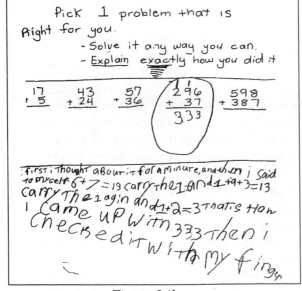

*Figure 24b*

to add large number without ten strips is a significant insight into Alissa's progress. When she becomes more confident using the strips, I can begin to have her record on paper just how the ten strips work.

Chris also used counting, but he wanted to challenge himself by solving the third problem. He started with 57 and the added the 36 to come up with his answer. Tessia also challenged herself with the problem *(see Figure 24b)*. Her writing explains clearly that she can *do* an algorithm, although I would question her *understanding* of it. When she wrote, "I carried the 1," I would question her to see if she understands that what she is carrying is actually a 10, not a 1. Josh understands this algorithm. He can solve it mathematically and write about how he solves it.

The importance of this quick assessment wasn't the accuracy of the answers. It was the children's explanations of how they solved the problem. Chuck and Megan both solved the same problem, but their strategies were quite different. When I assess and evaluate, I tend to focus more on strategy than on accuracy.

Yet, sometimes I do want to check accuracy and how much a child has learned or internalized. When we begin a topic or research project, I will ask the children to write down everything they know about the topic. For example, when we studied space a year ago, before we even began our study, I asked the kids to write down everything they knew about space. Some kids wrote, "I know nothing," and others wrote that they knew the sun and the moon and the stars are in space. I dated these and saved them. Then, at the end of the study, I again asked the kids to write everything they knew about space. This was a wonderful assessment of how much the kids had learned. I dated these papers, stapled them to the first ones the kids had written, and put them into their portfolios.

## Portfolios

I see *portfolio* as another term on its way to "term hell." There are two different kinds of portfolio. One is Portfolio Assessment, and the other is the Working Portfolio. *Portfolio Assessment* is a collection of the child's best work gathered together for the sole purpose of assessment. *Working Portfolios* are collections of work the child does all year. I use these two types of portfolios for my children as well as one other.

1. Portfolio Assessments (PA): This is a portfolio of authentic assessments I might give the child throughout the year. In this portfolio I might also include observations and the progress wheels. In this portfolio is a collection of work I have specifically chosen for assessing that child. I use this collection not simply as a collection of the child's work but for a more critical look at the child. This is where the child and I may choose to put a "best piece" of work.

2. The Working Portfolios (WP): These portfolios are collections of the child's work. The kids file their own work in four folders: writing, math, projects, and art. Their writing drafts are filed in their writing folders, which contain every piece of writing the child has done during Writing Workshop. This is also a great way to observe writing progress quickly. The math portfolio works the same way, as does the project portfolio, except for one difference: if a project or problem is too large to fit inside the folder, I ask the child to write about what they have done and put that writing into the portfolio. I have also take pictures of projects to go into these portfolios, but film and processing tends to get expensive, so I have found that the written explanation is sufficient. The art portfolios hold all the art work the child has done during art workshop.

These ever-growing files contain all the work the child has done during the year. Instead of sending work home, I ask the kids to keep it in these Working Portfolios so we can follow their progress by comparing their work from different parts of the school year.

3. The Pass-On Portfolio (PO): This is the portfolio that is to be passed on to the child's next teacher. (Some teachers call these *cumulative portfolios*. It serves as a sample of work that clearly shows where the child began, how far the child came, and where the child needs to go. This is where samples of writing that show progress should be included. I do not use PO Portfolios as an assessment tool for the next teacher. They are not a judgment piece, but rather a sample of work a new teacher can look at to get a *feel* for the child. These portfolios should be quite small, since no teacher will, or will want to, shuffle through a huge packet of work for twenty-six children. They should also

be selective, showing a piece of writing that demonstrates the child's knowledge of the writing process, an authentic math assessment, an evaluation by the child, and so on. I also use these portfolios as the carriers of my notes and/or record-keeping on the child. (I remove the progress wheel from the PA portfolio and stick it into the PO portfolio.)

In a PO portfolio I like to include samples of writing that show children's progress and their knowledge of the writing process. This could include one from the beginning of the year and one from the end of the year. I include a short explanation about why the pieces were included. The child also does this. Some teachers use spelling assessments as progress, others use spelling as part of the writing process. Both are valid forms of *spelling* assessment but not of writing assessment! Two or three samples of authentic assessments should be included. Knowing that a child received 83 percent on a math test would be of no help to me! Knowing what a child knows about a concept would be. Teachers often say, "But I don't know what to include." I advise them to decide on a few items that show the child's learning. Of course it is difficult to include a piece of work on all mathematical concepts. Most teachers don't want to see that. I included the fraction assessment in some of my students' portfolios.

I see teachers trying to use all of these portfolios at once. It helps to be clear on what you are saving, what needs to go to the child, and what needs to be passed on to the next teacher. In some cases, I find a piece of work that will fit into all these portfolios, and the child and I might decide together where it belongs.

PA is a tool I use to keep track of what the child knows. It is easy to look into this portfolio and see what a child understands about a particular concept. As I explained to the kids, the fraction problem I gave them might be something I would put into this portfolio. This was not a "right/wrong" type of assessment. It simply showed me what the children knew about fractions.

I *don't* think continuity in PO portfolios is all that crucial. All portfolios can and should be different: all children are different and their work should look different. Portfolios should respect the individuality of the child.

# I. Who Are the Gray-Area Children?

Gray-area children are sitting in classrooms all across the nation. Teachers often refer to these children as slow learners, at-risk students, or the "tweeners." They qualify for no special education services. Without accommodations made for their particular learning needs, they are in danger of falling between the cracks in the regular classroom.

## Gray-area children:

- are commonly known as "the gazers," who can't or won't pay attention.

- may appear to be immature, angry, unsettled, or unfocused, and may require constant redirection or one-to-one supervision.

- fear failure and may refuse to take part in learning.

- often come into our classes hungry, not only for food, but attention.

- may have "invisible disabilities," such as language problems, fetal alcohol syndrome, or attention difficulties.

*"Without accommodations made for their particular learning needs, they are in danger of falling between the cracks in the regular classroom."*

- perform at a slower pace than most children and require extra wait time.

- usually learn better when shown instead of told and work at a concrete, manipulative stage of development.

- may come to school with extra emotional baggage.

- may move from school to school throughout the year.

- often do not fit in socially with peers, either because of lack of experience or little support from home.

Their classwork may be disorganized, late in arriving, or incomplete. Desks and other belongings often appear to have been shot out of a cannon. They often have their shirt tails out, buttons open, zippers down, and their hair in knots.

It is our challenge as classroom teachers to work with these children, make sure they succeed in school, and help them feel good about themselves each day. We need to adapt existing curriculum, provide strategies that help them learn, and teach them new concepts through concrete, hands-on activities.

# I I. General Classroom Adaptations

## General Strategies

- Give students hands-on experiences. Use games, learning centers, projects, and speakers in place of worksheets or workbooks.

- Ask yourself, "Will these students need this information five years from now?" If the answer is no, reevaluate the purpose of the instruction.

- Use rebus picture directions.

- Vary tone and pitch of teaching voice.

- Place classroom jobs on individual strips of paper in an empty jar. Students reach in and choose a job to do alone or with a partner.

- Instead of having students constantly raising their hands to respond to questions, vary response modes. For example, students can touch their knees if the answer to 3 x 2 = 5. They may also nod their heads, or cross or uncross ankles to respond.

- Give students work options. "You may do a written end-of-the-chapter sheet or illustrate important events in the chapter."

- To retain important information, kinesthetic learners will often need to do something while restating important facts. Have them snap their fingers, clap their hands, or jump up and down while reciting information such as their phone number, the first ten states, etc.

- Forewarn students of upcoming transitions. Some typical samples might be:

    "We will work on journals for the same amount of time as (name of TV show popular with children)."

    "In five minutes we will begin to clean up centers."

    "In three minutes we will clean up."

    "It is now time to clean up. Let's see if we can be cleaned up by the time we finish singing_____."

- Distribute 3" x 5" index cards to children. One side of the cards says "no" and the other side says "yes." Children flip cards or hold them on their foreheads to respond accordingly.

# Developing Self-esteem

- Assist each student with meeting daily success in a variety of settings.

- Provide compliments in a variety of ways.

- Say at least one positive statement to each child daily.

- Give credit for completed work.

- Design "I am special" buttons for each child.

- Chart individual progress.

- Send written "I care" messages to each child daily, or send Happy Gram postcards home to each family at least once a month.

- Build learning expectations upon each learner's strengths.

- Allow students to circle the answers they want checked.

- Mark correct answers only.

- Provide partial credit for work attempted.

- Slow the pace of oral directions.

- Limit oral directions. Write directions on the board or overhead to accompany oral directions.

- Give one- or two-step directions at a time. Combine oral with written directions.

- Encourage students to talk themselves through tasks.

- Reduce classroom distractions. Many students are distracted by humming lights and clicking heaters.

- Avoid standing in front of busy, distracting bulletin boards.

- Avoid overdirecting. Use as few words as possible.

- Provide students with page and paragraph number for answers (see pages 112-113).

- Prove the child with a timer to track available time to complete tasks.

- Seat the child close to you during instruction. You may put an "X" on the rug with a specific child's name on it.

- Distribute workbook pages or worksheets one at a time rather than within the whole book. Children will not be distracted by the extra pages.

# Organization

- Be consistent so students know what to expect.

- Post a daily schedule visible to all children.

- Make individual "To do" lists (see page 141).

- Chunk assignments and provide directions for small, sequential steps. Instead of giving some children a chapter to read by the end of the week, break it into reasonable bite-size chunks. On Monday read pages 10-14, Tuesday read pages 15-19, Wednesday read pages 20-24, etc.

- Develop individual contracts (see pages 144-145).

- Develop individual goal sheets (see pages 138-140).

- Develop daily assignment books. Have parents or cross-age tutor sign the book on a daily basis.

- Give work samples. Hang a sample of what a completed project or paper should look like.

- Provide word banks on papers (see pages 122-123).

- Seat students in horseshoe format for visual accessibility.

- Enlarge print or spaces on work pages.

## Support

- Encourage parent participation in class.

- Provide at-home as well as school copies of texts.

- Check often for understanding.

- Give parents or peer tutors materials to rehearse with students before class.

- Encourage student discussion and collaboration.

- Use peer tutors, cross-age tutors, or study buddies for individual support.

- Allow for extra think time. In advance, give students a written copy of the question(s) you plan to ask them during discussion time.

- Encourage students to orally restate expected tasks to you or to a peer before beginning work.

- Provide immediate oral as well as written feedback.

- Allow for movement and frequent breaks.

- Allow students to take notes for a buddy. Copy your notes for those who are unable to take notes.

- Have more able students tape stories and texts for other classmates to use for rehearsal or as a follow-along activity. This provides auditory along with visual reinforcement. Students are encouraged to start or stop the tape as needed.

- Read tests orally to student.

- Contact a local retirement village for classroom volunteers. A school bus could pick up the retirees in the morning. The volunteers are then assigned a classroom to assist the teacher with projects, paper work, or as a student study buddy. These grandparent volunteers can be treated to a school lunch before riding the bus back to their retirement community.

# Developing Self-esteem

**Oral language**
**Written expression**

## I Have a Question

Cover an upright tissue box with brightly colored wrapping paper. Place white question marks over the wrapping paper. Leave the tissue slit open at the top of the box. Invite students to use the box as a place for questions they have regarding any school subject. When there is an extra 5-10 minutes of transition time, grab a question and collectively answer it as a class. Some teachers take this a step further and play "Stump the Teacher." Children put their own trivia questions in the box and attempt to stump the teacher whenever there is available time.

**Artistic expression**

## Where's Waldo?

Using the same format as the popular children's book, give children a small school snapshot of themselves. Have them paste their photos anywhere on a piece of construction paper. Now give children a magazine or catalog and have them cut out pictures. They then place their magazine pictures anywhere on the page while trying to camouflage their own snapshot. The entire class combines their pages together for a fun-filled way to find and identify their hidden friends.

**Oral language**
**Self-assessment**

## Show Me State(ment)

Instead of using workbooks, written tests, or worksheets, encourage children to involve their classmates with checking for understanding. One child could be in front of a group and say, "Show me two ways to solve 3 x 4" or "Show me two ways to express surprise in written language." This builds individual self-esteem by allowing students to take control of class review and encourages group collaboration.

# Developing Self-esteem

## Brag Bag

Artistic expression
Oral language
Self-assessment

During the first part of the school year, distribute to each child a large brown paper grocery bag. Invite children to decorate the bag with their names or initials in a creative way (turning letters into animals, initials into logos, etc.). Have children take their bags home and place in them any accomplishments or items they are proud to brag about. Children bring their brag bags to school for sharing time. It's amazing how much background information about children can be gained from this!

## Proud Book

Self-assessment

Encourage students to place the work they consider their best effort in a magnetic photo album, along with their name and date. Proud students can gather samples from the month or year and share with visitors.

## Look What I Did

Self-assessment

Place a small photo of each student on a classroom bulletin board. Put a push pin under that student's name. When students achieve something they are proud of, it is their very own display place in the room. They are permitted to go to the board and hang work, drawings, kindness statements, etc. (One boy from my pre-first hung his shoe laces there for two weeks after he learned to tie.)

# Developing Self-esteem

 **Self-assessment**

## Individual Timelines

Give each class member a prepared timeline for the entire year beginning in September. These individual lines can be hung on a bulletin board or placed inside a manila folder. The timeline is divided into the school months. Allow the child adequate space to write his/her accomplishment for the month.

 **Self-assessment**

## Brag Line

Hang a clothesline across the back of the classroom. At the end of each week, allow students to hang on the line anything they are proud of accomplishing that week. Keep a supply of snap-type clothespins available for children to use. This activity allows them to take ownership for what they have accomplished instead of a teacher-made bulletin board that says, for example, "See the best spellers in Room 23."

 **Self-assessment
Written expression**

## Classroom Timelines

In the front of the classroom, hang a large seasonal shape for that month (September — a large leaf, October — jack o'lantern, etc.). At the end of the month, pass out a 3" x 5" index card to each class member. Encourage students to write whatever important event or accomplishment they remember from the month. All the cards are hung over the seasonal shape and remain up for the year. These memories can then be converted into an end-of-the-year classroom memory book.

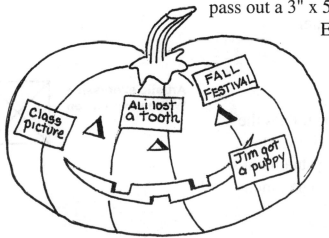

# Developing Self-esteem

## You Deserve a Hand

Have students trace and cut an outline of their hands and write their names in the center. Pass the hands around the room. Encourage classmates to write a positive statement on each finger. When each finger contains a compliment, return the hand to the owner.

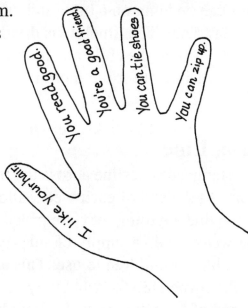

**Written expression**

## Punch Cards

Place name tags or cut-out animal shapes on students' desks. When you catch students being good, acting appropriately, or completing assigned tasks, punch the card with a hole punch. Design a reward board that might say something such as:

    10 punches = lunch with the principal
     8 punches = help in kindergarten
     5 punches = extra time on the computer

**Behavior**

## Pass the Bag

Have each student decorate a lunch bag. Pass the bag around the classroom to all members of the class. Encourage each student to write a positive statement about that friend and deposit it in the bag. The lunch bags end up with the original owner.

**Artistic expression**
**Written expression**

# Focusing Strategies

## Spotlight

Turn on the overhead projector. Stand in front of the bright light while talking or reading to students. Children who have difficulty focusing will be drawn by the light and will be able to focus on what you say.

**Behavior
Following
  directions
Oral language**

## The Ears Have It

Draw a large picture of an ear. Keep this picture under your seat, on the carpet, or in front of the room. When it is necessary for children to really listen to directions or lessons, hold up this ear to help them focus and listen.

This same ear can be used if you are ever faced with a primary classroom of tattlers. Hang an ear picture on a classroom bulletin board. Place a beanbag or rocking chair next to the ear. Encourage children to "tell it to the ear" when they need to tattle.

## The Eyes Have It

Before beginning instruction or giving directions, establish eye contact with all students. Verbal cues such as "ready" or "all eyes on me" encourage children to focus on the speaker.

# Focusing Strategies

## Highlighting Texts

Many students experience success in the classroom by having material in a text highlighted in a consistent fashion. One way to accomplish this is by using blue to highlight definitions, yellow to highlight specific facts, and pink to highlight main ideas. Once the color coding has been established, post a reference chart in the classroom. Share the task of highlighting with colleagues. One teacher could highlight science books for both classes; another could highlight social studies books. Many teachers find that they only have to highlight one or two books each year. This is an excellent way for parents to help.

Organization
Reading comprehension
 Facts
 Main idea
Study skills
Vocabulary

## 1 and 2

Make certain that students are focused on the directions. When giving multiple directions, obtain eye contact first. A typical scenario might look like this:

"Please look at me. I'm going to tell you two things to do."

Hold up two fingers.

Touch finger one.

"First, I want you to get out your clay figures."

Pause.

Touch finger two.

"Second, I want you to finish adding the toothpicks."

Following directions

# Organizational Strategies

**Number recognition**

## Tab It

Purchase heavy duty, removable subject tabs. Attach these tabs to pages 10, 20, 30, 40 etc., in a textbook. When students have difficulty getting to the correct page quickly, provide clues such as, "We will be working on page 46. Turn to the 40 tab and find 46 in that section."

## IRS Homework Envelopes

Take a large manila envelope. On the outside, write:

Did you remember to write your name? write the date? write the title? use capitals and periods?

The envelope is laminated and students check off their responsibilities in the same fashion as we check off information for the Internal Revenue Service.

## Desk Maps

Have students remove all extras from inside their desks, then organize necessary material in corners. Have them draw a map of the desk contents on a 5" x 8" index card. Place the desk map on top of the desk and challenge students to find things in their desk by looking at the map. When a specific article is called, children have until the count of five to retrieve that article without looking inside the desk. With younger children, the desk map can be drawn for them, and they can place items accordingly.

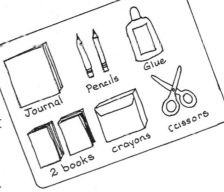

# Organizational Strategies

## Velcro Schedule

Place a strip of velcro on a student's desk. On 2" squares of paper draw pictures to represent the day's schedule. Place a 1" piece of velcro on back of the schedule cards. Attach pictures to the desk top strip of velcro. Allow the student to move the picture schedule on and off the velcro as the events are completed.

## Cut It Out

Use this strategy with students who cannot quickly turn to an assigned page in a consumable workbook. As each page is completed, clip the bottom right-hand corner off the page. When getting ready to find the next page, students put their index finger along the clipped off section and quickly find the next page.

**Workbooks/ worksheets**

From *I Can Learn! Strategies and Activities for Gray-Area Children*, by Gretchen Goodman.
Peterborough, NH: Crystal Springs Books, 1995. 1-800-321-0401. All rights reserved.

# A: ACCEPTANCE

Accepting children with diverse learning needs in the classroom today will help them feel secure in learning situations or social settings tomorrow.

The first step for those beginning inclusion is allowing time for teachers to share ideas, plan projects together, and develop goals to enhance the acceptance of all children in the classroom.

Accepting diversity as an asset is an essential part of making the plan work. Labels will disappear for both students and teachers and will no longer be the curriculum's driving force. All educators will become special educators and meet the individual needs of a wide range of learners.

If children are to learn how to accept others with diverse learning styles and needs, teachers must act as role models and teach by what they do – not merely by what they say. The positive manner of greeting children in the morning will set the tone for learning. By focusing on individual talents and gifts of each child entering the classroom, teachers will encourage students to work to the best of their abilities.

*"Accepting diversity as an asset is an essential part of making the plan work."*

# Acceptance Tips

1. Hold before-school gatherings for coffee and informal sharing among staff and administrators.

2. Maintain a diverse selection of trade books that address acceptance and differences. Sharing children's literature such as *The Ugly Duckling* by Hans Christian Anderson, *Dinah, The Dog With A Difference* by Esta de Fossard, and *Naomi Knows It's Springtime* by Virginia Kroll (see activity on page 4) can help heighten student acceptance of differences. (See children's bibliography for other titles.)

3. Check with support personnel to make sure they feel accepted and comfortable in the classroom.

4. Encourage children to express their feelings and reactions in journal writing.

5. Allow children to change reading buddies every few days.

6. Develop individual goals for students to increase self-esteem or self-motivation. (This week Carrie will find two new friends to book share with, or John's goal is to teach two friends how to snap.)

7. Develop an "I Can" bulletin board. Place individual pictures of class members on the board. Place a push pin under each picture. Invite children to choose a sample of their schoolwork each Friday that exemplifies what they can do.

8. Design classroom T-shirts. Students may collectively choose a class logo, "Miss Stopper's class cannot be stopped from learning," or "Learning with Miss Monos is a 1, 2 bonus." Children can use iron-on crayon pictures or puff paint for designing. T-shirts are worn first day of each month.

9. Encourage adults to speak about a student's placement as a grade or class, not a place. Aimee is in the primary school, not Aimee is in an autistic group.

10. Describe a child as a child first, not as a disability. "Ryan is an eight-year-old with severe disabilities," not "Ryan is a severely-disabled child."

11. Invite adult community members with disabilities to talk to the class. We had an adult with cerebral palsy read a story to our class. He then demonstrated how he needed to hold a piece of chalk to outline the story and how to use a facilitated communication device.

12. When possible assign all children the same chores throughout the school year.

13. Set up classroom furniture to accommodate special needs children within the hub of learning rather than in the back of the room.

14. Vary expectations for journal writing and reading according to children's needs and abilities. For example, while some children write lengthy journal entries, others can cut and paste pictures to show feelings. While groups of children read and share literature, others can look at pictures, listen to stories on tape, or match pictures to words.

# Acceptance Activity

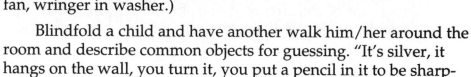

*Naomi Knows It's Springtime* by Virginia Kroll

## Purpose:

To enable children to accept different ways to interact with the environment and heighten their awareness of children with visual impairment.

## Procedure:

Introduce children to *Naomi Knows It's Springtime* (Boyds Mills Press, 1993) by reading the story and allowing children to then hear it on tape.

Play "I Hear" game. Tape a variety of household sounds and have children attempt to identify sounds without knowing what is producing them.

Give students picture cards of common household objects and encourage them to dramatize the object without a sound. (Popcorn popping in a popper – child pops up and down, a blade on ceiling fan, wringer in washer.)

Blindfold a child and have another walk him/her around the room and describe common objects for guessing. "It's silver, it hangs on the wall, you turn it, you put a pencil in it to be sharpened."

Describe some ways Mrs. Jensen would have responded differently if Naomi had been deaf.

Allow children to buddy up and go for "trust walks" around the school with one child leading a blindfolded partner.

Use names of classmates for a "knows" book. Jennifer knows her ABC's. Jennifer knows her phone number and address.

Borrow an ice cream freezer and make frozen chocolate custard that Naomi liked.

Cut apart "Naomi knows" sentences and match to pictures.

# Activities for Promoting Acceptance

1. Arrange students in a circle. Invite two children to stand in the center. Discuss similarities and differences.

2. Have two children pair up. They look at each other and take turns discussing what they like. Then the two children turn back-to-back, change something about their physical appearance, and see if the other person can identify the change.

3. Give children a challenging task (art project, sewing card). Set up the task so each child needs to ask two others for help. The two helpers sign the project to ensure that all classmates feel accepted enough to ask for help.

# Acceptance/Awareness Balloons

Hang a balloon cutout each week on the door of your classroom to dispel myths about differently-abled people. Take time to discuss the sentiments expressed. Hang the balloons on a large bulletin board, accumulate throughout the year.

Sample statements for balloons:

1. Everyone in here is as important as everyone else.

2. Each classroom member has something positive to contribute to our group.

3. Physical challenges are not contagious. (You can't "catch" one like you can't "catch" hair color.)

4. Everyone can and will make mistakes sometimes.

5. We are more alike than we are different.

6. What's inside us (feelings, emotions, ideas) are more important than what's outside us (hair color, eye color, size of our house).

7. We all have some kind of weakness and must learn how to overcome it.

8. Some differences are short-term (glasses, braces, dark baby teeth, a broken wrist) and some may be forever (deafness, blindness, muscle paralysis).

9. Mental and physical challenges don't erase feelings.

10. You can see some reminders of people's limitations (wheelchairs, hearing aids, white canes). Other limitations are invisible (memory problems, dyslexia, autism).

11. We can work together to help our friends be successful.

12. None of us is as smart as all of us.

13. Each day is a new beginning for our class.

14. Try not to guess what a person is like on the inside by looking at the outside. (Don't judge a book by its cover.)

15. Do your feelings or abilities change if you get a bump on your knee?

16. What if everyone with brown hair had to go to a separate classroom or eat alone?

17. Knowing we are alike and different will help us be successful adults.

18. If you couldn't see, would you still want to have the same friends?

19. Being different is not an excuse for lack of work.

20. What if we all did only what we are good in?

21. I wish I could change _____ about myself.

22. We sink or swim together as a team.

23. Two heads are better than one.

24. Do you have the same needs or desires when you are clean as when you are dirty?

25. If someone looks or acts differently because of an impairment, it is not a punishment for being bad.

26. We can talk about differences with our friends if we do it respectfully.

27. Having a handicap or disability is only a tiny part of a person's being – just like a piece of sand is a tiny part of a beach.

28. It is more polite to talk about differences kindly than it is to point, stare, or giggle.

29. Many children with different needs have to work twice as hard as you do to get their work done.

30. Who in this room is exactly like you?

31. Name three ways you are different now than when you were one-year-old.

32. More things in here are possible than impossible.

33. We all learn in different ways.

34. Changing a little might save a lot of work.

35. We all make progress every day.

From *Inclusive Classrooms from A to Z: A Handbook for Educators*, by Gretchen Goodman. Columbus, OH: Teachers' Publishing Group, 1994. All rights reserved by Crystal Springs Books, PO Box 500, Ten Sharon Road, Peterborough, NH 03458. 1-800-321-0401.

# Multiage Profiles

The Society For Developmental Education and N.A.M.E. (National Alliance of Multiage Educators) sent out requests for information to various schools involved in multiage education.

The schools were very generous in their response. Many sent report cards and other assessment tools, some sent curriculum outlines; one teacher even sent this year's schoolwide interdisciplinary theme, complete with sample letters to parents, a copy of a minigrant request, and a bibliography of theme-related children's books.

Because of the schools' generosity, we've come up with a resource book packed with practical, classroom-friendly ideas for the multiage teacher.

Probably the best resources we can give you, the multiage educator, are the names, addresses and phone numbers of the contributing schools. Each school welcomes visiting teachers and administrators, and is eager to show what multiage education is doing for its youngsters.

One advisory — call or write first! We have given you the name of a contact person at each school who will help you plan a visit to the school. Not only is calling a courtesy, but it will help optimize your time spent.

# BEARCAMP VALLEY SCHOOL AND CHILDREN'S CENTER

Our school serves a northeastern New Hampshire community that is primarily white and working class. The Bearcamp Valley School grew from an original pre-school and day care facility that has been in existence for 31 years; we have been multiage for six years. We are a private alternative school.

Our school has four classrooms, all multiage groupings. One large room houses four-to-six-year-olds, the equivalent to pre-kindergarten and kindergarten. Ages seven through thirteen share three rooms and are grade-equivalent to first through seventh.

## Why Multiage?

There was a growing need in the community to offer an alternative education for children who needed more individualistic learning situations, for parents who were concerned about their child's learning style being fostered and valued, and for children who were disaffected by a traditional learning center.

## Philosophy

The school's letter of intent written six years ago states:

> "It is our philosophy that multiage grouping will offer ongoing developmentally appropriate early childhood education. Teachers will know the children throughout their beginning years and will be guided by that knowledge when planning the curriculum for subsequent years. Each child will be valued for his or her unique pattern of growth, learning style, personality, interests, family orientation, and background. As each child's development (physical, emotional, social, and cognitive) is integrated, so too is his or her learning. Using the child as its first resource, the program will be structured with the flexibility that fosters his or her individual rate of growth, development, self-esteem and subsequent success. A confident learner will reach out for new information, extend his or her education and become a life-long learner.
>
> Multiage grouping encourages cooperation which in turn promotes an effective atmosphere for learning. Older children will experience pride, leadership, and the reinforcement of skills as they help and nurture younger children. Younger children will learn from modeling by older children and benefit from their encouragement and advance expertise."

*Using the child as its first resource, the program will be structured with the flexibility that fosters his or her individual rate of growth, development, self-esteem and subsequent success.*

Multiage grouping offers a new child a comfort zone to settle into and an area of challenge to rise to.

We have followed the progress of children who have transferred from Bearcamp Valley School's multiage program to graded classrooms in local public schools, and have learned they are doing very well. Several of our former students have been hailed as exceptional problem solvers.

## Staff Development

Teachers were hired for their philosophy and their already established conviction for multiaging, as this is the structure of the school. Teachers meet on a regular basis to discuss issues directly related to the multiaging aspect of our school and regularly attend or teach conferences on the subject.

## Curriculum / Assessment

There are two curricula at Bearcamp Valley School. The first is the one created by the teachers, a carefully planned progression of major themes such as "Community," or "Water," or "Dinosaurs and Birds," or "France and the Olympics"—which serve as unifying forces during four-to-eight-week periods of the school year. Within these themes, the teachers lead directed activities which raise the students' interest and involvement, and which draw upon each of the standard disciplines of literacy, math, science, art, social studies, etc.

The second curriculum is the one created by each individual student. Because each student has choices of what to do for some of his or her time each day, each student helps create his or her own individual curriculum.

Students practice through both curricula the skills necessary to learn, such as critical thinking, problem solving, research, cooperative communications, self-modification, etc. Teachers facilitate and provide the opportunities for these practices.

Student-to-teacher ratio is 8:1, with at least two teachers always working together. We have teacher aides and parent help that allow many one-on-one opportunities, we pose open-ended questions, and work on project-oriented tasks that are relevant to the students' needs and interests and that practice the skills necessary for students to become productive citizens.

We use student portfolios that consist of teacher-chosen pieces of work, student-chosen pieces of work, observations, formal and informal assessments, self-portraits, and commentaries written by the team.

## Dealing with Behavioral Issues

We honor the individual needs of students, while balancing the value of a cooperative environment. Behavioral problems are seen as teachable moments. We have problem-solving sessions that are discussed anonymously by placing written problems in a basket and randomly pulling them out to work through in the group. For situations that need immediate and private solutions, we have worksheets that ask each student specific questions about the incident. For instance, "What happened?" "How did

**BEARCAMP VALLEY SCHOOL**

PO Box 284
Durrell Road
Tamworth, NH 03886

**Phone: 603-323-8300**

**Entire school is multiage. Multiage groupings** by grade level: Pre-K, K, 1-7

**Open to visiting teachers and administrators**

**Contact:** Nancy Coville, founder, teacher and administrator
Document prepared by: Raetha Fitzpatrick, teacher

you feel about what happened?" "What would you like to happen now?" "What specifically will you do to keep this from happening again?" These sheets are used for times that are extreme and require a cooling-down period. The procedure is facilitated by a teacher and each child in turn has the opportunity to express her or his view and feelings on the incident.

## Taking School Outside the Classroom

We have two weeks a year of outdoor school for the whole school, in which we embrace all disciplines through outdoor studies including fort building, hiking, orienteering, games, an overnight, and more.

Each year we put on a school play that emphasizes some favored theme or themes. Leading up to the performance, we have many storytelling sessions and other drama-based activities.

The school goes on many source trips for general science studies; for instance: science centers, aquariums, demonstrations, villages of antiquity, etc. We also have many people come to the school and share their interests and expertise.

## Parent Involvement

We send home weekly newsletters; we allow time at the beginning and end of each day for parents (this is possible with team teaching); we enlist parents to accompany us on class trips; we welcome parents into the classroom often to share their own expertise; we conference with parents; and we provide parents with written commentaries of their child's progress.

## Specialists

Both the art and music teacher come into the classrooms. They are aware of the themes and integrate them into their area.

## Special Needs Students

We receive services for some children through the local public school. On the whole, every child is perceived as "special," and receives whatever tools and support are necessary for him or her to be successful.

## Team Teaching

Team teaching is the heart of our program. We have regular meetings. Teachers are teamed in ways to complement each other's strengths. Our philosophy is that "It takes a whole village to raise a child." We respect and celebrate each other's differences and are grateful that we can share the responsibility of teaching as well as the joy.

## Grouping for Instruction

We group students by needs and interests.

## Our Biggest Obstacle

Public relations—educating people on the value of multiaging and process learning—was a difficult obstacle. It is an ongoing process that has been in part received given time. This may seem like a simplistic statement but it has great value. We have seen people change their ideas and embrace our program over time, which has strengthened our convictions and encouraged us to grow.

## Our Biggest Issue

In terms of multiaging we continue to work toward a greater awareness of the general public about the benefits of multiaging. However, because we are a private school and parents choose to place their children in our program, we do not have multiaging-type issues that are difficult to deal with with our parents.

Funding continues to be our most difficult issue.

*"People who don't think class size matters, probably haven't been with five kids for more than three minutes in five years."*
— **Dr. Ernest Boyer**

*"Of course class size is important. You have to find the child before you can teach the child!"*

— **New Jersey Education Association**

Chadwick Elementary School is located in the Security/Rolling Road area of southwestern Baltimore County. The school, in 1991, celebrated twenty-five years of rich history dating back to July, 1966. It is a fairly stable community of municipal and federal employees who reside in private homes and apartment complexes. A new development of detached and semi-detached homes in the $95,000 to $120,000 range was completed in October, 1991. Two new developments in the same range have since been begun with completion dates of December, 1994.

Chadwick Elementary School is a one-story air-conditioned building composed of 16 classrooms and two portable classrooms, which houses children from pre-kindergarten through grade five. This year a modular addition consisting of two extra large kindergarten rooms, five regular classrooms, children's and adult bathrooms, and a storage room, will be constructed with a completion date of March first. Also this year, a permanent double modular classroom, with a completion date of January fifteenth, will be placed at the back of the school.

Chadwick offers full time services in vocal music, reading, library, physical education, art, and counseling, and part-time services in speech and instrumental music. Chadwick is a Chapter I school with a mobility index for 1992-1993 at 33 percent, and at 36 percent for 1993-1994. The school is currently 70 percent over-capacity with 532 students. Chadwick was built in 1966 to accommodate 325 students.

Our population consists of 72.26 percent African American students, 9.05 percent Asian students, and 2.26 percent Hispanic students. White children make up 16.03 percent of the school population. This represents a 4 percent increase of African Americans, a 2 percent increase of Hispanic students, and a 2 percent decrease of White children, with the Asian population keeping the same percentage as last year.

The majority of the school population lives within walking distance of the school.

Chadwick's professional team consists of thirteen African American females, eighteen White females and two White males. Our clerical and instructional support staff consists of two African American females, seven White females, and one White male.

In addition, cafeteria and custodial staffs employ one African American female, one African American male, two White females, and one White male.

## Multiage education

Multiage education has been in place for three years. The committee that worked on the plan researched and visited multiage programming for about 1½ years prior to beginning the first multiage class.

Our school became involved in multiage education for several reasons. Primarily, we looked at the retention rate in the primary grades and questioned what we could do to give those students an opportunity to reinforce skills and learn new strategies without repeating a whole year. Secondly, we looked at what we could do for those better than average students to provide the enrichment they need in a very comfortable learning environment.

*Our philosophy emphasizes the way children learn and it respects each individual child's specific needs, abilities, and interests.*

## Philosophy

Early childhood programs should provide a safe and nurturing environment that promotes the physical, social, emotional, and cognitive development of young children through developmentally appropriate practices. A multiage/continuous progress program provides all children with successful classroom experiences and, therefore, promotes a positive attitude toward learning.

Children at ages five to eight are at many different levels of development socially, academically, and physically. Schools are responsible for providing learning experiences suitable for each individual's developmental stage. Children should not be hurried into experiences too advanced for them, but neither should they be put in a holding pattern once they are ready for new, more difficult experiences. A nongraded environment for children ages five to eight allows teachers to provide a wide range of experiences and to help children advance successfully through several levels of achievement without waiting for a grade level year to pass.

Retention in the early grades has negative short- and long-term effects. Therefore, a positive approach to the diversity among children and the recognition of individual learning styles will result in long-term success.

Furthermore, children with limited English-speaking ability need to be encouraged to talk and interact with children as well as adults in order to facilitate communication learning. In keeping with this philosophy, Chadwick Elementary School has a multiage continuous progress program in which children ages five to eight are grouped together.

This grouping, in which teachers use a variety of materials and strategies, provides for differences in developmental levels. The focus is on the child engaging in active learning and decision making in a real life setting. Our philosophy emphasizes the way children learn and it respects each individual child's specific needs, abilities, and interests.

In the beginning the relationship between the graded classrooms and the multiage classrooms was strained. Those teachers felt that multiage was getting all the attention. However, as time has gone on and all the teachers have learned more about multiage, the closeness and cohesiveness that made the Chadwick faculty unique has returned.

Right now all of our primary grades are multiage. There is one traditional full day kindergarten and one multiage intermediate grouping.

The composition of our multiage classes is as follows:

- Three classes of ages 5 to 7 years
- One class of ages 6 and 7 years
- One class of ages 5 and 6 years
- One class of ages 8 and 9 years

## Staff Development

The team implementing the program networked in order to find out as much about multiage as possible. We contacted people in Kentucky, Florida, and New York, and at The Society For Developmental Education, and attended many

**CHADWICK ELEMENTARY**

1918 Winder Road
Baltimore, MD 21244

**Phone: 410-887-1300**
**FAX: 410-887-1381**

**Fully multiage**

**Multiage groupings
(by age):** 5-6, 5-6-7,
6-7, 8-9

**Open to visiting teachers
and administrators**

**Contact:**
Lois Balser
Rosalie Giese

conferences. We also visited Montessori schools (they are multiage) as well as the few programs that were within traveling distance. As time has gone on, we have had in-school staff development as well as county programs in order to develop a handbook for multiage in Baltimore County.

## Curriculum

The S.T.A.R.S. program at Chadwick Elementary School was implemented in September, 1993, after a year and a half of research. It is the model program for Baltimore county. It provides developmentally appropriate instruction in a multiage setting for students ages five through seven. Unlike many stereotypical elementary classroom settings, the S.T.A.R.S. program minimizes tracking and maximizes flexibility in grouping and alternative strategies to promote student achievement. Teachers use a variety of materials and strategies to provide for differences in developmental levels.

Students will spend part of their day working in small groups to refine skills. To facilitate a multiage approach to the curriculum, a variety of major thematic units have been developed and presented. This approach insures commitment to the teaching of skills within the context of themes and focuses on the developmental stages of the individual students. Furthermore, opportunities for young children to discover and explore concepts in mixed age groups and to share knowledge and experiences are encouraged, much like a family learning experience. This is a partnership between home and school.

## Multiage Literature Plan

Our multiage team has developed an organized plan for the use of literature for mixed age and abilities of students. This organized planning model includes strategies and activities to address the needs and abilities of all the students. This includes a five-day shared reading plan and independent activities and center activities for students to complete while the teachers conference.

## Team Teaching

Team teaching is an integral part of our multiage program. Each grouping has two teachers and one instructional assistant. We opted for larger numbers with two teachers so that we could team teach. The two teachers plan together, teach to their strengths, and assess students together.

One of our teams has been together for 22 years! The two teachers have found that they can meet the needs of their students this way. While one teacher conferences with groups of students, the other teacher stays with the students who are working on independent activities and at centers. They rotate this. In this way, there is always someone available for students.

The team members also divide the responsibility of teaching science/social studies and different math groupings. They assess and evaluate the students jointly, and both teachers sit in on parent conferences.

## Grouping for Instruction

The students are in many groupings during a day:

- One large group—for beginning group meeting, calendar study, math wall, project sharing. They are also in one large group for closing wrap-up at the end of the day.
- Two mixed-age groups for shared reading literature-based activities.

- From that point and for the rest of the language arts block in the morning, students may be in several groups—ability groups based on skills, reading ability, etc. They may be in interest groups determined by centers. They could also be working individually or in partner activities.

## Specialists

Our various specialists have found that they cannot follow their curriculum as it is written, so they have been very cooperative in adapting their program to coordinate with our themes as well as the needs and abilities of a multiage group. We meet with the special area teachers periodically to discuss our themes. The students leave the room as a mixed age group to participate in their special area activity at the end of the day.

## Special-Needs Students

Our philosophy and experience in multiage has shown that the advantage of this type of programming is that specific needs of students can be met. By grouping children and changing these groups as needed and not tracking children, we can handle the needs of all students. The beauty of multiage is that if a child needs additional reinforcement or enrichment, no matter what grade or age, it is available.

## Inclusion

We have inclusion students in our program. One challenge is that the special education resource person has to spread herself rather thin to supply services to all classes with inclusion students.

## Parent Involvement

Parent involvement is an integral part of any multiage program. Involvement includes:
1. Parent visitations
2. Parent volunteers
3. Interactive homework projects in which parents need to be involved
4. Periodic parent information meetings
5. Family math/reading/science nights

The PTA is an important component of the school. Over the past two years, membership has been established at 87 percent of the student body. This year's membership, for the first time, is 100 percent. The PTA has continued to maintain a group of dedicated parents who support the entire school program.

## Our Biggest Obstacle

Money! Money has always been an obstacle—funds to buy cubbies, centers, new reading materials, etc. Our principal was extremely resourceful, as was the first team of teachers that implemented the program. A library that was closing in our area donated shelves, and our PTA was very generous in helping us.

## Our Biggest Issue

The biggest issue facing us that we can do something about is transitions — that is, moving the 60 children in our teaching area from one subject area to another.

## Waivers/Mandates

When we started our multiage program, we did have to go to the Superintendent's staff to have full day kindergarten, which is not in all Baltimore County Schools. Since our school has site-based management, we have the choice of using the standard grading system or creating our own. We opted to do our own. The report card that we have used over the past year is still in the revision stage.

### Daily Schedule — Chadwick Elementary School

| | |
|---|---|
| 8:30 | Entrance Activities |
| 8:40-9:10 | Group Meeting |
| | Calendar |
| | Attendance |
| | Sharing |
| | Math Wall Activities |
| 9:10-9:40 | Whole Group Science/Social Studies |
| | Activities |
| 9:45-11:30 | Reading/Language Arts Block |
| | Shared Reading |
| | Independent Activities |
| | Flexible/Skills Groups and Conferencing |
| 11:35-12:10 | Lunch |
| 12:15-12:30 | Reading Club |
| 12:30-1:00 | Recess |
| 1:00-2:00 | Math |
| 2:05-3:00 | Special Area Activities |
| 3:00-3:10 | Wrap-Up/Dismissal |

*Parents can best help their children succeed in school when they themselves have had positive experiences with writing, reading, and learning. Parents can best help their children succeed in school when they know how to foster and connect the learning in the home environment with the learning in school. Rather than viewing parents, teachers, school, and home as distinct and separate, we need to honor the primary relationship they all have in common: learning and how to insure its success.*

*— James Vopat, The Parent Project: A Workshop Approach to Parent Involvement. York, ME: Stenhouse Publishers, 1994.*

# THEMES
# (3 YEAR PLAN)

| MONTH | YEAR I | YEAR II | YEAR III |
|---|---|---|---|
| September | Friendship | Animals That Talk | Health (Senses) |
| October | At the Farm/Food Groups | Kids Like Us | Space |
| November | Animals Woodland | Seasons | Animals/Desert & Rainforest |
| December | Our World - The Environment | Our World | Our World |
| January | Author Study (Frank Asch) | Scary Stories | Author Studies Tomie de Paola |
| February | Black History (Africa) | Brotherhood | Black History |
| March | Insects and Butterflies | Plants | Pets |
| April | Cats and Dogs | Fish | Transportation |
| May | Environment | Dinosaurs | Tools and Machines |
| June | Vacation Fun | Fairy Tales | Vacation Fun |

Chadwick Elementary School

Fond du Lac is located in east-central Wisconsin at the foot of Lake Winnebago, the third largest inland lake in the nation. Fond du Lac has a population of 39,000, and is three hours north of Chicago and 61 miles south of Green Bay. The residents are primarily people whose families have lived in the city for many generations. Fond du Lac is a city with a small-town feeling.

The industrial base deals primarily with manufacturing: Mercury Marine, whose product is marine motors, and Giddings and Lewis, whose product is machine tools; and food products: Tolibia Cheese, along with many mid-sized, mostly family-run dairy farms.

Fond du Lac is the home of Marian College, a mid-sized private college; Moraine Park Technical College; and the University of Fond du Lac, a two-year college.

The Fond du Lac School District enrolls approximately 7,507 students. There are nine elementary schools, K-6, with a population totaling a little over 4,000. The three junior high schools have a total population of 1,778, and one high school has over 1,600 students. There are also a number of private and parochial schools in town.

## Chegwin School

Chegwin is the fifth largest elementary school in the district and has the most diverse student population. It is located a few blocks from Main Street and is in the heart of the medical community and historical district. There are a large percentage of students receiving Title One services and a sizable population of Hmong [Vietnamese] students. It is the only school in Fond du Lac that is not organized in strictly traditional grade grouping.

## Curriculum

Our district curriculum is based on a continuous progress philosophy and meeting the individual needs of students. In the past two years, a literacy continuum has been developed by teachers and is used to define and describe the reading and writing development of students in K-3. This information is shared with parents during the two scheduled conferences each year. As teachers, parents, and community members become more comfortable with this type of reporting method, it will be expanded through the grades and into other content areas.

Teachers use a variety of resources to teach the language arts. Most use a combination of literature and a literature-based basal. Many teachers understand and implement a writer's workshop format to teach the art of writing. However, some take a very traditional approach to teach the language arts.

The math curriculum is built around NCTM's major goals. Early childhood teachers primarily use "Math Their Way." Intermediate teachers use the Addison-Wesley series along with a variety of teaching approaches (Marilyn Burns-type activities).

Science and social studies content was developed on a spiral, with many units revisited throughout the grades but in more sophisticated ways. Again, teachers have

> *"Never doubt that a small group of thoughtful, committed people can change the world. Indeed it's the only thing that ever has."*
>
> *— Margaret Mead*

a variety of materials available and teaching of units varies depending on the teacher's approach to instruction.

## The Strategic Plan

In 1994, members of the community, parents, students, and District staff and administrators joined together to create a Strategic Plan. The plan clearly identifies the purpose, focus, and direction of the Fond du Lac School District through the balance of the 1990s and into the 21st century. It is highly student-centered, with the driving force of this vision being "increased instructional effectiveness and higher levels of student achievement and performance."

One Action Plan was created to review the present educational structure and explore innovative designs to provide the most effective and relevant learning experiences for students. The document states:

> . . . We will provide children with the opportunity to participate in innovative specialized programs within existing schools, thus allowing for diversification of teaching methods and learning styles.

The Fond du Lac School Board voted unanimously in favor of the Strategic Plan in the fall of 1994.

## Staff Development

In the fall of 1993, several primary teachers at Chegwin attended an SDE multiage conference. SDE's teaching approaches and philosophy matched, for the most part, the school's philosophy. The teachers returned to school and shared information with their colleagues and their building principal, Ellen Ritchie.

The staff at Chegwin School decided to continue their journey toward multiage education by examining their beliefs about children, instruction and assessment.

With the support of Dr. Carolyn Keeler, Director of Curriculum and Instruction and other district administrators, a consultant was hired to provide inservice and ongoing classroom support for the remainder of the 1993 school year. This inservice dealt with theory, instructional demonstrations, and classroom practice, along with reading the literature about multiage practice. Nongradedness by Anderson and Pavan was the primary text used for focused discussions.

## From Planning to Implementation

Both those interested in multiage configurations and those who chose to continue to teach one-grade groupings were involved throughout the total process. While staff members operate under similar educational philosophies, not all teachers chose to move toward multiage configurations. Some were interested, but needed time to learn more about the concept.

A critical turning point was when teachers wrote a "Primary Position Paper" stating their philosophy based on sound instruction rather than on a grouping configuration alone:

**CHEGWIN ELEMENTARY**

109 E. Merrill Avenue
Fond du Lac, WI 54935

Phone: 414-929-2820
FAX: 414-929-3790

**Multiage Groupings**
(by age): 5-6, 6-7,
8-9, 10-11

**Looping: 6-7**

**Open to visiting teachers and administrators**

**Contact:** Marsha Winship

. . . We believe that neither multiage, unit-age, nor instructional methods alone can achieve optimal results. The three concepts must be understood and applied. Many strategies and systems that are used in a unit-age class are either the same or similar to those in a multiage class. Not everything done in the past needs to be thrown away or changed.

Approaching the configurations in this way meant working together and supporting each other's views, rather than turning the process into an either/or proposition.

From these meetings, staff members based their program on the following five research-based principles:

1. We match educational practices to the way children learn.
2. We create classroom environments that encourage exploration and risk-taking to facilitate active learning and development.
3. We hold the view that students represent a range of learners on a continuum of development.
4. We consider parent involvement a critical and essential element in the success of the program.
5. As educators, we are researchers and we use our data for making sound educational decisions about curriculum and individual student instruction.

The 1993-94 school year was spent continuing discussions to clarify philosophical positions. The time provided a forum for honest, albeit sometimes difficult, dialogue among staff members. This is an important element if school change is to be long-lasting and effective.

## Inclusion Plan

Also during the school year, a group of regular education and special-needs staff members wrote a proposal to receive state funding for a five-and six-year-old inclusion classroom. This proposal was fully funded, further validating the instructional and structural changes being implemented at Chegwin. This further broke the mold for providing instruction to special-needs children.

At the close of the school year, in place was a class for five- and six-year-olds, a looping configuration for six- and seven-year-olds, an eight- and nine-year-old class, and a ten-and eleven-year-old class. And interest was continuing to grow.

The 1994-95 school year proved to be even more challenging than we could have imagined. Presentations to the School Board were both frustrating and rewarding. Some members were supportive and some were not. We held a series of meetings to share ideas and inform parents of changes. Most parents supported this move, while a very small number made known their unhappiness toward this change both to the teachers and to the public.

However, we continued to grow in our commitment to our students and each other. We began the 1995-96 school year with the following configurations:

Two unit-age kindergarten classes
One 5-6 year old class
One looping configuration of 6-7 year olds

One unit-age first and second grade
Two 6-7 multiage classes
Two third unit-age classes
Two 8-9 year old multiage classes
Two fourth unit-age classes
Two fifth unit-age classes
Two 10-11 multiage classes
Two sixth unit-age classes

Throughout this time, staff members have supported each other and parents continue the positive support. Teachers now focus their efforts on curriculum issues, instructional approaches, parent communication, and team teaching.

## Flexible Grouping

We are committed to creating an environment that meets the needs of our individual students. While classrooms have specific differences in the way staff and students are organized during the school days, we agree that instruction is delivered through a process approach. Flexible grouping includes the integration of all students. Various learning styles are accommodated. Title I and special education teachers work to balance between in-class and pull-out instructional delivery models to meet the needs of both students and teachers. Instruction includes paired learning, cooperative learning, whole class and small group flexible instruction, direct instruction, modeling, guided practice, and independent practice.

The heterogeneous grouping of classes is a cooperative effort by staff members and the principal. Parents may choose to enroll their child in a multiage grouping or a unit-age grouping. So far we have been able to accommodate these requests. This will be reviewed each year due to possible staff changes, enrollment numbers, parent requests, etc.

The language arts (reading, writing, listening, and speaking) are taught in an integrated manner.

In math, teachers look for common strands, such as problem-solving, operations, geometry, measurement, etc. All students work on the same strand at the same time, although at different levels. Through sharing they are exposed to higher level concepts that they might be able to do independently. Whole class lessons of a math concept may serve as a springboard for small group skills work.

A two- or three-year cycle of unit study for Social Studies and Science allows teachers to make sure all the objectives are met without repeating themes and activities. Some assignments include different activities for varying learning levels of students. Most of the content units are integrated with Language Arts.

## Assessment

Assessment and evaluation is observed, recorded, and documented to show the progress of each student. This information becomes the basis for making instructional decisions.

The district's primary report card reflects an individual's growth and progress rather than grade level standards. Other reporting measures include the CAT (California Achievement Test) for students grades two through six, and the Third Grade Reading

Test, a state mandate. This year the Wisconsin Department of Public Instruction is implementing for the first time a comprehensive assessment for grade four.

## Parent Involvement

We believe that parent involvement is a critical component of the success for the restructuring taking place at Chegwin. We will continue to include and welcome parent participation in workshops, inservices, and conferences.

## Goals for the Future

Staff goals are to review the literature and maintain our philosophy. We believe that one must move through the process by choice. Just as our students are on a literacy continuum, we too are on a continuum of learning and application. Our individual approaches will be different and vary according to personal experiences, background, and situations. But we will continue to revise and refine our literacy model and school organizational plans, and no doubt will take different paths in meeting many of the same overall conceptual objectives.

*Visual literacy is a life skill. We need visual literacy in order to get by in our everyday lives. The contexts in which visual texts are encountered include finding our way, following instructions, filling in government forms, applying for work, choosing consumer goods, planning a vacation and so on. The visual texts associated with these tasks include maps, street directories, street signs and shop fronts, video terminal displays, weather maps, printed forms, advertising, retailers' catalogues, product labels, travel brochures, airline schedules etc. All of these forms combine verbal and visual information to make meaning and all are organised along principles of graphic design that can be taught explicitly.*

*— Steve Moline, I See What You Mean: Children at Work with Visual Information. York, ME: Stenhouse Publishers, 1995.*

# Summary at Ages 8 & 9 Curriculum

Emphasizes the study of Fond du Lac: community, community life, citizenship, government. Emphasizes the study of Wisconsin: geography, history, heritage, multicultural heritage, government.

## Geography

**City**

natural regions
Lake Winnebago
lakes

**Wisconsin**

forests
terrains
glaciated areas

Compare/Contrast the past with the present.

## Trades and Farming

- Agriculture as an industry (farming, dairy, lumbering)
- Fur traders/trading posts
- FDL Land Company

## People

**Early Immigrants/Settlers**
— Pier Family
— Dr. Darling
— German and Irish
— Galloways

**Modern-Day Immigrants**
— Black Americans
— Asian Americans
— Hispanic Americans

### How they Live/Lived

- Pioneer living vs. Modern day living
- Food and Cooking
- Travel
- Recreation
- Early schools vs. Modern day schools
- Galloway House
- Reservations

## Industry/Business/Manufacturing
- FDL vs. Wisconsin
- City parks vs. State parks
- Jobs available vs. skills needed

## Government
- What is it?
- Why important?
- Rules and laws
- Citizens' Rights
- Voting

### City-Manager

Appointed/elected officials
Departments
Community Services

### Three Branches of Government

Executive
Legislative
Judicial

# Major Goals for Writing

1. **Writing is a priority.** We provide daily opportunities for writing independently. We also promote and encourage writing by understanding the "forms" young children use to communicate an idea.

2. **Develop positive attitudes toward writing.** Leading our students to experience pleasure in writing and to have confidence in their ability to write creates voluntary, lifelong writers.

3. **To communicate ideas effectively and to incorporate skills into their writing.**

4. **To produce competent and independent spellers.**

5. **To appreciate authors at all stages of writing.**

"The process never ends because ideas never cease."

Primary Council, 1994

# Instructional Activities for Writing

- Students choose their own topics to write about and at times we conduct a teacher-directed writing activity. This may be to introduce students to a genre, or to model techniques such as using a web, to organize ideas or to write on a common theme which serves for discussion, and so on.

- A workshop often begins with a whole class mini-lesson. This is a brief meeting concerning an issue that reflects the needs of the students' writing content or skills.

- The teacher keeps a record of where each student is in the writing process. This procedure holds students accountable for what they are working on during writing workshop.

- Students go through a process which includes: thinking about a chosen topic, organizing ideas, drafting, making revisions, and editing for conventions. Writers go through phases of writing in different ways.

- Writing conferences are crucial to one's growth as a writer. A content conference helps students speak about and expand their ideas. Editing conferences focus on capitalization, omissions, punctuation, and spelling (COPS).

- We agree that meaningful spelling instruction includes the following:
    1. Providing students with a wide experience with print.
    2. Teaching spelling based on developmental understanding of how students learn to spell.
    3. Making a reading/writing/spelling connection.
    4. Recognizing when and how to teach/reinforce/model strategies, rules, letter patterns.
    5. Looking at how students apply knowledge of a particular spelling concept within their writing and move beyond it.
    6. Teaching proofreading skills.

- Writing workshops close with a "group share." This is a time for several student authors to share their writing. The teacher models how to ask appropriate and positive questions, and how to listen to another writer. The authors often ask for and receive specific feedback from their peers.

# Major Goals for Reading

1. **Reading is a priority.** The only way to get good at something is to practice. A study by John Goodlad (1984) reported that U.S. elementary students, grades K-6, spend only 6 percent of a typical school day actually reading. Nancie Atwell (1987) writes, *"The time we don't make for students' independent reading is probably our most harmful demonstration."* So, we read!!!

2. **Develop positive attitudes towards reading.** Leading our students to experience pleasure in reading and to have confidence in their ability to read creates voluntary, lifelong readers.

3. **Concept attainment** can be simply defined as placing things, events or ideas into categories (Bruner, 1966). This process can be seen in the way children learn first about the world around them, later as they achieve mastery of spoken language, and finally as they make sense of the world of print.

4. **Language development** parallels, reflects, and shapes concept acquisition. Together they provide the raw materials for literacy development. Children draw upon their oral language experiences in learning to read. It is imperative that teachers of reading have a general understanding of the pattern of oral language development.

   We support this development in young children by creating an atmosphere for learning that is print-rich and by accepting and applauding children's approximations of reading, writing, and speaking.

5. **Sight vocabulary.** This term refers to all printed words that are recognized instantly in various contexts. Nearly all the words encountered by a fluent reader are recognized at sight. Sight words develop over a period of time as a result of multiple exposures to printed words.

6. **Fostering reading for meaning.** Successful readers focus on meaning. Much of the instruction consists of a variety of activities and discussions dealing with elements that are common to both narrative and expository texts. Character traits, plot, setting, point of view, endings, organization, and structure are elements that students will encounter throughout their lifetimes as readers.

# Instructional Activities for Reading

As teachers, a great deal of our job is to **provide students with meaningful instruction** and understanding the students' perspectives — as well as our own. Therefore, instructional activities include, but are not limited to:

- Reading aloud to children, encouraging them to engage in activities that lead them to retell or extend the content of the story.

- Providing meaningful experiences with print, using enlarged texts (Big Books) where children read along and match their speech to the printed words. We also promote the use of the three cueing systems that reside in print and closely parallel the components of oral language.
  - Graphophonic: interrelationships between letter-speech sounds (phonics).
  - Semantic: enables beginning readers to use their knowledge of the meanings of known words to predict unknown words in context (meanings).
  - Syntactic: grammatical structure of the language (word order).

- Keeping simple records of reading; for example, a daily reading log.

- Sharing reactions to reading through book talks, discussions, and writing activities.

- Conducting periodic conferences with students to discuss impressions, assess comprehension, monitor reading progress, and stimulate further reading.

- Encouraging appreciation and understanding of favorite books through special projects.

- Creating authentic reasons for practicing and sharing oral reading. For example, choral readings of poetry, reading parts of a story to the class during a book talk, and rehearsing a story to retell.

These instructional activities help our students gain fluency, independence, and confidence as readers.

# Major Goals for Ongoing Student Assessment

**1.** *To document students' literacy development.*

Teachers have in place a more informal and naturalistic system for evaluating student work. These may include an informal reading inventory, literature logs, reading journals, conference notes, running records of students' miscues, periodic writing samples, and documenting spelling progress.

**2.** *To keep students appraised of their progress.*

Students are involved in developing a portfolio. We may use student interviews, written responses by students, and quarterly student evaluations. This helps them set personal goals. Each student thinks about what is successful about his/her work, what he/she can do to improve, or enhance progress.

**3.** *To help staff members evaluate their own teaching effectiveness.*

Teachers visit teachers in our district and in other school systems to discuss issues concerning assessment procedures. We discuss specific current literature in the field relating it to our personal experiences. We attend and participate in assessment meetings offered through professional organizations.

**4.** *To keep parents, school board members, and administration informed and to ensure them of our high standards and accountability.*

We arrange several informal meetings where assessment procedures, portfolios, etc., are presented and discussed. Involving community members results in a positive and crucial partnership.

*Does information have to be retained in order to make the effort to learn it worthwhile? I remember learning a lot that I do not remember today, but I also remember that, at the time I learned it, I thought it was worth thinking about and talking about in class, especially if I cared for the teacher. I did it for her. What I still remember about this experience today is not the long-forgotten information, but that she taught me to love to learn. That, not the specifics she taught, is what made my experience with her so valuable.*

*— William Glasser, M.D.*
*The Quality School Teacher:*
*A Companion Volume to*
*The Quality School. New York:*
*HarperPerennial, 1993.*

# Different Configurations

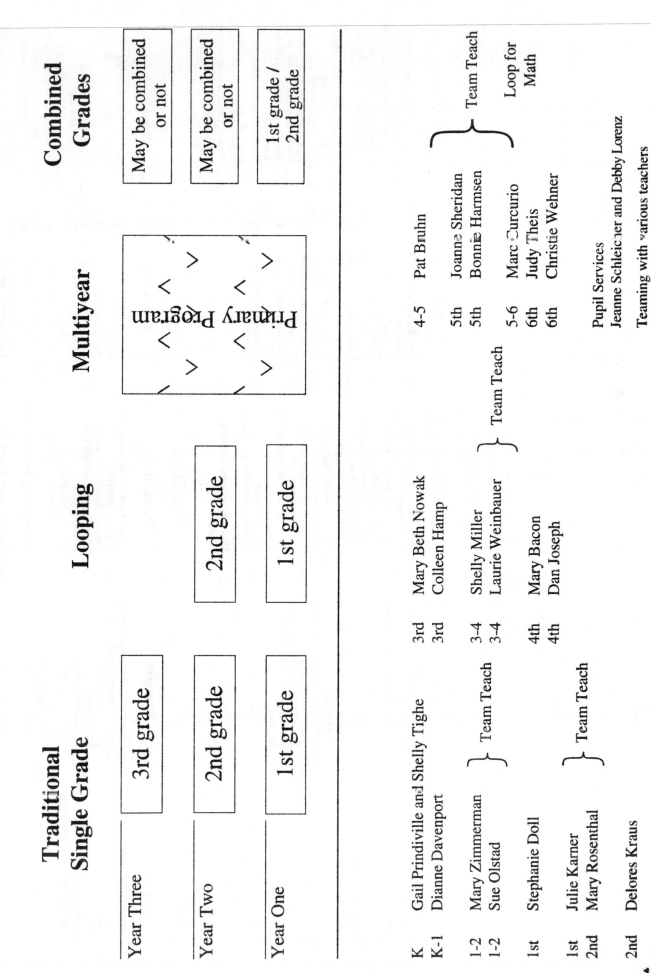

## Traditional Single Grade

| | |
|---|---|
| Year Three | 3rd grade |
| Year Two | 2nd grade |
| Year One | 1st grade |

## Looping

| | |
|---|---|
| | 2nd grade |
| | 1st grade |

## Multiyear

Primary Program

## Combined Grades

| |
|---|
| May be combined or not |
| May be combined or not |
| 1st grade / 2nd grade |

| | | |
|---|---|---|
| K | Gail Prindiville and Shelly Tighe | 3rd | Mary Beth Nowak | 4-5 | Pat Bruhn |
| K-1 | Dianne Davenport | 3rd | Colleen Hamp | | |
| 1-2 | Mary Zimmerman } Team Teach | 3-4 | Shelly Miller } Team Teach | 5th | Joanne Sheridan } Team Teach |
| 1-2 | Sue Olstad | 3-4 | Laurie Weinbauer | 5th | Bonnie Harmsen |
| 1st | Stephanie Doll | 4th | Mary Bacon | 5-6 | Marc Curcurio } Loop for Math |
| 1st | Julie Karner } Team Teach | 4th | Dan Joseph | 6th | Judy Theis |
| 2nd | Mary Rosenthal | | | 6th | Christie Wehner |
| 2nd | Delores Kraus | | | | |

Pupil Services
Jeanne Schleicher and Debby Lorenz

Teaming with various teachers
**Inclusion Model**

# FOND DU LAC SCHOOL DISTRICT
## KINDERGARTEN/GRADE 1 REPORT - 1995-96 SCHOOL YEAR

STUDENT: _____

SCHOOL: _____　　　　GRADE: K_____　1_____

*Information about your child as a reader and writer is intended to give you a "picture" of where your child is now and what kinds of behaviors you can expect next. Number indicates the quarter in which behavior is consistently and independently exhibited.*

1. First Quarter (ending in November)
2. Second Quarter (ending in January)
3. Third Quarter (ending in March)
4. Fourth Quarter (ending in June)

## READING

### Early Emergent
- ____ Recognizes name
- ____ Listens to stories
- ____ Chooses to look at books
- ____ Pretends to read
- ____ Enjoys rhymes and fingerplays
- ____ Understands what is read to him/her
- ____ Willing to take risks at this stage

### Emergent
- ____ Uses pictures to "read" a book
- ____ Joins in unison reading
- ____ Gives a memorized reading of a familiar book
- ____ Gives some attention to print in books
- ____ Reads signs and symbols from the environment
- ____ Can retell a sequence of events in a story
- ____ Repeats rhymes and fingerplays
- ____ Understands what is read to him/her

### Transitional
- ____ Identifies some sight words
- ____ Recognizes difference between letters, numbers and words
- ____ Identifies letter names
- ____ Beginning to associate some sounds with letters
- ____ Tracks from left to right
- ____ Knows where to begin and stop reading on a page
- ____ Attempts voice/print match with memorized readings
- ____ Makes predictions from pictures before reading
- ____ Can retell story
- ____ Becoming aware of punctuation (.?!" ")
- ____ Understands what is read to him/her

### Beginning
- ____ Developing a sight word vocabulary
- ____ Knows letter sounds
- ____ Makes first efforts at decoding
- ____ Demonstrates voice/print match
- ____ Uses background knowledge
- ____ Uses clues when reading (pictures, meaning, word order)
- ____ Able to "read" independently for a short period of time
- ____ Can read and retell story
- ____ Identifies punctuation marks (.?!" ")
- ____ Understands what is read to him/her

### Developing
- ____ Acquiring a large sight word vocabulary
- ____ Applies beginning decoding skills
- ____ Applies strategies (decoding, predicting, self-correcting, context, etc.)
- ____ Uses expression and punctuation cues in oral reading
- ____ Becoming a fluent reader
- ____ Able to read silently
- ____ Reads and develops story map (characters, settings, problems, solutions)
- ____ Reads for information and pleasure
- ____ Understands what he/she reads
- ____ Behaviors used with more difficult books

## WRITING

### Early Emergent
- ____ Chooses to experiment with writing
- ____ Draws to convey meaning
- ____ Writes with scribbles
- ____ Writes with letterlike forms
- ____ Willing to take risks at this stage

### Emergent
- ____ Chooses to write independently
- ____ Exhibits desire to see his/her words written down
- ____ Writes name
- ____ Copies words from environment without meaning
- ____ Writes with random letters
- ____ Writes left to right/top to bottom
- ____ Uses primarily capital letters
- ____ Copies the alphabet
- ____ Willing to take risks at this stage

### Transitional
- ____ Chooses to write for a purpose
- ____ Copies words from environment with meaning
- ____ Mixes upper and lower case letters
- ____ Uses beginning sounds
- ____ Uses beginning and ending sounds
- ____ Uses beginning/middle/ending sounds
- ____ Can print upper/lower case letters legibly
- ____ Willing to take risks at this stage

### Beginning
- ____ Uses a number of sentences in writing
- ____ Reads back writing consistently
- ____ Uses letters for each sound heard
- ____ Beginning to use vowels
- ____ Uses some standard spelling
- ____ Seeks out references to spell words (big book, chalkboard, word wall, picture dictionary)
- ____ Uses correct letter formation
- ____ Uses capitals for names
- ____ Uses capitals at beginning of sentences
- ____ Uses some punctuation (.?!)
- ____ Willing to take risks at this stage

### Developing
- ____ Begins to use the writing process: draft, revise, edit, final copy
- ____ Stories have a beginning, middle, and end
- ____ Sequences ideas in writing
- ____ Writing can be read by others
- ____ Uses more standard spelling
- ____ Spells high frequency words correctly
- ____ Uses phonics to spell unknown words
- ____ Uses vowels often
- ____ Uses endings (s, ing, ed)
- ____ Uses capitals appropriately
- ____ Uses punctuation correctly (.?!" ")
- ____ Willing to take risks at this stage

# FOND DU LAC SCHOOL DISTRICT
## GRADE 2 REPORT - 1995-96 SCHOOL YEAR

STUDENT: _____

SCHOOL: _____

*Information about your child as a reader and writer is intended to give you a "picture" of where your child is now and what kinds of behaviors you can expect next. Number indicates the quarter in which behavior is consistently and independently exhibited.*

1. First Quarter (ending in November)    2. Second Quarter (ending in January)    3. Third Quarter (ending in March)    4. Fourth Quarter (ending in June)

## READING

### Emergent

____ Uses pictures to "read" a book
____ Joins in unison reading
____ Gives a memorized reading of a familiar book
____ Gives some attention to print in books
____ Reads signs and symbols from the environment
____ Can retell a sequence of events in a story
____ Repeats rhymes and fingerplays
____ Understands what is read to him/her

### Transitional

____ Identifies some sight words
____ Recognizes difference between letters, numbers and words
____ Identifies letter names
____ Beginning to associate some sounds with letters
____ Tracks from left to right
____ Knows where to begin and stop reading on a page
____ Attempts voice/print match with memorized readings
____ Makes predictions from pictures before reading
____ Can retell story
____ Becoming aware of punctuation (.?!" ")
____ Understands what is read to him/her

### Beginning

____ Developing a sight word vocabulary
____ Knows letter sounds
____ Makes first efforts at decoding
____ Demonstrates voice/print match
____ Uses background knowledge
____ Uses clues when reading (pictures, meaning, word order)
____ Able to "read" independently for a short period of time
____ Can read then retell story
____ Identifies punctuation marks (.?!" ")
____ Understands what is read to him/her (story elements)

### Developing
#### (Advanced Beginning)

____ Acquiring a large sight word vocabulary
____ Begins to apply reading strategies (decoding, predicting, self-correcting, context, etc.)
____ Applies strategies independently (decoding, predicting, self-correcting, context, etc.)
____ Uses expression and punctuation cues in oral reading
____ Becoming a fluent reader
____ Able to read silently/independently
____ Reads and develops story/ map (characters, settings, problems, solutions)
____ Reads for information and pleasure
____ Understands what he/she reads

### Consolidating

____ Recognizes many words at sight
____ Applies word identification strategies successfully and independently (decoding, predicting, self-correcting, context, etc.)
____ Refines self-monitoring and self-correction strategies
____ Applies comprehension strategies
____ Can discuss story elements and support opinion with text
____ Reads independently

## WRITING

### Emergent

____ Chooses to write independently
____ Exhibits desire to see his/her words written down
____ Writes name
____ Copies words from environment without meaning
____ Writes with random letters
____ Writes left to right/top to bottom
____ Uses primarily capital letters
____ Copies the alphabet
____ Willing to take risks at this stage

### Transitional

____ Begins to write connected text
____ Chooses to write for a purpose
____ Copies words from environment with meaning
____ Mixes upper and lower case letters
____ Uses beginning sounds
____ Uses beginning and ending sounds
____ Uses beginning/middle/ending sounds
____ Can print upper/lower case letters legibly
____ Willing to take risks at this stage

### Beginning

____ Writes connected text
____ Beginning to write, then draw
____ Experiments with many genres (personal narrative, poetry, informational, fiction); may have a preferred genre
____ Seeks out references to spell words (big book, chalkboard, word wall, picture dictionary)
____ Uses correct letter formation
____ Uses capitals for names
____ Uses capitals at beginning of sentences
____ Uses some punctuation (.?!)
____ Writing includes phonetic, transitional, some standard spellings
____ Willing to take risks at this stage

### Developing
#### (Advanced Beginning)

____ Begins to use the writing process: draft, revise, edit, final copy
____ Stories have a beginning, middle, and end
____ Sequences ideas in writing
____ Writing can be read by others
____ Continues to develop content of writing in several genres
____ Uses endings (s, ing, ed)
____ Uses capitals appropriately
____ Uses punctuation correctly (.?!" ")
____ Spells high frequency words correctly
____ Uses transitional and standard spelling
____ Willing to take risks at this stage

### Consolidating

____ Continues to develop story structure in writing
____ Shows evidence of planned writing
____ Writes in many genres (personal narrative, fiction, poetry, information, etc.)
____ Has strategies for revising content (add on, insert, rearrange, delete)
____ Proofreads and edits writing for conventions
____ Writing includes transitional/standard spellings

The student population is currently 560 students and reflects the ethnic diversity of San Diego's mid-city population: 51 percent Hispanic, 14 percent Indochinese, 15 percent African American, 16 percent Anglo, and 5 percent American Indian. Over 19 languages are represented on our campus. Approximately 62 percent of our students require ESL support. Darnall participates in a schoolwide Title 1 program and over 89 percent of the students qualify for free or reduced breakfast and lunch.

The school opened in September of 1992 with a multiage focus and is continuing to refine it. We are in our fourth year.

Multiage education is a philosophy the staff readily aligned with. The staff also took advantage of an opportunity to design a school that reflected the best of their own educational experiences and expertise. That experience and expertise led directly to a multiage setting.

Our philosophy is evolving in that terms such as developmental learning, non-graded, continuous progress, and multiage/multiability are being worked through. There are no graded classrooms; all 22 classrooms are multiage.

The classrooms are divided as follows:

Early Primary Level, ages 4-7
Primary Level, ages 6-9
Elementary Level, ages 9-12

### Staff Development

Staff development consisted of on-the-job training, research, and collaboration. Since the beginning we have taken advantage of numerous staff development opportunities including seminars by Jim Grant [founder, Society For Developmental Education] and local trainings sponsored by the county and city office, and used High Scope and Wright Group materials, and "Math Their Way"/"Math: A Way of Thinking."

We encourage teachers of second language students who do not have a bilingual credential to take training and course work which results in an LDS—Language Development Specialist—credential issued by the state of California. ELIC and LLIFE are language arts/whole language training series which provide instruction for teachers, among other things, in the use of authentic evaluation of student portfolios in a non-graded setting. ELIC is for K-3 teachers; LLIFE is for 4-6 grade-level teachers.

### Darnall Holistic Learning Outcome

The Darnall Holistic Learning Outcome defines what every student is expected to know and be able to do as a result of curriculum and instruction, in order to be a productive, responsible citizen of the 21st century.

The following are *Givens:*

1. The culture of Darnall E-Campus will prevail.
2. Developmentally appropriate philosophy and curriculum will dominate instructional practice.

*The staff also took advantage of an opportunity to design a school that reflected the best of their own educational experiences and expertise.*

3. Staff will teach and work in concert with parents, community stakeholders and partners, as individuals and as members of groups.
4. Technology will pervade every aspect of learning and managing.
5. We will respect and value the cultural diversity within our community.
6. We will pursue the Holistic Learning Outcomes (HLO's) not only as individuals, but as members of groups.
7. The Holistic Learning Outcomes will inevitably overlap.

*Social, Community, Global Outcomes*   Every Darnall student will respect and acknowledge the interdependence of all human beings and our environment. In order to make the world a safer and healthier place to live, Darnall students will become lifelong contributors to the global community.

*Literacy*   Every Darnall student, as preparation for life-long learning in our rapidly changing world, will utilize Standard English to read, write, listen and speak to demonstrate their knowledge, understanding and application of the fundamental concepts across the curriculum.

*Self*   All Darnall students will recognize their own strengths and needs, care for, and take responsibility for themselves by:

- Making responsible choices and accepting the consequences
- Setting goals and following through
- Caring for their own physical and emotional well-being
- Using self-expression constructively
- Taking responsibility as life-long learners

*Creative Expression*   All Darnall students will understand and share in the cultural value and historical significance of the visual, performing and fine arts. All students will study, experience, and use a variety of means and media for creative expression. They will create, imagine, compose, design, and perform in enjoyable and constructive ways.

*Problem Solving*   Every Darnall student will become a capable problem solver as an individual and as a member of a group. To effectively consider and resolve problems, each student will be able to:

- Identify and state the problem(s)
- Gather information
- Seek input from others
- Consider opinions and analyze facts
- Recognize possible solutions and weigh their consequences
- Make an informed decision
- Support and accept the responsibility for the final decision
- As necessary, reevaluate and modify the final decision.

### Instructional Strategies

Instructional strategies include whole language, Reader's/Writer's Workshop, cooperative groups, sheltered strategies, core literature, math curriculum based on NCTM

**DARNALL E CAMPUS**

6020 Hughes Street
San Diego, CA 92115

**Phone: 619-582-1822**
**FAX: 619-287-4732**

**Entirely multiage**
**Multiage groupings**
**(by age):** 4-7, 6-9, 9-12

**Open to visiting teachers**
**and administrators**

**Contact:**
Martha Gerth
Loyal Carlon

standards, FOSS science training, and the Plan-Do-Review approach to Learning Centers. Plan-Do-Review is a daily time in class when students are able to select an activity ranging from computers, language arts, math, and art to drama and science. These centers change frequently. Students are expected to plan an activity within a chosen center, complete it, and then review it with other students, an adult, or in their journals.

Darnall employs a schoolwide, three-year theme cycle as the basis for its curriculum.

## Assessment

Assessment tools include student and staff portfolios; CLAS-like performance-based assessments; the Darnall Growth Record, which replaces traditional report card; and the California Learning Record.

## Programs at Darnall

We utilize a number of strategies and unique programs at Darnall, including:

- Triad and teaching support teams.
- Developmental strategies.
- A newcomer class, designed for developing English students and new immigrants from eight to twelve years of age who have not had much formal education. Most students in the newcomer class are refugees or recent Mexican immigrants and are placed in a multiage class. Instructor Deann Chenn and her part time instructional aide start at the very beginning levels and bring the students up to speed both in subject matter and in English so that at the end of their stay the students are ready to enter junior high. The program is highly successful. The current class has 32 students.
- Cross-cultural acceptance and awareness through the Families program. From 1:15 to 1:45 pm three times a week (Monday, Wednesday, and Friday), students from four to twelve years old are grouped heterogeneously—including ESL students and special needs students—to deal with peer tutoring, self-esteem training, community involvement, respect, etc. These groups stay together throughout their school career, so that when older students move on to junior high they already have contacts at the new school. Older students become very protective of younger students. There is a monthly Family sing-along and other activities.
- Primary language support team.
- Integration of sheltered, English, and bilingual students within teaching triads. The sheltered classes are for students transitioning from a second language to English. The instruction is in English, but the teaching strategies and pacing vary from the regular program. It is one of the three classes within a triad so students are naturally within an integrated setting.
- Triad planning weekly within teaching day.
- Intake assessments for all new students prior to placement.
- Our Hispanic Reading Program is funded by the district to provide teacher training and books for students who are transitioning from another language to English. The program also supplies funds for teachers to attend conferences.

## Student Selection

We have developed a descriptive form including academic, emotional, social, and physical traits along a continuum, and use those forms to place each individual student.

## Parent Involvement

We involve parents any way we possibly can—including volunteering, multicultural activities, field trips, home projects, donations, parent education classes, and through the Darnall Parent Association.

## Specialists in the Classroom

We have full-time physical education and music teachers. After-school clubs include the arts. The resource teacher is part of the teaching triad planning, as we mainstream all students. We also have community dance instructors participating in academic programs within the school.

During our prep rotation program, sudents attend one of their special classes—library, phys-ed or music—while teaching teams meet to plan learning centers and instructional strategies.

## Inclusion

We have full inclusion of special-needs students within the triad settings with resource specialist support. Inclusion is better facilitated within a multiage setting; however, many of these students need close supervision and one-to-one assistance, which is not always managed with peer tutoring. The resource specialist assists with teaching and curriculum development, and continues to design a support strategy that deals with these areas. There is always a need for materials. We also deal with diverse languages which often makes timely problem identification more difficult.

## Team Teaching

We incorporate team teaching within teaching triads across campus. Each triad is composed of one sheltered, one English, and one bilingual teacher. This allows for flexible groupings and natural movement, either by choice or assigned at times. Each triad has a shared planning time within the school day.

## Grouping for Instruction

Grouping within the classroom varies within the triads. There is a great deal of heterogeneous cooperative learning, plus small groups for subjects such as guided reading. Triad teachers group and regroup students in multiage settings throughout the day within the three classrooms they occupy depending on interest, ability, social and emotional development, etc.

Math is leveled using the multiage "Explorations" program as a curriculum with some triads.

## Our Biggest Obstacle

Finding the time to plan our programs is always a difficulty. Meeting the needs across age spans has been a problem; which we are solving by adjusting the age spans and by using developmental characteristics for placement. Class size and parent education are also issues we continue to deal with.

## Our Biggest Challenge

We have several issues that continue to challenge us:

- Defining our philosophy and how to meet the needs of such a language-diverse group.
- Knowing when to go with Primary language versus sheltered instruction.
- Figuring out the optimum distribution of ages within a multiage classroom — do multiage classrooms need an even distribution?
- How we can make students' transition into and out of the different levels smoother.
- Varying class size within triad structures.

## Waivers/Mandates

We became a California Charter School, and as such are not subject to many of the mandates that traditional schools must follow.

# Darnall E-Campus
# Developmental Characteristics

## Birth Date

### Early Primary
- Four years old as of September 1.
- Age range from 4 to 8 years old.

### Primary
- Six years old as of September 1.
- Age range from 6 to 9 years old.

### Elementary
- Eight years old as of September 1.
- Age range from 8 to 12 years old.

## Social

### Early Primary
- Egocentric, wants to be first.
- Has difficulty in seeing others' feelings and views.
- Dependent on authority.
- Likes to help.
- Few inhibitions.
- May prefer to play alone at times and with others at times.
- Beginning to understand consequences of own and others' behaviors.
- Likes to copy.
- Talkative.
- Difficult distinguishing real vs. unreal.
- Beginning to develop ability to take turns and share objects or play.
- Often feels anxiety when separated from familiar people, places, things.
- Beginning to develop friendships.

### Primary
- May feel some anxiety with the larger school community when separated from familiar people, places, things (going to camp, sleepovers, shopping malls).
- Becoming more outgoing.
- Developing closer friendships with others and may begin to play mainly with peers of same sex.
- Comparing self with others in terms of physical appearance (cultural heritage), gender, height, weight.
- Continuing to develop the ability to take turns and share.
- Developing ability to work in small groups and alone.
- Continuing to develop. Understanding consequences of his/her own and others' behaviors.
- Has experienced and feels comfortable in a variety of social settings (large, cooperative, independent, partners).
- May process verbally.

### Elementary
- May appear relatively calm and at peace with themselves.
- Occasionally becomes angry, sad or depressed, but short-lived.
- Often hides feelings of anxiety when introduced to new situations by appearing over-confident.
- Sensitive to criticism and displays feelings of success/failure depending on how adults and peers respond to them.
- Emotional identity is based largely on how peers and others respond to him/her.
- May not want to be disturbed when involved in an activity or game.
- Able to communicate feelings; may choose not to; might not be aware of origin of feelings.
- Torn between pleasing friends, teachers, family, and society.
- Grappling with independence and dependence.

## Emotional

### Early Primary
- Needs approval.
- Displays emotions readily.
- Defines the world as bad or good, all or nothing.
- Beginning to identify own sense of his/her emotions.
- Testing limits of authority and honesty.
- Impulsive.
- Possessive.
- Developing ability to sympathize.

### Primary
- May show bursts of emotion and impatience less frequently.
- Shows a general increased sense of self-confidence but has reticence about taking risks.
- Sensitive to criticism and displays feelings of success or failure depending on how adults respond to them.
- Needs to be praised.
- Needs to feel enjoyment and pride in knowing they can do one thing well.
- Needs to make, to do, to build, to explore.
- Becoming more able to understand own feelings and express them appropriately.
- Learning how to work cooperatively with others in order to problem solve.

### Elementary
- Often hides feelings of anxiety when introduced to new situations by appearing over-confident.
- Continues to be very sociable spending time with parents, friends of the same sex and often has a special friend.
- Becoming aware of strengths and weaknesses (may comment, "I can do that . . . I can't do that.")
- Often defines self by physical characteristics and possessions.
- Sensitive to criticism and displays feelings of success or failure depending on how adults and peers respond.
- Continues to develop ability to work and play with others.
- May not want to be disturbed when involved in an activity or game.
- Craves intimate group members/friendships.
- Developing abstract sense of humor.
- Self-conscious.

## *Intellectual*

### Early Primary

- Reasoning is dominated by perception.
- Intuitive rather than logical.
- Inability to conserve.
- Developing ability to distinguish reality and fantasy.

### Primary

- Developing ability to conserve.
- Understanding number.
- Thinking bound to concrete.
- Ability to distinguish reality and fantasy.

### Elementary

- Ability to conserve.
- Developing generality of thought.
- Beginning hypothetical and deductive reasoning.

## *Physical*

### Early Primary

- Developing fine motor control (scissors, crayons, pencils, pincer grasp).
- Developing eye/hand and left/right, ball skills.
- Developing right/left hand preference.
- Changes activities often.
- Develop gross motor skills — balance beam, gallop, run, jump, hop, push, catch, throw, swing.
- Sits and attends for short periods.
- Reversals common.
- Beginning to develop spatial awareness.
- Frequently rushing.
- Still developing control of body functions.
- Rate of physical growth may vary.
- Active.

### Primary

- Continuing to refine fine motor development.
- Visual difficulties may become apparent.
- Rate of physical growth may vary.
- Continuing to develop hand/eye coordination and may accomplish more complex tasks.
- Interest in group physical activities, may change often.
- Showing increased coordination of large and fine motor skills.
- Growth spurts may begin to interfere with coordination.
- Reversals becoming less common.

### Elementary

- May develop rapidly — spurt of growth before puberty.
- Continuing to develop hand-eye coordination.
- Continuing to develop ability to use either right or left side for batting, kicking or throwing.
- May need guidance in personal hygiene.
- Coordination may be awkward.
- Showing increased coordination, but growth spurts may begin to interfere.
- Developing ability to hit a ball.
- Developing more sophisticated understanding of body parts and functions.
- Beginning to develop ability to pace selves in high energy activities.
- Understands safety rules, but takes risks.
- Begins to play more complex group games and sports.
- May need to increase physical activity to maintain health.
- Develops loyalty to group or team.

*These developmental characteristics are identified to augment the academic continuums and student portfolios for the purpose of considering all aspects of a child's development. Together, these documents provide a basis for discussion on the placement of student in the most appropriate learning environments.*

Lake George (population 3,400) is located in the eastern Adirondack Mountains in New York State and is widely known as a resort community. Located halfway between Montreal and New York City, it combines the quiet and beauty of the mountains and lakes and is easily accessible to major metropolitan centers.

While our community would be classified as above average socially and economically, in recent years we have experienced an increase in student mobility, students with learning problems, and students involved in single-parent homes. This has led to an increase in counseling time, the addition of a social worker, and an increase in our remedial/special needs staff.

The Lake George School District has two schools—a K-6 elementary school with a full-time kindergarten and a junior-senior high school. The district's population is about 1,100-1,200 students, with between 550 and 580 in each of the two buildings. Fifteen to twenty percent of the student population in the elementary school are enrolled in free and reduced lunches. Approximately 15 percent of students are identified as special needs students; our per pupil cost is $6,138. Daily student attendance is 95.7 percent and our daily teacher attendance is 97.8 percent. Ninety-seven percent of our students are white.

## Multiage Since 1971

Edward F. Fiske, in his 1991 book *Smart Schools, Smart Kids*, states, "The longest running example of the multiage approach is Lake George Elementary School in Lake George, New York." The elementary school was constructed in 1968 and created a primary unit of six- and seven-year-olds in September 1971.

Back in June 1971 the school began its departure from a graded school because it viewed "multiage grouping as a positive step towards accommodating the wide range of students' ability and needs." (*News & Views*, June 1971)

The school is entirely multiage.

As a faculty, we recently described our continuous progress program at the Lake George Elementary School as

> ... educating children in a flexible environment which considers all aspects of a child's development—children progressing at their own individual rates without regard to age, grade, or a specific time frame. Evaluation and prescription are ongoing, providing a diagnostic framework for individual instructional needs. Children are grouped and regrouped according to their needs, ability, and achievement. Students are being evaluated in accordance with their own abilities rather than being compared to their peers.

The major goal of our elementary school is that all students must successfully achieve and continue to feel better about themselves. The brighter students must be challenged and not bored. The slowest students must achieve without frustration.

*"The longest running example of the multiage approach is Lake George Elementary School in Lake George, New York."*

There must be a continuity and consistency of programs throughout the students' elementary experience. It is this need that motivates our use of teaching teams and school-wide goals and objectives approved by our shared decision-making Cabinet.

## Team Teaching

Team teaching is a major element of the success of our elementary school. Much in-service and staff development occur when people work together to accomplish similar goals and objectives. When teachers team with other individuals, they get to know themselves better, and become more tolerant of other individuals.

Teaming at our elementary school occurs with two or three teachers working together in what we call "side by side teaching." Teams of teachers working with six-, seven-, and eight-year-olds combine with teams working with eight-, nine-, and ten-year-olds, and ten-, eleven-, and twelve-year-olds to form a cluster team. Three such clusters exist at our school.

A third level of teaming occurs when all kindergarten and primary teachers form a team. This process is duplicated with the teaming of Intermediate I staff members as well as with Intermediate II teachers.

Level 1 teaching teams deal basically with the direct instruction of students. Level 2 cluster teams deal with student organization, behavior management of students, and parental communications. Level 3 teaming deals basically with curriculum development. One must team if he or she is employed at Lake George Elementary School.

Teaming allows us to increase the number of reading and math levels so as to accommodate students in smaller groups. Teams of two or three teachers work with groups of students six- to eight-, eight- to ten-, and ten- to thirteen-years old. Each teaching team has the students for two years, with approximately half the students exiting the team's program as new students are added each year.

The school is divided into three cluster teams of seven or eight teachers, with approximately 175 students ranging in age from six to thirteen. While social studies and science are becoming more and more integrated as part of language arts and math, the state curricula in these three areas are taught by teaching teams in a two-year cycle. The traditional program for grades one and two are taught in a multi-age setting of groups of six-, seven-, and eight-year-olds, the traditional third and fourth program in inter-aged groups of eight- through ten-year-olds.

Our kindergarten is self-contained and team-taught in an open area by five teachers with one full-time and one part-time assistant. Some students spend an additional year in our kindergarten or three years with their teaching teams at other age levels, but because of the flexible grouping and continuous progress programs, do not feel a sense of failure, as it is not necessary for them to repeat previous work.

## Six-Day Schedule

At Lake George Elementary we make use of a six-day schedule. The first day of school is Day One, the next day is Day Two, and so on. After the sixth day, we start Day One again. This procedure equalizes the students' time spent with our specialists. Traditionally, if a group of students had art on Monday or Friday, they would miss out on two or three art days during the school year because of holidays, and the classroom teachers would miss an opportunity for planning time. More important, "snow days" and "no days" do not disrupt the school schedule. If a "snow day" occurs on Day Five, the next day becomes Day Five. Staff may use the same well-developed plans of the previous day. (Counseling sessions for students are held on the date they are scheduled.)

Multi-age grouping, teaming, the six-day schedule, and continuous progress programs help us provide the continuity and consistency of program throughout the students' elementary experience.

## Staff Development

The original staff development in the late '60s was a combination of workshops, conferences, and readings. Robert Anderson, a noted writer and national proponent of non-graded education, presented at the Lake George Elementary School in the late '60s.

In recent years, workshops, conferences, and readings, along with curriculum writing, continue to be our main source of in-service. Presently each staff member is accountable for 100 hours of staff development annually.

The following topics have been given a priority in recent years: cooperative learning, team teaching, whole language, goal setting, process writing, non-graded education, student management, learning disabilities, mainstreaming, and inclusion.

## Curriculum

*Language Arts:* In our school the average amount of time that a teacher devotes to language arts is approximately two- to two-and-a-half hours a day. Under the umbrella of language arts, we include the teaching and practicing of writing, reading, spelling, handwriting, and sustained silent reading.

Skills and strategies are taught primarily through teacher-initiated activities, mini-lessons, and teacher/student conferences. Our language arts programs, as all programs in our school, are based on individual pupil progress. We believe that each child moves toward mature literacy in developmental increments and that the mastery of language skills is a continuous process and may occur at different times for each child. Therefore, our program is designed to address the unique experiences and abilities of each child. The teacher/student conferences provide an ideal vehicle for meeting the various needs of each student. Practice of English skills and strategies is provided through large group activities (whole class), small group activities, and time for individual independent work.

*As educators, our intent is to prepare our students to be productive, life-long learners, preparation for which includes using higher order and critical thinking skills.*

As educators, our intent is to prepare our students to be productive, life-long learners, preparation for which includes using higher order and critical thinking skills. In language arts these skills are primarily addressed in our literature discussion groups. To some extent, all of our teachers are presently using real literature as a basis for reading instruction. We believe that attaining literacy is enhanced when language activities occur in meaningful contexts with meaningful purposes. Therefore, the use of authentic activities for writing instruction also provides a way to introduce higher-order and critical thinking skills.

In our school we advocate that children learn by using language. Learners come to school with a knowledge of the world and of oral and written language on which further learning is based. Therefore, we attempt to integrate language arts with other areas of the curriculum as often as feasible. For example, when students are studying Japan, they are reading books like *Sadako and the Thousand Paper Cranes* and writing Japanese haiku. When studying pond life in science, they are asked to write narrative reports of their field trip to the pond, correctly spelling words by using a glossary of scientific terminology.

Our school supports the philosophy that the skills of writing should be taught and assessed through authentic activities. Writing is integrated into all areas of the curriculum and is viewed as a tool for demonstrating competence. All of our teachers receive training in and are expected to teach writing as a process. To ensure that this happens, the language arts coordinator will observe every teacher at least once during the school year, model the teaching of the writing process, and, if needed, assist the teacher in becoming more proficient at teaching writing in this manner. Direct instruction of writing skills takes place during mini-lessons and teacher/student conferences.

Every year all classroom teachers are expected to collect three representative writing samples from each student (including all steps of the process). These samples are evaluated holistically, dated, and placed in a cumulative language arts folder. To accompany these language arts folders, we have devised two profile checklists for the teacher's use in keeping analytical data on the child's writing process. One profile is designated for the emergent author and the other for the more accomplished writer. Two to three times a year all classroom teachers are required to examine their students' language arts folders, complete the appropriate part of the writing checklists and review strengths and weaknesses with each student.

Computer technology is a major part of our curriculum and word processing is introduced to our students at the primary level. As the students become older, more and more final drafts are produced on the computer.

*Mathematics:* Lake George Elementary School has achieved a great deal of success in mathematics. The teachers at Lake George work hard at getting students motivated about math. The priority of the teachers is to develop understanding and apply mathematics to real-world problems. They also want their students to achieve success daily. The Addison-Wesley mathematics program allows for success by providing quality mathematics, teaching options, a comprehensive assessment program, and support materials. This program provides activities that interest students and give them an opportunity to develop an understanding of concepts and a sense of self-confidence.

The teachers show the students the relevance of math in their lives. Students get involved in activities that go beyond paper and pencil tasks. Many different manipulatives are incorporated into the teaching of all students. Students are give a variety of learning experiences and they work on problems that could have a number of solutions—not just one right or wrong answer.

Teachers follow an integrated approach. In each lesson that they teach, they try to allow students to be actively involved, provide time and guidance for critical thinking, encourage communication between students, and make it easy for students to work in small groups and independently. Each day our students should be doing, thinking, and talking math.

An encouraging, positive classroom atmosphere is probably the most important aspect of teaching problem-solving. Students are encouraged to try different approaches and come up with alternative methods and answers to problems. Problem-solving skills are also developed by providing the approach of understanding the question, finding data, making plans, estimating answers, solving the problem, and checking to make sure the answer makes sense. Our students are taught many different strategies such as drawing a picture, making a table, guess and check, finding a pattern, making an organized list, or choosing an operation. By learning to use all of these strategies our students are much more confident when dealing with the world's problems.

Our students have ample opportunity to communicate about mathematical ideas and situations. They have computer partners, math partners, small cooperative work groups, and large group sharing. We have found that when students work together they pool their resources, listen to other students explain thinking processes, see and hear alternative strategies, and, most importantly, experience math in a non-threatening, supportive environment. In our school, kindergarten averages 30 to 40 minutes a day of math activities; primary and intermediate I each averages 60 minutes a day, and intermediate II averages 70 minutes a day.

*Science:* Our science program at the elementary level is definitely a hands-on process approach. The state ESPET testing verifies our success in this approach. The Lake George Elementary School follows the state science curriculum, and we begin the instruction of science at the kindergarten level. A large degree of integration occurs between our art and our science programs.

Science textbooks are not used as basals other than as a resource help. Our basic science materials are Board of Cooperative Educational Services Elementary Science Program kits. Some of the topics covered are: classroom plants; sunshine, shadows, and silhouettes; brine shrimp; plant and animal life; crayfish; buoyancy; powder and crystals; electrical circuits; butterflies and moths; pond life; birds; electromagnetism; light; looking at liquids; plant responses; meet the creatures; environmental factors; and rocketry.

*Social Studies:* Social studies refers to the understanding of our world and its people. It is important to include cultural, economic, political, historical, geographical, and social aspects in this learning. Our social studies curriculum committee reviews and updates our program annually to be sure all of these areas are being taught and to assure a quality program.

Our social studies is designed to use a "hands on" approach to learning. While the guidelines of the New York State curriculum are carefully followed, textbooks are not our main tool for teaching. We place great value on integrating social studies with all other subject areas. Many related literature books are used for reading, writing and spelling activities. Graphs, charts, and maps are used in math areas. Cooperative learning activities are frequently used, as well as small group projects, computer programs, videos and field trips.

Our local area is especially rich in historical places such as Fort William Henry, Fort Ticonderoga, and the Saratoga Battlefield right in our backyard. Visiting these three locations greatly enriches the students' knowledge and understanding of our American history.

Geography is an ongoing study at all levels. Primary students begin with maps of their classroom, school, and then our community. Older students progress to a global knowledge. Our students participate in the National Geographic geography bee and a community international festival each year. They also exchange letters and videos with a sister city, Saga City, Japan.

> *Our students participate in the National Geographic geography bee and a community international festival each year. They also exchange letters and videos with a sister city, Saga City, Japan.*

The elementary school social studies programs are reviewed annually, and our students' knowledge and understanding are assessed the end of each level (primary, intermediate I, and intermediate II). Each year is a new adventure for our students as they learn about their world and its people.

*Health and Safety*: Health and safety are an integral part of our total school program in the areas of instruction and practical application. Formal lessons in health are presented weekly to our students by the school's nurse-teacher, with follow-up by teaching teams.

Strategies for health instruction are almost as varied as our students, allowing for their differences, enriching their health and safety education, and addressing their levels of critical thinking skills. Individual and group projects, field trips to the hospital emergency room or veterinarian, community resource people to interview and to invite as guest speakers, lectures, experiments, health games, adventure-based overnight programs in outdoor education, demonstrations (including our famous fire drill with fire trucks, hook and ladder extended, and fireman in full regalia), and a mini-speakout against substance abuse offer our students ample opportunities to challenge themselves and acquire health and safety knowledge. In addition, each of our intermediate II students receive a subscription to "Current Health I," which enriches our health curriculum.

Integration is inherent in our school's approach to health and safety instruction. By using the previously mentioned strategies, health and safety is integrated into language arts, social studies, math, science, physical education, and recess. Practical application of health and safety knowledge is practiced throughout the school. For example, our school parties offer nutritious snacks as opposed to candies; a fluoride swish program has a 99 percent participation rate by students; student and parent handbooks emphasize health and safety procedures; free soda is refused for our field/fun day and milk is purchased for the students; salt is not available to our students during lunch time.

## Specialists

Our specialists in the areas of art, music and physical education instruct our student in a multiage setting.

*Art:* The elementary art program schedule includes one hour every six days for students ages six to ten years old and one hour fifteen minutes for every six days for students ages ten to thirteen years old.

Visual arts "problems" are planned by the art teacher for students. Guidelines are given to the students. The guidelines are within a particular framework, using different media. Students are encouraged to experiment, organize, and express within the framework. The lessons foster a sensitivity to art elements and principles and often include a sequence of steps within the experience. Emphasis is also placed on the concepts of the particular curriculum being integrated, such as social studies, language arts, science, math or health. Directions are given verbally, written on the board, and demonstrated. In many lessons the art teacher asks the students to place themselves into a different time frame in order to allow the students to become aware of the physical environment and the customs and beliefs of different cultures and societies. Students could become an artist in ancient Egypt, an archaeologist, a Native American before 1490, etc. The children bring their own related experiences and past knowledge to the project, use their imagination, and add new ideas.

The computer is a recent addition to the art program. It is a medium used to increase the computer skills and confidence of the students, while emphasizing the creative visual arts elements of computer software.

As part of the visual arts enrichment activities, students are offered optional experiences after school. Designing and painting scenery for musical performances sometimes includes building props. Ceramics groups offer experiences for students on the potter's wheel and opportunities to create hand-built clay artwork. Also, high potential visual artists are offered after-school art experiences which include the computer.

*Music*: The elementary vocal music program schedule includes 30 minute classes twice every six days for primary, intermediate I and intermediate II students. Kindergarten children have music twice every six days for 20 minute class periods. Chorus is offered for intermediate I and II students as an after school extracurricular activity.

Music classes are based on the philosophies of Carl Orff, which encourage children to develop musically by creating, listening, and performing. The elements of music are explored through speech, movement, song and instruments. Because students are multiaged, it is necessary to teach different levels and abilities in one class. Lessons include concepts that are a review for some children and new for others. When a technical skill such as how to hold an instrument or how to read a rhythm pattern is involved, older students are excellent models for their younger peers. Because the Orff approach blends so beautifully with whole language theories, it is possible to enliven and enrich literature with song and movement, while providing an opportunity for many musical goals to be achieved.

The music teacher is challenged to sequence the instruction so that music skills are mastered by the student. Because the children spend two years at each level, there is some overlap of objectives; but integrating ideas from the classroom curriculum provides variety, and musical concepts can be easily reinforced.

*Physical Education:* We have two physical education teachers and a two-station gymnasium. Classes are scheduled for different lengths of time: 20 minutes daily for kindergarten, 30 minutes every other day for primary, 45 minutes every other day for intermediate I and 50 minutes every other day for intermediate II. Two homerooms come to physical education at the same time and both PE teachers see all the students in the school. Most lessons are taught in two separate groups of 20-25 each. Occasionally we have one large-group situation.

The younger students remain in their homeroom group for physical education. After each set of five or six lessons, the children switch teachers. Groups are multiaged, and we have found no problems caused by mixing ages.

With the older students, we have activity/sport units that last for varying amounts of time—from three days to several weeks. For each unit we change group members and/or teachers. We regroup in different ways: in some units we divide by physical skill level or age; in other units we use student interest; sometimes we assign groups randomly. We intentionally try not to use homeroom groups so that the students can experience different social contacts. A majority of class time is spent on skill work—we only play a "real game" a few times. Those who are interested in playing various sports must play after school. There is a late bus available, and all intermediate level students can sign up for after-school intramurals.

*Library/Resource Center:* The library/resource center in our school is an integral component of our overall education program and our school-wide philosophy emphasizing the importance of books. Our librarian is regarded as a teacher and participates in classroom and curriculum activities. She is a resource for both teachers and students, and she provides specific services for both groups of people.

Our library services over 60 teachers and staff members and over 550 students. The average monthly book circulation is over 4,600 books. The library contains over 18,000 books and 700 pieces of computer software. The number of professional journals and other publications is between 35 and 40.

A recent innovative change in our library has been the implementation of a computerized circulation system. This system has enabled the librarian to more efficiently handle the flow of materials in and out of the library. Our next addition will be File Server, connecting our library/resource center to individual classrooms.

## Gifted and Talented

While most of our students in need of advanced study or enrichment are accommodated in regular teaching teams through our continuous progress organization, we do employ a part-time teacher for our program known as High Potential. High Potential offers enrichment opportunities for both our "Talent Pool" and our school-wide population. Activities include presentation seminars, field trips, simulations, independent study projects, creative writing, team-building activities, hands-on experiments, community resources, publication of a school literacy magazine, and mini-courses. The emphasis is on thinking skills and problem-solving techniques.

## Special Needs Students

The elementary school has two self-contained classrooms for special needs students. Each classroom has students in a three-year age range, with a certified special education teacher and a teacher assistant. Though self-contained, each has direct involvement with one of our three family-grouped clusters. The mainstreaming of special needs students ranks extremely high on a list of student priorities.

Basically we offer two types of programming for special education students: the resource room, and the Option II classroom. The less severely disabled children are helped by our resource room teachers in two ways. The majority of the students are seen in a pull-out setting and worked with in groups of four to six children. However, a few students are worked with in the classroom, following a consultant-teacher model. For the more severely disabled we have two Option II classrooms, one for younger students and one for older. Each classroom is managed by one teacher and one full-time teaching assistant. Although these are self-contained for the most part, a great deal of mainstreaming takes place, enabling a number of special education children to be integrated into a regular classroom situation at some time during the school day.

Within these special education placements, the teachers attempt to keep the same instructional emphases as the rest of the school; for example, the use of big books, literature-based reading, writing process, and manipulative math. Obviously there is a need for additional teacher support, the use of more and sometimes different methods, and increased awareness of individual learning styles. However, the holistic, language-based philosophy of the building which guides the regular education program also exists in these special education programs.

One wonderful success story we have is of a multi-handicapped child who was mainstreamed into our school almost four years ago. This child is deaf, legally blind, and otherwise health-impaired. With the addition of a full-time aide, we have been able to completely mainstream this child into our regular program.

## Students Requiring Title I Services, LEP Students, and Students in Need of Remediation

The Title I program in our school is focused on reading and writing. Most of our children needing remedial support are seen by the full-time reading teacher, who has a teaching assistant working under her direction. In addition, a Reading Recovery teacher was trained during the 1994-95 school year. She currently works with our youngest primary students using the Reading Recovery program. She also sees some Title I, Intermediate I students.

Children are placed into remedial reading classes based on standardized test scores and teacher recommendations. Any student scoring below the 23rd percentile on the reading component of the Comprehensive Test of Basic Skills is provided supplemental reading assistance. As a screening, we also use the minimum level of competency of the New York State reading and writing tests. Each child has an individual folder in which the following type of materials are kept: learning logs with daily entries, diagnostic information, assessment reports, and letters of communication to parents. Our compensatory programs are totally supportive of what is happening in the classrooms.

## Inclusion

While we do not have an "inclusion program" as such at our elementary school, we do have mainstreaming to the maximum degree possible. Sound mainstreaming practices in a team teaching school is the philosophical basis for inclusion. We continue to maintain self-contained classrooms for special needs students because we feel that they are an important alternative for meeting the needs of some students. When you support an all or nothing attitude—that is, using only 100 percent inclusion—your program becomes rigid and lacks the flexibility to be successful with as many students as possible.

Our special needs education teachers team with the special needs instructional team as well as with one of the K-6 team of regular classroom teachers. This process helps us improve our quality of communication between staff members, which is sometimes missing in the practice of mainstreaming. The reason we moved from the graded to the non-graded school organization was that the graded school lacks flexibility. We should not make the same mistake by using total inclusion.

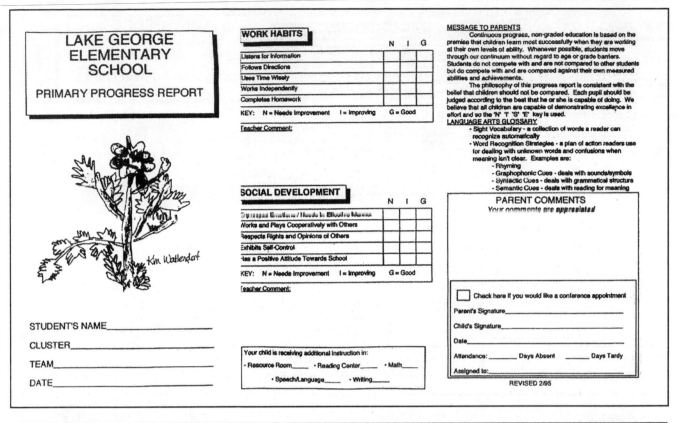

## LAKE GEORGE ELEMENTARY SCHOOL
### PRIMARY PROGRESS REPORT

STUDENT'S NAME_____

CLUSTER_____

TEAM_____

DATE_____

### WORK HABITS

| | N | I | G |
|---|---|---|---|
| Listens for Information | | | |
| Follows Directions | | | |
| Uses Time Wisely | | | |
| Works Independently | | | |
| Completes Homework | | | |

KEY: N = Needs Improvement   I = Improving   G = Good

Teacher Comment:

### SOCIAL DEVELOPMENT

| | N | I | G |
|---|---|---|---|
| Expresses Emotions / Needs in Effective Manner | | | |
| Works and Plays Cooperatively with Others | | | |
| Respects Rights and Opinions of Others | | | |
| Exhibits Self-Control | | | |
| Has a Positive Attitude Towards School | | | |

KEY: N = Needs Improvement   I = Improving   G = Good

Teacher Comment:

Your child is receiving additional instruction in:
- Resource Room_____   • Reading Center_____   • Math_____
- Speech/Language_____   • Writing_____

### MESSAGE TO PARENTS

Continuous progress, non-graded education is based on the premise that children learn most successfully when they are working at their own levels of ability. Whenever possible, students move through our continuum without regard to age or grade barriers. Students do not compete with and are not compared to other students but do compete with and are compared against their own measured abilities and achievements.

The philosophy of this progress report is consistent with the belief that children should not be compared. Each pupil should be judged according to the best that he or she is capable of doing. We believe that all children are capable of demonstrating excellence in effort and so the 'N' 'I' 'S' 'E' key is used.

### LANGUAGE ARTS GLOSSARY
- Sight Vocabulary - a collection of words a reader can recognize automatically
- Word Recognition Strategies - a plan of action readers use for dealing with unknown words and confusions when meaning isn't clear. Examples are:
  - Rhyming
  - Graphophonic Cues - deals with sounds/symbols
  - Syntactic Cues - deals with grammatical structure
  - Semantic Cues - deals with reading for meaning

### PARENT COMMENTS
Your comments are appreciated

☐ Check here if you would like a conference appointment

Parent's Signature_____

Child's Signature_____

Date_____

Attendance: _____ Days Absent   _____ Days Tardy

Assigned to:_____

REVISED 2/95

---

Student's Name_____

### LANGUAGE ARTS

| Stage of Reading | Beginning | Developing | | Independent |
|---|---|---|---|---|
| Basal Skill Level | Readiness 1 2 3 4 5 6 | 7 | 8 | 9   10 |

*Unmarked items are not being considered at this time*

| | Experiencing Difficulty | Beginning to Develop | Developing Satisfactorily | Highly Developed |
|---|---|---|---|---|
| Expresses Thoughts / Ideas in an Organized Manner | | | | |
| Enjoys Listening to Literature | | | | |
| Orally Responds to Literature (Retelling, Reacting) | | | | |
| Is Acquiring and Expanding Sight Vocabulary | | | | |
| Uses a Variety of Word Recognition Strategies | | | | |
| Selects Appropriate Reading Material | | | | |
| Engages in Reading Independently | | | | |
| Comprehends What Has Been Read | | | | |
| Responds Effectively to Literature in Written Format | | | | |
| Engages in Writing Independently | | | | |
| Demonstrates a Storyline | | | | |
| Writes on Various Topics | | | | |
| Writes Using Various Forms (Poetry, Letters, Stories) | | | | |
| Chooses to Share Writing | | | | |
| Revises Ideas When Appropriate | | | | |
| Uses Temporary Spelling to Write Unfamiliar Words | | | | |
| Uses Standard Spelling to Write Familiar Words | | | | |
| Identifies Temporary Spelling | | | | |
| Uses Spelling Resources for Unfamiliar Words | | | | |
| Applies Rules of Capitalization and Punctuation | | | | |
| Uses Penmanship Skills | | | | |

EFFORT: Needs Improvement   Improving   Good   Excellent

### LANGUAGE ARTS - Con't

Teacher Comment:

### MATHEMATICS

| Book | _____ | | | | | | | | |
|---|---|---|---|---|---|---|---|---|---|
| Chapter | 1 | 2 | 3 | 4 | 5 | 6 | 7 | 8 | 9 |
| Completed | 10 | 11 | 12 | 13 | 14 | 15 | 16 | 17 | 18 |

| | Experiencing Difficulty | Beginning to Develop | Developing Satisfactorily | Highly Developed |
|---|---|---|---|---|
| Recalls Basic Facts (+ - x ÷) | | | | |
| Is Accurate With Computation | | | | |
| Understands Concepts | | | | |
| Solves Word Problems | | | | |
| Reasons Well in Problem Solving | | | | |

EFFORT: Needs Improvement   Improving   Good   Excellent

Teacher Comment:

### SOCIAL STUDIES, SCIENCE, HEALTH

TOPIC_____

| | Experiencing Difficulty | Beginning to Develop | Developing Satisfactorily | Highly Developed |
|---|---|---|---|---|
| Participates in Class Discussions and Activities | | | | |
| Shows Understanding of New Facts / Concepts | | | | |
| Classifies and Records Information | | | | |
| Produces Worthwhile Projects | | | | |

EFFORT: Needs Improvement   Improving   Good   Excellent

Teacher Comment:

TOPIC_____

| | Experiencing Difficulty | Beginning to Develop | Developing Satisfactorily | Highly Developed |
|---|---|---|---|---|
| Participates in Class Discussions and Activities | | | | |
| Shows Understanding of New Facts / Concepts | | | | |
| Classifies and Records Information | | | | |
| Produces Worthwhile Projects | | | | |

EFFORT: Needs Improvement   Improving   Good   Excellent

Teacher Comment:

---

## Assessment and Evaluation

Portfolios provide student assessment for our primary teams; language arts checklists are used at all three instructional levels. Samples of student writings are collected three times a year starting with kindergarten.

## WORK HABITS

| | Experiencing Difficulty | Beginning to Develop | Developing Satisfactorily | Highly Developed |
|---|---|---|---|---|
| Is Organized | | | | |
| Plans, Organizes and Carries Through on Tasks | | | | |
| Strives for Neat Accurate Work | | | | |
| Listens for Information | | | | |
| Follows Oral Directions | | | | |
| Follows Written Directions | | | | |
| Works Independently | | | | |
| Completes Homework | | | | |
| Makes Responsible Decisions and Choices | | | | |

Teacher Comment:

## SOCIAL DEVELOPMENT

| | Experiencing Difficulty | Beginning to Develop | Developing Satisfactorily | Highly Developed |
|---|---|---|---|---|
| Communicates Ideas, Info. and Needs Effectively | | | | |
| Demonstrates Self-Confidence | | | | |
| Cooperates with Others | | | | |
| Displays Sensitivity and Respect for Others | | | | |
| Exhibits Self-Control | | | | |

Teacher Comment:

Your child is receiving additional instruction in:
- Resource Room_____  • Reading Center_____  • Math_____
- Speech/Language_____  • Writing_____

### MESSAGE TO PARENTS

Continuous progress, non-graded education is based on the premise that children learn most successfully when they are working at their own levels of ability. Whenever possible, students move through our continuum without regard to age or grade barriers. Students do not compete with and are not compared to other students but do compete with and are compared against their own measured abilities and achievements.

The philosophy of this progress report is consistent with the belief that children should not be compared. Each pupil should be judged according to the best that he or she is capable of doing. We believe that all children are capable of demonstrating excellence in effort and so the 'N' 'I' 'S' 'E' key is used.

### GLOSSARY
- **Inquiry Skills** - Obtaining Data, Organizing Data, Analyzing Data, Predicting and Evaluating
- **Listening Behaviors** - Eye Contact, Looks at Speaker, Proper Body Position and Facial Expression, Offers Feedback
- **Genre** - Type or style of reading material
- **Comprehension** - Constructs Meaning, Develops Interpretations, Makes Judgements
- **Reading Strategies** - Decoding, Self-Correction, Prediction, Rate, Re-Reading/Reading On, Self-Monitoring
- **Writing Mechanics** - Punctuation, Capitalization and Sentence Structure

### PARENT COMMENTS
*Your comments are appreciated*

Parent's Signature_____

Child's Signature_____

Date_____  Days Absent_____  Days Tardy_____

Assigned to:_____

☐ Check here if you would like a conference appointment

Revised 2/95

## LAKE GEORGE ELEMENTARY SCHOOL

### INTERMEDIATE I PROGRESS REPORT

Alex Lanfear

STUDENT'S NAME_____

CLUSTER_____

TEAM_____

DATE_____

---

## LANGUAGE ARTS

| Basal Skill Level | 7 | 8 | 9 | 10 | 11 | 12 |
|---|---|---|---|---|---|---|
| Spelling | | B | C | D | | E |

*Unmarked items are not being considered at this time*

| | Experiencing Difficulty | Beginning to Develop | Developing Satisfactorily | Highly Developed |
|---|---|---|---|---|
| Demonstrates Appropriate Listening Behaviors | | | | |
| Articulates Ideas Clearly | | | | |
| Makes Relevant Contributions to Discussions | | | | |
| Orally Responds to Literature | | | | |
| Speaks Confidently Before a Group | | | | |
| Reads a Variety of Genre * | | | | |
| Chooses a Variety of Reading Levels | | | | |
| Selects Appropriate Reading Material | | | | |
| Is Able to Read for Various Purposes | | | | |
| Uses a Variety of Reading Strategies * | | | | |
| Comprehends What Has Been Read * | | | | |
| Writes for Specific and Personal Purposes | | | | |
| Responds Effectively to Literature in Written Format | | | | |
| Pieces are Well-Developed and Organized | | | | |
| Takes Risks as a Writer | | | | |
| Uses the Process Writing Approach | | | | |
| Demonstrates Use of Reference Materials | | | | |
| Participates Effectively in Writing Conferences | | | | |
| Applies Writing Mechanics | | | | |
| Displays Legible Handwriting | | | | |
| Uses a Variety of Spelling Strategies | | | | |

EFFORT:  Needs Improvement   Improving   Good   Excellent

* See Glossary for Further Explanation

### Student's Name_____

### LANGUAGE ARTS - Con't

Teacher Comment:

### MATHEMATICS

| Book | | | | | | | | | | | Experiencing Difficulty | Beginning to Develop | Developing Satisfactorily | Highly Developed |
|---|---|---|---|---|---|---|---|---|---|---|---|---|---|---|
| Chapter Completed | 1 | 2 | 3 | 4 | 5 | 6 | 7 | 8 | 9 | | | | | |
| | 10 | 11 | 12 | 13 | 14 | 15 | 16 | 17 | 18 | | | | | |

| | Experiencing Difficulty | Beginning to Develop | Developing Satisfactorily | Highly Developed |
|---|---|---|---|---|
| Has Mastery of Basic Number Facts ( + - ) | | | | |
| Has Mastery of Basic Number Facts ( x ÷ ) | | | | |
| Demonstrates Accurate Computation Skills | | | | |
| Understands Concepts Presented | | | | |
| Understands Word Problems | | | | |
| Uses a Variety of Problem Solving Strategies | | | | |

EFFORT:  Needs Improvement   Improving   Good   Excellent

Teacher Comment:

## SOCIAL STUDIES, SCIENCE, HEALTH

TOPIC_____

| | Experiencing Difficulty | Beginning to Develop | Developing Satisfactorily | Highly Developed |
|---|---|---|---|---|
| Participates in Class Discussions and Activities | | | | |
| Shows Understanding of New Facts / Concepts | | | | |
| Uses Inquiry Skills to Solve Problems * | | | | |
| Participates Effectively in Group Activities | | | | |

EFFORT:  Needs Improvement   Improving   Good   Excellent

Teacher Comment:

TOPIC_____

| | Experiencing Difficulty | Beginning to Develop | Developing Satisfactorily | Highly Developed |
|---|---|---|---|---|
| Participates in Class Discussions and Activities | | | | |
| Shows Understanding of New Facts / Concepts | | | | |
| Uses Inquiry Skills to Solve Problems * | | | | |
| Participates Effectively in Group Activities | | | | |

EFFORT:  Needs Improvement   Improving   Good   Excellent

Teacher Comment:

TOPIC_____

| | Experiencing Difficulty | Beginning to Develop | Developing Satisfactorily | Highly Developed |
|---|---|---|---|---|
| Participates in Class Discussions and Activities | | | | |
| Shows Understanding of New Facts / Concepts | | | | |
| Uses Inquiry Skills to Solve Problems * | | | | |
| Participates Effectively in Group Activities | | | | |

EFFORT:  Needs Improvement   Improving   Good   Excellent

Teacher Comment:

---

We use the Computer Management System (Addison-Wesley) in mathematics. The system records pre- and post-test results, providing a printout for students, parents, and teachers of the students' mastery of identified math objectives. Reading and writing cards trace mastery of skills in the area of language arts. Parents receive progress reports three times yearly. Parent-teacher and parent-teacher-student conferences take place in November and December, with 99 to 100 percent parent participation. In addition, parents are

## WORK HABITS

| | Experiencing Difficulty | Beginning to Develop | Developing Satisfactorily | Highly Developed |
|---|---|---|---|---|
| Is Organized | | | | |
| Strives for Neat Accurate Work | | | | |
| Comes Prepared with Necessary Materials | | | | |
| Listens for Information | | | | |
| Attends During Instruction | | | | |
| Follows Directions | | | | |
| Works Independently | | | | |
| Completes Classwork | | | | |
| Completes Homework | | | | |

Teacher Comment:

## SOCIAL DEVELOPMENT

| | Experiencing Difficulty | Beginning to Develop | Developing Satisfactorily | Highly Developed |
|---|---|---|---|---|
| Talks at Appropriate Times | | | | |
| Demonstrates Self-Confidence | | | | |
| Cooperates with Others | | | | |
| Displays Sensitivity and Respect for Others | | | | |
| Exhibits Self-Control | | | | |
| Demonstrates Self-Motivation | | | | |

Teacher Comment:

### MESSAGE TO PARENTS

Continuous progress, non-graded education is based on the premise that children learn most successfully when they are working at their own levels of ability. Whenever possible, students move through our continuum without regard to age or grade barriers. Students do not compete with and are not compared to other students but do compete with and are compared against their own measured abilities and achievements.

The philosophy of this progress report is consistent with the belief that children should not be compared. Each pupil should be judged according to the best that he or she is capable of doing. We believe that all children are capable of demonstrating excellence in effort and so the 'N' 'I' 'G' 'E' key is used.

Your child is receiving additional instruction in:

• Resource Room_____    • Reading Center_____    • Math_____

• Speech/Language_____    • Writing_____

### PARENT COMMENTS
*Your comments are appreciated*

Parent's Signature_____

Child's Signature_____

Date_____    Days Absent_____    Days Tardy_____

Assigned to:_____

☐ Check here if you would like a conference appointment

Revised 2/95

## LAKE GEORGE ELEMENTARY SCHOOL
### INTERMEDIATE II PROGRESS REPORT

*Stuart Lake*

STUDENT'S NAME_____

CLUSTER_____

TEAM_____

DATE_____

---

## LANGUAGE ARTS

| Basal Skill Level | 10 | 11 | 12 | 13 | 14 |
|---|---|---|---|---|---|
| Spelling | C | D | E | F | G | H |

*Unmarked items are not being considered at this time*

| | Experiencing Difficulty | Beginning to Develop | Developing Satisfactorily | Highly Developed |
|---|---|---|---|---|
| Demonstrates Appropriate Listening Behaviors | | | | |
| Expresses Ideas Clearly | | | | |
| Makes Relevant Contributions to Discussions | | | | |
| Presents Information Orally | | | | |
| Reads a Variety of Literature | | | | |
| Reads at Appropriate Levels | | | | |
| Reads for Various Purposes | | | | |
| Accomplishes Independent Reading | | | | |
| Comprehends What Has Been Read | | | | |
| Understands Literary Concepts | | | | |
| Responds Effectively to Literature in Written Format | | | | |
| Uses Process Writing Approach | | | | |
| • Can Organize Thoughts and Ideas Before Writing | | | | |
| • Converts Ideas into Coherent First Draft | | | | |
| • Participates Effectively in Writing Conferences | | | | |
| • Revises Writing to Improve Content and Organization | | | | |
| • Edits Work to Improve Spelling, Punctuation, Grammar | | | | |
| • Shares Final Writing Piece | | | | |
| Demonstrates Mastery of Assigned Spelling Words | | | | |
| Applies Spelling Skills in Written Work | | | | |
| Displays Legible Cursive Handwriting | | | | |

EFFORT:   Needs Improvement   Improving   Good   Excellent

Student's Name _____

### LANGUAGE ARTS - Con't

Teacher Comment:

### MATHEMATICS

| Book | | | | | | | | |
|---|---|---|---|---|---|---|---|---|
| Chapter Completed | 1 | 2 | 3 | 4 | 5 | 6 | 7 | 8 |
| | 9 | 10 | 11 | 12 | 13 | 14 | 15 | 16 |

| | Experiencing Difficulty | Beginning to Develop | Developing Satisfactorily | Highly Developed |
|---|---|---|---|---|
| Has Mastery of Basic Number Facts (+ - x ÷) | | | | |
| Demonstrates Accurate Computation Skills | | | | |
| Understands Concepts Presented | | | | |
| Solves Word Problems | | | | |
| Uses a Variety of Problem Solving Strategies | | | | |
| Demonstrates Mental Math and Estimation Skills | | | | |

EFFORT:   Needs Improvement   Improving   Good   Excellent

Teacher Comment:

## SOCIAL STUDIES

| | Experiencing Difficulty | Beginning to Develop | Developing Satisfactorily | Highly Developed |
|---|---|---|---|---|
| Participates in Class Discussions | | | | |
| Shows Understanding of New Facts / Concepts | | | | |
| Participates Effectively in Group Activities | | | | |
| Demonstrates Use of Reference Materials | | | | |
| Takes Notes and Uses the Information Effectively | | | | |
| Comprehends Materials Read in Social Studies | | | | |
| Writes Reports, Reviews, Summaries, Essays | | | | |

EFFORT:   Needs Improvement   Improving   Good   Excellent

Teacher Comment:

## SCIENCE / HEALTH

| | Experiencing Difficulty | Beginning to Develop | Developing Satisfactorily | Highly Developed |
|---|---|---|---|---|
| Participates in Class Discussions | | | | |
| Shows Understanding of New Facts / Concepts | | | | |
| Applies Inquiry Skills to Solve Problems | | | | |
| Demonstrates Use of Reference Materials | | | | |
| Participates Effectively in Group Activities | | | | |
| Takes Notes and Uses the Information Effectively | | | | |
| Comprehends Materials Read in Science/Health | | | | |
| Writes Reports, Labs, Reviews, Summaries | | | | |

EFFORT:   Needs Improvement   Improving   Good   Excellent

Teacher Comment:

---

encouraged to meet with their child's teacher at any point during the school year.

We do not give students letter grades when reporting students' progress. We do not compare students with the ability of other students, but evaluate them on how well they do in comparison with their own ability. The message of letter grading is that no matter how hard you work, you will never be as good as someone else. Grading students and promoting self-concept are not compatible.

Students of Lake George Elementary School enjoy learning and are challenged by learning, because they know they will be judged successfully if they give us their best effort. Many teams send home weekly, biweekly, or monthly folders with samples of the classroom work and checklists covering work habits and academic performances.

In addition to the regular classroom progress report, parents receive individual reports in art, music, physical education, gifted and talented, and remedial instruction. State standardized tests are annually shared with parents and with the general public. Curriculum committees yearly perform itemized analysis of our state tests in reading, writing, math, social studies, and science. These analyses help us identify areas of weakness and result in changes in all curriculum areas.

State testing in social studies only takes place at level six. We are piloting our own social studies testing at levels two and four, that is, at the end of our primary and our intermediate II groupings. State testing in science is administered at level four. We have developed science testing for our primary and intermediate II students. Our test designs are congruent with the state model and allow us to monitor student progress in these areas throughout the youngsters' elementary school experience.

## Shared Decision-making

Decision-making at our school is centered with the Educational Cabinet, which is composed of elected team coordinators from each of the four clusters, an elected representative of the special education/remediation teams, and a representative of the teachers of art, music, physical education, and health. It is led by the elementary school principal, who has agreed to share any decisions that the teachers want to share, and to make any decisions that they want him to make.

The rationale for the Educational Cabinet is that:

- Cooperative decisions represent the best thinking of several people rather than one individual.
- People who must operate under a decision should have a part in making this decision.
- Commitment to a representative decision is always more persuasive than commitment to administrative decree.

The Cabinet's responsibilities include: establishing school-wide goals and objectives; coordinating curriculum to be consistent with established goals; planning, monitoring, and assessing implementation of the non-graded/continuous progress model; coordinating school-wide in-service; and monitoring and regulating its home-school community program.

Individual teaching teams monitor results of the annual standardized tests, student questionnaire, and parent survey, and build goals and objectives around identified weaknesses. They provide feedback on the effectiveness of faculty and in-service meetings and assess the performances of the elementary principal, psychologist, administrator/coordinator of the High Potential program, educational communications director, librarian, speech therapist, reading teacher, counselor, language arts coordinator, and teacher assistants/aides, as well as substitute teachers.

Teachers may also develop their own method of professional evaluation for the purpose of self-improvement. Staff members are a part of the interviewing teams for the selection of new teachers, assistants/aides, principal, and superintendent.

# Student Discipline

"It's exciting to see how many of the students care about what they're doing." "Every child was on task. The school is very productive; one can see this very quickly." "Children all well-behaved and on task and excited about learning."
*—Comments from 1991 visitors.*

Building respect and trust between staff and students is a basic principle at our school. However, the school's environment is not permissive or undisciplined. When necessary, students receive a high degree of teacher direction.

Our overall approach to discipline is the recognition and reinforcement of positive behaviors. Students gain recognition in our school by doing what is right rather than what is wrong. Positive behaviors are reinforced by phone calls to parents, comments on progress reports, oral comments at parent conferences, and name recognition in our daily bulletins and monthly newsletters.

Rules and procedures are clearly written in the student handbook, which states consequences for misbehavior. Whenever possible, rules are written in statements that tell students what they should do rather than what they should not do. At the beginning of each school year the handbooks are sent home to be reviewed by both parents and students. Parents then sign the handbooks, confirming that they are knowledgeable of the contents. Handbooks are returned to school to be used as a reference by the students for the remainder of the school year. In addition, parent handbooks are distributed to all student homes.

Team teaching in an open plan school allows students to experience adults working with each other in a cooperative way. It is excellent modeling for all students. Our school-wide goals and objectives require each teaching team to develop a minimum of three programs and activities to improve student self-concept, behavior, and independent skills. These must be explicitly taught and modeled; we cannot assume that as youngsters move through our elementary school and get older they will acquire these skills.

We have adopted the BEST program (Building Esteem in Students Today). The program is from the Institute of Human Resource Development, Notre Dame, Indiana. It features monthly themes which include the topics of responsibility, courtesy, honesty, health and drug prevention, goal setting, caring and sharing feelings, esteem, and school climate. The program provides teaching teams with useful classroom activities involving thinking skills, life skills, cooperative learning, and creative writing.

The areas of "sound character, democratic values, ethical judgment, good behavior, and the ability to work in a self-disciplined, purposeful manner" is assessed and monitored by the following questions which are part of our annual parent survey:

"The teachers in our school are concerned about my child  as an individual."
"Discipline seems fair and consistent."
"School rules and regulations affecting students in our school are reasonable."

Since between 81 and 95 percent of our parents respond to our survey, we feel that the responses reflect an accurate assessment of our parent population.

The following items are included in the student questionnaire completed anonymously by all our students ages 8 to 12:

"Do you try your best in school?"
"At school are you taught to be kind, thoughtful, and cooperative?"
"At school do other people really care about you?"
"In your class do you get a chance to make some decisions together?"
"Do students in your class obey the teacher?"
"Does your teacher unfairly punish the whole class?"
"Does your teacher favor some children over others?"
"When you do something wrong, does the teacher correct you without hurting your feelings?"

Students learn values and commitment to others through our school-wide participation in the following programs: Jump Rope for Heart, Operation Santa Claus, the Cerebral Palsy Skate-a-thon, the Walk-a-thon for the March of Dimes, sharing of gifts with St. Colman's Orphanage, and the collection of goods for the Estherville Animal Shelter and the Lake George food pantry.

Other major factors contributing to order and discipline throughout the school include:

- high expectations that students will behave well
- staff accepting responsibility to change students' behavior rather than simply punishing them
- the examples of positive behavior by our older students
- the excellent support and high expectations of our parents
- consistent enforcement of rules and procedures
- the understanding that students working successfully at their own levels of ability experience less tension and frustration and consequently create fewer discipline problems.

## Process for School Improvement

Charles Callahan, site visitor during our 1985-86 recognition procedure, stated,

> The principal has initiated an extensive network of monitoring—a kind of process evaluation—that on literally a day-to-day basis generates very specific feedback on how the school is doing . . . . It is a very large school with a complex system of evaluation and feedback where very little that goes on anywhere in the school is not monitored and adjusted on the basis of experience.

School improvements take place through the interaction of individuals. At Lake George Elementary School interaction is continuous. It takes place on all levels and in many ways; that is, teacher to teacher through teaming, student to teacher through daily group meetings, teacher to administrator through the educational cabinet, self-directed staff-development plans, committee chairpersons, faculty meetings, and feedback sheets. Interaction occurs daily; sometimes it is formal and other times informal.

Improvements happen formally by cabinet and/or school board action; by recommendations resulting from analysis of test results or studies from our various school or district committees; or by recommendations from the elementary principal as a result of feedback, tallies, suggestions from students or PTA representatives, or results of parent or student surveys.

Feedback sheets (written reactions) are used in the following ways:

- All cabinet, faculty and in-service meetings are assessed for stating and meeting objectives, being on-task, etc.
- Assembly presentations are evaluated by both teachers and students, relating to its effectiveness.
- Teachers evaluate the effectiveness of substitute teachers.
- Substitute teachers react to the teachers' lesson plans, what was covered during the class sessions, and the behavior of the students.
- Visitors to the school react to the purpose of their visit, general impressions of the school, and ways to improve our visitation program.
- Parents may respond on many issues in feedback sheets contained in our newsletters or annually in our parent survey.

The participation of the state and national recognition program is another form of our school improvement process. Our educational cabinet defined the following as rationales for repeating our involvement in the School Recognition Program:

"To assist us in identifying areas of needed growth for continuing school-wide improvements. To assure ourselves that we are maintaining a high level of excellence."

## Parental Choice

Since all our classrooms are multiage, parents do not have a choice between single-grade and multiage classrooms for their children. However, parents of incoming kinder-garten children do select their choice of one of the three multiage kindergarten clusters, after which the kindergarten teaching team groups the students for our primary classes, making them as heterogeneous as possible. The team considers which clusters the brothers and sisters of the kindergartners presently attend (in our family grouping plan, most parents want their siblings in the same cluster) and how students rate on our learning style profile, which identifies the dependent versus the independent. The team also considers speech and academic ability, the students' present reading ability, and whether or not they are identified as special needs students. Lastly, we are interested in seeing that the boy/girl ratio is somewhat equal in each primary team.

Parents of children of all ages have a choice of which teaching team they want to work with their child. We prefer that if parents want to make choices they should do so prior to the first of June for the coming school year. However, parents may make the choice to have their child with a particular teaching team at the end of the year or at any time during the school year. Presently about 18 percent of our kindergarten parents choose which teaching teams will instruct their children, while about one percent of our 1-6 population express a choice.

The opportunity for parent choice helps build an accountability system that motivates teaching teams to be successful with each child. Since parents are not told what professional doctor or lawyer they may or may not use, we feel they also have the right to select the professional teachers best suited to work with their children.

## Parent Involvement

At our 1986 National School Recognition ceremony, Mayor Robert M. Blais stated, "The parents are not only invited, but are persuaded to come and take part in the activities of the school. Our elementary school has asserted pressure on the teachers to teach, the students to learn and the parents to participate. This is a formula that I'm sure is often sought in all the school systems but seldom achieved as we have here."

Parental involvement continues to be a high priority at Lake George Elementary School. Parental collaboration, planning, feedback, decision-making, and involvement is achieved by a number of procedures and strategies. Our annual parent survey is responded to by better than 80 percent of our parents. It surveys such topics as:

"Our school is doing a good job of teaching children in the basic skills of reading, writing and math."
"There is an effort on the part of the school to help students to be kind, thoughtful, and cooperative."
"Teachers are responsive to parental concerns and questions."

Other topics refer to communication, school rules, discipline, responsiveness of the principal, time spent on homework, progress reports, etc. There are also two open-ended topics: "What do you like about the Lake George Elementary School?" and "What improvements do you feel are needed?" Results are compared with previous years' and presented to the school board, the educational cabinet, and the PTA executive board. Individual teaching teams are given their results in comparison to other teaching teams and their own previous years' results.

The school supports an extremely active PTA, and the principal works closely with the executive board. One hundred percent of our teaching staff are PTA members, with dues being paid by our local teachers' association. A large percentage of our teaching assistants and teacher aides are selected from our community of school parents.

Parents of Lake George Elementary School students are involved in many aspects of their children's school experience. Parents are included as members of decision-making committees dealing with such issues as the hiring of a superintendent of schools and a district principal, changes in our progress reports, our gifted and talented students, and the adaptation of an AIDS curriculum. Parents have presented lessons to our students on a variety of topics ranging from Alaska to the peregrine falcon. Parents volunteer as classroom aides, work in the library, and help supervise our book fairs. In addition to being field trip chaperones and homeroom mothers, parents coach our Olympics of the Mind teams, work with students on keyboarding skills, and meet with groups of teachers visiting our school.

Parents are always welcome in our school building. They are encouraged to observe lessons, and on several occasions parents have spent an entire day with their child. Ninety-four percent of those families responding to our parent survey agreed that they feel comfortable and welcome when visiting our school. Ninety-nine to 100 percent of our parents attended parent conferences, about 80 percent attended Let's Get Acquainted Nights, and 90 percent attended our open house.

A key to our strategy for parent relations is direct communication. We accomplish this by person-to-person contacts, using written communication as a last resort.

*Critics of whole language procedures often misunderstand what the strategies of process learning have to offer children at risk, insisting that these children in particular require the security of highly structured programs to succeed. On the contrary . . . it can be said with confidence that those children most at risk are the ones most deeply threatened by lack of purpose and wholeness in their engagements with the problems of becoming literate.*

*— Don Holdaway, Independence in Reading. Portsmouth, NH: Heinemann, 1990.*

## WRITING PROFILE

**INTERMEDIATE I**

AUTHOR: _____

+ Excellent
✓ Adequate
- Needs improvement

Revised 1994

| | | FALL | WNTR | SPRG | FALL | WNTR | SPRG | FALL | WNTR | SPRG |
|---|---|---|---|---|---|---|---|---|---|---|
| | DATE: | | | | | | | | | |
| | TCHR: | | | | | | | | | |
| **WRITING PROCESS:** Organizes thoughts and ideas before writing | | | | | | | | | | |
| Converts ideas into coherent first draft | | | | | | | | | | |
| Participates effectively in writing conferences | | | | | | | | | | |
| Revises to improve content and organization | | | | | | | | | | |
| Vocabulary | | | | | | | | | | |
| Sentences | | | | | | | | | | |
| Details | | | | | | | | | | |
| Conclusion | | | | | | | | | | |
| Paragraphs | | | | | | | | | | |
| **EDITS WORK TO IMPROVE:** Spelling | | | | | | | | | | |
| Punctuation | | | | | | | | | | |
| Grammar | | | | | | | | | | |
| Capitalization | | | | | | | | | | |
| Completes writing pieces | | | | | | | | | | |
| Shares/Publishes work | | | | | | | | | | |
| Zaner-Bloser Handwriting Rating | | | | | | | | | | |
| Displays legible handwriting in everyday work | | | | | | | | | | |

## CLARIFICATIONS

*Teachers should leave blank any area which is not appropriate to evaluate.*

| | |
|---|---|
| Writing conferences | Author is cooperative and prepared for teacher/student and peer conferences |
| Revises | Author is able to improve drafts independently, as well as use teacher/peer suggestions |
| Vocabulary | Author uses descriptive, varied language: tries out new words. |
| Sentences | Author writes well-formed sentences |
| Details | Author is able to develop ideas with support material ( details, examples, reasons, explanations, etc.) |
| Paragraphs | Author writes well-formed paragraphs |
| Spelling | Spelling is appropriate for age level |
| Punctuation | Punctuation is appropriate for age level. |
| Capitalization | Author uses capitals to begin sentences, and capitalizes other words appropriate for age level |
| Completion | Author brings most pieces to a final draft, within a reasonable amount of time |

## COMMENTS

DATE:_____

TCHR:_____

DATE:_____

TCHR:_____

DATE:_____

TCHR:_____

DATE:_____

TCHR:_____

164

# READING DEVELOPMENT CHECKLIST

NAME_____

Revised 1994

KEY
+    consistently uses
✓    beginning to use
-    does not use
(blank)    not appropriate to evaluate

| | FALL | WNTR | SPRG | FALL | WNTR | SPRG | FALL | WNTR | SPRG |
|---|---|---|---|---|---|---|---|---|---|
| DATE: | | | | | | | | | |
| TEACHER: | | | | | | | | | |
| **STAGE I - THE BEGINNING READER** | | | | | | | | | |
| Enjoys listening to literature | | | | | | | | | |
| Voluntarily chooses to look at books | | | | | | | | | |
| Understands environmental print and common words | | | | | | | | | |
| Has favorite stories and wants to hear them repeatedly | | | | | | | | | |
| Can orally retell a story read to them | | | | | | | | | |
| Can orally react to a story read to them | | | | | | | | | |
| Responds to literature in a creative manner | | | | | | | | | |
| Reads by matching memory of selection with words on the page | | | | | | | | | |
| Makes meaningful word predictions using context and syntax clues | | | | | | | | | |
| Views self as reader | | | | | | | | | |
| **SHARED BOOK EXPERIENCE** | | | | | | | | | |
| Listens attentively | | | | | | | | | |
| Joins in when able | | | | | | | | | |
| Can follow a line of print | | | | | | | | | |
| Responds to questions, text and picctures | | | | | | | | | |
| **STAGE II - THE DEVELOPING READER** | | | | | | | | | |
| Recognizes rhyme, repetition and rhythm | | | | | | | | | |
| Reads some print independently | | | | | | | | | |
| Is acquiring sight words | | | | | | | | | |

| | FALL | WNTR | SPRG | FALL | WNTR | SPRG | FALL | WNTR | SPRG |
|---|---|---|---|---|---|---|---|---|---|
| DATE: | | | | | | | | | |
| TEACHER: | | | | | | | | | |
| Uses picture clues | | | | | | | | | |
| Uses semantic clues | | | | | | | | | |
| Uses syntax clues | | | | | | | | | |
| Uses graphophonic clues | | | | | | | | | |
| Draws on prior experiences | | | | | | | | | |
| Makes meaningful substitutions when reading | | | | | | | | | |
| Notices miscues if they interfere with meaning | | | | | | | | | |
| Engages in reading independently | | | | | | | | | |
| Can respond to a story orally | | | | | | | | | |
| Can respond to a story in other forms (written, pictures, etc.) | | | | | | | | | |
| Selects appropriate books | | | | | | | | | |
| Takes risks as a reader | | | | | | | | | |
| **STAGE III - THE INDEPENDENT READER** | | | | | | | | | |
| Is expanding sight vocabulary | | | | | | | | | |
| Appropriately uses cueing systems (semantic, syntax, graphophonic ) | | | | | | | | | |
| Selects appropriate reading material | | | | | | | | | |
| Reads silently | | | | | | | | | |
| Self-corrects for meaning | | | | | | | | | |
| Comprehends at different levels (literal, interpretive, critical) | | | | | | | | | |
| Comprehends what has been read: can respond to a story orally and in written format | | | | | | | | | |

COMMENT

DATE_____

TCHR_____

_____

DATE_____

TCHR_____

_____

## EMERGENT AUTHOR PROFILE

LEVEL OF WRITING READINESS
Draws picture and
A) orally labels/discusses
B) labels by scribbling
C) composes with recognizable letters

* consistently uses
✓ beginning to use
- does not use

AUTHOR _____

| | Falll | Wntr | Sprg | Fall | Wntr | Sprg | Falll | Wntr | Sprg |
|---|---|---|---|---|---|---|---|---|---|
| Date: | | | | | | | | | |
| Teacher: | | | | | | | | | |
| Verbally expresses thoughts and ideas in an organized manner | | | | | | | | | |
| Level of writing readiness* | | | | | | | | | |
| Writes upper case letters | | | | | | | | | |
| Writes lower case letters | | | | | | | | | |
| Left to right directionality | | | | | | | | | |
| Top to bottom directionality | | | | | | | | | |
| Leaves spaces between words | | | | | | | | | |
| Reads back own writing | | | | | | | | | |
| Level of spelling development | | | | | | | | | |
| Uses temporary spelling effectively | | | | | | | | | |
| Spells sight words correctly | | | | | | | | | |
| Uses spelling resources for unfamiliar words | | | | | | | | | |
| Sentence sense | | | | | | | | | |
| Uses multiple sentences | | | | | | | | | |
| Demonstrates a storyline | | | | | | | | | |
| Chooses to share own writing | | | | | | | | | |
| Capitalization | | | | | | | | | |
| Punctuation | | | | | | | | | |
| Handwriting rating/ Uses penmanship skills | | | | | | | | | |
| | | | | | | | | | |

### Level of Spelling Development

A. No correlation between letters and sounds
**Generally spells a word by using:**
B. Initial consonants
C. Initial and final consonants

D. Initial, final, and middle consonants
E. Vowel placeholder
F. Mostly standard spelling

Revised 1994

167

# CLARIFICATIONS

## TEACHERS SHOULD LEAVE BLANK ANY AREA WHICH IS NOT APPROPRIATE TO EVALUATE

<u>Writes lower case letters</u>  Independently writes legible letters without rotations or reversals.
<u>Writes upper case letters</u>  Independently writes legible letters without rotations or reversals.
<u>Level of writing readiness</u>  Using the three readiness levels identified, mark A, B, or C to indicate where the author generally functions.
<u>Left to right directionality</u>  Writes sequentially from left to right.
<u>Top to bottom directionality</u>  Uses writing space from top to bottom.
<u>Reads back own writing</u>  Can read own writing aloud, if asked.
<u>Level of spelling development</u>  Using the developmental stages identified on the other side, mark A-F to indicate typical spelling in writing pieces.
<u>Spells sight words correctly</u>  Generally spells high-frequency words (often phonically irregular) correctly.
<u>Spaces between words</u>  Generally leaves spaces between words.
<u>Sentence sense</u>  Haw a feeling for the sentence as a unit of meaning.  Avoids fragments and run-ons.
<u>Uses multiple sentences</u>  Generally writes pieces of two or more sentences.
<u>Demonstrates a story line</u>  Usually develops and sticks to a single sequenced story line.
<u>Handwriting rating</u>  Rating scale based on Zaner-Bloser handwriting models.
<u>Uses penmanship skills</u>  Handwriting is legible.
<u>Capitalization</u>  Author uses capitals to begin sentences, and capitalizes other words appropriate for age level.
<u>Punctuation</u>  Punctuation is appropriate for age level.
<u>Chooses to share</u>  Often wishes to publish or orally share pieces.
<u>Uses temporary spelling effectively</u>  Adults able to read writing.

## COMMENTS

DATE_____

TCHR_____

DATE_____

TCHR_____

DATE_____

TCHR_____

DATE_____

TCHR_____

DATE_____

TCHR_____

DATE_____

TCHR_____

# Reading Development Checklist
## Intermediate I

NAME _____

| | Fall | Wntr | Sprg | Fall | Wntr | Sprg | Fall | Wntr | Sprg |
|---|---|---|---|---|---|---|---|---|---|
| Date: | | | | | | | | | |
| Team: | | | | | | | | | |

*Stage III-The Independent Reader*

**Vocabulary**

**Uses a variety of reading strategies**

| | | | | | | | | | |
|---|---|---|---|---|---|---|---|---|---|
| decoding | | | | | | | | | |
| self correction | | | | | | | | | |
| prediction | | | | | | | | | |
| rate | | | | | | | | | |
| background information | | | | | | | | | |
| rereading | | | | | | | | | |
| reading on | | | | | | | | | |
| self-monitoring | | | | | | | | | |
| content | | | | | | | | | |

**Reads a variety of genre**

**Reads a variety of levels**

**Selects appropriate reading materials**

**Able to engage in reading independently**

**Shows commitment to a book**

**Able to read for various purposes**

**Comprehension--literal:**

| | | | | | | | | | |
|---|---|---|---|---|---|---|---|---|---|
| tells main idea | | | | | | | | | |
| recognizes plot | | | | | | | | | |
| relates story sequence | | | | | | | | | |
| locates specific details | | | | | | | | | |
| identifies setting | | | | | | | | | |
| identifies characters | | | | | | | | | |
| reads and follows directions | | | | | | | | | |

**Comprehension--interpretive:**

| | | | | | | | | | |
|---|---|---|---|---|---|---|---|---|---|
| draws conclusion | | | | | | | | | |
| predicts outcomes | | | | | | | | | |
| understands cause and effect | | | | | | | | | |
| understands figures of speech | | | | | | | | | |
| infers meaning from context | | | | | | | | | |
| distinguishes between relevant and irrelevant information | | | | | | | | | |

**Comprehension--critical:**

| | | | | | | | | | |
|---|---|---|---|---|---|---|---|---|---|
| understands point of view of character | | | | | | | | | |
| makes judgments | | | | | | | | | |

# Lake George Elementary School Computer Outcome Report

Student Name _____   Date _____

*Date with month/year when evidence of completion is shown*

## Primary Objectives

### COMPUTER OPERATION

_____ 1. Student can identify the main parts of the computer including the CPU, monitor, disk drives, mouse, CD-ROM drive, and printer and can demonstrate knowledge of what they do.

_____ 2. Demonstrates the ability to properly handle and store computer software and CD-ROMs.

_____ 3. Student can start the computer up and given a selected program, can operate it successfully, quit when finished and shut the computer off.

### USE OF SOFTWARE FOR REINFORCEMENT

_____ 4. Uses computer programs prescribed by the teacher (or self-selected) for developmental and/or remedial instructional purposes.

## Intermediate I Objectives

### COMPUTER OPERATION

_____ 1. Student can identify and explain the following terms: software, hardware, files, programs, 3.5" disks, 5.25" disks, hard drive.

### TECHNOLOGY

_____ 2. Student can identify two ways technology has had a positive effect on our lives

### WORD PROCESSING

_____ 3. Student has produced two word-processed pieces of writing on the computer using a word processing demonstrating the ability to: create and name the file accordingly, save the file to disk. They should also demonstrate the ability to open existing word processing files, modify them, save changes and print.

### SELECTION OF APPROPRIATE HARDWARE/SOFTWARE

_____ 4. Student is able to choose the proper computer/software/printer combination to complete a classroom-related project.

### USE OF SOFTWARE FOR REINFORCEMENT

_____ 5. Uses computer programs prescribed by the teacher for developmental and/or remedial instructional purposes.

*NOTE: All writing pieces completed on the computer may be placed in the student's writing folder.*

## Intermediate II Objectives

### COMPUTER OPERATION

___ 1. Student can identify and explain the following terms: RAM, ROM, CD-ROM disks and drives, bits, bytes, megabytes, binary system, modem, telecommunications, printers (dot matrix, inkjet and laser), network, and system software (DOS, Windows, System 7, ProDOS).

### TECHNOLOGY

___ 2. Student will write a paragraph using a word processing program, telling how technology has changed the way we live today and why it is so important to our everyday life. *Optional: Have student use the computer and software to produce a project related to technology. Teachers may give their students some latitude in their design of this project.*

### WORD PROCESSING

___ 3. Student will produce a minimum of four word-processed pieces of writing on the computer using a word processing program, demonstrating the ability to: create and name the file accordingly, save the file to disk. They should also demonstrate the ability to open existing word processing files, modify them, save changes, use save as command, and print. In addition, at this level students need to show the ability to change the size and type of font in at least two of the pieces. They should also be able to demonstrate the use of a spell checker to proofread their work.

### DATA BASE

___ 4. Student can demonstrate the use of a data base program such as Filemaker, MacWorld, MacUSA to gather information on a selected topic.

___ 5. Student is able to use one of the CD-ROM reference disks to collect information on a selected topic. They should also be able to produce a file using the copy and paste commands.

### SELECTION OF APPROPRIATE HARDWARE/SOFTWARE

___ 6. Given a school-related project, be able to identify a program/computer/printer combination to accomplish the task. Student should be able to explain why the selection was made.

### USE OF SOFTWARE FOR REINFORCEMENT

___ 7. Uses computer programs recommended by the teacher for developmental and/or remedial instructional purposes.

### COMPUTER GENERATED ART

___ 8. Student will produce one piece of computer-generated art composed on Claris Works or a similar program in the classroom or in the Art Room. This can be in relation to work in any area of the school curriculum.

171

Madrona School is a Pre-K through 8th grade age, nongraded, multiaged school. We currently have 639 students. Our minority population is about 11 percent, with most of these being Asian, Hispanic, Native American and African American, in that order. The "free and reduced" lunch average is about 15 percent of the total population.

Students served range from severely physically and mentally disabled to the academically gifted and talented. We have 31 teachers and specialists on staff.

Our school began operating multiage classrooms in 1983 with two primary (1-2-3) centers and one intermediate (4-5-6) center. We are currently entering our twelfth year.

## Why Multiage?

In 1982-83, our school community did an extensive study of our school to establish some baseline data about the success of our students and to determine the perceptions of our parents, staff and community about the school.

At the same time we began a two-year study on effective educational practices and brain research, and made many visits to successful schools. We formed study groups as well as a site council to make recommendations for change—if needed.

We found that we needed to provide additional choices to our parents, students, and teachers. Our research suggested that nongraded, multiage classrooms would be a viable option for parents and staff. Our goal was to have choice within our building—not to change the entire school organization. After five years our school split into two separate schools, one graded and one nongraded and multiaged, because of increasing numbers of students entering the area.

## Parents Choose Multiage

We no longer have graded classrooms in our school. By choice, parents in our school began to select nongraded, multiage classrooms over graded classrooms. Students in these classrooms did better academically and socially; parents were impressed and wanted this option expanded. Before our schools split into two separate schools we had expanded the multiage offerings to 80 percent of our students and classrooms.

In the summer of 1988 our school population increased from 486 to 750 students with the opening of three large apartment complexes; our site-based decision (with school board support) was to split our school into two separate schools, one graded and one nongraded and multiaged. At this time Madrona Nongraded School was born and we became a magnet school for our school district, open to everyone.

Madrona has three early childhood centers, eight primary centers, eight intermediate centers, three middle school centers, and one special-needs classroom for severely disabled primary-aged students. The classes are composed as follows:

(3)   Pre-K/Kindergarten Centers serving 92 four- and
       five-year-old students

*Our goal was to have choice within our building—not to change the entire school organization.*

(3) Primary Centers, Team Taught, serving 144 six- , seven- , eight-, and some nine-year-old students. (Each center has 48 students and two teachers)

(1) Primary Center (with one teacher) serving 24 seven- , eight- , and some nine-year-old students.

(1) Primary/Intermediate Center, with two teachers, serving 52 seven- , eight- , nine- , ten- , eleven- , twelve- , and some thirteen-year-old students.

(2) Intermediate Centers, Team Taught, serving 56 ten- , eleven, twelve- , and some thirteen-year-old students.

(3) Intermediate Centers, Single Teacher, serving 168 ten- , eleven- , twelve- , and some thirteen-year-olds (56 students and one teacher in each center)

(3) Middle School Core Groups serving 140 students aged twelve, thirteen, and fourteen. (approximately 48 students and two teachers in each core)

## Philosophy

We follow the philosophy of nongraded education, which includes multiage practices as a viable organization.

## Staff Development

Prior to beginning each staff member did a self-assessment related to his or her individual background, assessing knowledge and skill related to each teacher's: understanding of nongraded and multiage philosophy; brain research; integrated learning; multiple intelligences; classroom management; instructional strategies; classroom environment; assessment and evaluation; and curriculum. Each staff member established personal professional growth plans to address over a number of years.

As a school we began by doing visits to other schools in order to help develop our vision. We decided that the number one priority for staff development was in learning more about the learning process and how it occurs within students. We particularly focused on brain research, integrated learning and learning styles. This became the foundation training needed to begin our new multiage, nongraded centers.

## Curriculum and Assessment

Our curriculum is partly based on our state's articulation of "essential learnings," as well as our school district's work on establishing standards and assessment options. Given all this, our school strives to offer a curriculum that is meaningful and flexible enough to meet differing needs and interests. In addition to guidelines provided from state and district sources we listen to our parents and community to help establish basic curriculum options. Our basic philosophy related to instruction is "Constructivist." We believe learning should take place in a meaningful context. We emphasize:

**MADRONA SCHOOL**

9300 236th St. SW
Edmonds, WA 98020

**Phone: 206-670-7979**
**FAX: 206-670-7985**

**Fully Multiage**
**Multiage groupings**
(by age): 4-5, 7-9, 7-13, 10-13, 12-14

**Open to visiting teachers and administrators**

**Contact:**
Joe Rice, Principal
Sherie Wahl,
Office Manager

- Teachers as facilitators
- self-directed learning
- integrated instruction/curriculum
- peer tutoring
- team teaching
- cooperative/collaborative learning
- classroom meetings
- parent/community networks
- direct instruction for basic skill development

and much more. We utilize lots of strategies, depending on the situation and need. (See "The Curriculum," and "The Instructional Strategies.)

Our assessment and evaluation procedures are varied and fairly comprehensive. They include the following four components:

- Observation of Process (watching kids work);
- Observation of Products Produced (assessment of work produced by students daily, projects, etc.);
- Classroom Assessments (teacher-made tests, end of chapter assessments, etc.; and
- Standardized Assessments/Tests (Levels Testing, CTBS, Annual 5th grade writing exam, etc.

The majority of our assessment efforts are built into daily work and not seen as a separate function. We generally do not have end-of-trimester exams in order to complete report cards and give grades. Teacher and students know exactly how they are doing through daily observation of process and products produced (see "The Assessment and Reporting.")

## The Madrona School Advantage

We have a school where students, parents and teachers have all chosen to be. We provide a choice within our school district for those wanting and perhaps needing an alternative to the "normal" school organization. We have students achieving at very high levels academically and are leading each to be self-directed learners. We are also utilizing parents as partners in the educational process and this is an important part of our success. Our greatest success is that we have a school based on what a community envisioned and worked to create. Teachers, students, parents and the community planned and implemented our nongraded, multiage organizational structure. We proceeded in a measured and organized fashion and based what we wanted on the research related to learning and the learner.

## Specialists in the Classroom

We do not separate the students into first, second and third grades as we send them to their "specials." The specialists have the same training and knowledge that the regular classroom teachers have related to working with multiage classrooms of students. The specialists focus on meeting the needs of the individual student instead of looking at them as a group of the same age needing the same thing at the same time. The planning is more difficult and time-consuming, but they feel the multiage classrooms bring them the same advantages that the regular teacher sees.

## Special Needs Students

Special needs students are handled in the same manner as other students. We try to match them up in a center that has room and is appropriate for their needs. We consider the need for a single room or a team-taught, double-size room with twice the number of students. Our special education teachers generally work within each classroom instead of using a pull-out model of service. This seems to work best to meet the needs of students and teachers. There are occasionally exceptions, and these students may be pulled aside for specific direct instruction where a quiet place is called for. Our learning support specialists work with the regular classroom environment as an additional teacher. Together the specialist and classroom teacher find the best way to meet the needs of students within the classroom. Our learning support teachers are all cross-funded from a combination of funding sources (special education, learning assistance, regular education, etc.) to allow for flexibility while working in each classroom.

## Inclusion

We do believe in and practice a more inclusive type of program. It works well for the great majority of special needs students. There are occasions when this is not the case and students need a separate place for work and study. Madrona has one classroom of severely disabled students that spend most of their time in that classroom and are then mainstreamed out for as much time as possible. This time varies from student to student.

Flexibility is the key in our school. Do what works best for the student instead of buying into one philosophy or program choice.

## Class Sizes a Challenge

Our class sizes are still too large to do all that we would like to do with our students. In addition, our multiage, nongraded program seems to be drawing a larger percentage of students with special needs. Parents perceive that a continuous progress program with students of varying ages is better for their child—offering more opportunities to be successful, moving ahead as skills are mastered instead of a grade level expectation. All of this is, of course, true, but also true for all students regardless of abilities and needs. We worry about maintaining balance within each classroom. Up to this point in time we have never had to 'skip' students on the waiting list based on special needs.

## Team Teaching

Team teaching is an element of our program. We have found that the ability of a multiage teacher to meet the needs of his or her students is enhanced when the teachers work as a team. In our school this takes the form of actual team teaching (two teachers working together with two classrooms combined) and with teams of teachers working in their individual classrooms but working collaboratively in planning and lesson development. Most of our classrooms are team-taught, with two teachers physically working with a larger number of students. Teachers take on the role of facilitator, provide direct instruction, monitor students working independently, and so on. Teachers identify their own teaching styles and try to match up with students who learn best in the manner in which they teach. All in all it is somewhat different in each classroom.

These teachers treat all of their students as theirs and do not separate them into the younger and older groups.

## Grouping for Instruction

Grouping can be done on the basis of need, ability, achievement, interest, study habits, learning styles, multiple intelligence groups, cooperative heterogeneous groups and even "one-person groups," in the context of the learning event. There is no one way that teachers follow exclusively. In general, we do try for smaller groups instead of whole-group instruction in order to provide more individual attention. Each classroom will utilize whole group instruction, small group instruction, peer tutoring, one-on-one instruction, students working independently, and so on. Of all the content areas Math instruction seems to be the one related most to some sort of ability grouping—even though this is not done exclusively.

## Student Selection

Our school is a magnet school (school of choice) within the Edmonds School District. Parents within the district complete a short application and come for a guided visit to the school. We compile lists of students by each grade level, with the first on the list being the first to apply.

When we have an opening for a student in the primary we go to the K, 1, 2, 3 lists and pick the first child on the list matching the age we need. The parent is contacted and offered an opportunity to join our school. We try to maintain balance within each center based on the following factors: ages represented; boy/girl mix; abilities/special needs; and diversity issues.

When we first began our program we did not have the entire school multiaged. We began with three teachers, who volunteered to teach multiage, and began by providing information to the entire school community (parents, teachers, students). Parents had a choice to join the multiage classes or stay in graded, single-aged classes.

Choice is very important! No one should be pressured to join. We believe the success of the students will be more than enough to create overwhelming interest. In our case it took four years to have 80 percent of the school multiaged. Since we've become a school of choice for the district, we now have 639 students and a waiting list of 600 students.

## Set Policy Recommended

I do recommend that a school have set policies related to student/parent selection as you begin your selection process. Make sure you have a diverse population that represents a similar mix as the single grade classrooms.

Make sure that those selecting students are from the entire school and not just the teachers teaching the class. Use the learning support teachers, principal, and other teachers as well. This will help hold down criticism when the multiage classrooms do so well—academically and socially—and focus the discussion away from "did they get the best students, the best parents, more money . . ." and so on.

## Parent Involvement

This is a very important area, and essential if you intend to do all that you want to do in your classrooms.

First and foremost, we know that parents want to be involved, but that the involvement choices need to be broad in order to match their time availability and interests. All of our centers offer opportunities for parents to work as tutors, teachers, drivers on field trips, correcting papers, doing bulletin boards and so on.

Each classroom offers a training and orientation program for the parents. We feel parents would appreciate specific jobs and tasks rather than come into a room and see what might need doing—if anything.

In addition to the above we have a fully developed school-wide volunteer program for parents and other community members headed by a paid (by the parents through fundraising) volunteer coordinator. Our coordinator works with individual room parent-coordinators and volunteers as a whole. Through this effort we promote school-wide activities such as holiday dances, fundraising, BBQ's, volunteer screening with local law enforcement (fingerprinting, background checks), parent education classes, and a host of other things. What a help this is to the teachers and principal!

## Our Biggest Obstacle

Our biggest obstacle was in providing the knowledge and skill needed through restructured training. There were not a lot of training opportunities available, especially in local teacher training institutions. We overcame this by not concentrating on nongraded, multiage training but on the training related to teaching in a multiage, nongraded environment. This meant focusing on brain research, integrated learning, learning styles, environment, and later assessment—sort of looking at the parts instead of the whole.

Another problem was related to the selection of students for the multiage classrooms— who was going to select the students? We ended up making it so that no parent, no student, and certainly no teacher would be forced to teach or learn in a multiage classroom unless he or she chose it.

Choice was the key. This also forced us to start small, instead of trying to implement it in many classrooms all at once. Setting up models and showing how they worked proved to be highly beneficial in creating interest with other teachers and parents.

## Our Biggest Challenge

Our biggest challenge seems to be finding enough TIME. Teachers need more planning time in order to do appropriate assessment activities, create curriculum, plan integrated thematic units of study, and all the other many things they need to do.

My biggest problem and concern, as a principal, is how to help them meet this need.

## No Waivers Required

I have not had to ask for any waivers on any law or procedure assessed by local or state agencies. In the very beginning we developed a comprehensive plan that articulated what we wanted to do to make our school better for students and our community. This plan was presented to the Superintendent and School Board. Because of the support we had gathered within our school and community, there were no problems in getting the go-ahead. The key is focusing on what is best for kids and having a support base of your teachers, parents and community.

# NONGRADING – A DEFINITION

Nongrading is a vertical pattern of school organization. It serves to move pupils upward from the time they enter school until the time they leave it. It provides for the continuous, unbroken upward progression of all pupils, the slowest and the most able.

## PHILOSOPHY STATEMENTS

1.  The role of the school is to develop self-directed independent learners.

2.  Each learner is entitled to an unbroken, continuous progression of learning steps. Each child should be under the right amount of pressure — not too much, as is the slower learner in the graded school, nor too little, as is the talented learner in the graded school.

3.  All students can learn, given the appropriate conditions. Suitable provision is made, in all aspects of the curriculum, for each unique child, including flexible groupings, curriculum, and instructional approaches.

4.  Students develop at different rates. The successive learning experiences of each student will be, to the greatest possible extent, pertinent and appropriate to the needs at the moment. Student needs, not teacher convenience or administrative convenience, guides the program.

5.  Children have different learning styles. Methods of instruction should be consistent with learning style differences.

6.  Children learn from each other. Peer tutoring, cooperative learning, and group projects are valuable tools in learning.

7.  Promotions and retentions are inconsistent with continuous progress. Success, with appropriate rewards, is assured for all kinds of learners as long as they attend to their tasks with reasonable diligence and effort.

8.  Students should be evaluated objectively according to their own potential, never compared. The reporting system is consistent with the philosophy that each child is a unique and precious individual. No A, B, C, D, and F report cards.

9.  Parents, students, and teachers share equal responsibility for the education of the students. Team participation is necessary for the full educational potential of the learner to be reached.

10. There is a more sophisticated curriculum planning, evaluation, and record-keeping on the part of the teacher than one normally finds in graded schools.

# MADRONA SCHOOL
# MULTI-AGE CONTINUOUS PROGRESS

## KEY ELEMENTS

✧ Shared Vision
Shared Commitment
Shared Decision Making
Shared Accountability

✧ Organizational Changes
- Multi-aged family units staffed by teacher teams
- Eliminate grade level distinctions

✧ Environment
- Room redesign — brain compatible
- Multi-aged — students stay within family for 2-3-4 years
- Inclusive

✧ Expanded Curriculum
- Multiple resources
- Integrated thematic curriculum
- Address social, aesthetic and physical development as well as academic concepts and skills
- Build upon the uniqueness of each child and each teacher
- Technology enhancements
- Foreign language instruction

✧ Varied Teaching Strategies
- Constructivist
- Teachers as facilitators plan, guide and modify instruction
- Self-directed learning
- Integrated thematic instruction
- Peer tutoring
- Performance based
- Team teaching
- Cooperative/collaborative learning
- Classroom meetings
- Parent/community networks

✧ Learning Styles
  • Reading styles (Carbo), learning style (Dunn), 4MAT (McCarthy), etc.
  • Multiple intelligences

✧ Internal/External Mentorship
  • Central focus for professional development
  • Develop teacher trainers/coaches
  • Network with others — share vision, expertise

✧ Assessment and Evaluation
  • New reporting system for parents — narrative, related to specific goals
  • System approach to assessment and evaluation —
      — observation of process (anecdotal records, interviews, conferences)
      — observation of products (reading logs, learning logs, audio tapes, interest inventories, self-assessments, performances, exhibitions, checklists, portfolios, video
      — classroom measures (end of chapter assessments, spelling tests, unit tests, etc.
      — criterion referenced testing, state or district mandated testing

✧ Assess What We Really Value
  • Knowledge
  • Risk taking
  • Collaboration
  • Self-confidence
  • Generative
  • Thoughtful
  • Resourcefulness
  • Organization
  • Industrious

✧ Partnership with Parents and Community

# THE CURRICULUM

The curriculum is the critical component of a school program. It must be flexible enough to serve all the needs of all students. It must promote growth along both horizontal and vertical lines. It must be current, encompassing critical issues. It must build process skills and higher order thinking skills. It must reflect current research on learning. It must allow the learner to build new learning upon past learning in a continuing fashion. It should allow concepts and skills to be developed in a wide spectrum of areas. It must promote the continuous learning of students of widely varying interests and abilities.

**It is our goal to design and implement a curriculum that:**

- Allows students a continuous progression of learning
- Has subject areas integrated into thematic units
- Builds on students' interests and sense of wonder
- Uses children's literature as its language focus
- Offers a multitude of resources and choices for students
- Emphasizes all communication skills in a whole language approach
- Includes self-pacing programs for continuous and individual progress
- Accommodates the varying learning styles and intelligences of the students
- Emphasizes higher order thinking skills
- Focuses on concepts and processes rather than isolated facts
- Provides enrichment and opportunities for acceleration of learning
- Will give students the opportunity to design curriculum when appropriate
- Expands basic curriculum areas to include technology and keyboarding

# THE INSTRUCTIONAL STRATEGIES

Traditional instructional strategies no longer meet student needs in our rapidly changing society. Current knowledge in brain research and learning mandates significant changes in the way students are taught, the activities they use, and the role of the classroom teacher. The philosophy of our program will determine the direction of these changes.

**It is our goal to implement instructional strategies that:**

• Change the teacher's role to facilitator rather than the source of knowledge

• Produce cooperation rather than isolation

• Allow students to learn from each other through peer tutoring

• Give students responsibility and independence in both learning and behavior

• Build understanding of action-consequence relationship

• Provide choice to the student in different areas of learning that will reflect learning-style differences

• Allow continuous learning through the use of learning centers

• Involve parents in classroom activities

• Give students responsibility and ownership of their environment

• Teach goal-setting from an early age

• Provide opportunities for mentorship

• Build leadership in all students

# THE ASSESSMENT AND REPORTING

Authentic assessment is centered around goals and is consistent with what we know about learning. It reflects the student's learning over time rather than at an arbitrary point. The reporting of pupil progress involves the use of a number of assessment tools. Students take an active role in evaluating their own progress and participating in conferences with parents.

**It is our goal to implement assessment strategies which include:**

- Elimination of retention

- Elimination of all comparision grading

- The use of student portfolios

- Student self-evaluation

- Reporting the mastery of individual learning objectives

- Student-maintained record-keeping systems

- Narrative reporting

- Student recognition program for all

- Student involvement in conferences with parents

- The use of performances or demonstrations

- The use of checklists to record progress

- Measuring progress according to goals

- Measuring progress according to movement along the continuum

- Peer Evaluation when appropriate

The Grand Blanc School District is a suburban district south of Flint, Michigan and north of the Pontiac/Detroit area. We have 5,700 students enrolled in five elementary schools, one middle school, and one high school. Our district has about 15 to 20 percent Black, Asian, Hispanic or other minority cultures. Our socio-economic climate runs the spectrum from wealthy to welfare.

A pilot multiage program was started at Reid Elementary in 1993 because we felt the students were boxed into a set graded curriculum, dictated down from the high school level. Our high school staff were not aware of what a kindergarten student was capable of doing or learning. We wanted to take the ceiling of learning off at each grade level and felt the best way to accomplish this was a multiage classroom. We had some teachers interested in trying this new adventure.

The mission of our school district says we will develop our students to their highest potential. The multiage classrooms use this as a philosophy and commitment. We believe students should be able to go beyond the core curriculum in both a horizontal and vertical enrichment curriculum. The graded classrooms are still following a lock-step core curriculum. Therefore, the multiage classroom is an alternative school within a school.

Reid Elementary has two multiage classrooms of three grade levels—third, fourth, and fifth—representing a student age range of seven through eleven. Our sister schools in the district, Cook Elementary and Myers Elementary, who began multiage in 1994, have one and two multiage classrooms, respectively.

Our district has many split classes of two grade levels. In the Grand Blanc District you have to have three grade levels in a classroom in order to be considered multiage.

### Staff Development

The most important qualification to teach multiage was a desire to change. We have no set requirements for staff development. Some of the teachers have become workshop junkies, while others are going at a slower pace. The district requires five staff development workshops: ITIP, Learning Styles, Cooperative Learning, Writing Workshop, and Creative Thinking/Problem Solving.

### Curriculum and Assessment

Our district has an Advisory Curriculum Council which is responsible for the district's core curriculum. Each teacher has latitude to develop enrichment to expand the core curriculum. The multiage classes use a developmentally appropriate program and individualize the curriculum. Many units are developed around a theme. Active learning and hands-on learning are encouraged. Rubrics are used for assessment and student-led conferencing is used to communicate with the parents.

### Team Teaching

Reid and Myers Elementary Schools both use team teaching. Teams are very carefully chosen and the teachers flow back and forth working to the strengths of each teacher.

### Enrichment Program

We meet the needs of all students in the class, and have an enrichment program for students who are above grade-level, offering curriculum above and beyond what most

*We believe students should be able to go beyond the core curriculum in both a horizontal and vertical enrichment curriculum.*

students receive. For instance, during the last school year a tutor came in to teach three fifth-graders seventh-grade algebra. We would also meet students' needs in reading.

One goal is to provide enrichment for all students through involvement with the community, parents, and business. Our multiage class is currently involved with the Business Department of the University of Michigan, which is helping the students produce and market an invention that the students are really excited about. The University has written a grant to obtain start-up funds for the students and will continue to be involved in all aspects of the business.

## Specialists in the Classroom

Art is taught by the classroom teachers. The multiage students are part of the regular school schedule for music and gym. The special education and Spanish specialists come right into the classroom.

## Inclusion

We have an inclusion program for our special-needs students. Even though the multiage classrooms have their share of special-needs students, there seems to be a perception by the special ed teachers that these students don't need as much service and therefore some needs are not met. Parents then have to decide whether to keep their child in the program or not. Very few parents have withdrawn their children.

## Parental Choice

Parents have a choice of placing their child in either a single-grade or a multiage classroom. When children enter the class at the third grade level, the school has been in the position of drafting one or two students in order to make the class size comparable to other classes. The principal and teachers collaborate to choose the students, then approach the parents and give them the final choice.

Once in, the students (and their parents) want to remain in the multiage class, so there is usually no opportunity for students to enter the class at the fourth or fifth grade level.

## Our Biggest Obstacle

Selling our ideas to the administration and curriculum council was our biggest problem when we started. It still is a problem. But, we now have a problem with the Middle School in that there is not a classroom with the same opportunities at the next level. We are working on having an alternative multiage program at the Middle School level.

We still have a parent education problem with the students that are assigned to the program. It takes constant parent counseling to get them up to speed with the program.

## Our Biggest Challenges

One of the goals of our multiage program is to improve the reading, writing, math and science scores on our Michigan Educational Assessment Program (MEAP) test.

We are also interested in expanding the enrichment program beyond the regular classrooms through involvement with the community, parents, and business.

## REID ELEMENTARY

2103 Reid Road
Grand Blanc, MI 48439

**Phone: 810-695-5103**
**FAX:  810-695-3288**

**Multiage groupings**
(By grade level): 3-4-5

**Open to visiting teachers and administrators**

**Contact:** Julie Martin or Charlee Litten

There are 250 students in grades K-12 in Rochester, Vermont. Ninety-nine percent of them are white.

Multiage education came into the Rochester School at the middle school level four years ago. Teachers and parents were noticing social interaction and behavior difficulties among students, which accelerated at the seventh grade level because of the homogeneous grouping and the fact that the same mix of kids are together from kindergarten through the twelfth grade. Categorization of students, cliques, and inappropriate behavior patterns emerged. The multiage configuration gave us an opportunity to adjust these social patterns and begin to mix kids creatively.

All middle school classes are multiage. All courses—reading, math, social studies, science, writing, Tech Ed, health, P.E., art, music, living arts and French—are taught in a multiage setting. We evenly mix the number of sixth, seventh and eighth graders in each group as well as male/female ratios. Students are rated (1,2,3) based on academic, socio-emotional, and cooperative skills, and mixed heterogeneously into groups.

### Staff Development

None. We did course work in thematic, interdisciplinary integrated curriculum and realized that it didn't really matter what grade the student was in, but rather where his or her instructional level was.

### Curriculum and Assessment

We use a three-year rotating curriculum which is theme-based. Every student will do all of the curriculum over the three years rather than a specific curriculum for a specific grade. Authentic assessment, rubrics, and projects are used extensively. Cooperative group learning is key in accommodating individual needs. Team teaching is a must as well as block scheduling.

The academic program at the middle school has two phases: the core curriculum phase and the exploratory phase.

*Core Curriculum Phase:* The Middle Level Education Program at Rochester provides its students the opportunity to:

1. Master basic skills in subject areas;
2. Develop effective communication skills, both oral and written;
3. Develop skills in the following areas:
   - A. Problem solving
   - B. Analyzing
   - C. Critical Thinking
   - D. Decision Making
   - E. Investigation
4. Accept accountability for their performance; and
5. Develop values through clarification.

*The multiage configuration gave us an opportunity to adjust these social patterns and begin to mix kids creatively.*

*Exploratory Phase:* Students will be exposed to a variety of learning situations and experiences that will cultivate their own special interests, aptitudes, and talents. An exploratory approach to the curriculum is essential for active participation.

## Grouping for Instruction

We group cooperatively, individually in math skills, and randomly. We use rubrics that set standards and students work to their ability.

## Positive Discipline

We work with middle school students extremely well. We provide flexibility, try to meet their individual needs, and empower them to be part of the decision-making process. We also use a [William] Glasser model discipline system, so that students will accept responsibility for their behavior. A student-centered discipline approach which involves making both oral and written plans has replaced the detention/rulebound system of past years.

Students are challenged at all levels—much more so than in a traditional, homogeneously mixed, mini high school. Students, teachers and parents seem happy with our program.

## Communicating with Parents

Most parents are eager for their child to enter the multiage environment for different social interactions. We keep the lines of communication open with parents with our school newspaper, letters home, report cards and conferences.

## Specialists in the Classroom

All special subjects (music, art, P.E.) are taught in a multiage setting, and the specialists have changed their curriculum to accommodate this. The first year we did multiage, some special subjects did not have a multiage environment, and negative behavior patterns reemerged. In the second year, all subjects were held in multiage classes.

## Inclusion

In this program we consider all students to have "special needs." Special education services are integrated within the classes during Blocks A and B (see daily schedule). Special education teachers and aides float among the groups of students, working in the classroom with all students and classroom teachers. During Short Block (see schedule) some students eligible for education are part of a pullout model for special instruction. During C Block other students who are eligible for special education receive support services.

The multiage program lends itself to inclusion; the challenge is to meet the specific needs of all students whether they are "coded" or not.

## Team Teaching and Cooperative Learning

Team teaching and cooperative learning are used extensively in the middle school. Reading, social studies and math problem solving use teacher-designed cooperative lessons as well as a formal cooperative learning package—TAI Math. TAI is an acronym for Team Accelerated Instruction, which was developed by Robert Slavin at Johns Hopkins University. A math

**ROCHESTER MIDDLE SCHOOL**

Route 100
Rochester, VT 05767

Phone: (802) 767-3161
FAX: (802) 767-1130

Multiage Groupings
(by grade level): 6-7-8

Open to visiting
teachers and
administrators

Contact:
Dave Allen
Debbie Matthews
Ilene Levitt

problem-solving program has been developed to accompany TAI, since it is only a skills program. Since we are a small school and teach both middle and high school, we team teach in many different combinations. Team size varies from two to seven teachers depending on the group. The team teachers decide collaboratively how each student's time will be spent.

## Our Biggest Obstacle

Our biggest obstacle was the K-5 teachers who did not want the multiage environment. Many of these teachers were also parents who were afraid that their smart kids would not have their needs met or would be mixed with the acting-out kids. We overcame this by doing a very successful multiage interdisciplinary trial unit that culminated in a play.

## Our Biggest Difficulty

Our biggest difficulty is transitioning students in and out of the multiage environment. Fear and prejudice affect transitions in, and some (not all) homogeneous high school classes affect transitions out. Negative self-esteem and old behavior patterns return with homogeneous grouping. i.e., high school English and math.

## No Waivers

We didn't ask permission or think of getting waivers of local or state mandates in putting together our multiage program. We just went ahead and did it. We also wrote a new curriculum.

Report prepared by Dave Allen and Debbie Matthews.

*Voices*

*The inclusive classroom is based on rights, learning and relationships. Mara-Sapon-Shevin (1991) argues that all children have the right:*

- *to learn with their age peers*
- *to be engaged in learning that is appropriate to their skills and needs*
- *to learn in heterogeneous groups as part of social learning*

*To these, we would add the following, and they will be critical to the teaching and learning processes developed in this book:*

- *teachers are facilitators of learning, not just givers of knowledge*
- *all children have gifts and their diversity enriches both learning and teaching*
- *authentic learning requires a positive self-esteem*
- *all children have the right to learn in a safe and welcoming environment*
- *parents of special needs children have a unique knowledge of, and deep commitment to, the education of their children*
- *educating special needs children is mutually beneficial for all concerned*
- *support must be provided*

*— Greg Lang and Chris Berberich,*
*All Children are Special:*
*Creating an Inclusive Classroom.*
*York, ME: Stenhouse Publishers, 1995.*

# Middle School Students
# Working in Cooperative Groups

All students are responsible for:

1. Listening to other team members;
2. Encouraging equal participation of all group members;
3. Staying on task;
4. Praising each other's successes;
5. Helping teammates with tasks;
6. Taking notes and getting handouts for absent members;
7. Being aware of adjusting your noise level;
8. Completing team tasks on time.


A cooperative group must fill each of the following roles:

| | |
|---|---|
| **Recorder:** | record ideas, decisions, products |
| **Gofer:** | find and get needed things |
| **Timekeeper:** | keep group on time and meet deadlines |
| **Taskmaster:** | keep everyone in the group on task |
| **Reporter:** | summarize and report to class and teacher as required |
| **Praiser:** | help and encourage all members of the group |
| **Checker:** | check for understanding and group agreement |


How to work in cooperative groups

1. Always meet at the beginning of the period to check organization for that day. Anyone absent? Who will fill in?

2. Get daily report back from Mr. Zucca. **Reporter** reads any teacher comments. Group reviews what must be done during the period.

3. After discussion, **Taskmaster** divides up the work. **Timekeeper** reminds everyone of when things must be done.

4. Work proceeds as planned.

5. **Timekeeper** reminds everyone of deadlines as needed.

6. At prearranged time, group reconvenes for daily report.

7. The whole class begins closure process. **Reporters** read daily report and turn it in to Mr. Zucca.

## BOOK CONTRACT EVALUATION

**Student:**_____          **Group Members:**

_____

_____

_____

### Focus Questions

| 1. | 2. | 3. | 4. |
|---|---|---|---|
| Student answered some of the questions, and/or did not follow the format. | Student followed the format and answered most of the questions, but did not complete all of the questions. | Student completed all of the focus questions in narrative form (2-5 sent.) with appropriate capitalization & punctuation. | Student met the requirements of level three and excelled in some way. |

### Glossary

| 1. | 2. | 3. | 4. |
|---|---|---|---|
| Student defined less than 25 words and/or did not follow the format. | Student defined most of the words from the list including the part of speech and a sentence. | Student defined all of the words from the list including the part of speech and a meaningful sentence. | Student met the requirements of level three and excelled in some way. |

### Project

| 1. | 2. | 3. | 4. |
|---|---|---|---|
| Student did not develop a project, and/or developed one which did not convey knowledge about the book. | Student developed a project which is connected to the book, and that conveys some knowledge about the book. | Student developed a project which is clearly connected to the book, and that conveys a thorough knowledge about the book. | Student met the requirements of level three and excelled in some way. |

### Presentation

| 1. | 2. | 3. | 4. |
|---|---|---|---|
| Student did not have project to present and/or there was no explanation about the story elements or how the project is related to the book. | Student presented project and knowledge about the book, but did not include story elements and/or how the project is related to the book. | Student presented project and knowledge about the book which included information about the story elements and explained how the project is related to the book. | Student met the requirements of level three and excelled in some way. |

|  | Focus Questions | Glossary | Project | Presentation |
|---|---|---|---|---|
| Group Score |  |  |  |  |
| Individual Score |  |  |  |  |
| Teacher Score |  |  |  |  |
| Overall Score |  |  |  |  |

# Ancient History, Change, Process, and Challenges:

## The Rochester Middle School Since 1988

| School Year | Schedule | Grouping & Students | Curriculum & Teaching Styles | Teacher Comments |
|---|---|---|---|---|
| 1993-94 | 3>90 minute blocks<br><br>1>50 minute block | — Truly heterogeneously mixed student groups, all ability levels grades 6-8 for A, B, and C Blocks.<br>— Students grouped by grade level in S- Block (for French only). | — Overall MS faculty planning improved.<br>— Instructional pairs work/ plan better.<br>— More cooperative learning.<br>— Better flexibility and use of resources towards overall curriculum goals. | — "The High School is becoming more like a second Middle School!"<br>— "What grade is she in?!" |
| 1992-93 | 3>90 minute blocks<br><br>1>50 minute block | — Four heterogeneously mixed student groups, grades 6-8. No ability or Grade Level classes for A, B, and S Blocks.<br>— Students grouped by Grade level during C-Block | — Curriculum Team taught and planned: A and B - Block teams of four, divided into sub-groups of two daily teaching partners with 36 students each block.<br>— Much summer and afterschool work, great creativity and stress. | — "Remember when we always spent the first four months complaining about the sixth graders?"<br>— "What are we going to do about C-Block?" |
| 1991-92 | Eight Period Day, 42 Minute Classes | — First Semester: By Grade and/or Ability Levels, Grades 6-8.<br>— Second Semester: Experimental Multi-Age and Ability Groups in some classes. | — Curriculum still "Traditional Junior High," but more teaming, Cooperative Learning, and Interdisciplinary work as the year progresses. | — "We might have something here . . . "<br>— "How do you break 75 kids in three different grades into four equal groups while retaining your sanity?" |
| 1990-91 | Eight Period Day, 42 Minute Classes | — By Grade and/or Ability Levels, Grades 6-8. | — "Traditional Junior High," Grade 6 more integrated, some creative "Team-building" activities, cooperative English/SS writing projects began. | — "The difference between Middle School and Junior High is we play more now — but we're still not sure about it all." |
| 1989-90 | Eight Period Day, 42 Minute Classes | — By Grade and/or Ability Levels, Grades 6-8. | — *** Rochester supposedly begins Middle School program. *** Curriculum remains "Traditional Junior High," Grade 6 Self-Contained except for Science and SS | — "So, you got stuck teaching in the Middle School? Too bad!" |
| 1988-89 | Eight Period Day, 42 Minute Classes | — By Grade and Ability Levels, Grades 7-8. | — "Traditional Junior High," Kids are treated more like "mini-High Schoolers" | — "This is the way it's always been done, and the kids usually turn out OK, so why change?" |

# Rochester Middle and High School Schedule

| |
|---|
| *A BLOCK 100 MINUTES* |
| *BREAK 20 MINUTES* |
| *B BLOCK 100 MINUTES* |
| *LUNCH 25 MINUTES* |
| *SHORT BLOCK 60 MINUTES* |
| *C BLOCK 100 MINUTES* |

## ROCHESTER MIDDLE SCHOOL STUDENT SCHEDULE

NAME_____ TA_____GRADE_____

| | | |
|---|---|---|
| A Block | Specials: Living Arts, Art, Music, Health, Physical Education | Mrs. Bushnell, Mr. Roberts, Ms. Chase, Mrs. Domas, Zeus Lary |
| B Block | Math, <br><br> Science | Mr. Swan, Mrs. Matthews Mr. Allen, Mr. Chadwick |
| S Block | Initiative, French, Keyboarding | Mr. Allen Mrs. Berube-Mayone, Mrs. Jesso |
| C Block | Reading, Writing, Social Studies Technical Education | Mrs. Matthews, Ms. Gephart, Mr. Moltz, Mr. Zucca |

**A Sample Schedule**

Middle School   1994-95   A-Block Schedule Proposal (by student group)

* key: "1,2,3" refers to the first three trimesters
  "^" separates first and second halves of the block

| Group | Monday | Tuesday | Wednesday | Thursday | Friday |
|---|---|---|---|---|---|
| A | 1 - Art/SS ^ Study<br>2 - PE<br>3 - FCS | 1 - Cooking<br>2 - Study ^ Art/SS<br>3 - Art ^ Study | Living Arts/Health | PE/Music-Chorus | PE/Music-Chorus |
| B | 1 - Study ^ Art/SS<br>2 - PE<br>3 - FCS | PE/Music-Chorus | PE/Music-Chorus | 1 - Cooking<br>2 - Study ^ Art/SS<br>3 - Art/SS ^ Study | Living Arts/Health |
| C | 1 - FCS<br>2 - Art/SS ^ Study<br>3 - PE | 1 - Art ^ Study<br>2 - Cooking<br>3 - Study ^ Art/SS | Living Arts/Health | PE/Music-Chorus | PE/Music-Chorus |
| D | 1 - FCS<br>2 - Study ^ Art/SS<br>3 - PE | PE/Music-Chorus | PE/Music-Chorus | 1 - Art/SS ^ Study<br>2 - Cooking<br>3 - Kybd ^ Art | Living Arts/Health |
| E | 1 - PE<br>2 - FCS<br>3 - Art/SS ^ Study | 1 - Study ^ Art/SS<br>2 - Art/SS ^ Study<br>3 - Cooking | Living Arts/Health | PE/Music-Chorus | PE/Music-Chorus |
| F | 1 - PE<br>2 - FCS<br>3 - Study ^ Art/SS | PE/Music-Chorus | PE/Music-Chorus | 1 - Study ^ Art/SS<br>2 - Art/SS ^ Study<br>3 - Cooking | Living Arts/Health |

**Rochester Middle School students have input into many decisions at the school, including scheduling considerations.**

193

# Rochester Middle School Curriculum

| Topic | Fall | Winter | Spring |
|---|---|---|---|
| theme | *Magic* | *Quest* | *Enlightenment* |
| event | Roman Banquet Nov. 30th | Play with Dana Yeaton | Invention Convention |
| historical period (social studies content) | ancient world — Egyptians, Macedonians, Greeks, Romans | Aztecs, Incas, & Mayans Middle Ages in Europe and Far East (400–1500) | Renaissance (1300-1800) French Revolution |
| symbol | Roman coin | coat of arms | da Vinci drawing |
| writing assignments | — Egyptian day in the life<br>— myth Greek/Roman comparison essay | — Middle Ages object point of view<br>— persuasive essay on one aspect of a culture | — research paper |
| technology | primitive tools layout pyramid Greek Arch. floor planning "Dream House" project | weapons & armor catapult competition castle architecture | problem-solving tools and materials<br><br>"INVENTION CONVENTION" |
| reading | *Lily and the Lost Boy* (required for Greece unit) + 2 choice books, fiction or non-fiction from *Magic* reading list | *Queen Eleanor* (required for Middle Ages unit) + 2 choice books, fiction or non-fiction from *Quest* reading list | 2 choice books, fiction or non-fiction from *Enlightenment* reading list |

# Geography Curriculum Outline

| Topic | Fall | Winter | Spring |
|---|---|---|---|
| teachers | | | |
| event | African night | World Travel Fair | play |
| area of the world (social studies content) | -Multi-cultural U.S.<br><br>-Africa<br><br>-Europe<br>-current events | -Asia<br><br>-Australia<br><br>-North America<br>-current events | -South America<br><br>-Central America<br><br>-Space<br>-current events |
| other subject areas-- connections | FCS--sew costumes<br>art--African masks | FCS -- food of different cultures | math & science -- space unit |
| reading | -*Chain of Fire*<br><br>+2 choice books | -*Dragonwings*<br><br>-*Walkabout*<br><br>+ 2 choice books | -*Maldonado Miracle*<br><br>-*Black Pearl*<br><br>+ 2 choice books |
| writing projects | -African Safari<br><br>-European Travel Packet (*Pagemaker*) | -Diary of an Asian Journey<br><br>-United States Road Trip<br><br>-persuasive writing | -Day in the Life (South America)<br><br>-science fiction |
| technology projects | mapping--<br>  -positioning<br>  -scavenger hunt<br>transportation--<br>  -vehicle safety & design | communications-<br>  -satellites<br>  -electronics<br><br>-Presentations for World Travel Fair | Rocketry |

# United States History Middle School Curriculum Outline

| Topic | Fall | Winter | Spring |
|---|---|---|---|
| teachers | artist-in-residence | | |
| historical period (social studies content covered in 6-week unit) | -Indians (pre-history to 1700's)<br><br>-Exploration & Colonization (1600-1770) | -American Revolution (1770-1800)<br><br>-Western Expansion & Civil War (1800-1875) | -Turn of the Century (1875-1940)<br><br>-"Late" Twentieth Century (1940-present) |
| event | Columbus play | | |
| media | | | |
| reading | -*Light in the Forest*<br>-*Pedro's Journey*<br><br>+ 2 choice books from reading list | -*April Morning*<br>-*Across Five Aprils*<br><br>+ 2 choice books from reading list | -*Story of Thomas A. Edison*<br><br>+ 2 choice books from reading list |
| writing | -Indian Letter<br><br>-Explorer's Diary | -Historical Fiction<br><br>-Civil War biography | -Invention research paper<br><br>-Field Guide to the Year ---- |
| technology | -Development of tools; Indian dwellings<br><br>-Water & Navigation; boat races | -Building & Construction; colonial village<br><br>-Communication & Information; use of *Pagemaker* | -Manufacturing & Industrialization<br><br>-Rocketry |

# Rochester Middle School Reading -- Curriculum Outline

## Ancient History & Humanities

### Year - Long Skill Objectives
- Content Area Reading
- Reading Speed and Fluency
- Reading Comprehension
- Vocabulary Development
- Oral Interactive Skills
- Study Skills / Time Management
- Written Expression
- Cooperative Learning
- Notetaking / Organization
- Map Reading Skills
- Creative Expression
- Library and Computer Research Skills
- Development of Computer Skills
- Cultural Appreciation and Tolerance
- Current Events

### Materials
- Teacher - Generated
- Trade books according to topic.
- Atlases and various map books.
- Resource center materials
- Almanacs
- Several software and CD - Rom applications on the Rochester Computer Network
- Student notebooks
- Creative and Artistic Materials

### Evaluation
- Book Contracts
- Projects
- Class Participation / Cooperative group work
- Homework completion
- Notebooks
- Effort
- Creativity
- Staying on Task

### Unit Outlines and Timeframe

**1. Prehistory and Ancient Egypt.**
One Month Unit:  Book choice and co-operative activities on  Mesopotamia, the Pyramids, Gods & Mummies, Geography, Egyptian Vocabulary, Modern Egypt, Egyptian Art & Scholarship, Archaeology.

**2. Ancient Greece.**
One Month Unit: Book *Lily and the Lost Boy* and co-operative activities on Ancient and Modern Olympics, Greek Government, Famous Greeks,  Greek Vocabulary, Greek Timeline, Modern Europe Mapping, Greek Plays, Gods & Myths, Alexander the Great, Athens & Sparta, the Trojan War.

**3. The Romans.**
One Month Unit: Book Choice and co-operative activities on Roman Vocabulary, Roman Culture and Government, Life of Roman Citizens, Christianity, Rome's Economic Triumphs and Failures, Mediterranean Geography, Roman Newspaper Project, BC / AD.

**4. The Middle Ages in Europe**
Two Months:Book *Eleanor of Aquitane* and co-operative activities on  The Crusades -- What & Where, King Henry II, Eleanor of Aquitaine, Charlemagne, the Vikings, Germanic Tribes and Peoples, Islam, William the Conqueror, Nationalism in Europe, Timelines, The Magna Carta and Parliament, Famous and Infamous Medieval People and Events.

**5. The Middle Ages in the Far East.**
One Month Unit: Book choice and co-operative activities on Chinese Dynasties, The Mongols, Oriental / Far East Vocabulary and People, Ancient Japanese Military systems (Shoguns, Samurai, ...), Japanese Feudalism, Japanese Geography, the Modern Orient.

**6. The European Renaissance.**
One and a half Months: Book *The Second Mrs. Giaconda* and co-operative activities on A Cultural Movement / Trend, Artists and Intellectuals, Intellectual Curiousity, Patrons, Nationalism and Trade, Renaissance People and Events, Geography of Renaissance Italy, Joan of Arc, the Reformation.

**7. American Aborigines.**
One and a half Months: Co-operative activities on the Incas, Aztecs, Mayas, North American Native Peoples, Gods and Culture, Natives against the White Mauraders, Year Wrap - up, Review, and Comparisons.

TYGM

# Rochester Middle School Reading -- Curriculum Outline

## Modern World / Geography

### Year - Long Skill Objectives
- Content Area Reading
- Reading Speed and Fluency
- Reading Comprehension
- Vocabulary Development
- Oral Interactive Skills
- Study Skills / Time Management
- Written Expression
- Cooperative Learning
- Notetaking / Organization
- Map Reading Skills
- Creative Expression
- Library and Computer Research Skills
- Development of Computer Skills
- Cultural Appreciation and Tolerance
- Current Events

### Materials
- Teacher - Generated
- Trade books according to topic.
- Atlases and various map books.
- Resource center materials
- Almanacs
- Several software and CD - Rom applications on the Rochester Computer Network
- Student notebooks
- Creative and Artistic Materials

### Evaluation
- Book Contracts
- Projects
- Class Participation / Cooperative group work
- Homework completion
- Notebooks
- Effort
- Creativity
- Staying on Task

### Outlines for Semester Topics / Units

**1. Fall : Continents and Oceans, Africa, and Antarctica**
Book: *Chain of Fire* and co-operative activities on Latitude and Longitude, Measuring Distance on Maps, Reading different types of Maps, Map Symbols, Scale, Using Map Grids to find Location, Introduction to the Continents and Oceans, In depth look at the nation of South Africa, Colonization, Other African Nations, Introduction to Basic Statistical Measures (Per Capita Income, Population Density, Literacy Rate, Life Expectancy, etc.), Current Trends in Africa, Issues and History of Antarctica.

**2. Winter : Europe, Asia, and Australia**
Book: *Zlata's Diary* and co-operative activities on Geographical terms, Much mapping of Europe, Statistical Comparisons of European nations, Modern European History (the demise of Communism, Bosnia, etc.), Introduction to various Environments / Topography, Focus Countries: Germany, France, United Kingdom, Russia and former USSR, India, China, Japan, Indonesia.

**3. Spring : North and South America, and the American States**
Book: *The Maldonado Miracle* and co-operative activities on Road maps, Geographical Oddities (Galapagos Islands, Easter Island, Amazon River, ...), The relationships between Political Instability and Economic Status, Native Peoples and Politics, The United States and the Americas -- Pushy or Paternalistic?, Examination / Analysis of Different Customs and their Origins / Implications, Examination / Analysis of different Socio - Political Communities (Nations, States / Provinces, Counties, Cities, Towns, Neighborhoods, In depth looks at Canada, the 50 States, and major North American Cities.

TYGM

# Rochester Middle School Reading -- Curriculum Outline

## U.S. History from a Vermont Perspective

| Year - Long Skill Objectives | Outlines for Six - Week Content Units |
|---|---|
| - Content Area Reading<br>- Reading Speed and Fluency<br>- Reading Comprehension<br>- Vocabulary Development<br>- Oral Interactive Skills<br>- Study Skills / Time Management<br>- Written Expression<br>- Cooperative Learning<br>- Notetaking / Organization<br>- Map Reading Skills<br>- Creative Expression<br>- Library and Computer Research Skills<br>- Development of Computer Skills<br>- Cultural Appreciation and Tolerance<br>- Current Events<br><br>*Materials*<br>- Teacher - Generated<br>- Trade books according to topic.<br>- Atlases and various map books.<br>- Resource center materials<br>- Almanacs<br>- Several software and CD - Rom applications on the Rochester Computer Network<br>- Student notebooks<br>- Creative and Artistic Materials<br><br>*Evaluation*<br>- Book Contracts<br>- Projects<br>- Class Participation / Cooperative group work<br>- Homework completion<br>- Notebooks<br>- Effort<br>- Creativity<br>- Staying on Task | *1. Indians and Prehistory (BC - 1600 AD)*<br>Book *Light in the Forest* and co-operative activities on Archaeology, Stages of Human Development in Vermont - - Paleo, Archaic, and Woodland Peoples, Vermont Natives, Basic VT Geography, Physiographic Regions, Timelines,<br>*2. Exploration / Colonization (1600 - 1770)*<br>Book choice and co-operative activities on Explorers, Samuel de Champlain, Investigation of other Potential VT Explorers, Forts in the Vermont Area, the New Hampshire Grants, Rogers' Rangers,<br>*3. The American Revolution and the Republic of Vermont (1770 - 1800)*<br>Co-operative activities on Troubles with NY, Ethan Allen, the Green Mt. Boys, Fort Ticonderoga, the American Revolution, Independent VT, VT Gov't, the U.S Constitution,<br><br>*4. The Nineteenth Century and the Civil War (1800 - 1876)*<br>Book *Across Five Aprils* and co-operative activities on "Freethinking" and Early Vermont Religions, 1816. Vermont Transportation, Pre - Civil War Facts & Figures, Sectional and Slavery, People and Places of the War Between the States, Civil War Timeline,<br><br>*5. The Turn of the Century (1876 - 1940)*<br>Co-operative activities on Societies, Clubs, and Spinsters, Railroading, Railroad Towns, The 1927 Flood, the Great Depression and the New Deal, the WPA, the Barre Auditorium, and the C.C.C.,<br><br>*6. Modern Vermont (1940 - Present)*<br>Book *The Story of Thomas A. Edison.* |

TYGM

The total population of our school is 421 students. Four percent of our students are Asian; 2 percent are American Indian; 26 percent are Hispanic; 35 percent are African American; and 54 percent are white. Forty-seven percent are male; 53 percent are female.

All of our students are military dependents. In order to come to Russell Elementary, they must live on the Camp Lejeune Military Base. Our school population comes from three housing developments: Watkins Village, Berkeley Manor, and Midway Park.

### Multiage at Camp Lejeune

There are two multiage teams at Russell Elementary: the "Bee Team," a primary team made up of first, second, and third graders; and the "Frog Team," made up of fourth and fifth graders. Both have been in place for three years.

The Camp Lejeune School System has had multiage teams at other schools with successful results. Establishing an intermediate multiage team at Russell Elementary resulted from two events.

First, Betty Smith, one of the founders, learned about multiage education in graduate school and had an opportunity to have discussions with veteran multiage teachers about the concept. At the same time teacher Donna Myslinski had been involved with a pilot program called "Project Child." In this program some students had already been together for two years, but were taught according to grade level. When "Project Child" disbanded because of personnel changes, Smith and Myslinski got together and created the Intermediate Multiage team for the next school year. It was a natural step to go from "Project Child" to Multiage.

### Philosophy

*The special teachers [art, music, P.E.] have experienced such benefits from our classes that they've decided to multiage their single-grade fourth and fifth grade classes as well.*

Our school's philosophy is that a multiage setting allows the students to learn according to their needs and abilities, not their chronological age. On the intermediate hall, we have three multiage classes and a team of three graded teachers. The teams work closely in order to create a community of learners. The students in the graded classrooms are multiaged with our students for social studies and science units with each of the six teachers spending five weeks with every child from both teams.

Russell Elementary currently has six multiage classrooms. The primary multiage is made up of three classrooms of second and third graders. The intermediate multiage is made up of three classrooms that consist of fourth and fifth graders.

Our students range from TMH (Trainably Mentally Handicapped) to gifted.

### Staff Development

The main staff development was provided by Betty [Smith] from what she learned from graduate classes. After beginning multiage, the first year we had an opportunity to attend a conference provided by The Society For Developmental Education, talk to other multiage teachers, conduct multiage team meetings with other schools, and observe at other schools. The multiage teachers were the ones who gave staff development to our faculty so that they could have a better understanding about multiage.

## Student Selection

Parents choose to sign their children up for either the multiage or single-grade classrooms. We have had the problem of having two many students sign up for multiage, and solve this by giving first priority to siblings of students already on the multiage team, and second priority to students who were on the primary multiage team.

## Curriculum and Assessment

Our curriculum is based on what is developmentally appropriate for each child. Our school system uses the Whole Language and Hands-On Math approach.

The students on the Frog team are taught using our fourth and fifth grade level objectives when appropriate. With some of our students, we must modify the work to make it easier, or in some cases, harder.

The students are grouped heterogeneously all day long. They are evaluated by teacher observation, cooperative learning groups, seminars, and pencil and paper tests. Our biggest emphasis is on authentic teaching and using authentic evaluation.

The students are required to take examinations based on their grade level; when it's time for standardized testing, we split our students up according to grade level.

## Grouping Students for Instruction

The students change classes throughout the day. The following is a list of classes and how they are formed.

*Social Studies/Science:* All fourth and fifth grade teachers teach Social Studies/Science. This means that students within the year will have six different subjects. The groups are formed based on the students' choice. Every student will go to all of the subjects but they have a choice of the order.

*Spelling:* The students are placed in heterogeneous groups by the teachers and change teachers every nine weeks.

*Reading:* We are very fortunate to have six teachers who help with reading, which allows for small groups. The Academically Gifted students must be together for reading and there are two teachers and one assistant who work with that group. They normally divide up into two small groups of 14. The remaining students are placed in heterogeneous groups based on the students' interests.

There are four teachers who teach the rest of the students. Three of the teachers are on the Frog team and the other teacher is a reading specialist. The teachers each choose a novel and the students choose which two of the teachers' choices they would like to read during a semester.

Each of the reading groups has approximately 12 to 14 students. Having such a small number in a reading group allows the teacher to individualize the curriculum to meet the needs of the students within her reading group. Grade level is not considered, only the students' interests and needs.

**RUSSELL ELEMENTARY SCHOOL**

798 Breater Blvd.
Camp Lejeune, NC
28547-2531

**Phone: (910) 451-3247**
**FAX: (910) 451-2200**

**Multiage Groupings**
(by grade level):
1-2-3, 4-5

**Open to visiting teachers and administrators**

**Contact:**
Dr. Judy Novicki

*Math:* Students are given a pretest and grouped in three flexible groups according to their needs. The groups change according to the concepts being taught. Grade level is not an issue when forming the groups.

*Art, Music, and Physical Education:* Our students are multiaged for their special classes. The special teachers have experienced such benefits from our classes that they've decided to multiage their single-grade fourth and fifth grade classes as well.

## Inclusion

Our team uses the Inclusion model. We heterogeneously mix students all day, except for the Academically Gifted students, who are grouped together for the Language Arts block.

Our team believes that all students should feel they belong on a team and have the opportunity to work with their peers. We modify work in the classroom to meet the special needs of the students. We do not form groups where students who have special needs are pulled out of the classroom. We want all students to feel like a "frog."

The biggest challenge we have is that one of our special-needs students must be pulled out of class for individualized math instruction each day. The classroom teachers take turns working with the child.

| CLASS SCHEDULE AND TEACHERS | | |
|---|---|---|
| **Monday:** | **Tues., Wed., Thurs,. Fri.:** | *Teachers:* |
| 8:30-8:50 Homebase | 8:30-8:50 Homebase | Social Studies/Science: |
| 8:50-9:45 Social Studies/ Science | 8:50-9:45 Social Studies/ Science | |
| 9:50-10:40 Math | 9:50-11:30 Spelling/Spanish Reading | Spelling: |
| 10:45-11:30 Clubs | | |
| 11:30-12:30 Lunch/Recess | 11:30-12:30 Lunch/Recess | Reading: |
| 12:40-1:15 Spelling/Reading | 12:30-1:20 Math | |
| 1:15-2:00 Reading | 1:25-2:10 Specials | Math: |
| 2:00-2:15 Break | 2:20-3:00 Writing Workshop | |
| 2:15-3:00 Writing Workshop | | Writing: |

## Team Teaching

Without a doubt, team teaching is the biggest benefit of working on the Frog team. At present we have a six-member team: Betty Smith, Donna Myslinski, Carolyn Davis, Stephanie Denova, and two assistants, Tina Rivera and Melissa Robinson. One of the teachers is certified to teach the gifted, one to teach reading K-12, one to teach special education, and one, a former social worker, who does very well dealing with family problems.

What makes our team so special is that we put all our talents together to provide the best education possible for our students. Our team's belief is that all of the 85 students belong to every teacher on the Frog team. We do not have a teacher who only teaches gifted students or one who only teaches the special needs students; all of the teachers teach everyone. If you were to ask a Frog student who his or her teacher is, most likely the child would name all the teachers.

We change classes for different subjects all day long so that each child has the opportunity to work with every teacher and each teacher has the opportunity to work with each child. This gives us the opportunity to modify and revise work to meet each child's needs.

We meet at least twice a week to plan and discuss team situations and events. We plan all events as a team, i.e., field trips, parties, author's teas, softball games, etc. We consider our team one big family.

The best part about our teaching team is that we are all so different in personalities and teaching styles, which allows the students to experience variety.

As teachers, we like the fact that each of us looks at things in different ways, which helps us come up with terrific ideas and solutions. We do not try to change each other, we accept each other as unique individuals. This has helped us professionally, because we realize that each child is unique and has his or her own unique personality.

## Transient Students

Russell Elementary School is located on Camp Lejeune, which is a Marine Corps base. Dealing with a transient population is a fact of our school; children come and go on a weekly basis. Children serve as tour guides to orient parents and the new student(s). They also answer questions that the student or parent may have.

Our team has a booklet explaining our program and procedures which we give to parents when they register their children. We also assign a buddy to the new student, so he or she has someone to "hang around" with. Within the first two weeks, we offer a conference to the parents to give them an opportunity to ask any questions they may have.

Our school is a very inviting place, and our goal is to make it feel like a "second home" to our parents and students. We strive to make that home-school connection, because we realize that if our parents and students feel welcome from day one, the school benefits greatly from the resulting support. And, as a school that serves a transient population, we are their support system.

We blend the fourth and fifth grade curriculums, allowing the children to work to their ability level; this way, we feel that when children are transferred out of the school they do not miss out on a chunk of their learning. When children do transfer out, the school forwards a summary of their progress as well as a teacher-written narrative of their learning in all subjects. This includes a math card, a narrative of math skills updated four times a year by the classroom teacher.

## Parent Involvement

We feel that our continuous communication with parents, peers and administration has been one of our most successful goals. Monthly newsletters and a calendar of events are sent home. A nightly homework log is sent home to be initialed by a parent. When homework or class assignments are missed, a note or phone call is made to parents. A contact log is kept on each child to be available when conferences are being held. Every teacher involved with the student is scheduled for parent meetings.

A central file is kept on each child that is filled with student work, teacher notes, etc. (When talking to parents, students and other staff members, we classroom teachers replace the pronoun "I" with "we". Practicing this concept promotes the concept of being a team.)

We always encourage parents to come in and volunteer in the classroom. We also have parents volunteer at the "teacher mart" run by the P.T.O. Our team also runs the school store, and parents volunteer to help in that.

We try to have a monthly event or activity that gets parents into the school. In the past we have held author's teas, softball games, family picnics, math day, writing stations, field trips, play performances, and Good Citizen activities. We try to get to know all of our families.

## Our Biggest Obstacle

—public relations! We had to get out the word about the multiage program to the parents and staff members. We overcame this by providing opportunities for staff and parents to learn and ask questions about the program.

## Our Biggest Challenge

—getting people to understand that we are not a combination grade and that we are not in competition with the traditional program.

Submitted by Betty Smith and Donna Myslinski

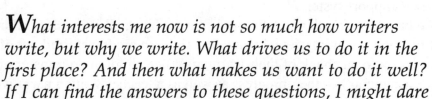

*W*hat interests me now is not so much how writers write, but why we write. What drives us to do it in the first place? And then what makes us want to do it well? If I can find the answers to these questions, I might dare to ask myself another: What are the implications for teachers of writing?. . . I'd be grateful if you'd think of yourself first as a writer and then as a teacher of writing, and ask yourself when you or your students last ached with caring over what you were writing, or wrote because it mattered, or wrote because you had a huge investment in your writing.

—*Mem Fox, Radical Reflections: Passionate Opinions on Teaching, Learning, and Living. San Diego, New York, London: Harcourt Brace & Company, 1993.*

# FROG TEAM COMPONENTS

## TEACHING TEAM

The multiage team has expanded this year to include Ms. Carolyn Davis as a result of adding a gifted class to Russell. Ms. Davis will be responsible for gifted language arts, math and economic objectives. Mrs. Rivera will continue to be the team assistant for Ms. Davis, Mrs. Smith, Mrs. Myslinski.

## SOCIAL STUDIES/SCIENCE ROTATION

The six units of social studies/science that are being taught this year are history, geology, weather, multicultural, economics and wellness. Each child in the fourth and fifth grade was involved in the scheduling of the units. The student will be involved for four to five weeks in each unit. A class project will be required for each unit. If you would like to be a guest speaker for any of these units, contact your child's homebase teacher.

## LANGUAGE ARTS

Mrs. Smith, Ms. Davis and Mrs. Myslinski will be teaching language arts using class novels, journals, newspapers and a newly purchased reading series. Each teacher has chosen novels and stories that revolve around the system wide themes of adaptation, influences and origin. Book evaluations are due the fifteenth of every month. Students are given fifteen minutes to thirty minutes a day and assigned fifteen minutes every night to read their independent books. Spelling words are made up from core lists, subject matter and writing errors. Writer's workshop implementing the writing process is the tool used to meet each child's developmental level. We will continue to have whole class lessons on grammar, punctuation and editing to meet benchmark objectives.

## MATH

The students will be divided into groups according to their needs. Math books were purchased this year as a class resource and home tool. The objectives will be taught as listed with Camp Legeune Learner Objectives but not necessarily in the same order as the book. Teachers will continue to use hands on activities, manipulatives and other resources to supplement the book.

## BOOKS

During the year your child may be issued textbooks or novels to enhance or support class instruction. We are asking that each child be responsible for the condition of the book. Covering the book with the brown grocery bags is an economical way to protect the cover. The inside pages of the book are not to be marked in any way. The cost of replacing the lost or destroyed books will be passed on to the parents. We are on a five-year book adoption process and have to keep a good year-to-year inventory.

## COMMUNICATION

We feel that our continuous communication with our parents has been one of our team's most successful goals. The homework notebook that is to be signed every night except Friday should futher enhance this goal. If you do not see your child's notebook two nights in a row and your child's teacher has not been in touch with you, please call or write a note immediately. Our policy is to contact the parent on the second day a notebook or class assignment is missing. We also try to send home good news notes or call as often as possible.

## SPECIAL EVENTS

Your child will be bringing home a monthly school and classroom calendar. We will make every effort to put on it all the events that involve our students at the school, team and class level. But always expect the unexpected when changes have to be made. When this happens, we will try to give you at least a twenty-four hour notice.

# CAMP LEJEUNE DEPENDENTS SCHOOLS

## K-12 WRITING FOLDER

Student_____

Writing is taught as a process in all classrooms in the Camp Legeune Dependents Schools. Though various parts of the process can be identified, it is important to note that these steps do not always proceed in a linear fashion. Students may move from one step to the next, then back to a step before moving on.

**Prewriting** or **rehearsal** is the stage in which students engage in activities to gather and organize ideas for writing. These ideas may come from the act of writing, from discussions with peers, from reading and listening to good literature, as well as from significant experiences students have had. During this time, writers may sketch out patterns in their ideas by drawing, talking, reading, mapping, interviewing, or engaging in other content area experiences.

**Drafting** is the writer's first effort at getting the piece on paper. At this point, nothing is permanent. In the process approach to writing, students write and refine their compositions through a series of drafts. The drafting stage is the time to pour out ideas, with little concern about spelling, punctuation, and other language mechanics, which are addressed later in the process.

**Revision** means just that: "re-vision," or re-seeing a piece. At this stage writers become readers, then writers again. "The writing stands apart from the writer, and writer interacts with it, first to find out what the writing has to say and then to help the writer say it clearly and gracefully." (Donald Murray) At this point the writer may involve others, both peers and the teacher, as she/he works to review the piece.

**Editing** is putting the piece of writing into its final form. Until this stage, the focus has been primarily on the content of student's writing. Once the focus changes to mechanics, students polish their writing by correcting spelling and other mechanical errors. These skills are taught most effectively during the editing process.

During **publishing** and **sharing,** students bring the composition to life by publishing their writing and sharing it with the appropriate audience.

The pieces in this Writing Folder reflect this writing process. Pieces included have been collaboratively chosen by the student and the teacher. All the steps of the process have been included in order to give a more accurate picture of the progression of the piece from prewriting to publication.

The front cover of Camp Legeune's Writing Portfolio folder.

# FROG TEAM

Dear Parents,

The purpose of this letter is to introduce our spelling program to you. We support the philosophy that views spelling as an integral part of the total language arts program. We believe children develop spelling strategies through purposeful daily reading and writing. Therefore, your child will be creating personal spelling lists from daily writing, high frequency words, and content area words, in the curriculum. Through research and our own teaching experiences, we have found that children are most interested in learning to spell words they need to use to communicate. We have also found that the more children read and write, the better they read, write, and spell.

We will emphasize three strategies in helping your child become a better speller:
- discovery and applying the rules and patterns
- proofreading
- using the dictionary and other resources

These are the same strategies adults use when trying to spell a word.

When your child asks you how to spell a word, here are some questions you can ask that may help him/her figure out the correct spelling:

Does it look right?
Can you try writing it another way?
How does the word start? How does it end?
Have you seen that word somewhere else?
What sounds do you hear?

After your child's attempts, verify the spelling by confirming the correct spelling or supplying it. Encourage your child to write the word as a whole, from memory, rather than copying it one letter at a time.

Keep in mind that we as adults are still developing the goal of perfect spelling. Our goal is to have the children become more aware of spelling strategies and to be able to express themselves legibly, competently, and confidently when writing. Remember, there is not reason to learn to spell if you don't write; writing must come first.

We welcome your cooperation, participation, and questions concerning the spelling program. Please feel free to contact us.

**Sample letter to parents about Russell School Program.**

# FROG
# TEAM

September 7th, 1995

Dear Parents,

Thank you for taking time to join us for parent orientation tonight. We appreciate you taking time out of your busy schedule to join us. Your support and input are important to us.

Tonight we will be focusing on two major areas. First, we will be taking an in depth look at your child's daily schedule. We will also explain how your child has become actively involved in making decisions about his/her learning choices. We believe that by giving your child opportunities to choose topics which are based on his/her interests that he or she will develop a lifetime love for learning.

The second area we would like to address this evening is curriculum. Each parent will be provided with a copy of the learner objectives for their child's grade level during the November parent conferences. These objectives reflect the desired learning outcomes for students at that specific grade level. We will be covering the material/topics listed, but will also be challenging your child to reach his/her fullest potential in all curriculum areas. We will discuss this revamp in more detail during individual parent conferences.

This year the Frog team is incorporating our new computer lab into our Writing Workshop time during the afternoon. Each child will have the opportunity to develop their writing ideas and polish up their editing/publishing skills. Mrs. Denova, Miss Robinson, and Mrs. Rivera will be working with the following teachers and writing workshops . . .

Mrs. Smith will be working on integrating multi-media approaches during the publishing stages of original story and report ideas. She will also be working on typing skills to help improve your child's word processing abilities.

Mrs. Myslinski will be providing your child with strategies that will help them edit and revise their stories and reports. She will also be covering English skills that will help expand their vocabulary and assist them in constructing more complex sentences. Cursive writing will be incorporated into the curriculum allowing students to develop their cursive handwriting skills.

Miss Davis will be helping your child to develop their own personal portfolio containing a variety of writing samples ranging from poetry to short stories. Students will be exploring a variety of book making techniques and publishing formats. The writing process will serve as an underlying structure for all styles covered during mini-lesson sessions and be used as guidelines for writing projects.

We appreciate your interest in education. If we fail to answer any questions that you may have tonight about the daily schedule or curriculum, please feel free to set up an appointment to discuss your concerns.

Sincerely,
The Frog Team

**Sample letter to parents: orientation night.**

# Camp Lejeune Dependents Schools
## SY 199_____ - 199_____
## INTERMEDIATE PROGRESS REPORT

| | |
|---|---|
| Student: _____ | **EXPLANATION OF MARKS:** |
| School: _____ | 0 = OUTSTANDING |
| Teacher: _____ | G = VERY GOOD |
| Grade: _____ | S = SATISFACTORY |
| | N = NEEDS IMPROVEMENT |

| | | Reporting Period | | | |
|---|---|:---:|:---:|:---:|:---:|
| | | **1** | **2** | **3** | **4** |
| **COMMUNICATION SKILLS** | | | | | |
| READING: | Achievement | | | | |
| | Effort | | | | |
| WRITTEN COMMUNICATION: | Achievement | | | | |
| | Effort | | | | |
| SPELLING: | Achievement | | | | |
| | Effort | | | | |
| ORAL LANGUAGE: | Achievement | | | | |
| | Effort | | | | |
| **MATHEMATICS:** | | | | | |
| | Achievement | | | | |
| | Effort | | | | |
| **SCIENCE/HEALTH:** | | | | | |
| | Achievement | | | | |
| | Effort | | | | |
| **SOCIAL STUDIES:** | | | | | |
| | Achievement | | | | |
| | Effort | | | | |
| **CITIZENSHIP AND STUDY SKILLS:** | | | | | |
| Takes responsibility for his/her own learning by: | | | | | |
| organizing materials | | | | | |
| using time wisely | | | | | |
| listening to and following directions | | | | | |
| following through on assignments | | | | | |
| Cooperates with teacher and obeys school rules | | | | | |
| Works and plays cooperatively with peers | | | | | |
| **SPECIAL AREAS ("S" OR "N" only) - Productively involved in:** | | | | | |
| Art | | | | | |
| Music | | | | | |
| Physical Education | | | | | |
| Spanish | | | | | |

Student

School

**FIRST REPORTING PERIOD**        Date_____
Teacher's Comments

_____
Teacher's Signature

_____
Parent's/Guardian's Signature

**SECOND REPORTING PERIOD**        Date_____
Teacher's Comments

Parent's/Guardian's Comments        Date:

_____
Teacher's Signature

_____
Parent's/Guardian's Signature

**THIRD REPORTING PERIOD**        Date_____
Teacher's Comments

**THIRD REPORTING PERIOD**        Date_____
Parent's/Guardian's Comments

_____
Teacher's Signature

_____
Parent's/Guardian's Signature

**FOURTH REPORTING PERIOD**

Teacher's Signature:_____        Date: _____

| ATTENDANCE | | | | | FINAL PROGRESS REPORT |
|---|---|---|---|---|---|
| Reporting Period | 1 | 2 | 3 | 4 | Next fall your child will report to grade_____. |
| Day Absent | | | | | |
| Days Tardy | | | | | |
| Days Present | | | | | Principal's Signature:_____ |

GOLD-1st Reporting Period   PINK-2nd Reporting Period   YELLOW-3rd Reporting Period   GREEN-4th Reporting Period

The Colchester School District is a one-town school system within the state of Vermont. Colchester is a middle-class town set on the shores of Lake Champlain. It is a suburb of the city of Burlington, Vermont's largest city, which has a population of 40,000. Colchester's population is about 14,000, making it a very large town by Vermont's standards.

Colchester has approximately 2,500 students in grades K-12. There are currently five school buildings. Class size is large—about twenty-three/twenty-five to one in the primary units. This ratio remains the same throughout most of the grades—never smaller, always larger.

Colchester has always allowed for teacher choice and decision making, thereby insuring the creation of many new and innovative teacher-designed classrooms each year.

The district involves all partners in its day-to-day work with curriculum, teacher evaluation, teacher licensing and strategic planning; that is, teachers, administrators, school board members and community members work side by side on all of the most important issues. Colchester is looked at as a leader in many educational arenas.

## Multiage in Colchester

Union Memorial School has had multiage classrooms for about twelve years. In the beginning, these classrooms were configured as combination classes, because of shifting populations at various grade levels—it was a quick fix to a housing difficulty. The multiage philosophy followed as teachers learned first-hand of the benefits brought to the classrooms by multiage groupings.

As teachers became more convinced of the benefits of multiage practices, they fought to keep their multiage classrooms even when class numbers no longer required them. Multiage blossomed at this point as other teachers were persuaded to try this style of teaching.

*As teachers became more convinced of the benefits of multiage practices, they fought to keep their multiage classrooms even when class numbers no longer required them.*

Our multiage classrooms are just as diverse as our single-grade classrooms. This can be viewed as an asset in most cases. Just as children need different learning environments, so do teachers need different teaching options. In all cases, the children are experiencing growth-over-time opportunities with the same teacher and extended time with a diverse student group.

The multiage classroom instructional style is as diverse as the teachers who teach them. Some are much more traditional, some are in-between with whole class thematic activities, while others are involved in multi-ability, multiage activities all day long.

Our school district's mission statement reflects the philosophical basis for the multiage classrooms. All curriculum work in our district is now aimed at solidifying this mission statement. It reads:

The mission of the Colchester School District—proud of its respect for individual needs and its commitment to integrated learning—is to ensure that all students will develop the academic proficiency, social skill, and character to be fulfilled, responsible, and involved citizens; we will accomplish this by providing diverse, challenging educational experiences in partnership with families and the community.

There have been times, several years ago, when there was friction between the multiage and single-grade classrooms. As with any new program, those of us who were involved and excited about our successes tended to share that enthusiasm with others. We talked, walked and ate multiage ad nauseum. Those "others" in our building felt left out, different, perceived as not as good.

As time went on, the multiage teachers began to tire of talking only about multiage practices and began to talk more about the process in our classrooms. We discussed writing workshop, hands-on science, and math. The conversation had shifted from teaching style to teaching. And we could all talk together again. After all, we all have classes, we all teach the academics—we did have things to talk about.

Currently there are 11 day-long classrooms for grades one through three. Of these, five are multiage 1-2 classes and one is a multiage 1-2-3 class. We also have six half-day kindergarten sessions with three teachers.

## Staff Development

Individual teachers took courses, attended workshops, and read extensively on holistic teaching techniques and philosophy. One staff member, who was teaching graduate courses on process classrooms, began to teach to other staff members. Within the past five or six years multiage education has become the focus of staff development.

**UNION MEMORIAL SCHOOL**

29 Main Street
P.O. Box 160
Colchester, VT 05446

**Phone: 802-878-2117**

**Multiage groupings**
(by grade level): 1-2, 1-2-3

**Open to visiting teachers and administrators**

**Contact:**
Mr. Joseph Oakes, Principal
Ellen A. Thompson, teacher, 1-2-3 multiage

## Curriculum and Assessment

Each teacher's method of presenting curriculum and assessing student performance is unique. Classroom instruction can typically be designed around year-long thematic studies chosen the previous year, through which school district curriculum requirements are met. Some topics studied have been: life in the arctic; tropical rainforests; Native Americans; Vermont's bicentennial; wet stuff; space; and flight. Currently we are involved in a study of "Mesmerizing Medieval Memories".

In the course of their theme studies children: become involved in research strands based on their own questions about the themes; listen to novel-length books which showcase the theme; receive theme-connected math lessons and games which involve multiple operations and problem-solving skills; take part in self-selected reading workshop time and writers' workshop time; learn science lessons which based on the theme studies; and help create their own curriculum.

The school district requires use of assessment tools such as miscues, spelling inventories, writing portfolios, a reading rubric, and math portfolios. Additionally, teachers may use tools showcased in the Primary Literacy Assessment Profile developed with teachers and consultants at the Vermont Department of Education. This profile asks that teachers address eleven key language arts questions ranging from concepts of print to engagement in the reading process. To do this, the teacher collects pieces of evidence on each of his or her students. It is no longer okay to just say it is so . . . one must prove it is so. These artifacts are collected and shared at teacher conferences and, once analyzed, can become the basis for a narrative report.

## Student Selection

In our school, all children, parents, and teachers have input into the classroom selection process. After parent conferences in April, a week is usually designated for parents of kindergarten students to visit other classrooms. They visit about three classrooms, which showcase different instructional styles. Typically, a very small number of parents actually take this option.

Next, all children in the school who are transitioning to a different class the next year are given a form for their parents to fill out. This form asks about their child's physical, emotional, and academic needs. It also asks parents to describe the environment in which their child would learn best. It also has a box to check off about multiage and/or single-grade preference. This information comes back to the principal, who then meets with the teachers involved and the specialist teachers (art, music, PE, library). Together they form the class lists.

## Specialists in the Classroom

The specialists at Union Memorial School are true supporters of multiage. They take all classes together; they do not split by ages. As an example, in the three-grade multiage classroom, the classroom teacher and the specialists plan the class's year-long theme study together, with each specialist showcasing a particular aspect of the project. The specialists are excellent with the children as a whole classroom community, and they have developed their curriculum to enhance the children's learning within the multiage environment.

## Inclusion

Each classroom at Union Memorial School has its share of remedial students, special education students, learning impaired, handicapped and/or emotionally disturbed students. Vermont is an inclusion state, so all of a community's students are educated in their home school. It is very rare to have pull-outs at this time, even within the school building.

In the case of the three-grade classroom, the special education people work within the classroom structure, and do not ability-group. The Title I reading teacher makes use of the class's theme and the multiage/multi-ability groups within the room to teach her language arts strategies and math concepts. She truly supports the academic program.

She also spends time with students on her caseload individually, reading and writing with them, and chatting with them about strategies to use. The special needs children get the additional support they require, yet are not made to feel different than or less able than their classmates.

In the past, not all special education teachers have been supportive. In one instance, the classroom teacher appealed to the administration to switch special educators for her classroom in hopes of finding a better match for herself in terms of teaching styles. The administrator agreed, and the results have been dramatic. The new special educator is so excited by the classroom atmosphere that she comes in during her preparation periods to learn and hear more. The children feel her enthusiasm and are not forced to choose between their teachers. The classroom teacher feels validated and accepted and now finds she can put her energy into her children rather than into defending her program. Just as children need to match their teachers, so do teachers need to match the other teachers with whom they work closely.

## Team Teaching

There are two teachers at Union Memorial school who team teach a multiage 1-2 classroom. They have adjoining rooms and share their kids, especially in the science/social studies areas. They hold conferences with parents and showcase their students' learning together. Their preparation periods are at the same time, allowing them time to plan together. Their children do go to their specialist classes as separate classes. These two teachers put a lot of time and effort into their teaming situation and it really works for them.

Another teacher team teaches once a week with the art specialist. Each teacher gives up preparation time to create an extended art block, and the classroom teacher often teaches art components, while the art specialist does storytelling.

## Grouping for Instruction

Teachers work with children in whole groups, small groups, and individually. One teacher has created a club for both math and language arts, and mixes children heterogeneously in terms of ability, age, and behavioral characteristics. During club times, lessons are shared in a mini-lesson format to the whole club. For some of the members it might be the first time they are exposed to the skill, for others it might meet a specific instructional need, and for other club members it might serve as a review.

## Waivers/Mandates

Vermont, as a portfolio state, does not have standardized testing by state mandate, nor does the school district require it. Staff at Union Memorial were actively involved in creating the Vermont State Writing Portfolio system, the district's language arts task force and the Primary Literacy Assessment Profile used statewide by interested teachers.

---

### Special Events Committee

The schoolwide Special Events Committee is made up of classroom teachers and specialists. Each year the committee searches out a focus for the whole school to involve itself in. Often it is a mini-theme which all classes will research and work on for a designated period of time. Last year's Circus Arts theme is an example of how this committee works.

During this theme study each of the specialists worked the theme into their curriculum. The music department taught the children circus songs; the physical education department taught juggling, tumbling and tricks; in art children created a miniature circus of three-dimensional figures based on the circus collection at the Shelburne Museum; and the library provided books about the circus for the children to read. All the classes went to the Shelburne Museum to view the circus collection of miniatures and carousel animals. Each classroom showcased a circus animal outside its room. And the entire school participated in an evening circus performance, complete with a three-ring circus, singing acts, and face painting.

By putting together this mini school-wide theme study each year, the special events committee ensures that thematic teaching occurs in every classroom, that the school children are all showcased at Parents Night, and most importantly that the learning is shared with the Colchester Community. Because this group works out all the details in committee and even writes a grant to support the project, the actual impact on each classroom teacher is minimal. Teachers can concentrate on their own classes' participation in the school-wide project.

# COLCHESTER SCHOOL DISTRICT

## Union Memorial School

Name: _____

Teacher: _____

Grade: _____

Placement Next Year: _____

Teacher: _____

Grade: _____

School: _____

## LANGUAGE ARTS

| Approximate Grade Level | | | | |
|---|---|---|---|---|
| Above | ___ | ___ | ___ | ___ |
| On | ___ | ___ | ___ | ___ |
| Below | ___ | ___ | ___ | ___ |

### LISTENING

Listens with understanding .......................... ___ ___ ___ ___
Enjoys listening to stories .......................... ___ ___ ___ ___

### SPEAKING

Expresses self clearly .......................... ___ ___ ___ ___
Participates in discussion .......................... ___ ___ ___ ___

### READING

Selects books at appropriate level .............. ___ ___ ___ ___
Reads independently .......................... ___ ___ ___ ___
Reads for meaning .......................... ___ ___ ___ ___
Uses a variety of reading strategies .............. ___ ___ ___ ___
Demonstrates understanding .......................... ___ ___ ___ ___
Sustains silent reading .......................... ___ ___ ___ ___

### WRITING

Expresses self in writing .......................... ___ ___ ___ ___
Sequences ideas .......................... ___ ___ ___ ___
Demonstrates growth in grammar skills ........ ___ ___ ___ ___
Demonstrates growth in penmanship .......... ___ ___ ___ ___
Learns assigned spelling words .......................... ___ ___ ___ ___
Applies spelling skills to written work .......... ___ ___ I ___

EFFORT .......................... 

## SOCIAL STUDIES/SCIENCE

Topics:

Participates .......................... ___ ___ ___ ___
Understands concepts .......................... ___ ___ ___ ___

**EFFORT** .......................... 

**216**

## MATH

| Approximate Grade Level | | | | |
|---|---|---|---|---|
| Above | ___ | ___ | ___ | ___ |
| On | ___ | ___ | ___ | ___ |
| Below | ___ | ___ | ___ | ___ |

Concepts:

Addition .......................... ___ ___ ___ ___
Subtraction .......................... ___ ___ ___ ___
Multiplication .......................... ___ ___ ___ ___
Division .......................... ___ ___ ___ ___
Problem Solving .......................... ___ ___ ___ ___

**EFFORT** .......................... ___ ___ ___ ___

MUSIC .......................... ___ ___ ___ ___
PE .......................... ___ ___ ___ ___
ART .......................... ___ ___ ___ ___

## WORK HABITS

Works neatly .......................... ___ ___ ___ ___
Is attentive .......................... ___ ___ ___ ___
Stays on task .......................... ___ ___ ___ ___
Completes assignments on time .................... ___ ___ ___ ___
Follows oral directions .......................... ___ ___ ___ ___
Follows written directions .......................... ___ ___ ___ ___
Works independently .......................... ___ ___ ___ ___
Works in groups .......................... ___ ___ ___ ___

## SOCIAL & EMOTIONAL GROWTH

Gets along well with others .......................... ___ ___ ___ ___
Accepts rules and limits .......................... ___ ___ ___ ___
Accepts personal responsibility .................... ___ ___ ___ ___
Respects rights, property, & feelings of others ___ ___ ___ ___
Demonstrates self-control.......................... ___ ___ ___ ___

# Colchester School District
## Union Memorial School

NAME_____  GRADE_____

## TEACHER COMMENTS

1.2.3. 96

| Time | MONDAY | TUESDAY | WEDNESDAY | THURSDAY | FRIDAY |
|---|---|---|---|---|---|
| | ← FREE CHOICE TIME → | | | | ← BOOK CLUB TALLY → |
| 8:40–9:15 | Attendance · Lunch Count · Hot Lunch $1.25 | choc/juice 35¢ milk 25¢ | Book Club Tally | | SNACK |
| 9:15–9:40 | Morning News Share · Today's News · Secret Message · Proof Rdg. | Poetry | Morning News share · Today's News · Secret Message · Proof Rdg. | Poetry | morning News share · Today's News · Secret Message · Proof Rdg. |
| 9:40–10:25 | Reading Club — status of the class · self-selected reading · conferences · instructional clubs | MUSIC ♪ 9:40–10:25 | Reading Club — status of the class · self-selected reading · conferences · instructional clubs | LIBRARY 9:40–10:20 | Writing Club — status of the class · independent writing · conferences · instructional groups |
| 10:30–10:50 | ← RECESS → | DUTY / RECESS | RECESS / DUTY → | ← RECESS → | ← RECESS → |
| 10:50–11:45 | Reading Club (cont) | Key Word Time · Get new words · write/illustrate or · word analysis activity | Reading Club (cont.) | Reading – OR – Writing Club | Writing Club |
| | | (or math) | (or math) | | |
| 11:45–12:25 | ← LUNCH → | ← LUNCH → | ← RECESS → | ← LUNCH * → | |
| 12:25–12:40 | ← Traveling Books → | ← Traveling Books → | ← Traveling Books → | ← Traveling Books → | |
| 12:40–1:10 | P.E. 12:35–1:20 | STORY | STORY | STORY | STORY |
| 1:10–1:25 | | SILENT READING · Writing Club | SILENT READING | SILENT READING | SILENT READING |
| 1:25–2:15 | Cursive/manuscript · spelling/poetry | | ART | mini-science experiment | MATH |
| 2:15–3:00 | MATH | MATH | MATH (or math) | MATH | P.E. 2:15–3:00 |
| 3:00–3:10 | ← DISMISSAL → | ← STACK CHAIRS → | ← STACK CHAIRS → | ← DISMISSAL → | ← STACK CHAIRS → |

AM Recess Duty 10:30–10:50 — Tues/Thurs
Monday — Planning Mtg. 6:00 PM UMS

*every other Friday, TEAM mtg - 11:45–12:25

Ellen 95-96

# COLCHESTER SCHOOL DISTRICT
# TITLE VI MINI GRANT PROPOSAL
# 1995-1996

PROJECT TITLE: Mesmerizing Medieval Memories

PROJECT COORDINATOR:
    Name: Ellen A Thompson
    Position: Teacher — Multiage 1•2•3

    School: Union Memorial School

    Phone: 878-2117      878-1127
    (school)          (home)

NUMBER OF PARTICIPANTS IN EACH CATEGORY:    Students 25 - 351

Administrators 1        Teachers 4+   Community        members 50+ (many)

TOTAL BUDGET REQUEST:    $911.95

## REQUIRED SIGNATURES

ADMINISTRATIVE SIGNATURE         :_____
(indicates awareness by
 building administrator)

APPLICANT'S SIGNATURE:        _____

TODAY'S DATE:        _____

Please answer all questions on these grant application forms. Do not attach additional documents or letters of explanation. Thanks!

## 1. What do you plan to do with your mini grant? Summarize your project in one short paragraph indicating how your mini grant relates to our district's mission and strategic plan.

This year of "*Mesmerizing Medieval Memories*" will integrate all areas of the curriculum into a year long literature and activity based thematic study of medieval times for my 25 students in grades 1-2-3. These memories will take many forms throughout this school year. Everything from castle life, the food eaten, the weapons used, the songs sung, the instruments played, the stories told, to the architecture of the castles will be explored. This mini grant would help to secure several hands on components that would enhance the learning for these students as well as the learning for their fellow students at Union Memorial School.

This study will truly illustrate the strength of student-teacher-parent generated curriculum as it is developed around this theme study in this classroom. Parents and children have been invited to explore and develop this topic of medieval times, allowing for true ownership of the learning.

"The mission of the Colchester School District—proud of its respect for individual needs and its commitment to integrated learning—is to ensure that all students will develop the academic proficiency, social skill, and character to be fulfilled, responsible, and involved citizens; we will accomplish this by providing diverse, challenging educational experiences in partnership with families and community."

This statement is the heart and backbone of this grant, *Mesmerizing Medieval Memories*. It is through this theme study that all of the areas of the mission statement are addressed. In particular, its connection for parents and community in a challenging integrated learning situation designed to capitalize on the individual strengths and needs of the students in this classroom.

## 2. What will you accomplish as a result of your project? State your specific learner outcomes. What will students be able to demonstrate as a result of participation in this project?

- The students will read and be read to quality children's literature that centers on the medieval times.
- The children will write stories that reflect their growing knowledge of story as modeled to them in many forms and genres.
- The children will generate questions which will be researched throughout the year, creating student "experts" who will transfer their knowledge to others.
- The children will experience the music of these times with Ms. Mutz through recordings, songs and the use of recorders as a musical instrument.
- The children will experience the art of storytelling with students in other grade levels through their use of a story telling technique, the "story sack".
- The children will experience class field trips to area castles and museums, guest speakers, as well as the annual three-day campout.
- The children will learn all of their academic skills in an integrated manner whenever possible.
- The children will learn how to count money, make change and pay bills through their participation in the class restaurant.
- The children will learn of the importance of physical fitness activities through their creation of a medieval festival.
- The children will explore the genre of fairy tales in great detail. They will compare and contrast different versions of the same tales and will try their hand at writing their own "fractured" tales modeled after work by author Jon Scieszca.
- Castles will be built . . . in Legos, blocks, sand and even soap!

### 3. List the activities you plan to schedule for this project in chronological order.

This theme study will incorporate all areas of the curriculum in an integrated manner as per our mission statement. Because of the nature of this classroom and the involvement of the students, other specialists and the parent group, the activities listed below are really just the beginnings of this study. Events, books, ideas will evolve and grow as we all work together in true partnership for the learning.

#### September—December . . .

This will be the true beginning for the children in room 6. They will be learning the ways of the room, the school and medieval times. Novels will be read that explore this time period, really hooking children in to the lifestyles and living conditions for these people. Books such as *Castle in the Attic, Battle for the Castle, Catherine, Called Birdy* and *The Boggart*. Much factual material will be explored also. Trips to the Wilson Castle in the Rutland area will be arranged as well as exploring videotapes produced by ETV on this subject. A field trip to a local horse farm will help the children to understand the importance of horses during this time and will allow them to understand them as an example of animal life. They will make use of computer technology in this area through the use of *Castles II* and *King Arthur's Magic Castle*. The children will be writing their own stories which will be bound and showcased at their Authors' Tea in the spring. They will create shields, flags of heraldry, gargoyles, stained glass window designs—all in an effort to transform the classroom into a castle-like structure.

#### January to June . . .

During this half of the year, the activity level will increase dramatically as the children research their questions about the time period, create picture books of their own, plan out and run their latest restaurant creation to be modeled after a medieval feast, visit other castles in the area, work with museum medieval kits from the Fleming Museum in Burlington and best of all . . . experience a medieval fest with the help of the group *The Society for Creative Anachronism*. It is hoped that this group can come out during the month of March and April to help instruct the children about life in these times. This group would also, with the help of parents, children and teacher put on a fest for the entire student body at Union Memorial School during their week long celebration of children's literature. This group would help to bring to life the many characters these children will have experienced all year long. And finally, the annual campout! At this time, it is being planned for the Gloucester, Massachusetts area in a campground right next door to the Hammond Castle . . . but I have been told about a certain empty castle in Belgium . . . so you never know!

### 4. How will this project be evaluated? What strategic plan strategy(ies) will be advanced as a result of your project? Who will be involved in this evaluation?

The children will produce many products which will showcase their knowledge acquired. These will take many forms from published books to literacy portfolios to restaurants to storytelling, to journal entries to works of art. Their knowledge gained will be shared with the community at large through the use of our class newspaper and articles in the *Colchester Chronicle* and the *Colchester News Magazine*. Their academic growth will be highlighted in their individual writing and math portfolios. Specific growth will be charterd by myself in the area of literacy through my use of the *Primary Literacy Assessment Profile*.

Children will be evaluated according to their developmental needs. Success is insured through the use of open-ended, hands on, real activities which involve the whole child, allowing them success at their own level of achievement.

Parents will be in true partnership. They will evaluate activities, plan the restaurant and the campout.

Specifically, this mini grant addresses several areas of the school district's strategic plan.

Strategy One—Action Plans 10, 11—Here the children will continue their work with portfolios and the use of authentic pieces of assessment as a means to drive instruction. Portfolios will be shared with parents and other interested groups in our community. Our near-famous Portfolio Party will be held during the spring and will be opened to more people as a means to showcase this type of assessment program.

Strategy Two—Action Plans 1A, 1B, 5—Goal setting has been occurring in room 6 for a long time but the process has not been formalized. This strategy could easily fit into this classroom and this theme study. It is an area that will be explored in more detail. Parents will be included in on this process.

Strategy Four—Action Plans 1, 4, 7—Ensuring Use of Effective Instructional Strategies is the reason for my use of year long theme studies enhanced by the partnership of students, teachers, parents and community members. This type of instructional program can be a model for the use of effective strategies. This model, along with others, could support teacher visitations from within and without the district. This type of instructional program takes into account the diversity of student needs within the regular classroom. It addresses the ways to challenge gifted students while still allowing them to work with their age appropriate peers. This year, I have at least two children who would fall into a gifted category if one were so designated within the district.

Strategy Five—Action Plans 2, 5—This theme study brings with it much in the way of technology. Exploring new data through *America on Line* services, CD Rom programs with video text, use of video and the school's inter-classroom network system are all scheduled for this year. I would like to challenge my parent group to participate in the matching grant opportunity offered at IBM.

Strategy Seven—Action Plan 2—As always informing the community of the learning in this little kingdom of room 6 is a real priority for the parents and teachers involved. Regular articles will be part of the regular business in this classroom—teacher generated, student generated, and parent generated.

**5. In what ways does this project <u>enrich</u> or <u>supplement</u> the basic instructional program you offer to your students? Note any other resources you will need to complete this project.**

This project will address all of the basic curriculum areas. It will go beyond the basic strands and will integrate with art, music and physical education components. It will fit nicely with our school-wide theme study of celebrating children's literature. By opening up the students to the intensity of a year long theme study, the sky is the limit. The children will have many opportunities to explore areas which are important to them as learners.

**6. Has part or all of this project been previously funded through Title VI/Chapter 2? If yes, please specify when. Also, share how this grant differs from your previously funded project.**

No.

## PROPOSED BUDGET

### ITEMIZE THE SPECIFIC RESOURCES YOU NEED TO FUND THIS MINI GRANT.

| 1. Materials and Supples | Cost |
|---|---|
| Video series - VT ETV<br>The Middle Ages plus manual | 33.75 |
| Video -<br>   Gargoyles-<br>Fleming Museum Teaching Kit | 24.95<br><br>20.00 |
| **2. Equipment** | **Cost** |
| | |
| **3. Contracted Services**<br>**(consultants, workshop leaders, community resources)** | **Cost** |
| Under negotiation<br>   Organization fees for "The Society for Creative Anachronism"<br>   Guest Artist* - Story teller / Jester "Alexander, King of Jesters"<br><br>*To be shared with Whole School at Medieval Festival | 350.00<br>350.00 |
| **4. Other (Please specify)** | **Cost** |
| Scholarships for 2 students for class campout<br><br>Wilson Castle - admission costs<br>(parents will drive) @2.10 per student<br>            4.75 per adult | 40.00<br><br><br>52.50 children<br>40.75 adults |
| **TOTAL BUDGET** | 911.95 |

NOTE: we will fund raise *most* costs for class campout at Hammond Castle and campout in Massachusetts.

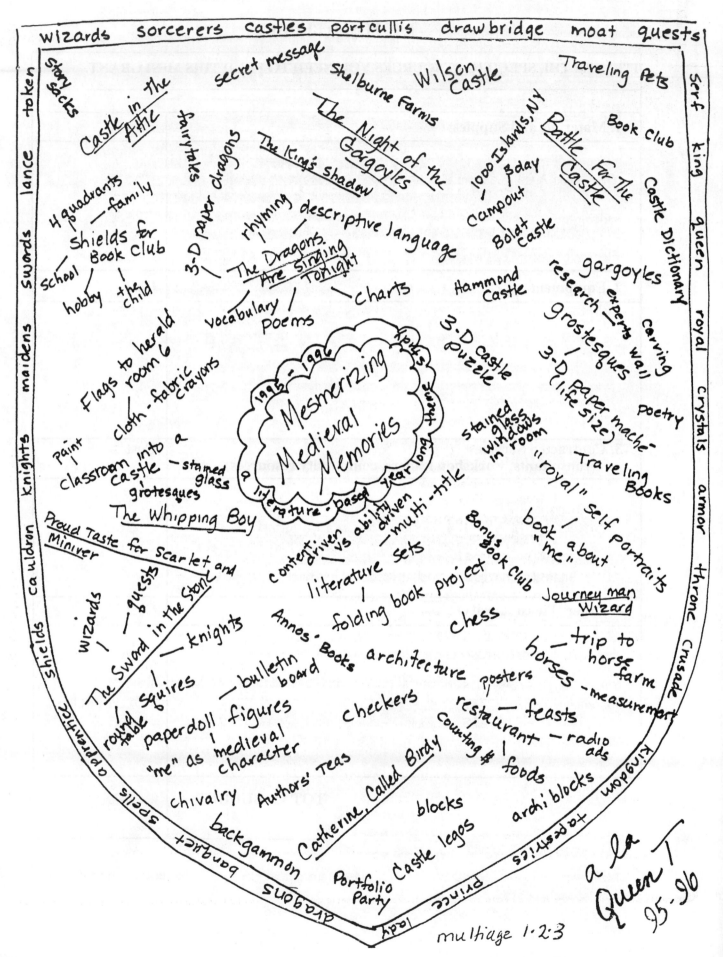

wizards sorcerers castles portcullis drawbridge moat quests

token lance swords maidens knights cauldron shields

serf king queen royal crystals armor throne crusade

story sacks
Castle in the Attic
secret message
Shelburne Farms
Wilson Castle
Traveling Pets
Book Club

fairytales
4 quadrants — family
Shields for Book Club
school hobby the child

3-D paper dragons
The King's Shadow
The Night of the Gargoyles
rhyming descriptive language
The Dragons Are Singing Tonight
vocabulary Poems
charts

1000 Islands, NY
3 day Campout
Boldt Castle
Battle For The Castle

Castle Dictionary
gargoyles
research experts carving wall
grostesques
3-D paper mache (life size)
poetry
Hammond Castle
3-D Castle Puzzle

1995 - 1996 **Mesmerizing Medieval Memories** a literature-based year long theme

Flags to herald room 6
Paint cloth - fabric crayons
classroom into a castle — stained glass
grotesques
The Whipping Boy

stained glass windows in room
Traveling Books
"royal" self portraits
book about "me"

context-driven vs ability-driven multi-title
literature sets
folding book project
Bonus Book Club
chess
Journeyman Wizard
trip to horse farm

Proud Taste for Scarlet and Miniver
wizards — guests
The Sword in the Stone — knights
round table squires
paperdoll figures
"me" as medieval character
chivalry
bulletin board
Anno's Books
architecture posters
checkers
Authors' Teas
Catherine, Called Birdy
backgammon

horses — measurement
restaurant — feasts
counting foods — radio ads
blocks
Portfolio Castle legos
archi blocks
Portfolio Party

224

multiage 1·2·3

a la Queen T 95-96

multiverse spells banquet dragons lady fool prince forest kingdom

August 22, 1995

Dear boys and girls (moms and dads, too),

It is hard to believe that school will be starting next Wednesday, August 30th. The summer has been so hot and glorious - great swimming weather. I only hope it will cool down a little when we all gather again in room 6. I have missed you all and I am really looking forward to getting to know all of our newest members of the class.

I have been working in the classroom and it is beginning to really shape up. The iguana cage has been moved by the classroom door. Now everyone will be able to peek at them when they pass our doorway! They enjoyed their quiet summer at school, but I know they are looking forward to all of you returning, as I am! I have been cleaning and sorting and even throwing out things. Yes, old fogies, this is really Ms. T writing this letter. I just had to clean up in order to fit in all of the new books and games that I purchased for this school year.

Our theme study for the year will indeed be the Middle Ages, complete with castle studies and construction, knights and shining armor, heraldry, jousting tournaments, visits to area castles, illuminations and the study of fairy tales as a story form. In fact, we will even turn room 6 in to a castle of our very own. Mrs. Jop is in on the plan along with Jim (my new husband)! And, of course, our newest traveling pet will be our dragon puppet that Devin gave me last year. Start thinking of royal names. And...our campout...well, William's whole family has been hot on the trail. They visited the Hammond Castle in Massachusetts and brought back lots of information about tours and nearby campgrounds. Thank you Grippin's all!

Once again, I traveled all over the summer speaking with teachers in states as far away as Texas and as close as Connecticut. It was great to share our classroom with them. They just love to hear about our multiage adventures. Many of the teachers are just beginning to set up their classrooms as multiage units. Hearing about all of you made them even more excited than they were before!

We have a new-comer to our classroom family...Cassidy William Moore was born this summer. Now Courtney will have two brothers to tell us stories about at *Today's News* in the classroom.

Ms. Companion will join us from the University of Vermont as our student teacher until December. She will be learning all about the classroom. She will bring with her lots of ideas for our castle year, too. Ms. Companion will have a chance to try out her teaching wings. This will be an exciting time for all of us!

And...oh, yes...Jim and I got married this summer!!! We had a wonderful ceremony and reception at the Boat House in Burlington. We flew off for a week in Bermuda. It was so beautiful there. We're hoping to be able to return. But, me...I'll still be Ms. T, so you don't have to learn how to spell (or even say) Holzschuh. Jim is finding that Thompson is a much easier name to spell, too. Maybe he'll become another Mr. T!

I better close now, so that I get this in the mail to you BEFORE school actually begins.

See you soon,

Love Ms T

PS
Lunch money is collected on the first day of each week. Hot lunch is $1.25, juice/chocolate milk is $.35 and regular/skim milk is $.25. Please send your child's money in for the whole week in a clearly labeled envelope. Thanks.

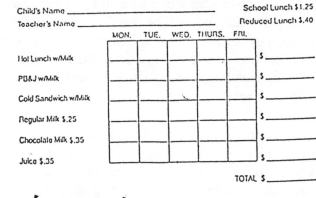

| | MON. | TUE. | WED. | THURS. | FRI. | |
|---|---|---|---|---|---|---|
| Hot Lunch w/Milk | | | | | | $ |
| PB&J w/Milk | | | | | | $ |
| Cold Sandwich w/Milk | | | | | | $ |
| Regular Milk $.25 | | | | | | $ |
| Chocolate Milk $.35 | | | | | | $ |
| Juice $.35 | | | | | | $ |

Child's Name _____
Teacher's Name _____

School Lunch $1.25
Reduced Lunch $.40

TOTAL $ _____

Lunch Envelope Sample

September 11, 1995

Dear Parents,

This school year is off to a wonderful start! Our theme study is going to prove to be one of the most exciting that I have ever experienced thus far in my teaching career. Every time I turn around someone has a new idea to share. I am really looking forward to it all.

The children are getting a long grandly. We are learning the classroom structures and are getting in to all of our academic areas. The group gets a long well and everyone seems really enthused about school.

**Don't forget...**your night is coming up this week! **Parent's Night is this Thursday evening, beginning at 6:30 PM. All adults are invited.** This is our chance to share stories about the classroom, meet Mrs. Companion - our student teacher from UVM, and learn about the new things in store for all of us in room 6. **Old fogies - we need you there, too - your stories are the very best of all!**

Put Thursday on your calendar....it will be lots of fun.

Sincerely,

Queen T

PS Don't forget tomorrow's important meeting at the high school - TOWN MEETING to borrow 60% of the moneys needed to run the school based on last year's budget. This is not a budget vote. This is a vote to borrow money to keep our schools open.

PPS  September 21 is the OPEN HOUSE date for Union Memorial School.

# PARENTS' NIGHT
## 1995-1996

September 14, 1995
6:30 PM - 7:30 PM

**Introductions...**
 Ellen
 Amy
 Old, middle and new fogies (parents!)

**Multiage Setting...**
 Why?

**Academics... (videotape)**
 Reading
 Writing
 Math
 Science/social studies

**Year Long Theme Study...**
 Why?

**Campout...**
 !!!????!!!!
 Last year's stories

**Classroom Help...**
 What?
 When?
 Where?

**Questions...**

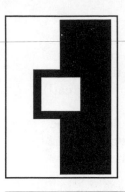

# WHAT HAS HAPPENED SO FAR . . . ?

by Ellen Thompson

The literature-based theme study of *Mesmerizing Medieval Memories* has gotten off to a quick start in my multi-age classroom. Collection of materials began last spring, with children, parents and teacher starting to collect ideas and activities to put together for this year. The result has already been outrageous. It seems the very idea of medieval times, complete with heraldry and pageantry, brings forth lots from the people involved. Parents have researched castles and campgrounds, as well as books and music. Everyone is involved in some way.

In the classroom, several large events have transpired. Some of these events will have tie-ins later in the year as we prepare for our community-oriented celebrations.

Our first read-aloud of the year was *The Castle in the Attic*, written by Elizabeth Winthrop. The children adored this book, virtually sitting on the edges of their seats waiting breathlessly for each page to be read. What a great beginning for our year's study! From this book several ideas came to the surface. The very idea of how a castle is constructed, what a knight wears, what a quest is, what a sorcerer can do, the role of ladies and squires. As we read aloud, the class and I noted the new vocabulary that we were hearing. We discussed its meaning and "saved" it on a chart for use later on. We will construct a *Castle Dictionary*, complete with definitions and illustrations for use in our classroom and perhaps the school library. We will begin this activity when we have enough new terms taken from our theme talk and readings for all to help define.

From here, we began to think about ourselves and what our role might possibly be if we were living in that era. We explored pictures of costumes, read about different roles within their society and just generally tried to imagine what we would look like if we lived then. During art class, Ann Joppe-Mercure and myself team teach throughout the school year. That is, we have juggled our schedules where we both give up preparation time to ensure that we have at least a double block of time for art class. And then "we" teach it. Sometimes Ann is the storyteller and sometimes I am the artist. Our roles move and change as we plan and encourage one another to take risks within our teaching. For the children, they get to see firsthand two friends doing what they love . . . teaching young children . . . together! For this reason, many of our more dramatic activities often occur in the art room, but these are shared responsibilities from the teachers in question. Probably the depth and breadth of these activities has taken on much more powerful dimensions because of this teaming.

In the art room while the rest of the school was working on "paper doll" likenesses of themselves, then children in room 6 created their likenesses dressed in medieval costumes. The children became ladies, knights in full armor, jesters and even wizards with at least one queen thrown in for good measure. Yes, my name this year is **Queen T!**

These paper doll figures, once cut out, became the makings for a medieval fair bulletin board back in room 6. The individual children are clearly recognizable.

As luck would have it, there was a dragon guarding the wizard's castle in *The Castle in the Attic*. The children knowing my fondness for dragons were excited to create a dragon of their own. Using Annie's expertise with forms, we created a one piece of paper folded 3-dimensional dragon that could be decorated in extravagant colors and then brought back to the classroom to live on its walls.

These dragons were decorated by using indelible marker and markers or crayons. The children first used line designs to create patterns and then colored in these patterns. Annie, of course, was sneaking in an art lesson. We were creating friends.

The children in the classroom have a weekly homework assignment, that of "BOOK CLUB". Here they read at home or are read to at home by others and record their minutes on a weekly chart. The chart comes to school each week. Once a week, we save time to add up the minutes read at home using calculators. The children then record their minutes read on an individual chart. Minutes are recorded in units of 100, so for every 100 minutes a new sticker is added. This year the children created shields for their book club minutes. Their shield was made out of construction paper. They are divided into four quadrants, one for their name, one for a picture of their family, one for a best school related thing and the last for a special hobby or interest. These are hung around the room and are quickly getting covered with "hundreds of minutes."

All of my read-alouds are included in other parts of the school day. In particular, this book was a mainstay for our three times a week "secret message." "Secret message" is usually referred to as a minimal cues message. I use the story to write my message, using no cues at all except the number of letters in words and marks of punctuation (It looks like hangman!) Usually a question is asked and when the puzzle is completed, a discussion will follow which reinforces the reading. This activity and discussion happens at 10:00 A.M.; storytime happens at 12:30 P.M.

With *The Castle in the Attic* coming to a close, we decided to create our own royal family. Here the children painted self-portraits in the art room. Again the children were really able to capture their attributes in their paintings. I added a silver crown from shiny contact paper and voila . . . a royal family! Currently these are hanging outside the classroom door as a welcome wall for those passing by. Later when they come down, we will create a book about ourselves. The self-portraits will be their cover pages.

As the close of the book, the children were truly sorry to have it end. They requested time to reflect on the story and their favorite parts. This took the form of a quiet drawing time. The children drew their favorite parts while listening to harp music (great!) in the background.

Throughout the room you could hear the children quietly sharing their thoughts on the book. They loved it and needed the time to tell others of their joy.

As we begin our new school year, there are always times when the older children in my multiage need to share the "traditions" of our classroom life together with the younger children. This theme study allowed us to do this quite royally! We decided that we would decide on thirteen traditions or events that truly heralded our class, things that were unique to room 6. With our list in hand, the children worked in partners to create a flag of heraldry for each item. The flags are constructed of bright solid colors with geometric fabric shapes added. In the center the children drew with fabric crayons a picture of their item. The flags are double-sided and currently hang in the hallway outside the classroom door. They take up the whole length of the classroom. They chose to immortalize: the iguanas; Broccoli and Ruby; Malachi, the parakeet; the annual bubble gum bubble blowing contest; the Thanksgiving feast; the class-run restaurant; the camp-out; and much more!

Another weekly occurrence which is always theme-related is the sharing of poetry. We began this year with four poems selected from *The Dragons are Singing Tonight,* written by Jack Prelutsky. These are written on chart paper and are read to and with the children. We have sung them, illustrated them, found rhyming words, imagined the stories these dragons would be able to tell, and have acted them out as a group. We know these poems by heart. The children have also created a booklet which included copies of each poem with follow-up activities which include penmanship practice. Much needed in a multiage 1-2-3 classroom!

During the children's own reading time, we worked on a large whole class book project. I would best describe this as a type of literature circle activity based much on the ideas presented by Dorothy Watson. I did this a little differently. First, I chose about forty theme-related books from our picture book collection. These were all story books rather than factual books. As we began the project, I "book talked" the books, that is, I went through all forty and shared tidbits about each book. I have to admit, I couldn't resist and actually read two of the books aloud! My weakness! The children listened and thought about which books they might like to read or have read to them. I shared with the final project at this time, too, as it is important that they use their knowledge of the project to better pick a book that will match the project expectations for them. They knew that they would need a book that they could "tell" back in four pictures.

The children then worked within their reading/writing clubs to actually try out the books and finally pick one for the project. Their clubs are multiage and multiability. There are four members in each club. The club members were to work together on reading the books.

You see, the children did not have to pick a book out that they could read themselves, they had to pick a book that they could "tell" in pictures. This is a "content-based" literature set, not an ability-based literature set. Therefore, club members would designate readers or partners readers or silent readers, but everyone had to explore as many stories as they could. Finally, when all the club members had a book picked, the club could move to the final project.

The final project involved creating four pictures: one from the beginning of the story, two from the middle and one from the end. The pictures were drawn on a long piece of construction paper which had been folded to create six panels. The children created a border design much like those found in medieval times around each of their pictures.

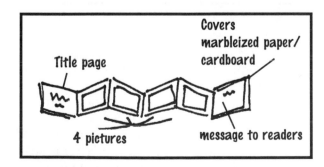

The title of the book and author were typed and glued on the first panel. A tiny message was printed on the last panel: "Did you like my book? Please write me a message." Hardcovers were created for these accordion-folded books with cardboard and marbleized papers. The folding books will be used at the fall NERA "Building Bridges to Literacy" Conference. Hopefully these young artists will gather many messages from the participants at the Carol Otis Hurst luncheon.

Another theme-related activity which occurs in the room goes along with our at-home *BOOK CLUB* reading, but this reading actually happens at school and is dubbed *BONUS BOOK CLUB*. As in all classrooms, I often have children who are not read to at home. Often it is not their fault. So, rather than have them never be able to put up a sticker on their *BOOK CLUB* shield, I have created this as a means to give them all some extra minutes with a good story. The children are called by clubs by a parent or an instructional aide or my student-teacher. They find a comfortable spot and the adult reads aloud a theme-related story or factual book. At the end of reading, they record their time spent and deposit these slips in to the official *BOOK CLUB* box. It is great fun to listen to these little groups. The children love it and it is a perfect activity for the others who are in my room. Plus, it allows for another opportunity to fill the children with the theme information. I can not "do" it all, nor do I want to!

My next read aloud is, of course, *The Battle for the Castle*, written by Elizabeth Winthrop. For once, I think I believe the sequel is even better than the first book. We are mesmerized by it. We are capturing more theme-related vocabulary for our class chart. It looks like we will be able to start our dictionary soon.

The class has been able to experience a real live castle. Last week we visited the Wilson Castle in Proctor, Vermont. It was a great experience. This castle was constructed in the 1850s by an American for his new English wife. She wanted an English castle, so all of the building material was shipped to Vermont. It has stained glass, three turrets, beautiful furniture, and a *knight's window* on the north wall. One never wants the sun to rise or set on this window! The children were duly impressed. The two hour drive during the peak of foliage season was well worth it for the 12 adults who drove us there, too!

Another book that has been shared in

detail is Eve Bunting's *The Night of the Gargoyles*. Next Wednesday, we will begin constructing 3-D gargoyles, well, actually 3-D grotesques! Gargoyles have long necks to carry water, grotesques are usually faces used to adorn buildings. These grotesques will be constructed out of paper mache in a manner we have used before to create masks. The children will explore grotesques in Eve Bunting's book and on a videotape I have found. They will decide their face and build it in the art room. Finally they will be painted with shades of gray to replicate the stone they would have been carved from in days of yore. These grotesques will come back to room 6 to begin our biggest project of all—that of turning the room into a castle!

## Our plans include:

- painting the walls to show the stone work used in a castle, with castle tops and flags flying
- hanging grotesques
- creating stained glass story windows out of our classroom windows, complete with a knight's window on the north wall flags of heraldry (already completed)

This has been cleared with my school principal . . . long ago! When we act . . . we will act fast!

And that is where we are right now, as of October 14, 1995. We have many big plans which will crop up as the year progresses. Look for our newest restaurant featuring the foods from a medieval feast during January and February of 1996. This will involve menu planning, learning how to handle (and make) money, cooking and serving as well as how to

do radio ads and posters. We will be creating theme-related stories and books to be heralded at our near famous Authors' Teas. And our campout is taking on new dimensions with the latest idea of camping in Alexandria Bay, New York, the home of the Boldt Castle. This castle was built on Heart Island as a present for the owner's wife. It is only accessible by boat. There is a State Park Camping area on a neighboring island!

# List of Theme-Related Titles

*The Sorcerer's Apprentice*, Nancy Williard. 1993 The Blue Sky Press, NY.

*Heckedy Peg*, Don and Audrey Wood, 1987 Harcourt Brace Javonovitch, San Diego, CA.

*Eyewitness Book: CASTLE*, Christopher Gravett. 1994. Alfred A. Knopf, NY, NY.

*The King's Commissioners*, Aileen Friedman. 1994. Scholastic, Inc., NY.

*The Dragon of an Ordinary Family*, Margaret Mahy. 1992. Dail Books for Young Readers, NY, NY.

*The Whipping Boy*, Sid Fleischman, 1987. Troll Associates, NJ.

*The Battle for the Castle*, Elizabeth Winthrop. 1993. Bantam, Doubleday, Dell, NY, NY.

*The Library Dragon*, Carmen Agra Deedy. 1994. Peachtree Publisher, GA.

*The Selfish Giant*, Oscar Wilde. 1995. G.P. Putnam's Sons, NY, NY.

*Henry's Gift: The Magic Eye*, David Worsick. 1994. Andrews and McMeel, MO.

*The Sorceror's Apprentice*, Marianna Mayer. 1989. A Bantam Skylark Book, NY.

*My Father's Dragon*, Ruth Stiles Gannett. 1948. Random House, NY.

*Elmer and the Dragon*, Ruth Stiles Gannett. 1950. Random House, NY.

*The Dragons of Blueland*, Ruth Stiles Gannett. 1951. Random House, NY.

*Saint George and The Dragon*, Margaret Hodges. 1984. Little, Brown and Co., MA.

*Cathedral*, David Macaulay. 1973. Trumpet Club, NY.

*Pish, Posh, Said Hieronymus Bosch*. Nancy Williard. 1991. Harcourt, Brace, Jovanovitch, CA.

*Amazing Buildings*, Philip Wilkinson. 1993. Dorling Kindersley, London.

*The Half-A-Moon Inn*, Paul Fleischman. 1980. Harper Trophy, NY.

*The Boggart*, Susan Cooper. 1995. Aladdin Paperbacks, NY.

*Just in Time for the King's Birthday*, E.B. Chance. 1970. Scholastic Book Services, NY.

*Castle, David Macauley*. 1977. Houghton Mifflin, MA.

*The Midwife's Apprentice*, Karen Cushman. 1995. Clarion Books, NY.

*Catherine, Called Birdy*. Karen Cushman. 1994. Harper Trophy, NY.

*The Sorceror's Apprentice*, Ann McKie. 1983. Ladybird Books, ME.

*Cross Sections, Man-Of-War*, Stephen Biesty. 1993. Dorling Kindersley, London.

*Castles, Pyramids and Palaces*, Carol Young and Colin King. 1989. Usborne Publishing, Ltd., London.

*Forts and Castles*, Brian Williams. 1994. Penguin Books, NY.

*Eyewitness Books, Knight*. Christopher Gravett. 1993. Alfred A. Knopf, NY.

*A Medieval Feast*, Aliki. 1983. Harper Trophy, NY.

*Castles*, Naomi Reed Kline. 1985. Caratzas, NY.

*Castles*, Gallimard Jeunesse. 1990. Scholastic, NY.

*Armies of Medieval Burgundy*, Nicholas Michael. 1988. Osprey Publishing, London.

*Eyewitness Books, Book,* Karen Brookfield. 1993. Alfred A. Knopf, NY.

*Incredible Cross Sections*, Stephen Biesty. 1992. Alfred A. Knopf, NY.

*Incredible Castles and Knights*, Christopher Maynard. 1994. Shap Shot Book, NY.

*A Medieval Castle*, Fiona MacDonald and Mark Bergin. 1990. Peter Bedrick Books, NY.

*Castles to Cut Out and Put Together*, J.K. Anderson. 1995. Bellerophon Books, CA.

*A Medieval Alphabet to Illuminate*. 1994. Bellerophon Books, CA.

*Castles of Scotland to Cut Out and Put Together*, J.K. Anderson. 1993. Bellerophon Books, CA.

*Kings and Queens of England to Color*, David Brownell and Harry Knill. 1994. Bellerophon Books, CA.

*A Coloring Book of the Middle Ages*. 1995. Bellerophon Books, CA.

*Paper Soldiers of the Middle Ages*, David Nicolle. 1992. Bellerophon Books, CA.

*The Story of a Castle*, John S. Goodall. 1986. Margaret K. McElderry Books, NY.

*The King's Fountain*, Lloyd Alexander. 1989. E.P. Dutton, NY.

*The Middle Ages*, Edmund Gillon. 1971. Dover Publications, NY.

*When the Giants Came to Town*, Marcia Leonard. 1994. Scholastic, NY.

*The King's Shadow*, Elizabeth Alder. 1995. Farrar Straus Giroux, NY.

*The Adventures of King Midas*, Lynne Reid Banks. 1976. Avon Camelot Books, NY.

*Tomorrow's Wizard*, Patricia MacLachlan. 1982. Scholastic, NY.

*A Present for Prince Paul*, Ann Love. 1995. Child's Play.

*The King Who Rained,* Fred Gwynne. 1970. Trumpet Club, NY.

*Knights and Armor Coloring Book*, A.G. Smith. 1985. Dover Publishing, NY.

*Castles of the World*, A.G. Smith, 1986. Dover Publishing, NY.

*The Kitchen Knight*, Margaret Hodges. 1990. Holiday House, NY.

*King Crow*, Jennifer Armstrong. 1995. Crown Publishers.

*Little Salt Lick and the Sun King*, Jennifer Armstrong, 1994. Crown Publishers, NY.

*Illuminations*, Jonathan Hunt. 1993. Aladdin Books, NY.

*The Toll-Bridge Troll*, Patricia Rae Wolff. 1995. Harcourt Brace and Co., CA.

*The Secret of Trembleton Hall*, Ursala and Gisela Durr. 1995. North-South Book, NY.

*The Fish Who Could Wish*, John Bush and Korky Paul. 1991. Cane/Miller Book Publishers, NY.

*The Reluctant Dragon*, Kenneth Grahame. 1983. Holt, Rinehart and Winston, NY.

*The Prince Who Wrote a Letter*, Ann Love. 1995. Child's Play.

*Sir Gawain and the Loathly Lady*, Selina Hastings, 1985. Mulberry Books, NY.

*Iron John*, Eric Kimmel. 1984. Holiday House, NY.

*Good Grizelle*, Jane Yolen. 1994. Harcourt Brace and Co., NY.

*Journeyman Wizard*, Mary Frances Zambreno. 1994. Harcourt Brace, NY.

*Cowardly Clyde*, Bill Peet. 1979. Houghton Mifflin, MA.

*Castles*, Francesca Baines. 1995. Franklin Watts, NY.

*The King's Equal*, Katherine Paterson. 1992. Trumpet Club, NY.

*The Wonderful Counting Clock*, Cooper Edens. 1995. Simon and Schuster, NY.

*Block City*, Robert Louis Stevenson. 1988. Puffin Books, NY.

*Anno's Math Games II*, Misumansa Anno. 1989 Philomel Books, NY.

*Anno's Math Games*, Mitsumasa Anno. 1987 Philomel Books, NY.

*Anno's Mysterious Multiplying Jar*, Mitsumasa Anno. 1983. Philomel Books, NY.

*Anno's Hat Tricks*, Mitsumasa Anno. 1982. Philomel Books, NY.

*Anno's Counting House*, Mitsumasa Anno. 1982. Philomel Books, NY.

*Anno's Counting Book*, Mitsumasa Anno. 1977. Harper Trophy Book, NY.

## Fairy Tales

*Annos' Three Little Pigs*, Mitsumasa Anno. 1985. The Bodley-Head, London.

*The Jolly Christmas Postman*, Janet and Allan Ahlsberg. 1990. Little, Brown and Co., Boston.

*The Jolly Postman*, Janet and Allan Ahlsberg. 1991. Little, Brown and Company, Boston.

*Politically Correct Bedtime Stories*, James Finn Garner. 1994. Macmillan Publishing, NY.

*Once Upon a More Enlightened Time*, James Finn Garner. 1995. Macmillan Publishing, NY.

*Cinder Edna*, Ellen Jackson. 1994. Lothrop, Lee and Shepard, NY.

*The Frog Prince,* Jacob and Wilhelm Grimm. 1812. North-South Books.

*The Happy Prince*, Oscar Wilde. 1989. Simon and Schuster, NY.

*Prince Cinders*, Babette Cole. 1987. G.P. Putnam's Sons, NY.

*The Rough Faced Girl*, Rafe Martin. 1992. G.P. Putnam's Sons NY.

*The Three Little Pigs*, James Marshall. 1989. Dial Books, NY.

*The Stepsister*, Naomi Lewis. 1987. Dial Books, NY.

*Somebody and the Three Blairs*, Marilyn Tolhurst. 1990. Orchard Books, NY.

*The Three Little Wolves and the Big Bad Pig*, Eugene Trivizas. 1993. Scholastic, NY.

*The True Story of the Three Little Pigs*, Jon Scieszka. 1989. Scholastic, NY.

*The Golden Goose*, Susan Saunders. 1987. Scholastic, NY.

*Rude Giants*, Audrey Wood. 1993. Trumpet Club, NY.

*Rumpelstiltskin*, Brothers Grimm. 1979. Troll Associates, NJ.

*Peter and the Wolf,* retold by Victor G. Ambrus. 1986. Oxford University Press, England.

*Twelve Dancing Princesses*, Brothers Grimm. 1979. Troll Associates, NJ.

*The King, The Dragon and The Witch*, Jerome Corsi. 1972. Ginn and Co., NY.

*Three Billy Goats Gruff*, Ted Dewain. 1994. Scholastic, NY.

*Peeping Beauty*, Mary Jane Auch. 1993. Holiday House, NY.

*Yeh-Shen*, Ai-Ling Louie. 1982. Philomel Books, NY.

*Three Jovial Huntsmen*, Susan Jeffers. 1973. Bradbury Press.

*The Egyptian Cinderella,* Shirley Climo. 1992. Harper Trophy Books, NY.

*Hansel and Gretel*, James Marshall. 1990. Dial Books, NY.

*Rapunzel*, Barbara Rogasky. 1982. Holiday House, NY.

*Puss and Boots*, Charles Perrault. 1990, Farrar, Straus, Giroux.

*Cinder-Elly*, Frances Minters. 1994. Penguin Books, NY.

*Lon Po Po*, Ed Young. 1989. Philomel Books, NY.

*Cinderella*, Charles Perrault. 1989. Henry Holt, NY.

*The Three Little Javelinas.* Susan Lowell. 1992. Scholastic, NY.

*The Three Little Pigs.* Gavin Bishop. 1989. Scholastic, NY.

*Princess Furball.* Charlotte Huck. 1989. Greenwillow Books, NY.

*Jim and the Beanstalk*, Raymond Briggs. 1970. Sandcastle Books, NY.

*Cinderella*, Nola Langner. 1972. Scholastic, NY.

*Little Red Riding Hood*, Trina Schart Hyman. 1983. Holiday House, NY.

*The Sleeping Beauty*, Trina Schart Hyman. 1977. Little, Brown and Co., Boston.

*The Three Little Pigs and The Fox,* William H. Hooks. 1989. Macmillan, NY.

*Red Riding Hood*, Beatrice Schenk de Regniers. 1972. Aladdin Books, NY.

*The Three Little Pigs*, Jean Claverie. 1989. North-South Books, NY.

*The Twelve Dancing Princesses*, Marianna Mayer. 1989. Morrow Junior Books, NY.

*Berlioz The Bear*, Jan Brett. 1991. Scholastic, NY.

*Snow White in New York*, Fiona French. 1986. Oxford University Press.

*Cinderella Penguin.* Janet Perlman. 1992. Puffin Books, NY.

*The Korean Cinderella.* Shirley Climo. 1993. HarperCollins, NY.

There are very distinct differences in the rationale of the multiage programs in the West Park and Raisin City school districts. The move to multiage at West Park was teacher-driven and resulted in the formation of California's 44th Charter School. This move was wholly supported by the administration and board of trustees. The Charter has been functioning for three years, has seen many changes, and continues to grow. The Charter involves about 40 percent of the staff and students at West Park School. It operates as a separate school on the same campus as the traditional school.

The multiage program at Raisin City developed partially as a result of a new superintendent [author Hanlon] being hired by the district. Additionally, the board and staff were convinced that some major changes were necessary to revitalize the educational process. Among the first changes to occur were to move from a traditional calendar to a single-track, year-round calendar, and the shift to a totally multiage school.

## Year Round Schools

Both West Park and Raisin City are year-round schools, operating on a 45-day in, 15-day out schedule; in other words, students and teachers get three weeks vacation every nine weeks. During the first week of each three-week vacation period, students can come in for remediation or enrichment programs. Teachers have the option of teaching during the first week, attending conferences or seminars, or using the entire three-week period as vacation time.

In addition, every Monday, the students go home early to give teachers two hours of free time for collaborative planning and inservice training.

The school year starts in July, and goes through the end of September. The first three-week vacation happens the last week of September and the first two weeks of October.

There is absolutely less teacher burnout than in a nine-month school program; the teachers know they're never more than nine weeks away from a break. Most teachers state they would not give up the year-round, single track program.

*Both . . . are year-round schools, operating on a 45-day in, 15-day out schedule.*

Parents' biggest initial concern is child care; but most parents are surprised to find they have an easier time finding good child care for three weeks at a time, rather than three months at a time. Both schools set their vacation times up to coordinate as much as possible with vacations at other schools, to avoid scheduling conflicts for families with children in other schools. The September-October break does not coincide with any at other schools, but the winter break is the same as elsewhere, and the spring break coincides for the week-long spring break of other schools in the area.

Superintendent Hanlon advises schools considering year-round education to invite nonprofit and for-profit day-care providers into the school to discuss the day-care needs of children attending year-round schools.

## Special Education

The California school system recognizes two main types of special needs students, and Raisin City and West Park's special education program reflects that. Both schools have in place a Resource Specialist Program, or RSP, and a Special Day Classroom (SDC) program.

The Resource Specialist Program assists children who need some extra help, but not a full day program. The children are pulled out of their regular classrooms for a period of between 45 minutes to a maximum of three hours a day. During that time period the RSP students participate in a classroom composed of a small group of children with a special education teacher, in a multiage setting. The classroom teachers and the RSP teacher share information about each student. The special help usually involves math and the reading process.

In the Specialist Day Classroom, children spend 51 percent of their day in special (multiage) classes, then are mainstreamed into regular classes for the rest of the day. Mainstreaming is required by state and federal mandate.

---

### OUTCOMES

West Park and Raisin City School Districts

The student will be able to:

- communicate
- collaborate
- use technology
- problem solve/think critically
- research
- make ethical decisions within all content areas.

### COMMUNICATE

Communicate effectively and express thoughts, feelings, and beliefs through a variety of methods; and react appropriately to the thoughts, feelings, and beliefs of others.

### COLLABORATE

Work as a member of a team, using effective interpersonal skills, toward a mutual purpose or goal.

### PROBLEM SOLVE/THINK CRITICALLY

Apply investigative, analytical, and solution strategies to life-long learning.

### RESEARCH

Locate, access, and analyze information utilizing a variety of methods and sources for a specific purpose.

### USE TECHNOLOGY

Maintain a basic awareness and use of current technology.

### MAKE ETHICAL DECISIONS

Develop the ability to make reasoned and ethical decisions.

---

# WEST PARK

The vast majority of our students are from low socioeconomic homes. The ethnic breakdown is: Hispanic, 75 percent; White, 15 percent; Black, 5 percent; other ethnic groups, 5 percent.

The school became involved in multiage education because the staff felt that the traditional methods of teaching weren't working for many of our students. After doing some research on teaching techniques and visiting other sites that were trying alternative methods, we decided that we would move in the multiage direction. We felt that this method gave a clear option to students and parents. We also felt that, with the state's push to greater interdisciplinary studies, multiage education provided the best opportunity to be successful.

## Philosophy

Our philosophy focuses on giving parents and students an option as to the environment in which learning occurs best. We want to provide an alternative for students who function better when they can be more vocal and active, and perhaps better see the relationship between what they are learning and how they will use that learning. We also feel that the multiage program allows for students to take a greater responsibility for their learning.

While our staff does not team teach in the truest sense of the word, our teachers do work together in developing themes, planning special activities, etc.

The relationship between the multiage and traditional schools has, at times, been strained. This is due in part to the fact that many of the new and exciting techniques and concepts used by the multiage staff have been copied by the traditional staff. It has created a competitive environment that can be very healthy for a school—if it doesn't get out of hand. At this point in time there exists a peaceful co-existence between the two schools.

## Student Selection

Since the West Park Charter School is entirely multiage, the choice parents and students have is between this school and the traditional school on the same campus. To get into the charter school, students and their parents must agree to abide by the Charter agreement (included). As part of the Charter agreement, parents must volunteer time in the program.

## Staff Development

Our staff did research on alternative teaching techniques and methods. We followed this up with site visits to several schools that were starting the multiage approach. We attended multiage conferences and workshops held by The Society For Developmental Education and met with practitioners to develop our own methods and concepts. We also spent time planning what and how we were going to start this unique program.

## Curriculum

We use the interdisciplinary approach. Our staff has developed thematic units created around a different topic each year. We use standardized tests, portfolios and performance activities to evaluate our student progress and program effectiveness. We also use surveys to get parents' input and feelings about the program.

Thematic units are presented to the class as a whole; students then work in learning centers and in small groups and individually, collaboratively and with the teacher, at their own level.

## Benefits of Multiage Education

Multiage education has shown many subtle, but positive changes, in the performance of children at West Park. The kids' attendance records are better, and behavior referrals are fewer, than in single-grade classrooms at the school. This may be ascribed in part to the more flexible, family unit structure in the multiage classes, as well as the fact that there is more parent involvement with the multiage classes. This may be because the children in the multiage classes are there by choice of the parents, rather than by school placement.

Our staff has succeeded in making learning exciting again, for both the teacher and the students. We have broadened our experiences to include activities like Red Cross swimming lessons and Camp Friday Night, and have developed a farm on the campus. The excitement has shown itself in an increase in our actual daily attendance and hopefully in increased test scores.

## Camp Friday Night

Once every quarter, West Park participates in Camp Friday Night. Students do not attend school during the day on Friday, but come at 3:30 or 4:00 p.m., spend an hour or so on an activity, then have dinner and speakers, and participate in activites that teach leadership skills, interaction, and social skills. The kids (and the teachers) bring their sleeping bags and stay overnight; TVs and VCRs are set up in the cafeteria, and the kids can stay up all night talking and watching movies if they want to.

In the morning, a group of parent volunteers comes in to fix breakfast, then the children break into groups and choose a service project; so far children have planted flowers, washed buses, and raked leaves. One group of children built picnic benches. The children generally work from around 9:00 am to noon, then go home.

The kids also get a T-shirt that says West Park Friday Night. The kids love the program; the parents love it—a lot of parents say they wish they could do it every Friday night.

## Our Biggest Obstacle

For us, the biggest obstacle was convincing the rest of the staff that the move to multiage was not going to negatively affect them.

## Our Biggest Challenge

Our biggest challenge now is to make the Charter School program work. We are working to improve our communications with the parents, refine our themes, and deal with the teacher work load that comes with being multiage and Charter.

**WEST PARK CHARTER ACADEMY**

2695 S. Valentine
Fresno, CA 93706

**Phone: 209-233-6501**
**FAX: 209-233-8626**

**Multiage groupings**
(by grade level):
K-1, 2-3, 4-5, 6-7
Limited English Class
(mixed ages/grades)

**Open to visiting teachers and administrators**

**Contact:** Bernie Hanlon, Superintendent

# CHARTER AGREEMENT

West Park Charter Academy
2695 S. Valentine • Fresno, CA 93706
209-233-6501• FAX 233-8626

The purpose of this contract is to strengthen the bonds between West Park Charter Academy, its parents and students. It will clarify the roles, obligations, and expectations of involved parties.

## West Park Charter Academy will:

1. Recognize the rights of parents to participate in all decisions affecting the children.
2. Provide clear, concise reports to parents on student progress.
3. Contact parents as needs arise concerning behavior and/or academic progress.
4. Respond quickly to parental concerns.
5. Provide quality educational opportunities for each child.
6. Provide a safe, nurturing environment conducive to learning.
7. Provide a strong curriculum that encourages risk-taking.
8. Provide competent role-models to facilitate learning.
9. Accept parents as full partners in the educational process.
10. Encourage parent participation in the decision-making of school policy.
11. Encourage parent participations.

## Parents Agree To:

1. Supervise and assist students in the completion of their homework.
2. Support and reinforce school and classroom rules.
3. Take an active role in student performance, instruction, or other issues.
4. Be an active member of the school community.
5. Attend school events—including Back-To-School Night, Open House, Parent Conferences and other school functions.
6. Provide at least 3 hours per month of volunteer time to the school.
7. Commit to program participation for one year.

## Students Will:

1. Understand that they have responsibility for their education.
2. Will pursue their studies at school and at home and will complete all work to the best of their ability.
3. Demonstrate respect for school property and the property of others.
4. Follow school rules.
5. Demonstrate respect for their parents, and their community.
6. Be a positive role-model for others.
7. Contribute 2 hours of service to the school or community each month.
8. Demonstrate a high level of respect toward school employees, other adults on campus and fellow students.

Failure to comply with this contract may lead to student's dismissal from the Charter.

We the undersigned agree to the terms of the contract.

_____        _____
Student Signature                                          Date

_____        _____
Parent Signature                                            Date

_____        _____
Superintendent                                              Date

# RAISIN CITY

The majority of our students come from low income families. The ethnic breakdown is as follows: 85 percent Hispanic; 10 percent White; and 5 percent a mixture of other cultures.

It was obvious that we needed to change the way we were doing the business of education. Too many of our kids were not reaching their full potential as learners for a variety of reasons: a lack of parent involvement or a sense of responsibility for their children's education, the changing dynamics of the family, and the students' own lack of ownership in their own education.

Staff members began to explore other program possibilities such as multiage by attending local conferences and visiting local workshops, and by visiting local districts that were implementing a multiage approach. We felt that this change would better serve our student population.

Our philosophy is simply to offer the best educational opportunities possible to all our students. We feel that multiage education does that.

The school has been entirely multiage for three years. We have a total of 12 classes.

We use an interdisciplinary approach, with an emphasis on the acquisition of basic skills, and aimed at our six identified student outcomes (included). We use standardized tests, portfolios, and performance activities.

## Curriculum

We use the same general approach as West Park, using thematic units, learning centers, and small-group, collaborative, and individual work. We also use surveys to get parents' input and feelings about the program.

We use standardized tests, portfolios and performance activities to evaluate our student progress and program effectiveness.

## Limited English Class

We are proud of our Limited English class, which teaches the core subjects in the students' native language in the morning and follows up with English in the afternoon. The English classes concentrate on language development.

Of the Hispanic students, 69 percent have Spanish as their primary language. The school also deals with students speaking Cambodian, Laotian, Vietnamese, and Punjabi, among others, as their primary language. The small, rural school does not always have access to Spanish-speaking teachers, because the school district often loses them to larger school districts who can afford to pay more money and tend to get all the qualified Spanish teachers. We are mandated to train all staff to teach ESL children. Some of our teachers are bilingual.

The school has no access to a Punjabi teacher, but does have a Punjabi tutor in three days a week working with small groups of children for a period of 45 minutes to an hour a day. The school shares the tutor with two other school districts.

The school encourages kids to keep their first language, while learning English; the way you make it in this country is to be fluent in English. The goal of the school is to be able to mainstream children into regular classes, fully functional in English. There are varying degrees of success in this, depending on the level of the students.

## Impact of Multiage on Standardized Test Scores

Raisin City School is located in a rural area, serving a population of very low income. Kids are coming to school further and further behind; they do not have parents reading to them; many one-to-five-year-olds are not exposed to family trips or cultural experiences, in or out of the home.

Parents are not keeping the good kids at home; they're sending us what they've got. These kids aren't stupid; they're not dumb; they're disadvantaged. But, given time to work with them, these students do make significant academic progress.

Raisin City students were tested with the CTBS—Comprehensive Test of Basic Skills—two years ago, and then one year ago. The same students who had been tested in reading in first, fourth, and seventh grades were tested again in second, fifth, and eighth grades—with a dramatic rise in scores. the range in scores was from 95 percent in the lowest quartile in first year, first grade, to only 17 percent in the lowest quartile in second year, eighth grade (see charts). Math scores were also positively affected. Multiage seems to be at least one tool that is effective. It's not just doing multiage or year-round education or whole language; it's those things in combination with other things.

## Parent Involvement

Parents are encouraged to participate in the classroom, in parent Math nights, and in several on-site workshops.

## Our Biggest Obstacle

Our biggest obstacle was convincing parents that multiage was a positive and necessary change. We got agreement from them after sharing research on multiage education, discussing how current strategies weren't as effective as they once were, and making site visits.

## Our Biggest Challenge

We want to continue to improve our program, get more parents involved in classroom and home activities, and show improvement in standardized test scores.

## Mandates

Trying to meet all the federal and state education mandates can be a continuing challenge. Rules are so rigid that it is difficult to try something innovative. Many teachers feel frustration at being told they can't try something they feel would improve their classes. My feeling is, make me prove to you that what we're doing works; and if it doesn't, *then* come down and kick my butt!

**RAISIN CITY SCHOOL DISTRICT**

P.O. Box 69
Raisin City, CA 93652

**Phone: 209-233-0128**
**FAX: 209-486-0891**

**Multiage groupings**
(by grade level):
K-1, 1-2, 2-3, 4-5, 6-7-8

**Open to visiting teachers and administrators**

**Contact:**
Bernie Hanlon,
Superintendent

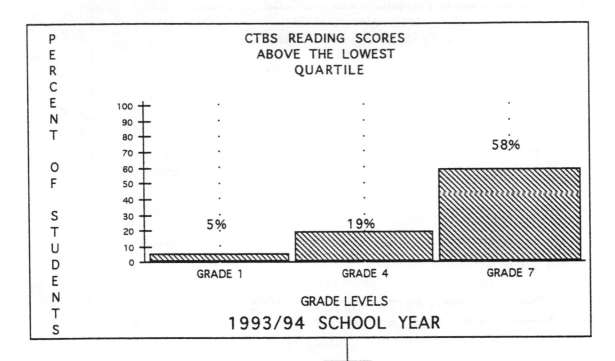

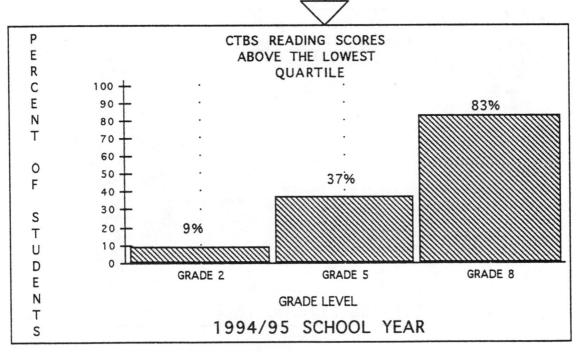

The top graph illustrates the CTBS reading scores for the 1993/94 school year. The bottom graph illustrates the CTBS reading scores for the 1994/95 school year. The grade levels were chosen to show the growth that occurred in one year for the same students. The students who were in grade one during the 1993/94 school year were in grade two during the 1994/95 school year. The graphs show that there was most significant growth in the seventh grade students from 1993/94 (58%) to 1994/95 (83%).

The CTBS test is a comprehensive test of basic skills.

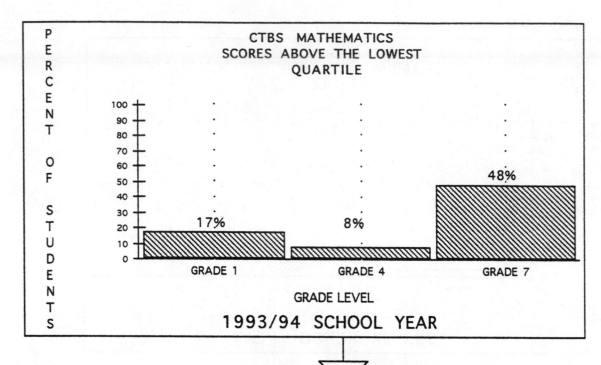

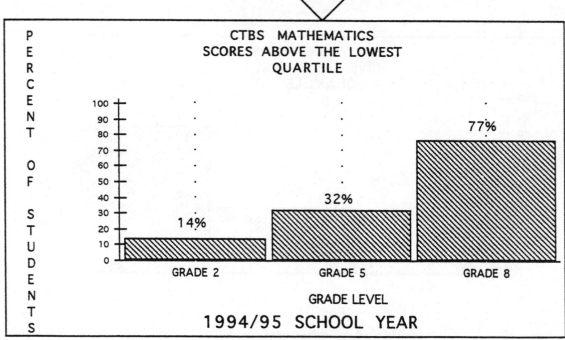

The top graph illustrates the CTBS mathematics scores for the 1993/94 school year. The bottom graph illustrates the CTBS mathematics scores for the 1994/95 school year. The grade levels were chosen to show growth that occurred in one year for the same students. The students who were in grade one during 1993/94 school year were in grade two during the 1994/95 school year. The graphs show that there was most significant growth in the seventh grade students from 1993/94 (48%) to 1994/95 (77%).

The CTBS test is a comprehensive test of basic skills.

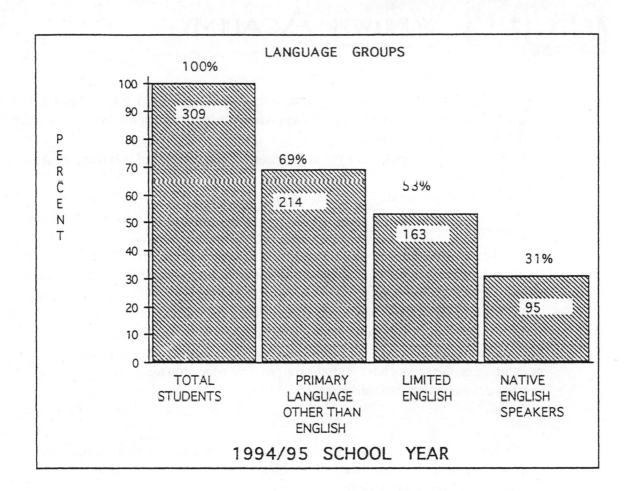

**LANGUAGE GROUPS**

100%

| PERCENT | | | |
|---|---|---|---|
| 100% — 309 | 69% — 214 | 53% — 163 | 31% — 95 |
| TOTAL STUDENTS | PRIMARY LANGUAGE OTHER THAN ENGLISH | LIMITED ENGLISH | NATIVE ENGLISH SPEAKERS |

**1994/95 SCHOOL YEAR**

*The way you make it in this country is to be able to speak English—we need to encourage kids to retain their own language and culture, while becoming fluent in the English language.*

*— Bernie Hanlon, Principal*
*Raisin City and West Park*
*School Districts, California*

Windsor Academy, an alternative school which is part of the Columbus school system, is located off Cleveland Avenue in the heart of the Windsor Terrace Housing Complex.

One-third of our population lives in Windsor Terrace. One-third is bussed from the North 4th Street/Summit-Chittenden to Hudson Avenue Area. Our final third are ESL (English Second Language) students, which include 160 students from 18 different countries.

The student population is approximately 65 percent African-American, 25 percent ESL, and 10 percent White. Approximately 98 percent of our students are recipients of free or reduced-price breakfast and lunch. Enrollment fluctuates because of our 57 percent mobility rate; the current enrollment figure is 530 students. The average daily attendance is approximately 92.3 percent.

Windsor's school focus is physical and academic excellence; our aim is to develop the mind and body together. Our students learn that when your body is healthy, well-rested, and well-fed, your mind works well. Windsor Academy integrates physical movement into all content areas; the school has two full-time physical education teachers. The phys ed program is developmentally appropriate.

## Staff

We have 36 certified teachers, consisting of 30 women and six men; about 30 percent are African American. We also have 20 Classified Staff (assistants and aides), 15 women and five men; 75 percent are African American.

Some teachers choose to team teach, doing rotations for certain subjects. All but math regroupings are multiage.

## Why Multiage Education?

Windsor Academy has been practicing multiage education for seven years. The school began multiage because two staff members had student-taught in multiage classrooms. They started it, and others joined in; the result was that multiage went schoolwide. We now have 13 multiage classrooms.

*We teach to the individual child; the building works as a whole towards accelerating learning.*

We consider multiage a solid, positive educational philosophy. We teach to the individual child; the building works as a whole towards accelerating learning.

We also recognize that a range of levels occurs as much in our single-grade classrooms as in our multiage classrooms.

## Composition of Multiage Classes

The school is organized, pre-kindergarten through fifth grade, in multiage family groupings. Our multiage classes consist of K-1, 1-2, 3-4, and 4-5 blends. Our 2-3 multiage just changed to 2,3,3 single grade classrooms due to an open enrollment and a huge increase in third-graders.

We have two units for developmentally handicapped (DH) children, and two units for children with specific learning disabilities (SLD).

*Our students wear uniforms in our public school.*

Placement decisions are made based on where the teachers feel a child would best fit. We keep a balance of high, medium, and low ability levels in each grade for each room; we then try to balance the male/female population.

Parents have a choice of placing their child in a particular classroom only on a very individual basis; it is not a public option.

## Staff Development

We participated in a panel discussion with staff members who had implemented multiage for one or two years. We also attended a multiage conference, and studied books about multiage.

## Curriculum and Assessment

Because Windsor Academy is now a school-wide project school, all federal funds alloted based on free and reduced lunch numbers can be used for the school's educational program which was designed on-site. The school hired its own reading and language arts person, and set aside money for lots and lots of books—you can never have enough books—and equipment and supplies like magnetic letters, overhead projectors, and magnadoodles.

Our daily schedule provides us uninterrupted blocks of time—90 minutes for language arts blocks and 45 minutes for math blocks. (An example framework for our language arts blocks is included.)

We use Columbus Public Schools alternative reading assessment tool, and we keep writing folders.

Standardized testing is a big problem, because we have to make the classrooms straight grades during that week, and students may be tested by someone who is not their regular teacher. That's why teaming is so important—so the students become familiar with every teacher.

We have excellent ESL instructors who focus on growth over time. Our ESL teachers do a 90-minute block with ESL students daily, and this provides the classroom with much needed support with these unique learners.

## Specialists—And Special Needs

Our specialists (music, art, etc.) only come into the classroom when a special integration project is going on. Specials are scheduled so as to provide classroom teachers with time daily for planning and team meetings. The specialists do make themselves aware of thematic units classroom teachers are doing.

We have simple mainstreaming, during specials and rotations between team members, for certain topics. The special needs teachers have multiage within their rooms. We cannot get to a full inclusion program; because our teachers have so many gray-area students in their classrooms, they already deal with

## WINDSOR ACADEMY

1219 East 12th Avenue
Columbus, OH 43211

**Phone: 614-365-5906**
**FAX: 614-365-6939**

**Multiage groupings**
(by grade level):
K-1, 1-2, 3-4, 4-5

**Open to visiting teachers and administrators**

**Contact:** Gayle Brand, instructional facilitator

gray-area students in their classrooms, they already deal with many special needs.

"Pull-outs" for students with special needs in the regular classroom only occur during content studies blocks.

## Grouping

We use flexible grouping of students based on student needs and interests. Ability grouping also exists when needed. Some multiage classes do switch students for math, because of our math series requirements, mainly in the intermediate grades.

## Homework

Homework is required.

---

### *Serving a Transient Population*

Our biggest challenge is keeping our classes balanced in terms of high, medium, and low-achieving students of each grade, and in terms of class size. We are still working on this, because our population is so transient! We balance the classes in the spring, and by September, those kids don't come back. A lot of changes in student enrollment occur around the first of the month—when bills come due—and after the holidays.

With students coming and going so frequently, many of them do not get the full benefit of their schooling, but we do feel, that when students do come to Windsor Academy, they develop a liking for school. We treat new students the same as if they've been with us all year long.

Many of the children receive free breakfast and free lunch; they all receive the warmth and love of an adult human. They feel safe here. Of course, as multiage educators we are able to meet incoming students where they're at academically.

The multiage structure cuts down on off-task issues at the beginning of each year, with the "old" students actively helping newcomers adjust to the classroom.

### Parent Involvement

When students do return in the fall, a relationship has already been established between the school and the family. Many parents are school-phobic when they visit us; but once we manage to get them in here they love it; they come in and in and in.

Our parent involvement has increased slightly every year. Our teachers do lots of communicating through notes, home visits, and phone calls. The parents are always welcome.

*Inschool Scouting*

### In-School Support Systems

The Intervention Assistance Team (IAT) is made up of Windsor Academy teachers, counselors, the principal, and in-house social workers. The IAT arranges for student physicals, which are required for enrollment in the school; transports students to hospital (i.e., for physical therary, etc.) when necessary, and arranges for testing procedures and intervention when a teacher refers a student to the IAT for developmental or academic issues.

The Care Connection provides social services for the students and their families within the building.

### Scouting

Because many children cannot participate in after-school extracurricular activities, Windsor Academy also provides in-house Boy Scouts and Girl Scouts programs during school hours. The school has a scoutmaster in the building. Boy Scouts and Girl Scouts are part of the students' social studies grade.

# WINDSOR ACADEMY OF ACADEMIC & PHYSICAL EXCELLENCE

## GRADES 1 - 5   ACADEMIC YEAR _____

STUDENT _____   ROOM _____
GRADE _____

**GRADING CODES**

- E --- Excellent
- S --- Satisfactory
- I --- Improvement Needed - Working at grade level

AT GRADE LEVEL

- P --- Progressing - Not at grade level
- N --- Not Progressing

BELOW GRADE LEVEL

- N/A --- Not addressed at this time

**EFFORT CODES**

- 1 --- Strong Effort
- 2 --- Normal Effort
- 3 --- Little or No Effort

### READING

| | 1 | 2 | 3 | 4 | FG |
|---|---|---|---|---|---|
| Applies Appropriate Strategies | | | | | |
| • early strategies (K-1) | | | | | |
| • monitors what is read | | | | | |
| • interprets sources of information | | | | | |
| • self corrects | | | | | |
| Understands and responds to what is read | | | | | |
| Develops vocabulary | | | | | |
| Completes homework | | | | | |

### LANGUAGE ARTS

| | 1 | 2 | 3 | 4 | FG |
|---|---|---|---|---|---|
| Expresses ideas orally | | | | | |
| Uses writing to express ideas | | | | | |
| Uses the writing process | | | | | |
| Completes homework | | | | | |

### SPELLING

### HANDWRITING

COMMENTS:

1. _____
2. _____
3. _____
4. _____

### MATH

| | 1 | 2 | 3 | 4 | FG |
|---|---|---|---|---|---|
| Understands numbers and number relationships | | | | | |
| Uses appropriate information to solve problems | | | | | |
| Recognizes patterns | | | | | |
| Understands principles of geometry | | | | | |
| Understands principles of algebra | | | | | |
| Demonstrates measurement skills | | | | | |
| Completes homework | | | | | |

COMMENTS:

1. _____
2. _____
3. _____
4. _____

### ENGLISH AS A SECOND LANGUAGE

### ART

### MUSIC

### CONTENT STUDIES

| | 1 | 2 | 3 | 4 | FG |
|---|---|---|---|---|---|
| SCIENCE | | | | | |
| SOCIAL STUDIES | | | | | |
| HEALTH | | | | | |
| PHYSICAL EDUCATION | | | | | |

COMMENTS:

1. _____
2. _____
3. _____
4. _____

### MESSAGE TO PARENT

| | 1 | 2 | 3 | 4 |
|---|---|---|---|---|
| NOTE ENCLOSED | | | | |
| CONFERENCE REQUESTED | | | | |
| RETENTION BEING CONSIDERED | | | | |

### RECORD OF ATTENDANCE

| | 1 | 2 | 3 | 4 | Total |
|---|---|---|---|---|---|
| TIMES TARDY | | | | | |
| DAYS PRESENT | | | | | |
| DAYS ABSENT | | | | | |

### BEHAVIORS

| | 1 | 2 | 3 | 4 |
|---|---|---|---|---|
| Shows appropriate behavior in class | | | | |
| Shows appropriate behavior in other areas | | | | |
| Accepts responsibility for own actions | | | | |
| Respects rights and property of others | | | | |
| Practices self-discipline | | | | |
| Follows directions | | | | |
| Works independently | | | | |
| Listens attentively | | | | |
| Has necessary materials for work | | | | |

COMMENTS:

1. _____
2. _____
3. _____
4. _____

YOUR CHILD IS:

PROMOTED TO GRADE _____   ROOM _____

PLACED IN GRADE _____   ROOM _____

RETAINED IN GRADE _____   ROOM _____

PRINCIPAL _____

TEACHER _____

# A Framework for Early Literacy Lessons

| Element | Values | Supporting Research |
|---|---|---|
| **1. Reading Aloud to Children** (rereading favorite selections) | Motivates children to read (shows purpose)<br>Provides an adult demonstration<br>Develops sense of story<br>Develops knowledge of written language, syntax and of how texts are structured<br>Increases vocabulary and linguistic repertoire<br>Supports intertextual ties through enjoyment and shared knowledge, creates community of readers | |
| **2. Shared Reading** Rereading big books<br>Rereading retellings<br>Rereading alternative texts<br>Rereading the products of interactive writing | Demonstrates early strategies<br>Builds sense of story and ability to predict<br>Demonstrates process of reading<br>Provides social support from the group<br>Provides opportunity to participate, behave like a reader | |
| **3. Guided Reading** | Provides opportunity to problem-solve while reading for meaning ("reading work")<br>Provides opportunity to use strategies on extended text<br>Challenges the reader and creates context for successful processing on novel texts<br>Teacher selection of text, guidance, demonstration, and explanation is available to the reader | |
| **4. Independent Reading** | Children read on their own or with partners from a wide range of materials<br>Some reading is from a special collection at their reading level | |
| **5. Shared Writing** | Children compose messages and stories; teacher supports process as scribe<br>Demonstrates how writing works | McKenzie |
| **6. Interactive Writing** | Demonstrates concepts of print, early strategies, and how words work<br>Provides opportunities to hear sounds in words and connect with letters<br>Helps children understand "building up" and "breaking down" processes in reading and writing<br>Provides opportunities to plan and construct texts<br>Increases spelling knowledge | |

| Element | Values | Supporting Research |
|---|---|---|
| **7. Guided Writing and Writers' Workshop**<br>Teacher guides the process and provides instruction | Demonstrates the process of writing, including composing, drafting, and editing<br>Provides opportunity for explicit teaching of various aspects of writing<br>Gives students the guidance they need to learn writing processes and produce high quality products | |
| **8. Independent Writing**<br>Individual re-tellings<br>Labeling<br>"Speech balloons"<br>Books and other pieces | Provides opportunity for independence<br>Provides chance to write for different purposes<br>Increases writers' ability to use different forms<br>Builds ability to write words and use punctuation<br>Fosters creativity and the ability to compose | |
| **9. Letters, Words, and How They Work** | Materials and experiences are provided to help children learn to use visual aspects of print | |

**Extensions and Themes:** Drama, Murals, Story Maps, Innovations on Text, Surveys, Science Experiments, and others.

- Provides opportunities to interpret texts in different ways
- Provides a way of revisiting a story
- Fosters collaboration and enjoyment
- Creates a community of readers
- Provides efficient instruction through integration of content areas

**Documentation of Progress**

- Provides information to guide daily teaching
- Provides a way to track the progress of individual children
- Provides a basis for reporting to parents
- Helps a school staff to assess the effectiveness of the instructional program

**Home and Community Involvement**

- Brings reading and writing materials and new learning into children's homes
- Gives children more opportunities to show their families what they are learning
- Increases reading and writing opportunities for children
- Demonstrates value and respect for children's homes

*Oral language is the foundation for all elements of the framework.*

# COLUMBUS PUBLIC SCHOOLS
## WINDSOR ACADEMY
### Daily Schedule

| | TEAM 1 | TEAM 2 | TEAM 3 | TEAM 4 | TEAM 5 | |
|---|---|---|---|---|---|---|
| TEAMS | PRE-K, K, K K-1, K-1, K-1 | 1-2, 1-2, 1-2, 1-2 Primary DH | 2, 3, 3, Primary LD | 3-4, 3-4, 3-4 Int. DH | 4-5, 4-5, 4-5, 5 Int. LD | |
| 8:45-9:00 | PERIOD OF PREPARATION | | | | | 8:45-9:00 |
| 9:00-9:30 | HOMEROOM/OPENING ACTIVITIES/READING RECOVERY | | | | | 9:00-9:30 |
| 9:30-10:15 | SPECIALS | LANGUAGE ARTS AND READING BLOCK | LANGUAGE ARTS AND READING BLOCK | LANGUAGE ARTS AND READING BLOCK | LANGUAGE ARTS AND READING BLOCK | 9:30-11:00 |
| 10:15-11:45 | LANGUAGE ARTS AND READING BLOCK | CONTENT STUDIES | CONTENT STUDIES | SPECIALS | CONTENT STUDIES | 11:00-12:00 |
| 11:45-12:00 | 15 Min. Extra | | | | | |
| 12:00-1:00 | LUNCH/ RECESS | LUNCH/ RECESS | LUNCH/ RECESS | LUNCH RECESS | LUNCH/ RECESS | 12:00-1:00 |
| 1:00-1:45 | CONTENT STUDIES | MATH | SPECIALS | MATH | CONTENT STUDIES | 1:00-1:45 |
| 1:45-2:30 | CONTENT STUDIES | SPECIALS | CONTENT STUDIES | CONTENT STUDIES | MATH | 1:45-2:30 |
| 2:30-3:15 | MATH | CONTENT STUDIES | MATH | CONTENT STUDIES | SPECIALS | 2:30-3:15 |
| 3:15-3:30 | DISMISSAL | DISMISSAL | DISMISSAL | DISMISSAL | DISMISSAL | 3:15-3:30 |

# The **Windsor Academy** for Academic and Physical Excellence

### Windsor Literacy Clinic

- *Daily 90 minute blocks*
- *"Intensive Care Unit"*
- *Reading Recovery Clinic*
- *Reduced Class Size*
- *Resource Room*
- *Instructional Facilitator*
- *Inclusion*
- *Resource Teachers*

### Professional Development School

- The Ohio State University
- Urban Professional School
- *Literacy Links*
- Professional Partnership
- Schools that Work for Kids & Teachers
- *Peer Coaching*

### Physical Education/ Health

- *Comprehensive Pre-K-5 Physical Education Program*
- Health Fair
- Intramural Program
- Big Run Experience
- Structured Recess
- Track Meet
- Field Days
- Camp (Outdoor Education)

### English Second Language Center

- Model ESL Program/Center

### Family Support Center

- Full time Counselor
- IAT
- Care Connection Children's Hospital Child Diocesan
- Home Visits

### Parent Involvement Program

- *Parent Liaison*
- *Volunteer Program*
- Workshop Training
- Fundraising
- PCAC
- Parent Support Group

### School/ Business Partnership

- AKZO
- Nationwide
- Tutoring Program

### Library/ Technology

- *Full-time Librarian*
- *Upgrade:* Audio Visuals; TV's; VCR's; Laser Discs; Zapshot Camera
- PRONET
- INTERNET
- *Computer Instruction (Phase-In)*

### Assessment

- Alternative Reading Assessment
- Portfolios
- Writing Assessments
- Proficiency Testing
- District-wide Testing
- Periodic Assessment

### Cultural Arts Extended Day/ Year Programs

- Double Dutch
- Assemblies
- Scouting
- Choir
- *Orchestra*
- Field Trips
- Fun Festival
- Art-Music Specialist
- *Summer School*

### Other Programs/ Activities

- DARE
- Egypt Girls
- Ebony Boys
- Morning Announcements
- School-wide Themes
- Peer Mediation/ Conflict Resolution
- Right to Read
- *GED Preparation*

### PR Marketing

- *Uniforms*
- Newsletter
- Media
- Academy Store
- Fundraiser

*Bold/Italic = New Concepts*

W e are a small town of approximately 6,500 people in the northeast corner of Connecticut. It is a bedroom town for many business people, as well as a rural farming community. We have around 900 students in grades Pre-K through 8. In January we will be opening a new middle school for grades 5-8; grades Pre-K through 4 will remain in the present building. At this time both schools have their own principal.

This is the third year we have had multiage 1-2 classes, and the first year we have had a 3-4 multiage and a looping program in K-1.

In April of 1993, two staff members attended the SDE (Society For Developmental Education) conference in Nashua, New Hampshire, and came back very excited about multiage education. They approached the administration and received permission to pursue the idea with the Board of Education and the community.

At the time one of the teachers was a first grade teacher, and one was teaching second grade. It did not create job shifts for anyone else, it did not cost extra money, and both teachers had taught at both grade levels, so they were encouraged to give it a try.

## Philosophy

A child who comes into a multiage program in Woodstock stays in the program for two years. The child is challenged at his or her developmentally appropriate level and moves through the curriculum at a pace appropriate for him or her. All children cover the same material as single-grade children, but the timing and sequence may differ from the single grade classroom.

*... no one teaching method or strategy works for all children. We look at the child as an individual and for what works best for him or her.*

If we are covering the same topics as the single-grade classrooms, we might share speakers, field trips, and activities. We also frequently share materials with the single-grade classrooms. However, since our schedules cannot be the same, there is very little time to plan together with single-grade classrooms.

We have three multiage 1-2 classes and two multiage 3-4 classes. We have one Pre-K, two kindergartens (including one kindergarten which is looped with a first-grade class), four single-grade first grades (including the one looped with the kindergarten class), three single-grade second grades, three single-grade third grades, and three single-grade fourth grades.

Our multiage 1-2 classes have children ages five to eight at this time; these children would be considered first and second graders. Our multiage 3-4 classes have children seven to nine; these children would be considered third and fourth graders if they were in single-grade classes.

## Staff Development

Prior to the 1993 summer break, the two staff members planning on doing multiage in the fall shared their plans and the program's research base material with the K-4 staff. The multiage teachers encouraged the staff to read the material and answered questions about the process they underwent to get approval for the program. They encouraged the staff to voice any concerns they had for the program. The multiage teachers answered questions to the best of their ability; the school purchased materials for everyone to use. The administration voiced support for the program, as well as for the two multiage staff members.

## Curriculum and Assessment

Our curriculum is based on the Connecticut state curriculum; we give the Connecticut Mastery tests for on-grade and off-grade levels. We base our math curriculum on the NCTM standards. We are implementing a new science curriculum, and we are developing a comprehensive social studies curriculum. Our Language Arts program encompasses reading, writing, speaking and listening, and is viewed as a process.

We have a workshop approach to many subjects; the children work at their own level. Our writing process takes children from the earliest stages of scribble writing to the advanced stages of story writing, editing, and publishing.

We use many tools to assess the child's developmental and academic levels and we report the child's progress to parents at least twice a year in conferences, and twice more in written form. We use developmental spelling assessments including the Features List and Richard Gentry's list. We use the Morrison-McCall Spelling Scale and Marie Clay's dictation sentences, as well as the San Diego Quick Word Assessment. We have also developed rubrics for our core literature books for each grade level; each child receives a score on the rubrics which is recorded on his or her progress report.

We also assess using writing prompts. All children in a given grade level are given the same writing prompt, and each child receives a score according to the writing rubrics that we have established. Copies of these forms can be provided.

Our math curriculum includes skills that need to be developed, reinforced and mastered at each grade level. Teachers use observation, anecdotal notes, paper and pencil tests and problem solving to assess children's progress in math.

Our multiage classes use centers and a workshop approach to hands-on, activity-based learning. Our children are encouraged to problem solve in cooperative learning groups and to become independent, responsible learners. We work with children in all types of groups and employ many different strategies when teaching children. We find that, with a diverse group of children, no one teaching method or strategy works for all children. We look at the child as an individual and find what works best for him or her.

## Student Selection

Our philosophy is that every child can benefit from a multiage classroom; however, the child whose parents are against a multiage placement will not do well in one. Our selection process as evolved over the last three years. All kindergarten parents now fill out a form indicating whether they would like their child placed in a single-grade first followed by a single grade second, a multiage for two years, or a looping to first if that child is in the "looping" kindergarten. They may also choose to leave the decision to the discretion of the present teacher.

The 3-4 multiage does the same with all second-grade parents (and third grade parents this year, as it was a new program). After the parent forms are collected, the multiage teachers, the kindergarten teacher, the special education teachers, speech and language teachers, Occupational Therapy and Physical Therapy specialists and the principal sit down as a team and form class lists for the next year.

We create classes that are balanced for male/female, academic level of performance, and number of special needs students. We also look at possible emotional/behavioral conflicts and consider the parents' feelings on placement of siblings or twins. Our multiage classes break down demographically to be comparable to the single-grade classes.

## Parental Choice

Parents state a preference, but we cannot guarantee all multiage requests. After the first year, there was a big demand by parents for multiage spaces. The administration responded by adding another 1-2 multiage and increasing our class sizes from 19 to 22. This year we had a number of requests for 1-2 multiage placements that could not be filled, nor were there enough spaces available to consider the pool of people who chose to leave the decision to the discretion of the teacher.

## Grouping

Children are grouped heterogeneously in our classrooms, which gives us a diverse collection of children of many different ages and developmental levels. Within the class, children are instructed as a whole group, in small groups, individually, by technology, by interests, by same-age, by different-age, and randomly. Grouping in our classrooms depends on the task and the students needs' in our rooms.

## Specialists in the Classroom

When we began multiage, our art teacher was out on an extended illness leave, and she had a long-term sub. Our music teacher wasn't sure she wanted to deal with two grades at one time. Our physical education teachers had no choice; they had to take our classes as a whole entity. Music and art classes were held for second graders at one time and first graders another time.

This situation was very difficult for us because we never had any planning time; we always had half a class with us. Neither did we have any common planning time. We began to feel that our classes were not developing the sense of community that we were looking to create. They did not see themselves as a "class"; they were first graders and second graders sharing a teacher.

We discussed the situation with the music teacher, and she agreed to teach the classes as 1-2 classes. Art class continued to be taught separately as first and second grades until our regular art colleague returned. She has had a difficult time with multiage as the art curriculum is very lock-step, grade specific.

All of the specialists have worked to develop curriculum that allows our multiage 1-2 classes to be taught together. As this is the first year of the 3-4 multiage and the specialists feel the skill level and curriculum delivery would be very difficult with a 3-4 multiage, we created a schedule so specials take place back-to-back for 3-4. All third graders go to art together and then to music together, and all fourth graders go to music first and then to art together. This also happens with the P.E. and Library special time slots. It seems to be meeting the needs of the specialists as well as the children.

## Gifted And Talented Programs

Our gifted and talented programs for academics, music, art, and creative writing are open to all students in the building who qualify, whether they are in a single grade or multiage. They are pullout programs that children are recommended for by themselves, their parents or their teachers.

## Special-Needs Students

Special-needs students are found in the same numbers in our classrooms as they are in single-grade classrooms. We have had emotionally disturbed, Down syndrome, ADD, ADHD, learning disabled, Autistic (PDD), hearing-impaired, and language-deprived children in our classrooms. Some of these children have teacher assistant's help depending on the severity of the situation. Special-needs children are fully included in all aspects of our program. Programming in our classes is done on an individual basis for just about all children, so modifications for special needs children are really not noticed by other children or the casual observer.

Our special-needs children are included in all aspects of our programs, with appropriate modifications when needed. These children are with us for almost their entire day. Sometimes an Occupational Therapist or Physical Therapist specialist (which is an outside service) will pull the child for therapy, but this might be ½ to 1 hour a week.

Our special education resource teacher now comes into the classroom to work with "her" children and a small group of other children during reading. The resource room assistant also comes and works with another targeted group. This is helpful to all children in the class. Our speech and language specialist is also piloting a program of inclusion in our classrooms this year. She will come into the classroom and work with small groups of targeted children in the classroom.

Some children have teacher assistants assigned to them either full or half time. These people are in the classroom to help the child and can be used to monitor work, help adjustments, or work with small groups of children in the class. The special-needs child spends a large part of his day with his peers in his classroom.

## Team Teaching

The three teachers of the 1-2 multiage classes consider ourselves a team. We have an extended period of time where all three classes are at two back-to-back specials, which gives us time each week to devote to each other and our classroom planning.

We plan our centers together and divide up the preparation of materials and other tasks for all three classes. We share ideas for reading workshop, math workshop, writing workshop, social studies, science, and health activities. We plan and implement ideas for theme and/or curriculum driven "ticket time".

## Ticket Time

Children choose which area of focus they want to follow for a certain subject area. The children are grouped by their choices and spend time with children from the other two multiage 1-2 classes, studying their chosen area by rotating to one of our three classrooms.

At the end of ticket time we have "Multiage Sharing" — the three classes get together as a community of learners and share what we have learned separately in ticket time. Multiage Sharing is also a forum for sharing published books, poems, and art work, and provides time as a group for shared lessons, initiations and closures.

The teaming that happens in our multiage classes is also being developed by our 3-4 team. It is an important part of a multiage community.

## Parental Involvement

We invite our parents to a Parent Open House at the beginning of the year, where we outline the goals and objectives of the program and answer any questions they have about the process of learning in our classroom. Parents help at home by being part of the W.E.B. Log (Wonderfully Exciting Books) program, in which the child is encouraged to read to his or her parents, or anyone else at home. The parent records the name of the book and a positive comment for the young reader.

Parents also help by providing materials needed in the classroom. Parents help in the classroom by listening to children read books and their own stories, typing children's work in the writing process on the computer, monitoring learning in small center groups, and giving spelling tests for our individualized spelling program. Parents help extend lessons by sharing their expertise in many areas. They also help by supporting our program in the community. They are essential to the success of our program!

## Our Biggest Issue

The biggest issue facing us now is the lack of support for our programs from some colleagues teaching in single-grade classrooms. Some seem to feel threatened by the multiage program; when the administration voiced support for a new 3-4 multiage program, many colleagues teaching in single grades worried that they would be pressured into teaching multiage and did not want to do it. Some colleagues who felt negatively toward the multiage program were vocal to parents about not placing their children in it.

Teaching in a multiage classroom is a lot of work, and when you are planning a new program, forming a new team, and taking a big personal risk, you need all the support you can get. It is difficult to deal with other professionals who do not support new and different ideas that you feel are right for yourself and the children you are teaching.

We continue to work to bridge the rifts that have formed among colleagues.

## Waivers/Mandates

We did not have to secure any waivers or bypass any mandates that I know of. During the required Connecticut Mastery Tests, our 3-4 multiage teachers split the classes; and one teacher took fourth graders and administered that test, and the other teacher took all of the third grades. For our grade-specific health curriculum we split the classes by grade level, and split the teaching of the lessons for the "Here's Looking At You 2000" health curriculum kit.

# Woodstock Public School
# Language Arts Assessment — K-4

The following is a list of L.A. assessments expected at each grade level:

**Kindergarten:** The first four assessments on the first grade list should be used in kindergarten on an individual basis at the teacher's discretion. Scored Reading Comprehension Questions, Attitudinal Surveys

**First Grade:** Gentry Developmental Spelling, Morrison-McCall Spelling Scale, Reading Recovery Dictation Task, San Diego Sight Word Assessment, Scored Reading Comprehension Questions, Writing Prompts, Attitudinal Surveys

**Second Grade:** Gentry Developmental Spelling, Morrison-McCall Spelling Scale, Reading Recovery Dictation Task, San Diego Sight Word Assessment, Scored Reading Comprehension Questions, Writing Prompts, Attitudinal Surveys

**Third Grade:** Features Developmental Spelling, Morrison-McCall Spelling Scale, Reading Recovery Dictation Task, San Diego Sight Word Assessment, Scored Reading Comprehension Questions, Writing Prompts, Attitudinal Surveys

**Fourth Grade:** Features Developmental Spelling, Morrison-McCall Spelling Scale, Reading Recovery Dictation (only on an individual basis), San Diego Sight Word Assessment, Scored Reading Comprehension Questions, Writing Prompts, Attitudinal Surveys

All of the actual forms and student work should be passed on in the language arts folder. It is up to the next year's teacher to discard any or all of these forms. The reading comprehension questions and writing prompts must stay in the student's folder. As would the attitudinal surveys. All of the other information will have been transferred onto the progress report.

The 1995-96 school year will be the pilot year for the scored comprehension questions. Grade levels need to work together to accumulate samples of scored student work that will show the progression from September to June. These samples will be used to form an anchor set for each grade level.

# Language Arts Folder Table of Contents

Teacher initials: _____ _____ _____ _____ _____

Year: _____ _____ _____ _____ _____

| | K | 1 | 2 | 3 | 4 |
|---|---|---|---|---|---|
| 1. L.A. Progress Report | | | | | |
| 2. Developmental Spelling Chart with student copies | | | | | |
| 3. Morrison McCall Spelling Scale with student copies | | | | | |
| 4. Dictation with student copies | | | | | |
| 5. San Diego chart | | | | | |
| 6. Scored reading comprehension materials | | | | | |
| 7. Writing prompts | | | | | |
| 8. Attitudinal surveys | | | | | |
| Write your initials and the year. Check off each material once it is enclosed in the child's folder. | | | | | |

# *Spelling Assessments —*

Two types of spelling assessments are administered quarterly; a developmental spelling test and the Morrison-McCall Spelling scale.

The Developmental Spelling Test, created by Gentry and Gillet (Teaching Kids to Spell, 1993), is administered in first and second grades and kindergarten, as needed. The features Spelling Lists are administered in grades three and four. These tests are used to diagnose at which stage of the spelling process the child is functioning. The stages used are precommunicative, semiphonetic, phonetic, transitional, and conventional.

The Morrison-McCall Spelling Scale consists of eight lists of words. Each list consists of fifty words which gradually increase in difficulty. A grade equivalency from first to "college" is derived from the number of correct responses from a list. First and second grades may use lists one through four while third and fourth grades may use lists five through eight.

All of these tests are administered in the same manner. The teacher says a word, gives the sentence provided with the word, then repeats the word. This process is continued to the end of the list for the developmental spelling tests. The teacher may use his/her discretion as to how many of the words will be administered from any Morrison-McCall list in order to attain a fair grade level equivalency score.

## *Reading Comprehension —*

Comprehension is obviously the most important aspect of reading. A reader is clearly not reading if he or she does not understand the text. Students must realize that there is a purpose for reading and that purpose changes according to the circumstances. They are reading to learn, to build something, to cry, to investigate, etc. or for pure enjoyment. We must be careful to not send the message to students that they are reading for the sole purpose of answering specific questions.

However, we must in some way be accountable for their reading comprehension. A simple retelling would be most informative but not always most practical. The following reading comprehension questions will inform us on the student's ability to comprehend the literature that has been designated to his or her grade level and at the same time they will also give the students practice on answering questions similar to those on the Connecticut Mastery Tests.

Shortly after the student has read the core books, the teacher should give him or her the comprehension questions in writing. Help reading the questions or dictating the answer may be necessary and should be noted. The student should use the reading comprehension form enclosed to write his or her answers. Younger students may obviously need unlined white paper to draw their pictures. The forms should be dated and the class should answer the questions within a reasonable time period.

Please note that due to the number of books available, each class within a grade may read the core literature during different marking periods. Each student must have a comprehension score for each marking period. Scores should be transferred to the progress report. After the 1995-96 school year an anchor set will be available to help when scoring.

## Reading Comprehension Questions — Kindergarten

*The Three Little Pigs —*

— Tell about or draw two characters from the story of *The Three Little Pigs*.

*The Three Billy Goats Gruff —*

— Tell about or draw where the billy goats went and why did they go there?

*The Three Bears —*

— Tell about or draw two differences between this story and *The Three Little Pigs* or *The Three Billy Goats Gruff*.


## Comprehension Rubrics — Kindergarten

*The Three Little Pigs —*

2   Response correctly lists two characters from the story *The Three Little Pigs*.

1   Response correctly lists one character from the story *The Three Little Pigs*.

0   Response is vague or irrelevant OR  no attempt to respond.

*The Three Billy Goats Gruff —*

2   Response correctly lists where the billy goats went and why.

1   Response correctly lists where the billy goats went OR why they went there.

0   Response is vague or irrelevant OR no attempt to respond.

*The Three Bears —*

2   Response correctly lists two ways this book is different from either *The Three Little Pigs* or *The Three Billy Goats Gruff*.

1   Response correctly lists one way this book is different.

0   Response is vague or irrelevant OR no attempt to respond.

# Reading Comprehension Questions — First Grade

### Rosie's Walk —

— Write or draw at least two things that would have been different if Rosie went on her walk in the Winter.

### Chicka Chicka Boom Boom —

— Tell two things that happened when all of the letters got to the top of the tree.

— Write two things that the tree would say to the letters if it could talk.

### Henry and Mudge —

— Give two words that would describe Henry's grandmother.

— Name two things that were different when you slept somewhere other than your own bed. Explain.

# Comprehension Rubrics — First Grade

### Rosie's Walk —

2    Response correctly lists two things that would be different if Rosie went for her walk in the Winter.

1    Response correctly lists one thing that would be different if Rosie took her walk in the Winter.

0    Response is vague or irrelevant OR  no attempt to respond.

### Chicka Chicka Boom Boom —

2    Response correctly lists two things that happened when all of the letters got to the top of the tree and two things that the tree would say to the letters if he could talk.

1    Response correctly lists one thing that happened and two things that the tree would say or two things that happened and one thing that the tree would say OR response correctly answers only one question.

0    Response is vague or irrelevant OR no attempt to respond.

### Henry and Mudge —

2    Response correctly lists two words to describe Henry's grandmother and two things that were different when they slept somewhere other than than their own bed.

1    Response correctly lists one describing word and two things that were different or two describing words and one thing that was different OR response correctly answers only one question.

0    Response is vague or irrelevant OR no attempt to respond.

# Reading Comprehension Questions — Second Grade

*Frog and Toad are Friends —*

— Tell two ways Frog and Toad show that they are friends.
— Tell about two ways that you could show that you were a good friend to others.

*The Drinking Gourd —*

— Name two reasons why Big Jeff and his family were following the Drinking Gourd.
— Explain two ways the underground railroad is like a real railroad.

*Ox-Cart Man —*

— Name two reasons why the ox-cart man has made his trip.
— Name two things that he bought and explain why he bought them.

*The Art Lesson —*

— Tell two reasons why Tommy was disappointed when he started school.
— In the end both Tommy and the Art teacher were happy. Explain why.

# Comprehension Rubrics — Second Grade

*Frog and Toad are Friends —*

2   Response correctly lists two ways that Frog and Toad are friends and two ways that you could show that you were a good friend to others.
1   Response correctly lists one way that Frog and Toad are friends and two ways to show you are a friend OR two ways that Frog and Toad are friends and one way to show you are a friend OR response correctly answers only one of the questions.
0   Response is vague or irrelevant OR  no attempt to respond.

*The Drinking Gourd —*

2   Response correctly lists two reasons why Ben and his family were following the Drinking Gourd and two ways the underground railroad is like a real railroad.
1   Response correctly lists one reason why Big Jeff and his family followed the Drinking Gourd and two ways the underground railroad is like a real railroad OR two reasons why Big Jeff followed the underground railroad and one way the underground railroad is like a real railroad OR response correctly answers only one of the questions.
0   Response is vague or irrelevant OR no attempt to respond.

*Ox-Cart Man —*

2   Response correctly lists two reasons why the Ox-Cart Man made his trip and two things that he bought and why.
1   Response correctly lists one reason why he made his trip and two things he bought and why OR two reasons why he made his trip and one thing he bought and why OR response correctly answers only one of the questions.
0   Response is vague or irrelevant OR no attempt to respond.

*The Art Lesson —*

2   Response correctly lists two reasons why Tommy was disappointed and why both Tommy and the Art teacher were happy in the end.
1   Response correctly lists one reason why Tommy was disappointed and why both Tommy and the teacher were happy OR two reasons why Tommy was disappointed and why only Tommy or the teacher were happy OR response answers only one of the questions.
0   Response is vague or irrelevant OR no attempt to respond.

# Reading Comprehension Questions — Third Grade

*Fables—*
— Compare any two animals in Arnold Lobel's *Fables*. Tell two ways they are alike or different.
— Choose one moral from a fable. Explain what the moral means using two examples from one of the fables.

*The Boxcar Children —*
— In the story *The Boxcar Children* the children travel to the dump to look for treasures. Describe two of the treasures that they find.
— There are four main characters in *The Boxcar Children*. Describe one of the children. Tell two things that he or she does, likes, or says.

*Helen Keller —*
— Helen Keller did many important things to help deaf and blind people in her lifetime. Tell two important things she did.
— As a child Helen Keller lived in a dark and silent world. She learned many things to help her live in this world. Tell about two important things Helen learned to do.

*Sarah Plain and Tall—*
— In a letter Sarah tells them that she is not mild mannered. Write about two or more things that happened to show that this is true.
— When Sarah comes to the prairie tell at least two things that show that the children are nervous about meeting Sarah for the first time.

# Comprehension Rubrics — Third Grade

*Fables —*
2 Response correctly lists two ways that two animals are alike or different and two examples explaining the meaning of a moral from a fable.
1 Response correctly lists one way that two animals are alike and two explanations OR two ways animals are alike and one explanation OR response correctly answers only one question.
0 Response is vague or irrelevant OR no attempt to respond.

*The Boxcar Children —*
2 Response correctly describes two of the treasures they found and two characteristics of one of the children.
1 Response correctly describes one of the treasures and two characteristics OR two of the treasures and one characteristic OR response correctly answers only one of the questions.
0 Response is vague or irrelevant OR no attempt to respond.

*Helen Keller —*
2 Response correctly lists two things Helen Keller did to help deaf and blind people and two important things Helen learned to do.
1 Response correctly lists one thing Helen Keller did to help and two things she learned to do OR two things she did to help and one thing she learned to do OR response correctly answers only one question.
0 Response is vague or irrelevant OR no attempt to respond.

*Sarah Plain and Tall —*
2 Response correctly lists two things that happened to show that Sarah was mild mannered and two things that show the children were nervous.
1 Response correctly lists one thing that happened and two things that show they were nervous OR two things that happened and one thing that showed they were nervous OR response correctly answers only one question.
0 Response is vague or irrelevant OR no attempt to respond.

# Reading Comprehension Questions — Fourth Grade

### Dear Mr. Henshaw —
— Mr. Henshaw gives Leigh the advice that all "characters in a story should solve a problem or change in some way." What problems did Leigh solve and how did he change throughout the story?
— Throughout most of the story Leigh is angry with his father for many reasons. Explain Leigh's anger toward his father. How does Leigh resolve these feelings?

### Charlotte's Web —
— How did Charlotte and Fern save Wilbur's life? Cite specific examples from the book.
— The signs in the book were very important to Wilbur's survival. How did each sign contribute to his survival and make him illustrious?

### Ben and Me —
— Defend Amos' decision to break his agreement with Ben in Chapter 8. Be sure to explain the agreement and the circumstances that brought Amos to this point with Ben.

### Little House in the Big Woods —
— Throughout the book, Pa seemed to try to teach the Ingalls children "lessons". He did this by telling stories. Tell about one of the stories Pa told. What was the lesson that he wanted the children to learn?
— Keeping in mind how long ago this story took place, explain how this story would be different if Laura had a brother.

# Comprehension Rubrics — Fourth Grade

### Dear Mr. Henshaw —
2   Response correctly lists problems that Leigh solved and how Leigh changed in the story AND Leigh's anger toward his father and how he resolves his anger.
1   Response correctly lists only one part of question one OR only one part of question two OR response correctly answers only one question.
0   Response is vague or irrelevant OR no attempt to respond.

### Charlotte's Web —
2   Response correctly lists how Charlotte and Fern save Wilbur's life with at least two examples AND how each sign contributes to Wilbur's survival and makes him illustrious.
1   Response correctly lists only one example of how they saved his life OR how only some signs contribute to his survival and not all OR response correctly answers only one of the questions.
0   Response is vague or irrelevant OR no attempt to respond.

### Ben and Me —
2   Response correctly defends Amos' decision to break his agreement AND the agreement and the circumstances are both addressed.
1   Response correctly defends Amos' decision and only the agreement is mentioned OR only the circumstances are mentioned OR the agreement and the circumstances are mentioned but the decision is not defended.
0   Response is vague or irrelevant OR no attempt to respond.

### Little House in the Big Woods —
2   Response correctly lists a story Pa told and the lesson AND at least two things that would be different if Laura had a brother.
1   Response correctly lists a story Pa told without the lesson and two ways the story would be different OR a story Pa told and the lesson and only one way the story would be different OR response correctly answers only one of the questions.
0   Response is vague or irrelevant OR no attempt to respond.

# Woodstock Elementary Language Arts Progress Report

Name_____ Grade_____ Teacher_____

## Developmental Spelling Assessment:    Circle: Gentry or Features

Consists of 10 words(Gentry) or 14 words(Features) used to "diagnose" which stage of the spelling process a child is in:

| (Pre) | Precommunicative= | Using random lettering. |
|-------|-------------------|-------------------------|
| (S) | Semiphonetic= | Using mainly the consonants heard in a word, especially the first and the last. |
| (P) | Phonetic= | Every sound in a word is represented by a letter. |
| (T) | Transitional= | Very close approximation of the spelling of the word. |
| (C) | Conventional= | Correct spelling. |

*Scores reflect into which stage the majority of the words fell.*

| Baseline(Opt) | 1st quarter | Second | Third | Fourth |
|---------------|-------------|--------|-------|--------|

Dates administered: _____        _____        _____   _____

## Morrison-McCall Spelling Scale:

Eight lists consisting of 50 words each. The words gradually increase in difficulty to give a grade equivalancy from first to college levels. The children do *not* have to do all 50 words.

| Baseline(Opt) | 1st quarter | Second | Third | Fourth |
|---------------|-------------|--------|-------|--------|

Dates administered: _____        _____        _____   _____

## Dictation Sentences:

These sentences are used in coordination with the above assessments to get an overall usage of sounds in words and spelling. The number of sounds and words in the sentences are as follows:

First grade= 37 sounds and ___ words.        Fourth= At teacher discretion
Second Grade= 64 sounds and 18 words.
Third grade= 64 sounds and 17 words.

*The top score shows how many sounds were represented. The bottom score shows how many words were spelled correctly.*

| | Baseline(Opt) | 1st quarter | Second | Third | Fourth |
|---------|---------------|-------------|--------|-------|--------|
| Sounds | | | | | |
| Words | | | | | |

Dates administered: _____        _____        _____   _____

## San Diego Quick Word Assessment:

Words are grouped by grade level to give a grade equivalancy reading level of *sight* words.

| Baseline(Opt) | 1st quarter | Second | Third | Fourth |
|---|---|---|---|---|

Dates administered: _____    _____    _____    _____

## Reading Comprehension Scores:

Questions for the core books were formulated and each student was asked to answer them to the best of their ability. The answers were then scored according to the comprehension rubrics.

| | 1st quarter | Second | Third | Fourth |
|---|---|---|---|---|

Book Title:

Score:

Date: _____    _____    _____    _____

## Writing Comprehension Scores:

Students participate in school wide writing periods. During this time all children grades k-4 are given the opportunity to write about a given topic.  The prompt is different for each grade level and students are given forty-five minutes to write. Student work is then scored according to the writing rubrics.

| | 1st quarter | Second | Third | Fourth |
|---|---|---|---|---|

Prompt Title:

Score:

Date: _____    _____    _____    _____

# Multiage Glossary

**artificial assessments**    The evaluation of a child's learning accomplishments through standardized tests and paper-pencil worksheets. Artificial assessments are wholly incompatible with child-centered practices.

**authentic assessment**    The evaluation of a child's learning within the context of his or her daily work. Can include portfolios, teacher observation, one-to-one or small group questioning by the teacher, reading aloud, projects completed at learning centers, and other methods.

**block scheduling**    The scheduling of large blocks of time devoted to a subject; for instance, two hours devoted to language arts or math during the course of a day, rather than dividing the day up into small segments and scheduling 35 minutes for geography, 20 minutes for spelling, etc.

**combination/split classes**    Classes created, usually for financial reasons, which contain more than one grade level, but have two separate curriculums, one for each grade. The teacher ends up teaching two curriculums, correcting two sets of papers, planning two different sets of activities, etc. Often mislabeled multiage education; it's not.

**continuous progress**    A curriculum which allows a child to progress through the curriculum at his or her own rate, without conforming to an externally imposed time limit on learning a fixed amount of subject matter in a fixed amount of time.

**cooperative learning**    Learning that takes place in groups and involves several children working in cooperation with each other to accomplish a task or set of tasks. Cooperative grouping enhances learning of subject matter while teaching social skills.

**developmentally appropriate practices**    Educational practices that are age- and individually appropriate and are matched to the developmental level of the child, rather than expecting a child of a certain age to accomplish a set amount of learning. Recognizes that children of the same age are at widely differing developmental levels, and need to be taught "where they're at."

**graded practices**    Practices which assign specific curriculum content to specific grades. Examples of graded practices include: group standardized testing, comparative reporting, unfair competition, tracking by ability, retention/promotion/social promotion, and age/grade segregation of students. Some multiage programs are being required to retain their graded practices, which goes against the multiage philosophy.

**inclusion**    The policy of making special-needs children members of a regular classroom. The underlying assumption is that special-needs children have a right to start out in a regular classroom, and are removed only if it is deemed necessary.

   Some inclusive classrooms bring special education personnel into the regular classroom to serve the needs of certain children; others use pullouts during the day. Some schools use a combination of techniques.

**integrated curriculum**    Learning that combines subjects such as reading, art, math, science, geography, into a single unit; most often theme-based.

**learning centers**    Areas of the classroom set aside for certain activities and containing materials and instructions for those activities. Can be subject-related: reading centers, math centers; or theme-related: bats, bugs, dinosaurs. Very conducive to multi-level activities.

   Learning centers tend to be long-term, with the activities within the centers changing as necessary to reflect theme units and curriculum requirements. They offer open-ended, hands-on activities with a deemphasis on worksheets, and are invitational for all students in a classroom. Learning areas set aside and geared to reinforcing specific skills are often distinguished as work stations.

**learning styles**    The notion that children (and adults) learn in different ways: some better by hearing, some by seeing; some people are concrete learners, some are abstract. Formalized in Howard Gardner's theory of multiple intelligences, but not limited to that theory, learning styles reflect individual differences in students as well as cultural and family influences.

**literature-based reading**   The process of teaching reading through exposing children to good literature. Skills are taught using stories, poems, and songs as examples, rather than by using worksheets or over-relying on basals.

**looping**   A multiyear structure in which a teacher teaches a first grade class, for example, then follows her students to second grade, while the second grade teacher moves to first grade and picks up a new class. Looping has the benefit of a long-term relationship between teacher and child. Though not a multiage classroom, looping provides many of the same benefits.

**multiage continuous progress classroom**   The practice of blending two or more grades, four or more chronological ages, staying with the same teacher for more than one year. Multiage practices foster developmentally appropriate instruction and provide a more challenging educational experience.

**multiple intelligences**   The concept that there exists different intelligences; and that all children and adults possess these intelligences in greater or lesser degrees, and can increase their ability in all these intelligences with appropriate learning experiences. Originated by Howard Gardner, who has now listed eight intelligences: musical intelligence; bodily-kinesthetic intelligence; logical-mathematical intelligence; linguistic intelligence; spatial intelligence; interpersonal intelligence; intrapersonal intelligence; and environmental intelligence.

**multiyear education**   see looping and multiage education.

**nongradedness**   a way of organizing schools so that children learn a seamless curriculum, on a continuous basis, at their own pace, and not artificially placed in a specific grade. All classrooms, even multiage classrooms, have some graded elements still in place and should more accurately be considered "less graded."

**portfolio**   A collection of work samples by students which demonstrates the accomplishment of particular skills, and documents progression of skills. A good source of information when evaluating a student's work (for report cards, for instance.)

**retention**   Keeping a student in a grade for an additional year, while his or her classmates move on to the next grade. Retention is an intervention to correct wrong grade placement. Retention is indigenous to timebound, graded structures. A true multiage, continuous progress structure avoids grade-level retention but still provides an extra year for students who need more time.

**social promotion**   Moving a student on to the next grade level, even though the child's developmental needs are not considered, and the child has not accomplished academically what he or she needs at the present grade level. Done to keep the student with his or her peers and to avoid the cost of providing the student with an extra learning time. Unfortunately, the student often ends up falling further and further behind, and may ultimately drop out of school. Social promotion is an economic concept, rather than an education concept.

**team teaching**   A structure in which two or more teachers share the teaching and planning responsibilities for a particular class or classes. A variety of grouping-for-instruction possibilities within the classroom are aided by a team teaching arrangement.

   All teachers in a team take responsibility for all students in all areas of curriculum. This provides two or more perspectives on learning and assessment, and more than one set of eyes to observe children. A team of teachers can integrate different approaches to learning and diagnosis and devise a variety of teaching strategies.

**theme-based instruction**   Instruction in which the core curriculum subjects are taught in the context of integrated theme units. A thematic unit on weather, for instance, could include recording and graphing temperature variations (science, math); logging weather observations (reading, writing); reading stories about weather (reading); pulling vocabulary words from logs (spelling); and drawing pictures of cloud formations (science, art).

**timebound**   Tied to a set number of days and hours in which to learn a fixed amount of curriculum. Most traditional school systems expect their students to learn in 13 years, 180 days a year, in 5¼-hour days, everything they need to learn.

**time-on-task**   A recurring education fad that cycles every few years. It involves assigning a specific length of time to complete a task—twelve minutes of math, fifteen minutes of science, twenty minutes of reading. This administrative concept is wholly incompatible with multiage, continuous progress education, and is a developmentally inappropriate practice.

**tracking by ability**   Grouping students by ability and holding them together for long periods of time. Tracking tends to create a caste system that discriminates against minorities, poor, at-risk students, and students who are linguistically different. Children who are tracked at age five tend to stay in the same category throughout their school careers.

   This is not the same as short-term grouping by ability for a specific purpose for a short period of time, often referred to as ad hoc grouping. This type of short-term grouping includes cooperative grouping; learning styles grouping; problem solving grouping; grouping by interest; and skills reinforcement grouping.

   Tracking is considered a developmentally inappropriate concept that is not in the best interests of students.

**whole language**   The philosophy that children learn literacy best by integrating reading, writing, speaking and listening. This is accomplished using a variety of whole language strategies including the writing process, inventive spelling, literature immersion utilizing a variety of genres, guided reading/guided writing and other strategies. Whole language teachers integrate word decoding skills (phonics) and other lessons in skills into their literature-based programs.

**work stations**   Areas of a classroom set aside for certain activities. Similar to learning centers, but where learning centers are open-ended, work stations are usually short-term, designed for reinforcing skills previously taught by the teacher, and are used by students at the invitation of the teacher. The teacher tries to incorporate as many of the multiple intelligences as is naturally possible in the activities to give children choices of how to reinforce their skills.

**year-round education**   A school schedule that operates year-round, rather than having three months off in the summer. This schedule helps avoid loss of learning that can occur over the long summer vacation. Year-round calendars provide a cost-effective way to utilize buildings and staff. Schools organized around a year-round schedule respond to the learning needs of students; i.e., students need to learn year-round. The traditional school is controlled by the agrarian calendar (the farmer's planting and harvesting cycle) and is organized for administrative purposes.

   Year-round schools use many different calendar configurations, adapted to their own local needs. Year-round education, combined with a continuous progress, multiage structure, is a powerful tool for student success.

   Year-long scheduling does not mean lengthening the school day, the school year or both. Students still spend 180 days in school, but within a different structure.

# Resources

## Multiage Organizations

**National Alliance of Multiage Educators (N.A.M.E.)**
Ten Sharon Road, Box 577
Peterborough, NH 03458
1-800-924-9621

*N.A.M.E.* is a networking organization for educators who want to share ideas, information, and experiences with others who have a similar interest in multiage and continuous progress practices. *N.A.M.E.* is also a source of information on books and audiovisual materials about multiage. Membership is open to those considering multiage as well as those already teaching and supervising it.

**International Registry of Nongraded Schools (IRONS)**
Robert H. Anderson, Co-director (with Barbara N. Pavan)
PO Box 271669
Tampa, FL 33688-1699

*IRONS* is housed at the University of South Florida. It has been established to gather information about individual schools or school districts that are either in the early stages of developing a nongraded program or well along in their efforts. Its purpose is to facilitate intercommunication and research efforts. There is a phase one membership and a full membership.

**Multiage Classroom Exchange**
*Teaching K-8*
40 Richards Ave.
Norwalk, CT 06854

*The Multiage Classroom Exchange* puts teachers in contact with others who are interested in swapping ideas, activities, and experiences relating to the multiage, progressive classroom.

To join, send your name, address, age levels you teach, years of experience with multiage education, and a self-addressed, stamped envelope to the address listed. You'll receive a complete, up-to-date list of teachers who are interested in exchanging information.

**California Alliance for Elementary Education**
Charlotte Keuscher, Program Consultant
California Department of Education
721 Capitol Mall, 3rd Floor
Sacramento, CA 95814
email: ckeusche@smtp.cde.ca.gov

The Elementary Education Office and the *California Alliance for Elementary Education* have published the second and third installments of The Multiage Learning Source Book.

The second installment is a guide for teachers, principals, parents, and community members who are involved and interested in multiage learning. It contains descriptions of what multiage learning is and is not, questions staffs and parents need to explore before and during the implementation stage, samples of how schools have communicated to their communities about multiage learning, classroom curriculum vignettes, anecdotes from schools that have successfully implemented multiage learning under a variety of conditions, descriptions of multiage programs throughout the state, and current and relevant research and articles.

The third installment deals with evaluation of a multiage program and assessment in multiage classrooms. Copies of the Source Book are distributed free of charge to California Alliance for Elementary Education members.

**California Multiage Learning Task Force**
(see California Alliance for Elementary Education)

Much of the multiage learning effort in California is guided by the Multiage Learning Task Force, which is made up of California Alliance for Elementary Education teachers, principals, parents, board of education members and university professors. The group has provided guidance and material for The Multiage Learning Source Book and are practitioners of multiage learning.

Networks supporting multiage education are being developed throughout California, coordinated by the Elementary Education Office, which assists the startup of the groups. Once started the groups operate independently.

**Under Construction**
Jane Meade-Roberts
202 Riker Terrace Way
Salinas, CA 93901
Phone: 408-455-1831 (to leave message)

*Under Construction*'s goal is to assist teachers, parents and administrators gain an understanding of how children and adults construct knowledge, and to support experienced teachers who are working to understand constructivist theory and its implications for teaching. (Constructivism is a scientific theory of learning, based on Piaget's theory of cognitive development, that explains how people come to build their own knowledge and understand the things and people in their own world.)

The organization feels that multiage classrooms are wonderfully suited for helping adults learn more about how children develop and construct knowledge. Many of the teachers and parents in the group are currently involved in multiage classrooms or are interested in developing their understanding of constructivism so that they may begin a multiage learning environment for children in their own school.

*Under Construction* is an umbrella for several groups working toward this end. The Constructivist Network of Monterey County, which meets monthly, is largely composed of university personnel and some schoolteachers. The network provides a speaker series for the community. A focus group includes teachers involved in coaching and classroom visitations. The organization is collaborating
with the local adult school to provide classes for parents of children in multiage classrooms, and has just begun to work with a new local university, with the object of working with people in the community. An advisory board oversees the organization.

The organization is funded by the Walter S. Johnson Foundation.

**Kentucky Department of Education**
1908 Capital Plaza Tower
500 Mero Street
Frankfort, KY 40601
502-564-3421

*The Kentucky Department of Education* has created a wealth of material, both written and in video form, about Kentucky's multiage programs. (Some are listed in the bibliography of this book.) For a list of available materials, contact the publications department at the above address.

# Specialist Staff Organizations

**National Association for Sport and Physical Education**
1900 Association Drive
Reston, Virginia 22091-1599

The *NASPE* is an association of the American Alliance for Health, Physical Education, Recreation and Dance (AAHPERD). To order materials, call 1-800-321-0789.

**Music Educators National Conference**
1806 Robert Fulton Drive
Reston, VA 22091
703-860-4000

**Center for Music and Young Children**
217 Nassau Street
Princeton, NJ 08542
609-924-7801

The *Music Educators National Conference* provides support for music educators from pre-kindergarten through the post-graduate level.

The *Center for Music and Young Children* has a multiage focus, but deals with children from birth through kindergarten only.

**National Art Education Association**
1916 Association Drive
Reston, VA 22091-1590
703-860-8000

**American Association of School Librarians**
15 East Huron Street
Chicago, IL 60611
312-944-6780

The American Association of School Librarians is one of eleven divisions of the American Library Association.

# Newsletter

**MAGnet Newsletter**
805 W. Pennsylvania
Urbana, IL 61801-4897

The *MAGnet Newsletter* provides information about schools that have implemented multiage practices.

## ERIC

*ERIC* (Educational Resources Information Center) is a clearinghouse or central agency responsible for the collection, classification, and distribution of written information related to education. If you need help finding the best way to use ERIC, call ACCESS ERIC toll-free at 1-800-LET-ERIC. If you need specific information about multiage education, call Norma Howard at 1-800-822-9229.

*A Value Search: Multiage or Nongraded Education* is available for $7.50 and can be ordered from Publication Sales, ERIC Clearinghouse on Educational Management, 5207 University of Oregon, Eugene, OR 97403-5207. A handling charge of $3.00 is added to all billed orders.

## Workshops and Conferences

**The Society For Developmental Education**
Ten Sharon Road, Box 577
Peterborough, NH 03458
1-800-924-9621
FAX 1-800-337-9929

*The Society For Developmental Education* (SDE) presents one- and two-day workshops as well as regional conferences throughout the year and around the country for elementary educators on multiage, inclusion education, multiple intelligences, character education, discipline, whole language, authentic assessment, looping, readiness, math, science, social studies, developmentally appropriate practices, special education, and other related topics.

SDE also offers customized inservice training to schools on the topics of their choice.

SDE sponsors an International Multiage Conference each July. For information on workshop/conference dates and locations, or to arrange for inservice training, write or phone SDE at the address or phone/FAX numbers listed above.

# *Bibliography*

## Multiage Education

American Association of School Administrators. *The Nongraded Primary: Making Schools Fit Children*. Arlington, VA, 1992.

Anderson, Robert H., and Pavan, Barbara Nelson. *Nongradedness: Helping It to Happen*. Lancaster, PA: Technomic Press, 1992.

Banks, Janet Caudill. *Creating the Multi-age Classroom*.  Edmonds, WA: CATS Publications, 1995.

Bingham, Anne A.; Dorta, Peggy; McClasky, Molly; and O'Keefe, Justine. *Exploring the Multiage Classroom*. York, ME: Stenhouse Publishers, 1995.

Bridge, Connie A.; Reitsma, Beverly S.; and Winograd, Peter N. *Primary Thoughts: Implementing Kentucky's Primary Program*. Lexington, KY: Kentucky Department of Education, 1993.

Burruss, Bette, and Fairchild, Nawanna. *The Primary School: A Resource Guide for Parents*. Lexington, KY: The Prichard Committee for Academic Excellence and The Partnership for Kentucky School Reform, 1993. PO Box 1658, Lexington, KY 40592-1658, 1-800-928-2111.

Chase, Penelle, and Doan, Jane. *Full Circle: A New Look at Multiage Education*. Portsmouth, NH: Heinemann, 1994.

Davies, Anne; Politano, Colleen; and Gregory, Kathleen. *Together is Better*. Winnipeg, Canada: Peguis Publishers, 1993.

Fogarty, Robin, ed. *The Multiage Classroom: A Collection*. Palantine, IL: Skylight Publishing, 1993.

Gaustad, Joan. "Making the Transition From Graded to Nongraded Primary Education." *Oregon School Study Council Bulletin*, 35(8), 1992.

————."Nongraded Education: Mixed-Age, Integrated and Developmentally Appropriate Education for Primary Children." *Oregon School Study Council Bulletin*, 35(7), 1992.

————."Nongraded Education: Overcoming Obstacles to Implementing the Multiage Classroom." 38(3,4) *Oregon School Study Council Bulletin*, 1994.

Gayfer, Margaret, ed. *The Multi-grade Classroom: Myth and Reality*. Toronto: Canadian Education Association, 1991.

Goodlad, John I., and Anderson, Robert H. *The Nongraded Elementary School*. New York: Teachers College Press, 1987.

Grant, Jim, and Johnson, Bob. *A Common Sense Guide to Multiage Practices*. Columbus, OH: Teachers' Publishing Group, 1995.

Grant, Jim; Johnson, Bob; and Richardson, Irv. *Multiage Q&A: 101 Practical Answers to Your Most Pressing Questions*. Peterborough, NH: Crystal Springs Books, 1995.

Gutiérrez, Roberto, and Slavin, Robert E. *Achievement Effects of the Nongraded Elementary School: A Retrospective Review*. Baltimore, MD: Center for Research on Effective Schooling for Disadvantaged Students, 1992.

Hunter, Madeline. *How to Change to a Nongraded School*. Alexandria, VA: Association for Supervision and Curriculum Development, 1992.

Kasten, Wendy, and Clarke, Barbara. *The Multi-age Classroom*. Katonah, NY: Richard Owen, 1993.

Katz, Lilian G.; Evangelou, Demetra; and Hartman, Jeanette Allison. *The Case for Mixed-Age Grouping in Early Education*. Washington, DC: National Association for the Education of Young Children, 1990.

Kentucky Department of Education. *Kentucky's Primary School: The Wonder Years*. Frankfort, KY.

———. *Multi-Age/Multi-Ability: A Guide to Implementation for Kentucky's Primary Program*. Frankfort, KY: Kentucky Department of Education, 1994.

Maeda, Bev. *The Multi-Age Classroom*. Cypress, CA: Creative Teaching Press, 1994.

McAvinue, Maureen. *A Planbook for Meeting Individual Needs in Primary School*. Frankfort, KY: Kentucky Department of Education, 1994.

Miller, Bruce A. *Children at the Center: Implementing the Multiage Classroom*. Portland, OR: Northwest Regional Educational Laboratory; 1994.

———. *The Multigrade Classroom: A Resource Handbook for Small, Rural Schools*. Portland, OR: Northwest Regional Educational Laboratory, 1989.

———. *Training Guide for the Multigrade Classroom: A Resource for Small, Rural Schools*. Portland, OR: Northwest Regional Laboratory, 1990.

National Education Association. *Multiage Classrooms*. NEA Teacher to Teacher Books, 1995.

Nebraska Department of Education and Iowa Department of Education. *The Primary Program: Growing and Learning in the Heartland*. Second edition. Lincoln, NE, 1994.

Ostrow, Jill. *A Room With a Different View: First Through Third Graders Build Community and Create Curriculum*. York, ME: Stenhouse Publishers, 1995.

Politano, Colleen, and Davies, Anne. *Multi-Age and More*. Winnipeg, Canada: Peguis Publishers, 1994.

Province of British Columbia Ministry of Education. *Foundation*. Primary Program Foundation Document. Victoria, British Columbia, 1990. This and the accompanying Resource Document provide extensive resources that would be of great help in any multiage program.

———. *Primary Program Resource Document*. Victoria, British Columbia, 1990.

Rathbone, Charles; Bingham, Anne; Dorta, Peggy; McClaskey, Molly; and O'Keefe, Justine. *Multiage Portraits: Teaching and Learning in Mixed-age Classrooms*. Peterborough, NH: Crystal Springs Books, 1993.

Society For Developmental Education. *Multiage Classrooms: The Ungrading of America's Schools*. Peterborough, NH, 1993.

Virginia Education Association and Appalachia Educational Laboratory. *Teaching Combined Grade Classes: Real Problems and Promising Practices*. Charleston, WV: Appalachian Educational Laboratory, 1990.

# Multiage Education – Audio/Video

Anderson, Robert, and Pavan, Barbara. *The Nongraded School*. Bloomington, IN: Phi Delta Kappa. An interview with the authors of *Nongradedness: Helping It to Happen*. Video, 30 minutes.

Association of Supervision and Curriculum Development. *Tracking: Road to Success or Dead End?* Alexandria, VA: ASCD. Audiocassette.

Cohen, Dorothy. *Status Treatments for the Classroom*. New York: Teachers College Press, 1994. Video.

George, Yvetta, and Keiter, Joel. *Developing Multiage Classrooms in Primary Grades*. Ft. Lauderdale, FL: Positive Connections, 1993. Video, 22 minutes.

Goodman, Gretchen. *Classroom Strategies for "Gray-Area" Children*. Peterborough, NH: Crystal Springs Books, 1995. Video.

Grant, Jim. *Accommodating Developmentally Different Children in the Multiage Classroom*, 1993. Keynote address at the NAESP Annual Convention. Audiocassette available from Chesapeake Audio/Video Communications, Inc. (6330 Howard Lane, Elkridge, MD 21227, product #180).

Katz, Lilian. *Multiage Groupings: A Key to Elementary Reform*. Alexandria, VA: Association for Supervision and Curriculum Development, 1993. Audiocassette.

Lolli, Elizabeth J. *Developing a Framework for Nongraded Multiage Education*. Peterborough, NH: Crystal Springs Books, 1995. Video.

Oakes, Jeannie, and Lipton, Martin. *On Tracking and Ability Grouping*. Bloomington, IN: Phi Delta Kappa.

Thompson, Ellen. *The Nuts and Bolts of Multiage Classrooms*. Peterborough NH: Crystal Springs Books, 1994. Video, 1 hour.

———. *How to Teach in a Multiage Classroom*. Peterborough, NH: Crystal Springs Books, 1994. Video, 25 minutes.

Ulrey, Dave, and Ulrey, Jan. *Teaching in a Multiage Classroom*. Peterborough, NH: Crystal Springs Books, 1994. Video.

# Developmental Education

Ames, Louise Bates. *What Do They Mean I'm Difficult?* Rosemont, NJ: Modern Learning Press, 1986.

Ames, Louise Bates, Baker, Sidney, and Ilg, Frances L. *Child Behavior (Specific Advice on Problems of Child Behavior)*. New York: Barnes & Noble Books, 1981.

Ames, Louise Bates, and Chase, Joan Ames. *Don't Push Your Pre-Schooler*. New York: Harper & Row, 1980.

Ames, Louise Bates, and Haber, Carol Chase. *He Hit Me First (When Brothers and Sisters Fight)*. New York: Dembner Books, 1982.

———. *Your Seven-Year-Old (Life in a Minor Key)*. New York: Dell, 1985.

———. *Your Eight-Year-Old (Lively and Outgoing)*. New York: Dell, 1989.

———. *Your Nine-Year-Old (Thoughtful and Mysterious)*. New York: Dell, 1990.

Ames, Louise Bates, and Ilg, Frances L. *Child Behavior*. New York: Barnes & Noble Books, 1955.

———. *The Child from Five to Ten*. New York: Harper & Row, 1946.

———. *Your Two-Year-Old (Terrible or Tender)*. New York: Dell, 1980.

———. *Your Three-Year-Old (Friend or Enemy)*. New York: Dell, 1980.

———. *Your Four-Year-Old (Wild and Wonderful)*. New York: Dell, 1980.

———. *Your Five-Year-Old (Sunny and Serene)*. New York: Dell, 1979.

———. *Your Six-Year-Old, Loving and Defiant*. New York: Dell, 1979.

———. *Your Ten-to-Fourteen Year-Old*. New York: Dell, 1981.

Ames, Louise Bates, Ilg, Frances L. and Haber, Frances L. *Your One-Year-Old (The Fun-Loving 12-to-24-month-old)*. New York: Delacorte, 1982.

Ames, Louise Bates, et al. *The Gesell Institute's Child from One to Six*. New York: Harper & Row, 1946.

Bluestein, Jane. *Being a Successful Teacher—A Practical Guide to Instruction and Management*. Belmont, CA: Fearon Teacher Aids, 1988.

Bluestein, Jane, and Collins, Lynn. *Parents in a Pressure Cooker*. Rosemont, NJ: Modern Learning Press, 1990.

Boyer, Ernest. *The Basic School: A Community for Learning*. Ewing, NJ: Carnegie Foundation for the Advancement of Learning, 1995.

———. *Ready to Learn: A Mandate for the Nation*. Princeton, NJ: The Foundation for the Advancement of Teaching, 1991.

Brazelton, T. Berry. *Touchpoints: The Essential Reference. Your Child's Emotional and Behavioral Development*. Reading, MA: Addison-Wesley, 1994.

———. *Working and Caring*. Reading, MA: Addison-Wesley, 1985.

———. *To Listen to a Child: Understanding the Normal Problems of Growing Up*. Reading, MA: Addison-Wesley, 1986.

Bredekamp, Sue, ed. *Developmentally Appropriate Practice in Early Childhood Programs Serving Children From Birth Through Age 8*, expanded edition. Washington, DC: National Association for the Education of Young Children, 1987.

Charney, Ruth Sidney. *Teaching Children to Care: Management in the Responsive Classroom*. Greenfield, MA: Northeast Foundation for Children, 1991.

Elovson, Allanna. *The Kindergarten Survival Book*. Santa Monica, CA: Parent Ed Resources, 1991.

Grant, Jim. *Childhood Should Be a Pressure Precious Time*. (poem anthology) Rosemont, NJ: Modern Learning Press, 1989.

———. *Developmental Education in the 1990's*. Rosemont, NJ: Modern Learning Press, 1991.

———. *"I Hate School!" Some Common Sense Answers for Parents Who Wonder Why*. Rosemont, NJ: Programs for Education, 1994.

———. *Jim Grant's Book of Parent Pages*. Rosemont, NJ: Programs for Education, 1988.

———. *Worth Repeating: Giving Children a Second Chance at School Success*. Rosemont, NJ: Modern Learning Press, 1989.

Grant, Jim, and Azen, Margot. *Every Parent's Owner's Manuals. (Three-, Four-, Five-, Six-, Seven-Year- Old)*. Rosemont, NJ. Programs for Education.

Hayes, Martha, and Faggella, Kathy. *Think It Through*. Bridgeport CT: First Teacher Press, 1986.

Healy, Jane M. *Endangered Minds: Why Children Don't Think and What We Can Do About It*. New York: Simon and Schuster, 1990.

———. *Your Child's Growing Mind: A Guide to Learning and Brain Development From Birth to Adolescence*. New York: Doubleday, 1987.

Holt, John. *How Children Fail*. New York: Dell Publishing, 1964, 1982.

Horowitz, Janet, and Faggella, Kathy. *Partners for Learning*. Bridgeport, CT: First Teacher Press, 1986.

Lamb, Beth, and Logsdon, Phyllis. *Positively Kindergarten: A Classroom-proven, Theme-based Developmental Guide for the Kindergarten Teacher*. Rosemont, NJ: Modern Learning Press, 1991.

Mallory, Bruce, and New, Rebecca, eds. *Diversity and Developmentally Appropriate Practices: Challenges for Early Childhood Education*. New York: Teachers College Press, 1994.

National Association of Elementary School Principals. *Early Childhood Education and the Elementary School Principal*. Alexandria, VA: NAESP, 1990.

National Association of State Boards of Education. *Right From the Start: The Report of the NASBE Task Force on Early Childhood Education*. Alexandria, VA: NASBE, 1988.

Northeast Foundation for Children. *A Notebook for Teachers: Making Changes in the Elementary Curriculum*. Greenfield, MA, 1991.

Reavis, George H. *The Animal School*. Rosemont, NJ: Modern Learning Press, 1988.

Singer, Dorothy, and Revenson, Tracy. *How a Child Thinks: A Piaget Primer*. Independence, MO: International University Press, 1978.

Wood, Chip. *Yardsticks: Children in the Classroom Ages 4-12*. Greenfield, MA: Northeast Foundation for Children, 1994.

# Cooperative Learning

Cohen, Dorothy. *Designing Groupwork: Strategies for the Heterogeneous Classroom*. New York: Teachers College Press, 1994.

Curran, Lorna. *Cooperative Learning Lessons for Little Ones: Literature-Based Language Arts and Social Skills*. San Juan Capistrano, CA: Resources for Teachers, Inc., 1992.

DeBolt, Virginia, with Dr. Spencer Kagan. *Write! Cooperative Learning and The Writing Process*. San Juan Capistrano, CA: Kagan Cooperative Learning, 1994.

Ellis, Susan S., and Whalen, Susan F. *Cooperative Learning: Getting Started*. New York: Scholastic, 1990.

Fisher, Bobbi. *Thinking and Learning Together: Curriculum and Community in a Primary Classroom*. Portsmouth, NH: Heinemann, 1995.

Forte, Imogene, and MacKenzie, Joy. *The Cooperative Learning Guide and Planning Pak for Primary Grades: Thematic Projects and Activities*. Nashville, TN: Incentive Publications, 1992.

Glover, Mary, and Sheppard, Linda. *Not on Your Own: The Power of Learning Together*. New York: Scholastic, 1990.

Johnson, David, and Johnson, Roger. *Cooperation and Competition: Theory and Research*. Edina, MN: Interaction Book Company, 1989.

———. *Learning Together and Alone*. Englewood Cliffs, NJ: Prentice Hall, Inc, 1991.

Kagan, Spencer. *Cooperative Learning*. San Juan Capistrano, CA: Resources for Teachers, Inc., 1994.

Reid, Jo Anne; Forrestal, P.; and Cook, J. *Small Group Learning in the Classroom*. Portsmouth, NH: Heinemann, 1989.

Shaw, Vanston, with Spencer Kagan, Ph.D. *Communitybuilding In the Classroom*. San Juan Capistrano, CA: Kagan Cooperative Learning, 1992.

Slavin, Robert. *Cooperative Learning*. Englewood Cliffs, NJ: Prentice Hall, 1989.

———. *Cooperative Learning*. Boston: Allyn and Bacon, 1995.

# Curriculum

Bredekamp, Sue, and Rosegrant, Teresa, eds. *Reaching Potentials: Appropriate Curriculum and Assessment for Young Children*, Vol. 1. Washington, DC: NAEYC, 1992.

Dodge, Diane Trister; Jablon, Judy R.; and Bickart, Toni S. *Constructing Curriculum in the Primary Grades*. Washington, DC: Teaching Strategies, Inc., 1994.

Fogarty, Robin. *The Mindful School: How to Integrate the Curricula*. Palatine, IL: Skylight Publishing, 1991.

Hall, G.E., and Loucks, S.F. "Program Definition and Adaptation: Implications for Inservice." *Journal of Research and Development in Education* (1981) 14, 2:46-58.

Hohmann, C. *Mathematics: High Scope K-3 Curriculum Guide*. (illustrated field test edition.) Ypsilanti, MI: High Scope Press, 1991.

Maehr, J. *Language and Literacy: High Scope K-3 Curriculum Guide*. (illustrated field test edition.) Ypsilanti, MI: High Scope Press, 1991.

National Association of Elementary School Principals. *Standards for Quality Elementary and Middle Schools: Kindergarten through Eighth Grade*. Alexandria, VA, 1990.

Rowan, Thomas E., and Morrow, Lorna J. *Implementing the K-8 Curriculum and Evaluation Standards: Readings from the "Arithmetic Teacher."* Reston, VA. National Council of Teachers of Mathematics, 1993.

Short, Kathy, and Burke, Carolyn. *Creating Curriculum*. Portsmouth, NH: Heinemann, 1981.

Stevenson, S. Christopher and Carr, Judy F. *Integrated Studies in the Middle School: Dancing Through Walls*. New York: Teachers College Press, 1993.

Whitin, D.; Mills, H.; and O'Keefe, T. *Living and Learning Mathematics: Stories and Strategies for Supporting Mathematical Literacy*. Portsmouth, NH: Heinemann, 1990.

## Learning Centers

Cook, Carole. *Math Learning Centers for the Primary Grades*. West Nynack, NY: The Center for Applied Research, 1992.

Ingraham, Phoebe Bell. *Creating and Managing Learning Centers: A Theme-Based Approach*. Peterborough, NH: Crystal Springs Books, Fall 1996.

Isbell, Rebecca. *The Complete Learning Center Book*. Beltsville, MD: Gryphon House, 1995.

Poppe, Carol A., and Van Matre, Nancy A. *Language Arts Learning Centers for the Primary Grades*. West Nynack, NY: The Center for Applied Research in Education, 1991. 234 pages.

————.*Science Learning Centers for the Primary Grades*. West Nyack, NY: The Center for Applied Research in Education, 1985.

Wait, Shirleen S. *Reading Learning Centers for the Primary Grades*. West Nynack, NY: The Center for Applied Research, 1992.

Waynant, Louise, and Wilson, Robert M. *Learning Centers: A Guide for Effective Use*. Paoli, PA: Instructo Corp., 1974.

## Learning Styles/Multiple Intelligences

Armstrong, Thomas. *In Their Own Way: Discovering and Encouraging Your Child's Personal Learning Style*. New York: Putnam, 1987.

————.*Multiple Intelligences in the Classroom*. Alexandria, VA: Association for Supervision and Curriculum Development, 1994.

Banks, Janet Caudill. *Creative Projects for Independent Learners*. CATS Publications, 1995.

Bloom, Benjamin S. *All Our Children Learning: A Primer for Teachers and Other Educators*. New York: McGraw-Hill, 1981.

————,ed. *Developing Talent in Young People*. New York: Ballantine, 1985.

Carbo, Marie. *Reading Styles Inventory Manual*. Roslyn Heights, New York: National Reading Styles Institute, 1991.

Carbo, Marie; Dunn, Rita; and Dunn, Kenneth. *Teaching Students to Read Through Their Individual Learning Styles*. Needham Heights, MA: Allyn & Bacon, 1991.

Gardner, Howard. *Frames of Mind: The Theory of Multiple Intelligences*. New York: Basic Books, 1985.

———.*Multiple Intelligences: The Theory in Practice*. New York: Basic Books, 1990.

———.*The Unschooled Mind: How Children Think and How Schools Should Teach*. New York: Basic Books, 1990.

Gilbert, Labritta. *Do Touch: Instant, Easy Hands-on Learning Experiences for Young Children*. Mt. Ranier, MD: Gryphon House, 1989.

Lazear, David. *Multiple Intelligence Approaches to Assessment: Solving the Assessment Conundrum*. IRI/Skylight Publishing, Inc., 1994.

———. *Seven Pathways of Learning: Teaching Students and Parents About Multiple Intelligences*. Tucson, AZ: Zephyr Press, 1994.

———. *Seven Ways of Knowing: Teaching for Multiple Intelligences*. Palatine, IL: IRI/Skylight Publishing, Inc., 1991.

———.*Seven Ways of Teaching: The Artistry of Teaching With Multiple Intelligences*. Palatine, IL: IRI/Skylight Publishing, Inc., 1991.

Vail, Priscilla. *Gifted, Precocious, or Just Plain Smart?* Rosemont, NJ: Programs for Education, 1987.

———.*Learning Styles: Food for Thought* and *130 Practical Tips for Teachers K-4*. Rosemont, NJ: Modern Learning Press, 1992.

## Other Books of Interest to Multiage Educators

Batzle, Janine. *Portfolio Assessment and Evaluation: Developing and Using Portfolios in the K-6 Classroom*. Cypress, CA: Creative Teaching Press, 1992.

Clemmons, J., Laase, L., Cooper, D., Areglado, N., and Dill, M. *Portfolios in the Classroom: A Teacher's Sourcebook*. New York: Scholastic, Inc., 1993.

Coletta, Anthony. *Kindergarten Readiness Checklist for Parents*. Rosemont, NJ: Modern Learning Press, 1991.

———.*What's Best for Kids*. Rosemont, NJ: Modern Learning Press, 1991.

Davies, Anne; Politano, Colleen; and Cameron, Caren. *Making Themes Work*. Winnipeg, Canada: Peguis Publishers, 1993.

Elkind, David. *All Grown Up & No Place to Go*. Reading, MA: Addison-Wesley, 1984.

———.*The Hurried Child*. Reading, MA: Addison-Wesley, 1981.

———.*Miseducation: Preschoolers at Risk*. New York: Alfred A. Knopf, 1987.

Erb, Thomas O., and Doda, Nancy M. *Team Organization: Promise—Practices and Possibilities*. Washington, D.C.: National Education Association of the United States, 1989.

Fisher, Bobbi. *Joyful Learning: A Whole Language Kindergarten*. Portsmouth, NH: Heinemann, 1991.

George, Paul. *How to Untrack Your School*. Alexandria, VA.: Association for Supervision and Curriculum Development, 1992.

Goodman, Gretchen. *I Can Learn! Strategies and Activities for Gray-Area Children*. Peterborough, NH: Crystal Springs Books, 1995.

———.*Inclusive Classrooms from A to Z: A Handbook for Educators*. Columbus, OH: Teachers' Publishing Group, 1994.

Graves, Donald, and Sustein, Bonnie, eds. *Portfolio Portraits*. Portsmouth, NH: Heinemann, 1992.

Harp, Bill, ed. *Assessment and Evaluation in Whole Language Programs*. Norwood, MA: Christopher Gordon Publishers, 1993.

Karnofsky, Florence, and Weiss, Trudy. *How To Prepare Your Child for Kindergarten*. Carthage, IL: Fearon Teacher Aids, 1993.

Keshner, Judy. *The Kindergarten Teacher's Very Own Student Assessment and Observation Guide*. Rosemont, NJ: Modern Learning Press, 1996.

Kohn, Alfie. *No Contest: The Case Against Competition*. Boston, MA: Houghton Mifflin, 1992.

Kozol, Jonathan. *Savage Inequalities: Children in America's Schools*. New York: Crown, 1991.

Lang, Greg and Berberich, Chris. *All Children are Special: Creating an Inclusive Classroom*. York, ME: Stenhouse Publishers, 1995.

Lazear, David. *Multiple Intelligence Approaches to Assessment: Solving the Assessment Conundrum*. IRI/Skylight Publishing, Inc., 1994.

Ledell, Marjorie and Arnsparger, Arleen. *How to Deal with Community Criticism of School Change*. Alexandria, VA: Association for Supervision and Curriculum Development, 1993.

National Education Commission on Time and Learning. *Prisoners of Time*. Washington, DC: U.S. Government Printing Office, Superintendent of Documents, 1994.

Oakes, Jeannie. *Keeping Track: How Schools Structure Equality*. New Haven: Yale University Press, 1985.

Pavelka, Patricia. *Making the Connection: Learning Skills Through Literature*. Peterborough, NH: Crystal Springs Books, 1995.

Rasell, Edith, and Rothstein, Richard, Editors. *School Choice: Examining the Evidence*. Washington, DC: Economic Policy Institute, 1993.

Society For Developmental Education. *Creating Inclusive Classrooms: Education for All Children*. Peterborough, NH: 1994.

Stainback, S., and Stainback, W. *Curriculum Considerations in Inclusive Classrooms: Facilitating Learning for All Students*. Baltimore: Paul H. Brookes, 1992.

————.*Support Networks for Inclusive Schooling*. Baltimore: Paul H. Brookes, 1990.

Stainback, S, Stainback, W., and Forest, M., eds. *Educating All Students in the Mainstream of Regular Education*. Baltimore: Paul H. Brookes, 1987.

Tomlinson, Carol Ann. *How to Differentiate Instruction in Mixed-Ability Classrooms*. Alexandria, VA: Association for Supervision and Curriculum Development, 1995.

Uphoff, James K. *Real Facts From Real Schools: What You're Not Supposed To Know About School Readiness and Transition Programs*. Rosemont, NJ: Modern Learning Press, 1990, 1995.

Uphoff, James, K.; Gilmore, June; and Huber, Rosemarie. *Summer Children: Ready (or Not) for School*. Middletown, OH: The Oxford Press, 1986.

Wheelock, Anne. *Crossing the Tracks: How "Untracking" Can Save America's Schools*. New York: New Press, 1992.

Wortman, Bob, and Matlin, Myna. *Leadership in Whole Language: The Principal's Role*. York, ME: Stenhouse Publishers, 1995.

# Index

# NOTES

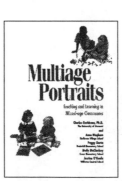
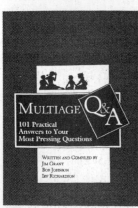